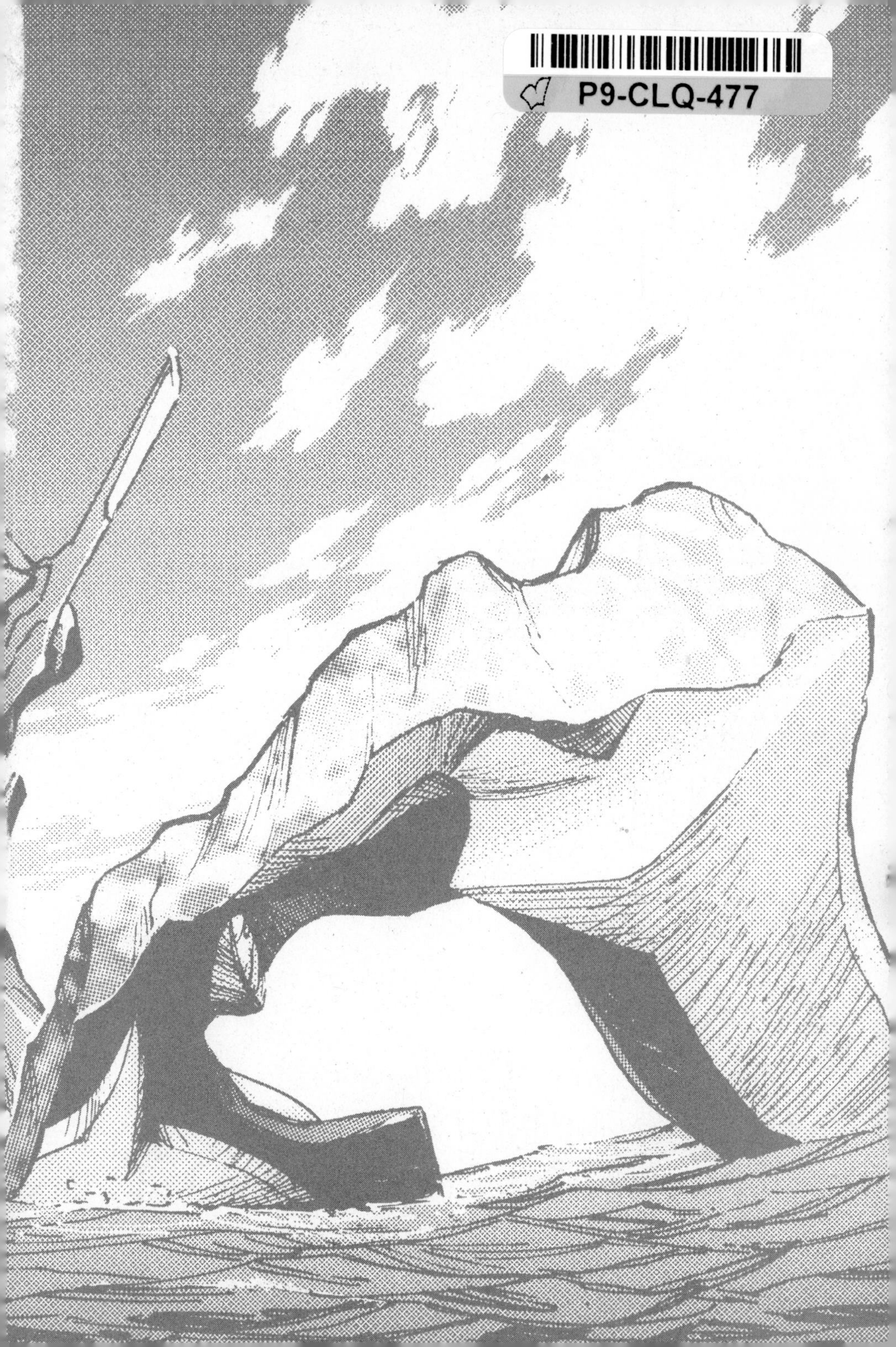

«This is a giant robot saga -- the same way **Twin Peaks** was a cop show...the psychological drama is genuinely engaging, and the art and story first-rate.»
Comics Buyer's Guide

«It's a powerful story by series character designer **Yoshiyuki Sadamoto** about character, responsibility, and the measure of a man. Read it and find out why the series is so popular.»
Sci-Fi Universe

«Despite that **Evangelion** was first an anime, Gainax producer **Yoshiyuki Sadamoto**'s manga is more than faithful to the story: it adds an additional storytelling element, by telling the stories more from Shinji's point of view. The result is a new feeling of the series that can't be had anywhere else...»
Anime News Network

«Fantastic art by **Yoshiyuki Sadamoto**, much heavier character development and more detailed story makes this comic a must if you want to know what **Hideaki Anno** and Gainax really wanted to do with the TV series. A must for all fans of the series.»
Protoculture Addicts

«**Yoshiyuki Sadamoto** is on form as always, playing with his zipatone with as much subtlety as the shades of grey in the very story itself...this comic is recommended reading for all real Evangelion fans...»
Manga Max

«**Neon Genesis Evangelion** is a good manga and the right choice for those who are looking for a good story. If you don't mind the differences from the anime, this version is worth your time.»
EX: The Online World of Anime & Manga

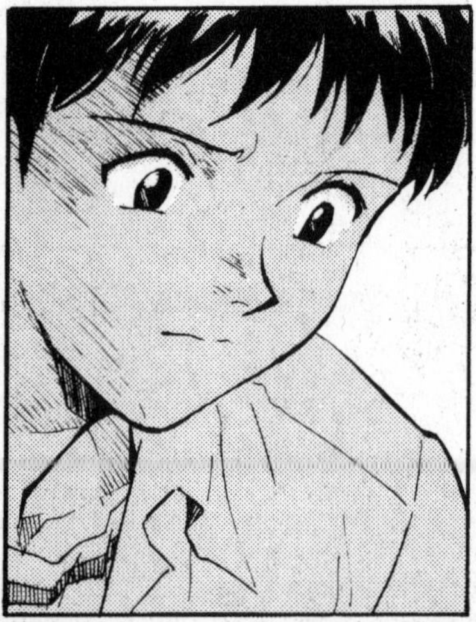

NEON GENESIS EVANGELION

Volume 4

Neon Genesis EVANGELION
Vol. 4

CONTENTS

This volume contains NEON GENESIS EVANGELION Book Four #1 through #7 in their entirety.

Story & Art by Yoshiyuki Sadamoto
Created by GAINAX

English Adaptation by Fred Burke

Translation/Lillian Olsen
Touch-Up Art & Lettering/Wayne Truman
Cover Design/Hidemi Sahara
Editor/Carl Gustav Horn
Assistant Editor/Annette Roman

Managing Editor/Annette Roman
Editor-in-Chief/Hyoe Narita
Publisher/Seiji Horibuchi
Director of Sales & Marketing/Oliver Chin

© GAINAX 1997
First Published in 1997 by KADOKAWA SHOTEN PUBLISHING CO., LTD. Tokyo. English translation rights arranged with KADOKAWA SHOTEN PUBLISHING CO., LTD., Tokyo.

Printed in Canada

Published by Viz Communications, Inc.
P.O. Box 77010
San Francisco, CA 94107

10 9 8 7 6 5 4 3 2
First printing, November 1999
Second Printing, March 2000

Get your free Viz Shop-By-Mail catalog!
(800) 394-3042 or fax (415) 348-8936

NEON GENESIS EVANGELION GRAPHIC NOVELS TO DATE

NEON GENESIS EVANGELION VOL. 1
NEON GENESIS EVANGELION VOL. 2
NEON GENESIS EVANGELION VOL. 3
NEON GENESIS EVANGELION VOL. 4

NEON GENESIS EVANGELION

Volume 4

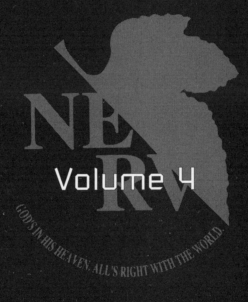

GOD'S IN HIS HEAVEN. ALL'S RIGHT WITH THE WORLD.

Story & Art by
Yoshiyuki Sadamoto
Created by
GAINAX

Name: SHINJI IKARI
Identity: EVA UNIT-01 PILOT, NERV/ MIDDLE SCHOOL STUDENT
Age: 14
Notes: Shinji was the "Third Child" chosen to pilot the monstrous Evangelion series: biomechanical weapons developed by the clandestine UN paramilitary agency known as NERV to fight entities code-named "Angels." Despite having no previous knowledge of NERV or combat, and despite his estrangement from NERV's commander, Shinji has already defeated three Angels.

Name: GENDO IKARI
Identity: SUPREME COMMANDER, NERV
Age: 48
Notes: Shinji's father; this ruthless and enigmatic man is the guiding force behind both the development of NERV's Evangelion system, designed to defeat the prophesied return of the Angels, and the even more secret Instrumentality Project. Gendo reports on occasion to the Instrumentality of Man Committee, a shadowy group seeking to control the mysteries of the Dead Sea Scrolls.

Name: CAPT. MISATO KATSURAGI
Identity: OPERATIONS CHIEF, NERV
Age: 29
Notes: Even though Capt. Katsuragi is third in command at NERV, after Commander Gendo and Sub-Commander Fuyutsuki, and oversees the Eva pilots in combat in her role as tactical planner, there are many things about the organization that have been kept from her. A carouser and slob in her off-hours, Misato has become surrogate family for Shinji, with whom she shares an apartment.

Name: REI AYANAMI
Identity: EVA UNIT-00 PILOT, NERV/ MIDDLE SCHOOL STUDENT
Age: 14
Notes: The "First Child" chosen to pilot an Evangelion, and first to use it in combat, sustaining severe injuries in Unit-01 while fighting the Third Angel. Although Rei barely expresses emotion, she at first regarded Shinji as an interloper. Since she and Shinji fought the Fifth Angel together, they have grown closer, yet Shinji is still mystified at how Rei relates to Gendo in a way he himself cannot.

Name: DR. RITSUKO AKAGI
Identity: CHIEF SCIENTIST, NERV
Age: 30
Notes: Technical supervisor for NERV's "Project E (Evangelion)," Dr. Akagi is a polymath genius who rode the wave of scientific revolution that followed the cracking of the human genetic code at the end of the 20th century. Her disciplines include physics, biotechnology and computer science. Dr. Akagi was a friend of Misato's in college.

Name: KOZO FUYUTSUKI
Identity: SUB-COMMANDER, NERV
Age: UNCERTAIN—ABOUT 60
Notes: Gendo's second-in-command and right-hand man. Before the Second Impact, Fuyutsuki was a biology professor in Kyoto, Japan, during which time he first met Gendo, who married his prize student. He and Dr. Akagi may be the only ones at NERV besides Gendo to know the complete story behind Evangelion and the Instrumentality Project.

Name: KENSUKE AIDA
Identity: MIDDLE SCHOOL STUDENT
Age: 14
Notes: A devoted fan of military affairs, Aida plays war games in Army costume out in the country, habitually carries a Sony camcorder to capture shots of hardware or combat, and engages in computer hacking to acquire information for his "mania." He has expressed the wish that someone like Misato would "order him around."

Name: TOJI SUZUHARA
Identity: MIDDLE SCHOOL STUDENT
Age: 14
Notes: Best friend of Aida; speaks with a pronounced accent from his home town, Osaka. His father and grandfather are both part of NERV's research labs. At first he blamed Shinji for injuries his sister suffered during the attack of the Third Angel and even punched him out; now both Aida and he are friends with Unit-01's pilot.

Stage 1:

ASUKA COMES TO JAPAN

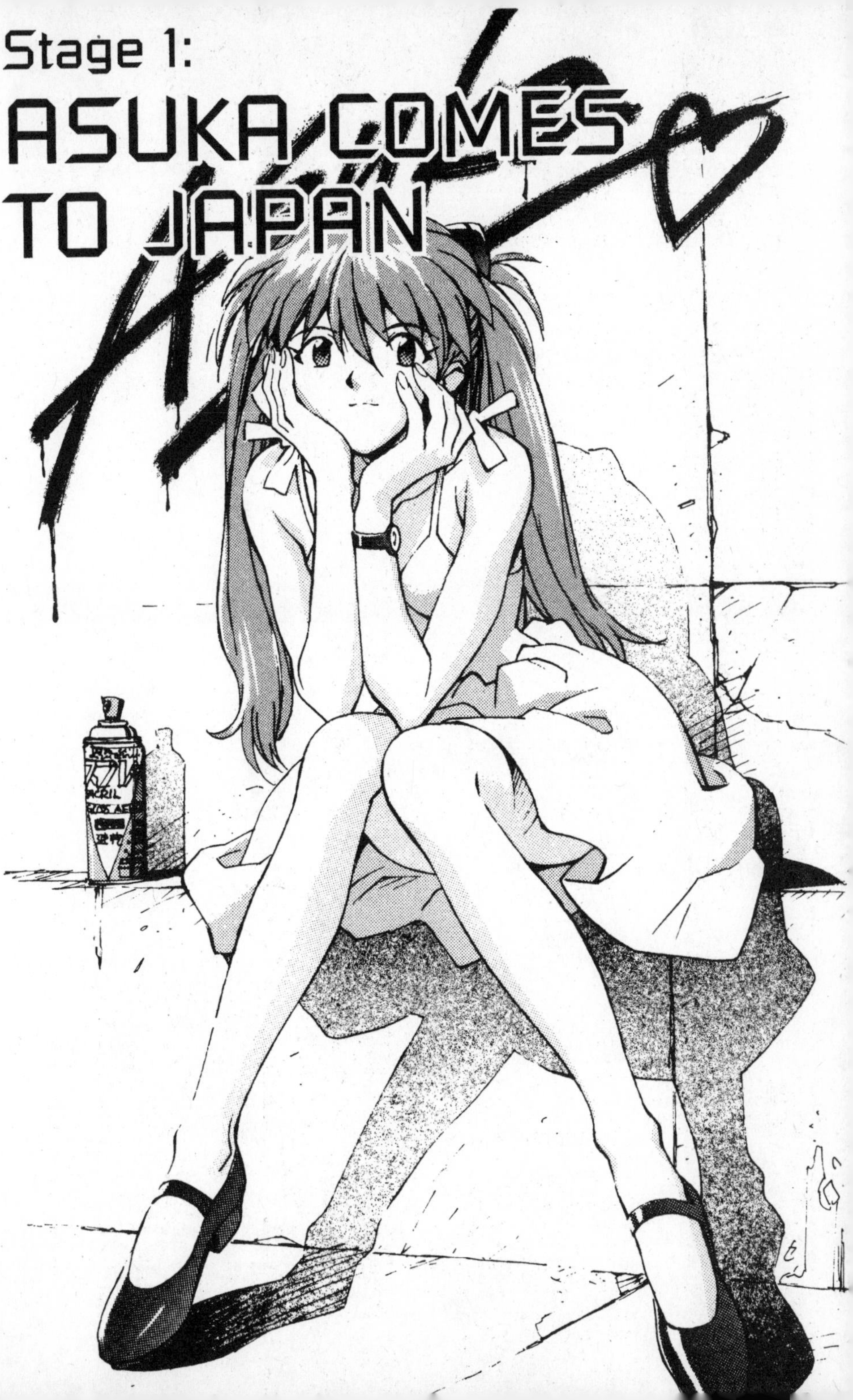

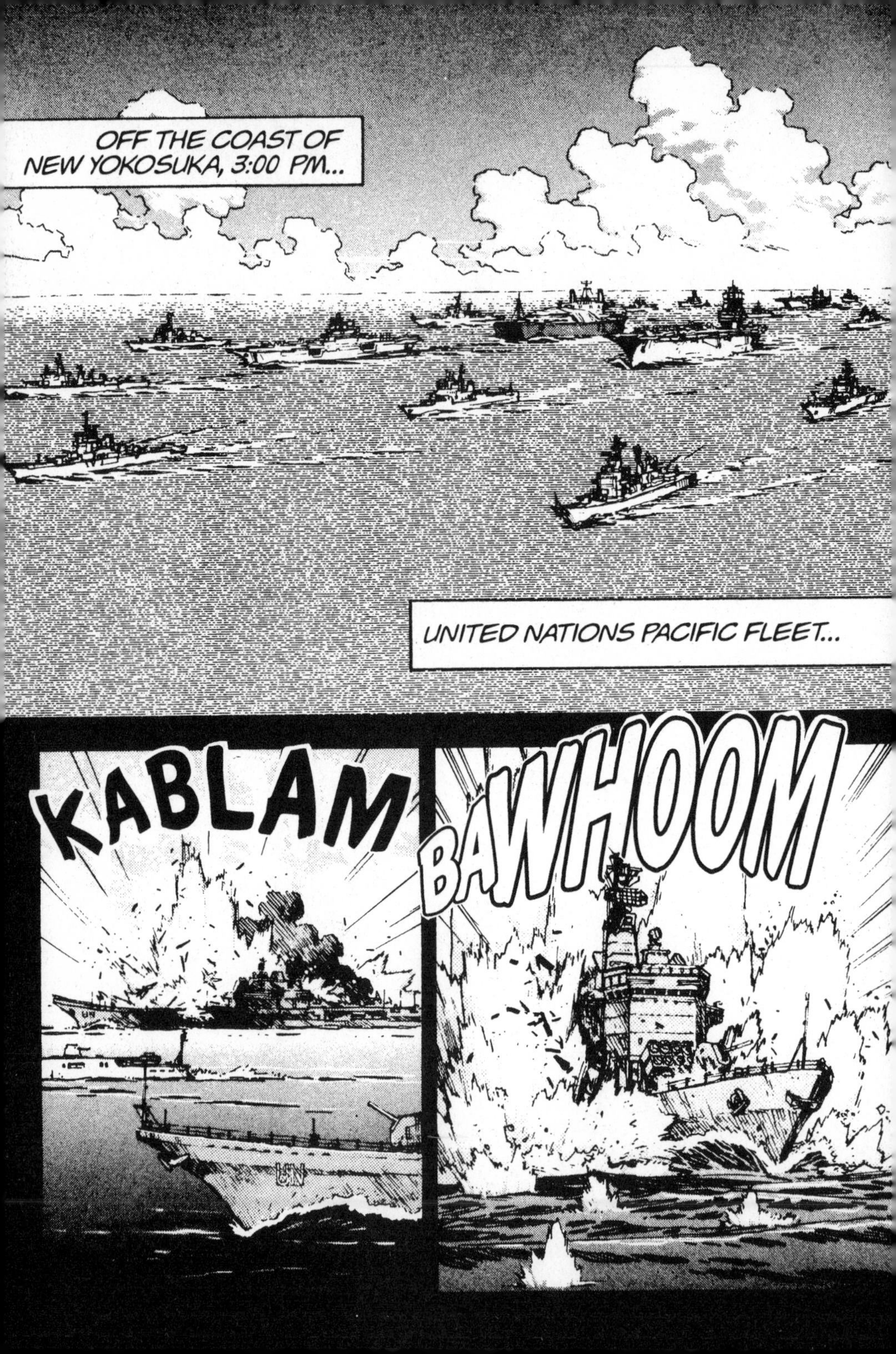
OFF THE COAST OF NEW YOKOSUKA, 3:00 PM...
UNITED NATIONS PACIFIC FLEET...
KABLAM
BAWHOOM

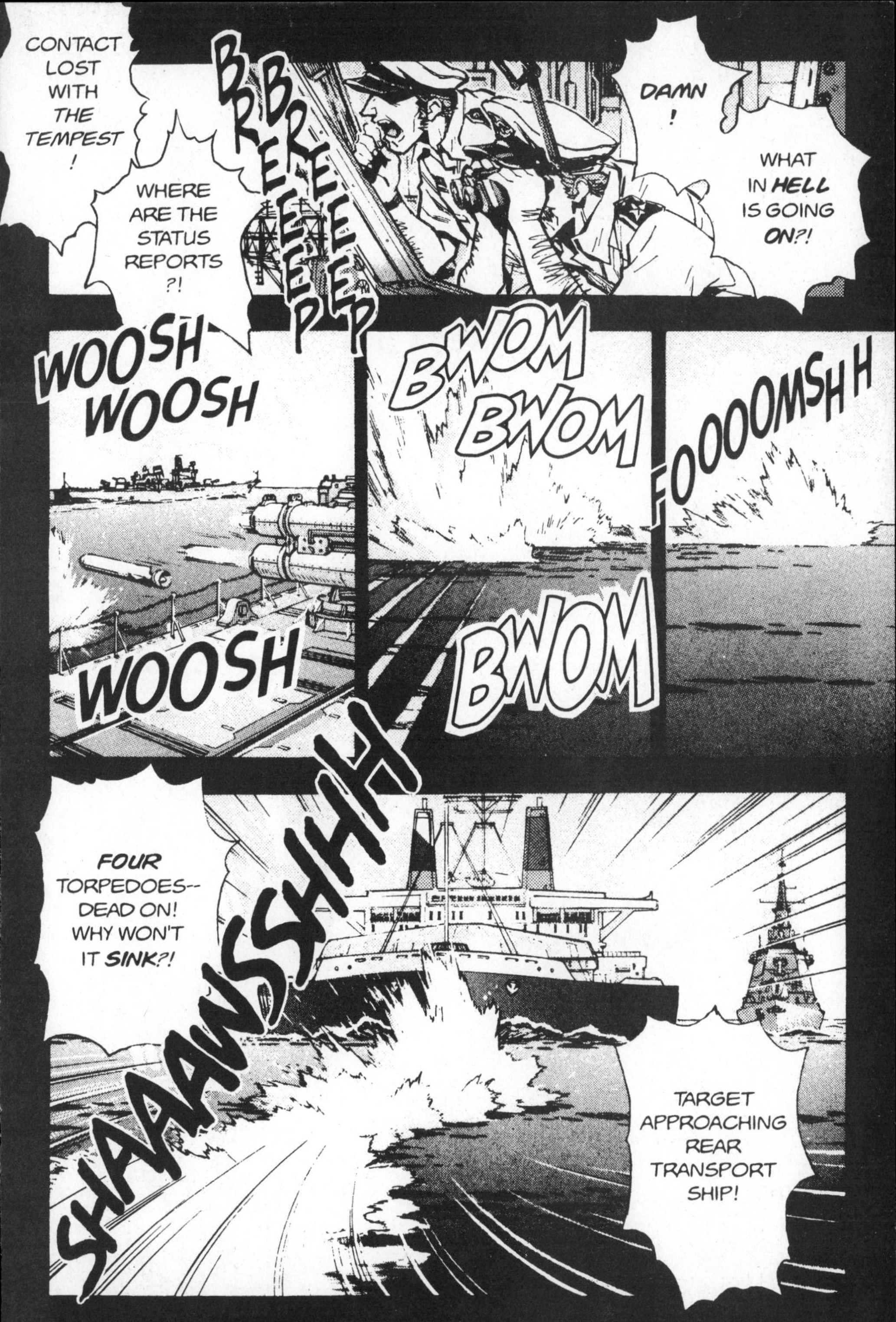
CONTACT LOST WITH THE TEMPEST!
BREEEP
BREEEP
WHERE ARE THE STATUS REPORTS?!
DAMN!
WHAT IN HELL IS GOING ON?!
WOOSH WOOSH
WOOSH
BWOM BWOM
BWOM
FOOOOMSHH H
SHAAAWSSHHH
FOUR TORPEDOES-- DEAD ON! WHY WON'T IT SINK?!
TARGET APPROACHING REAR TRANSPORT SHIP!

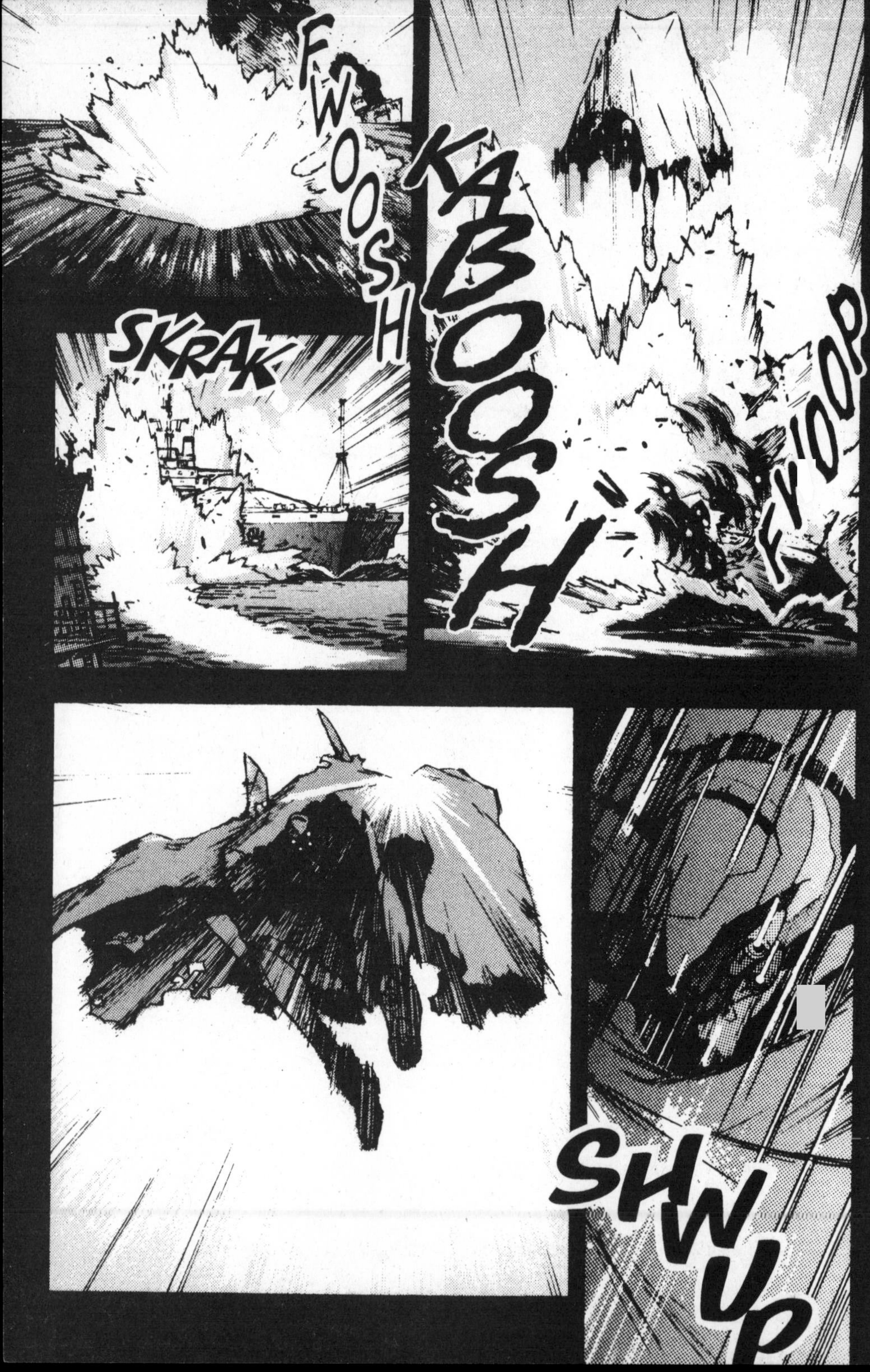
FWOOSH
SKRAK
KABOOSH
FYOOP
SHWUP

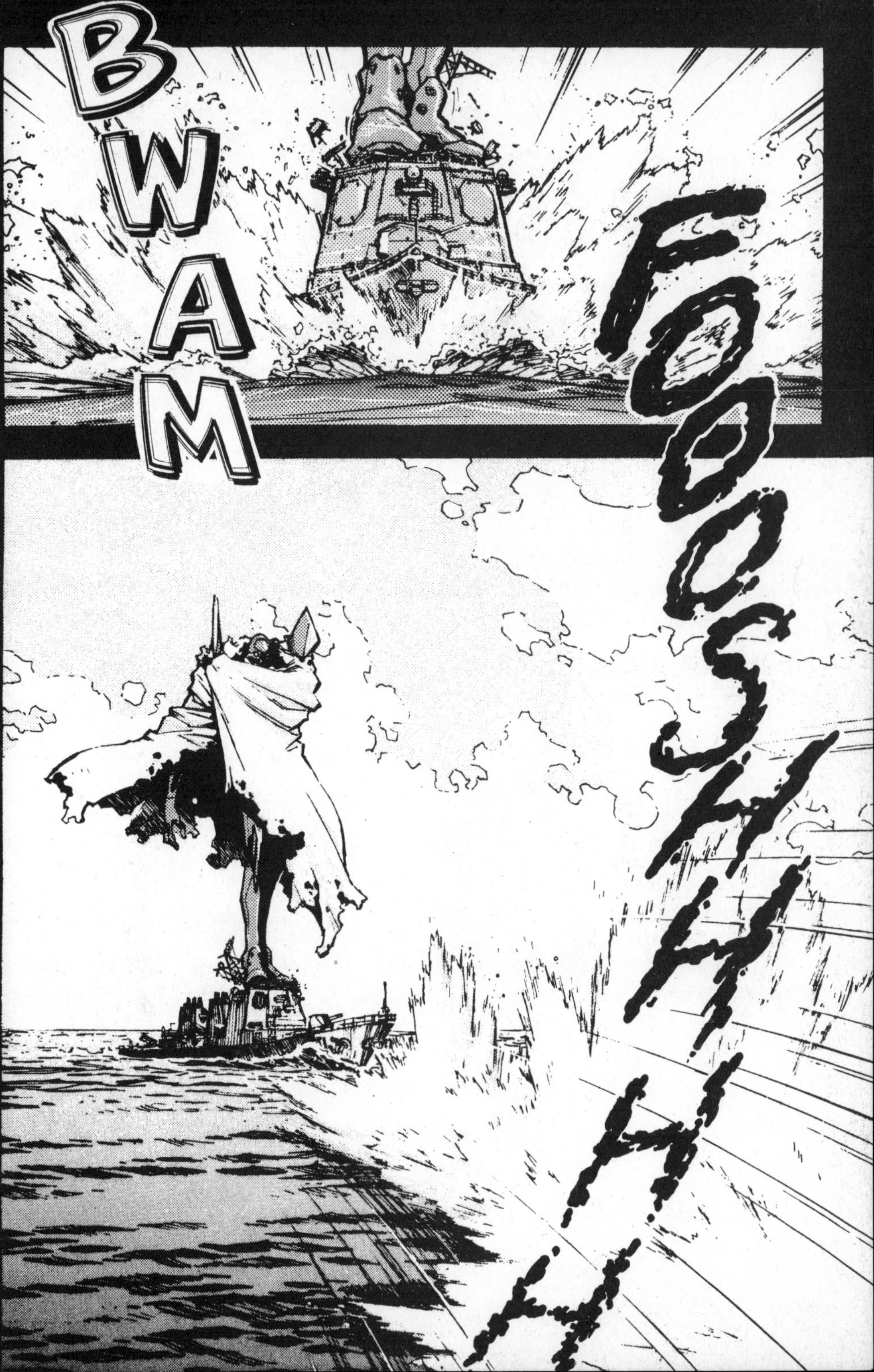
BWAM
FOOOSHHHH

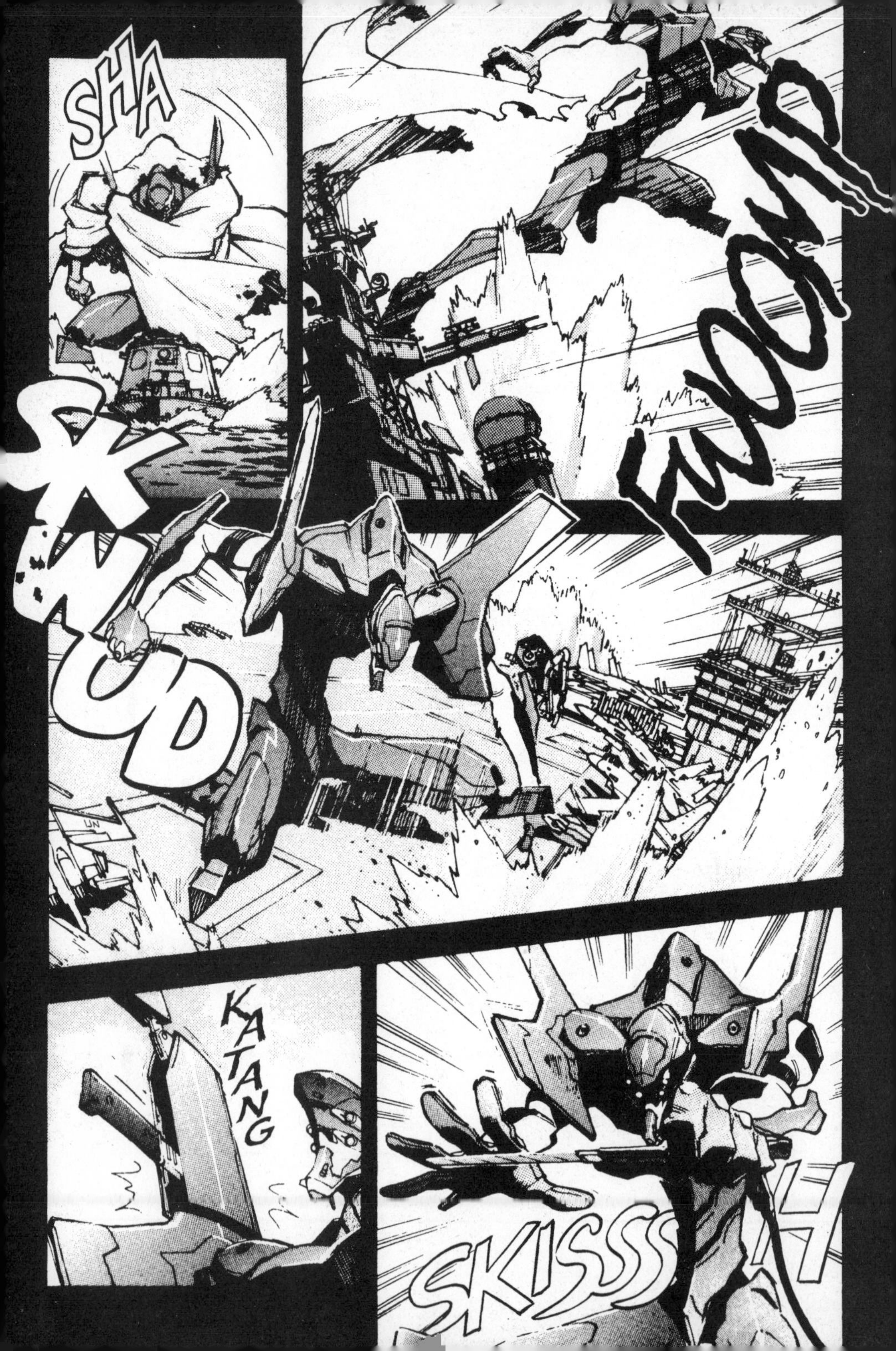
SHA
FWOOMP
THUD
KATANG
SKISSSH

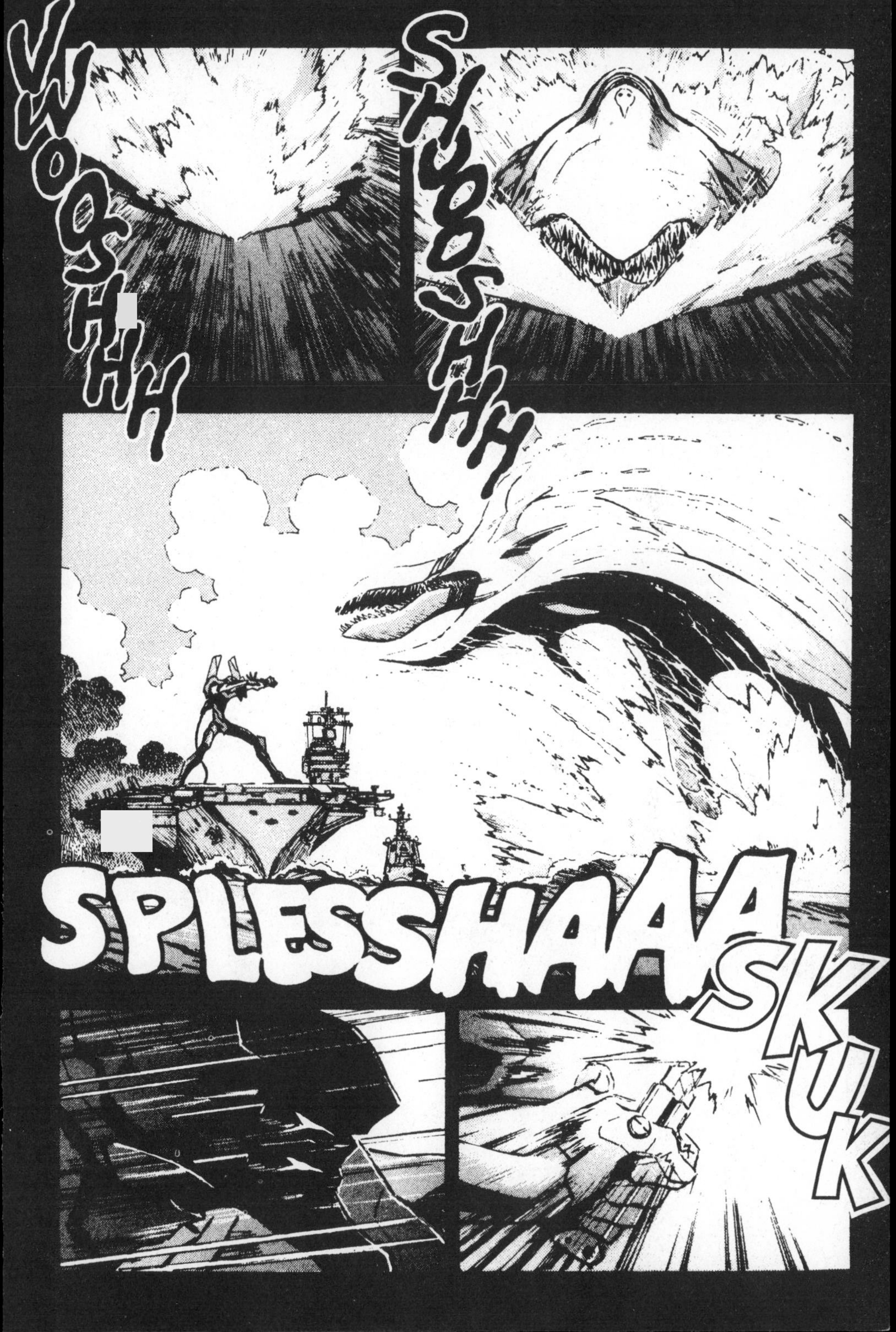
VWOOSHHH
SHOOSHHHH
SPLESSHAAA
SKUK

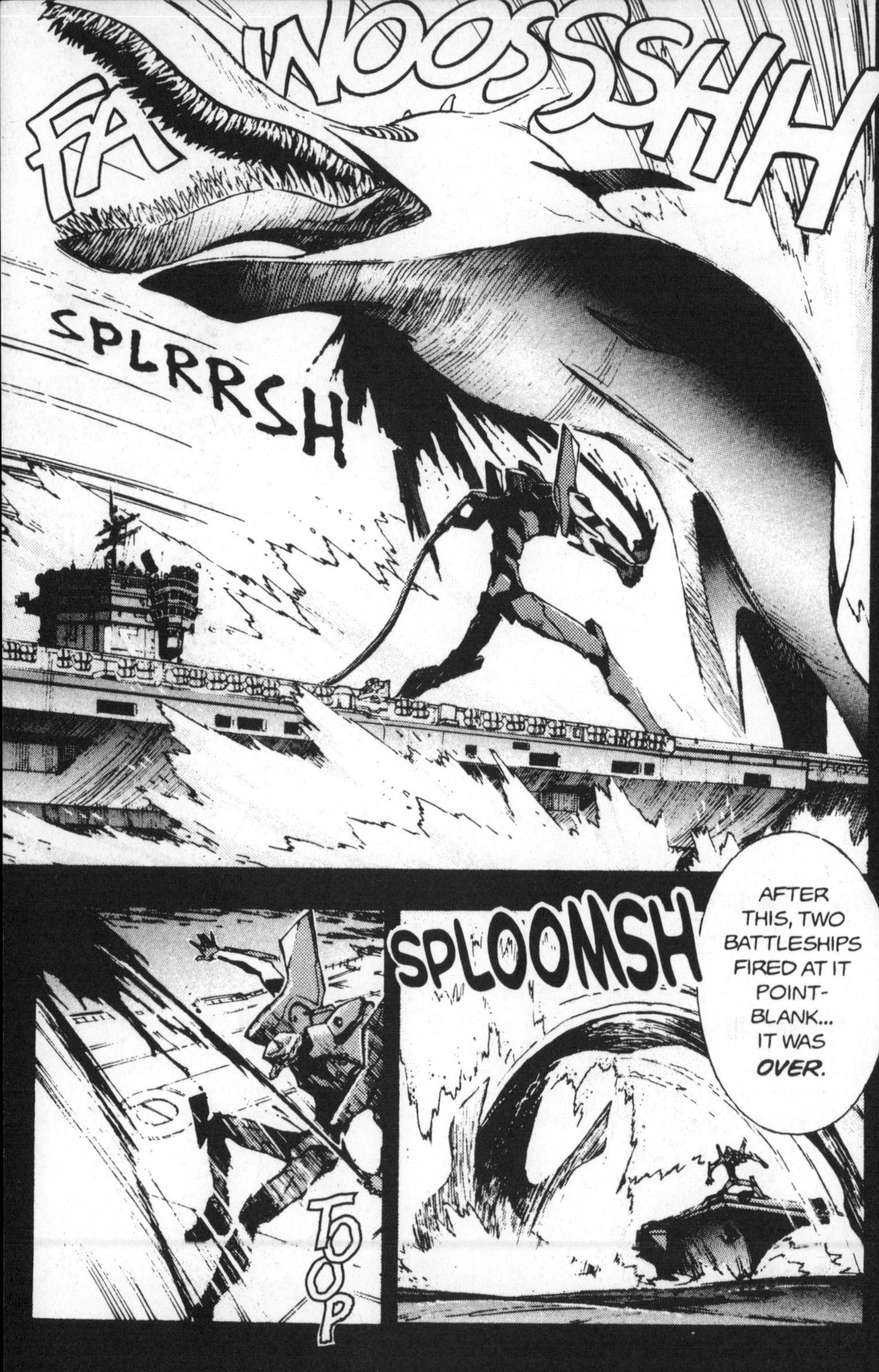
FA WOOSSHH
SPLRRSH
TOOP
SPLOOMSH
AFTER THIS, TWO BATTLESHIPS FIRED AT IT POINT-BLANK... IT WAS **OVER.**

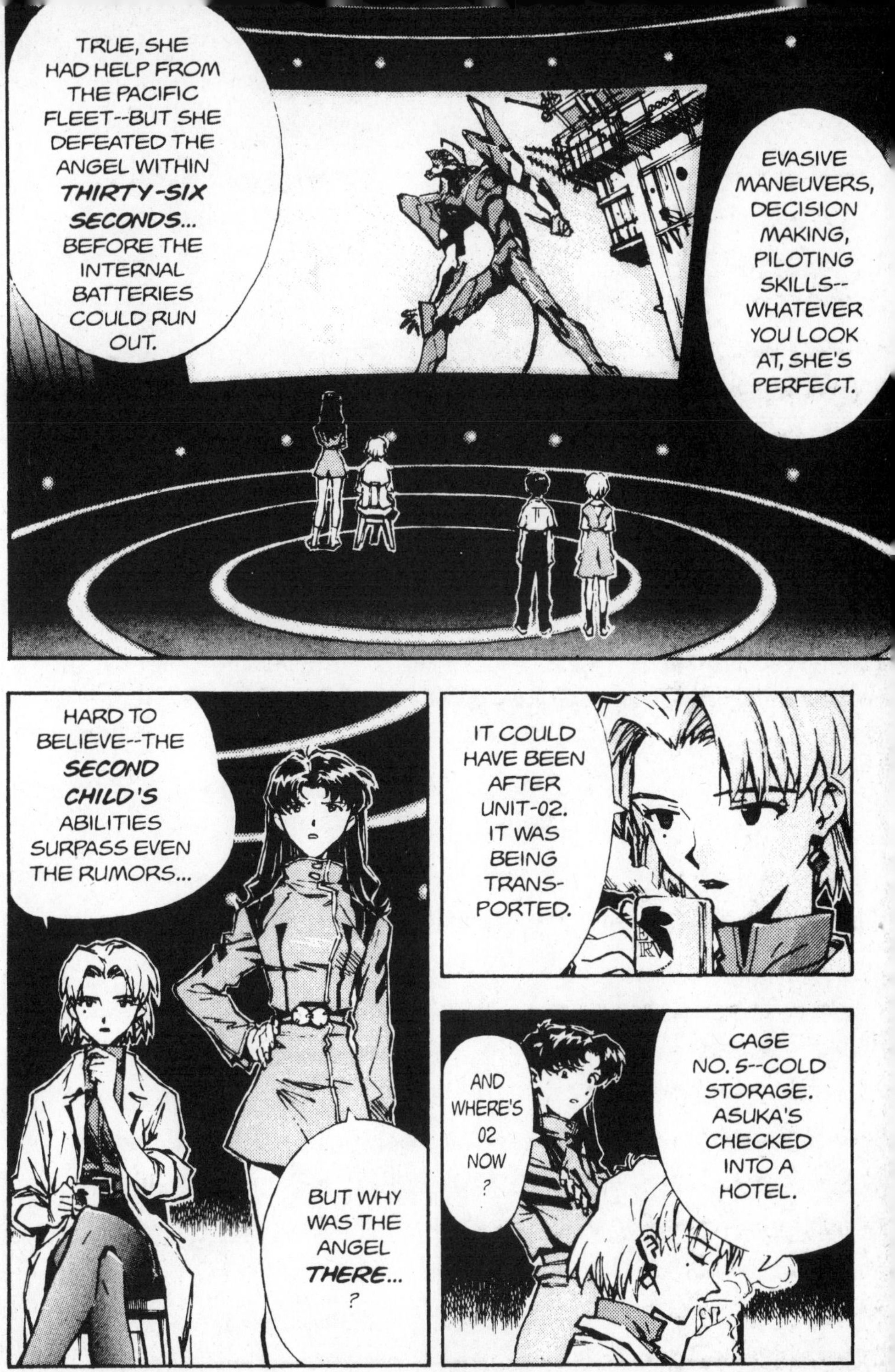

TRUE, SHE HAD HELP FROM THE PACIFIC FLEET--BUT SHE DEFEATED THE ANGEL WITHIN THIRTY-SIX SECONDS... BEFORE THE INTERNAL BATTERIES COULD RUN OUT.
EVASIVE MANEUVERS, DECISION MAKING, PILOTING SKILLS--WHATEVER YOU LOOK AT, SHE'S PERFECT.
HARD TO BELIEVE--THE SECOND CHILD'S ABILITIES SURPASS EVEN THE RUMORS...
BUT WHY WAS THE ANGEL THERE... ?
IT COULD HAVE BEEN AFTER UNIT-02. IT WAS BEING TRANS-PORTED.
AND WHERE'S 02 NOW ?
CAGE NO. 5--COLD STORAGE. ASUKA'S CHECKED INTO A HOTEL.

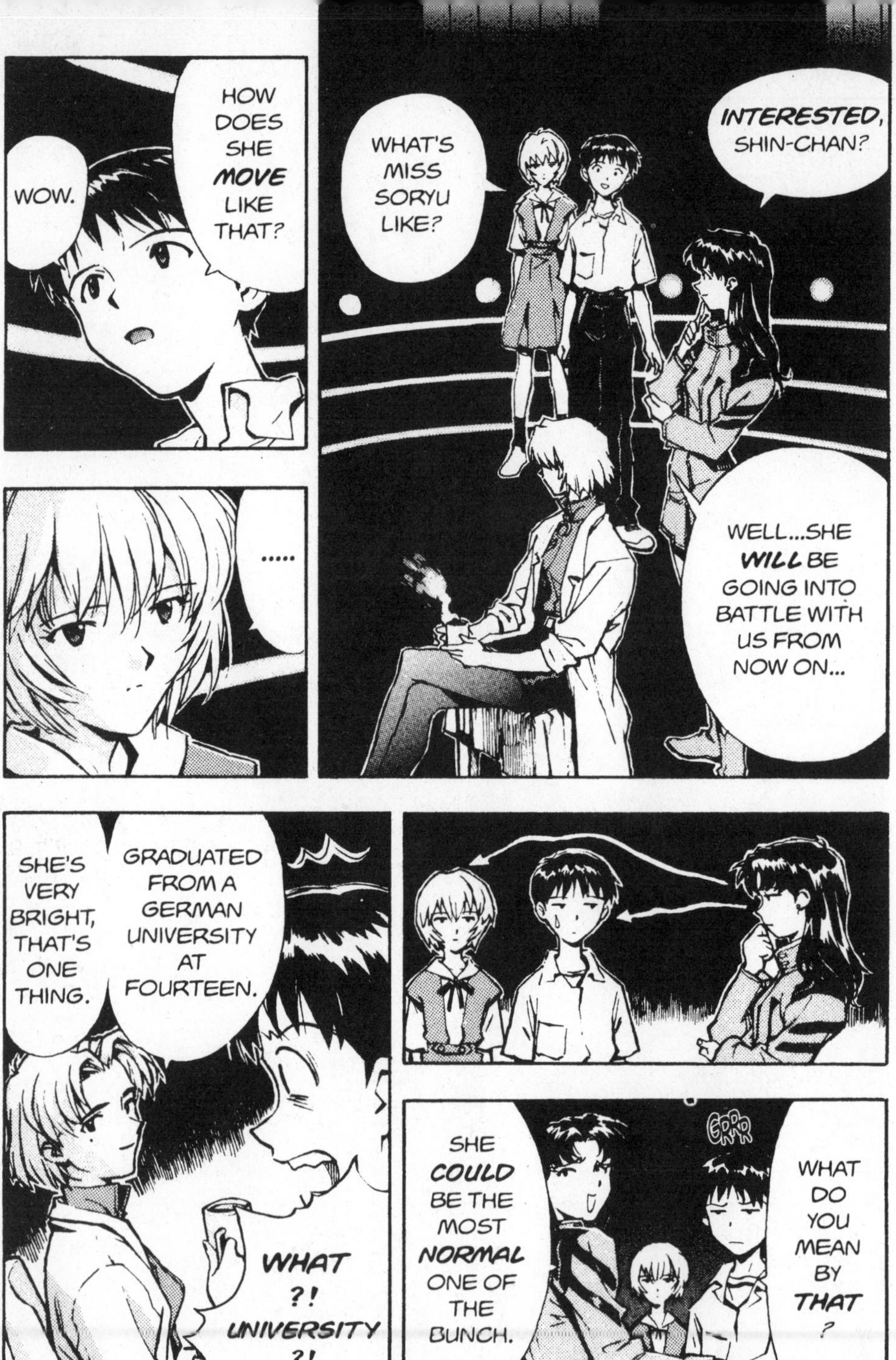
WOW.
HOW DOES SHE MOVE LIKE THAT?
.....
WHAT'S MISS SORYU LIKE?
INTERESTED, SHIN-CHAN?
WELL...SHE WILL BE GOING INTO BATTLE WITH US FROM NOW ON...
SHE'S VERY BRIGHT, THAT'S ONE THING.
GRADUATED FROM A GERMAN UNIVERSITY AT FOURTEEN.
WHAT?! UNIVERSITY?!
GRRR
SHE COULD BE THE MOST NORMAL ONE OF THE BUNCH.
WHAT DO YOU MEAN BY THAT?

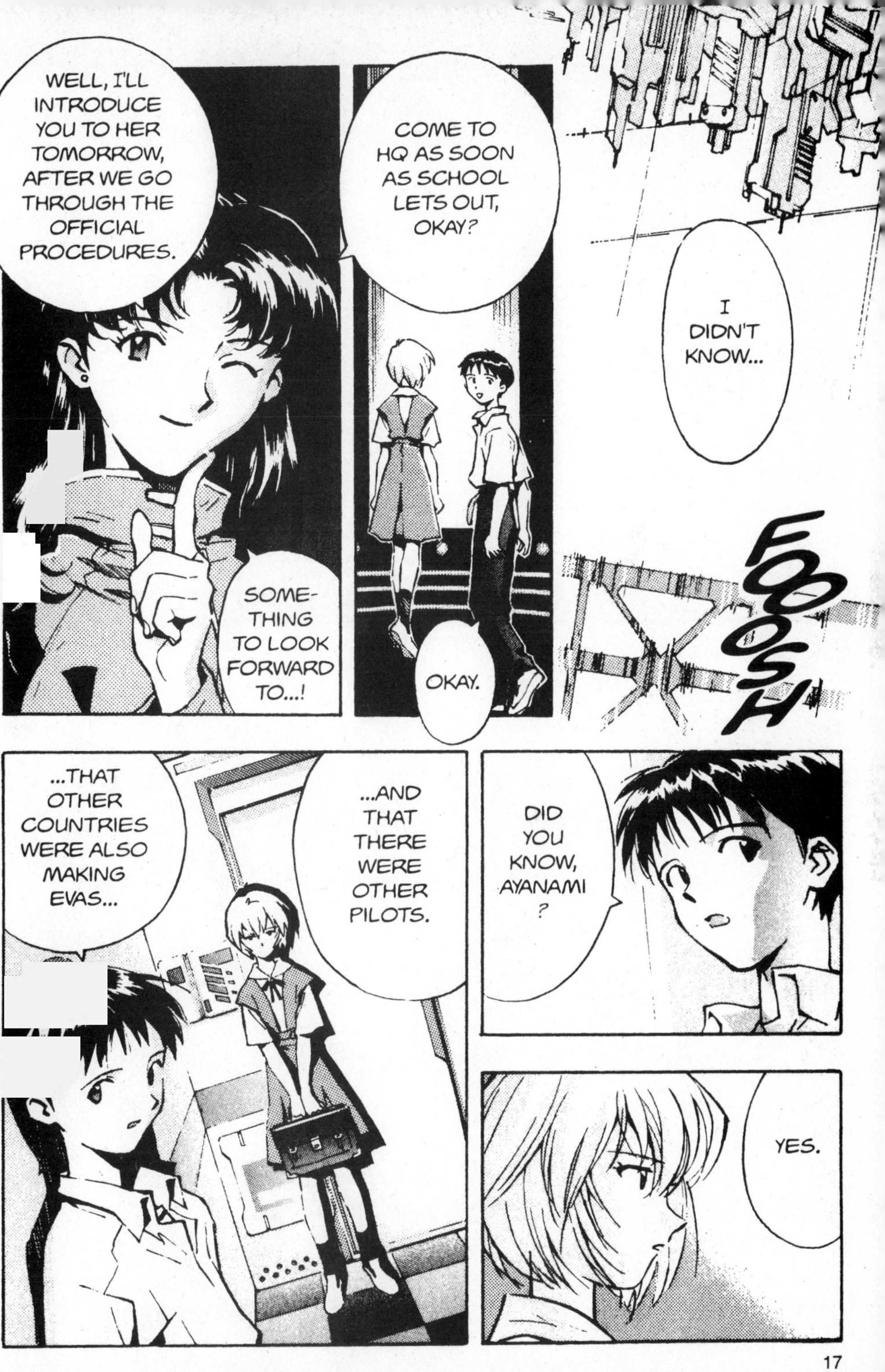
WELL, I'LL INTRODUCE YOU TO HER TOMORROW, AFTER WE GO THROUGH THE OFFICIAL PROCEDURES.
SOME-THING TO LOOK FORWARD TO...!
COME TO HQ AS SOON AS SCHOOL LETS OUT, OKAY?
OKAY.
I DIDN'T KNOW...
FOOOSH
...THAT OTHER COUNTRIES WERE ALSO MAKING EVAS...
...AND THAT THERE WERE OTHER PILOTS.
DID YOU KNOW, AYANAMI?
YES.

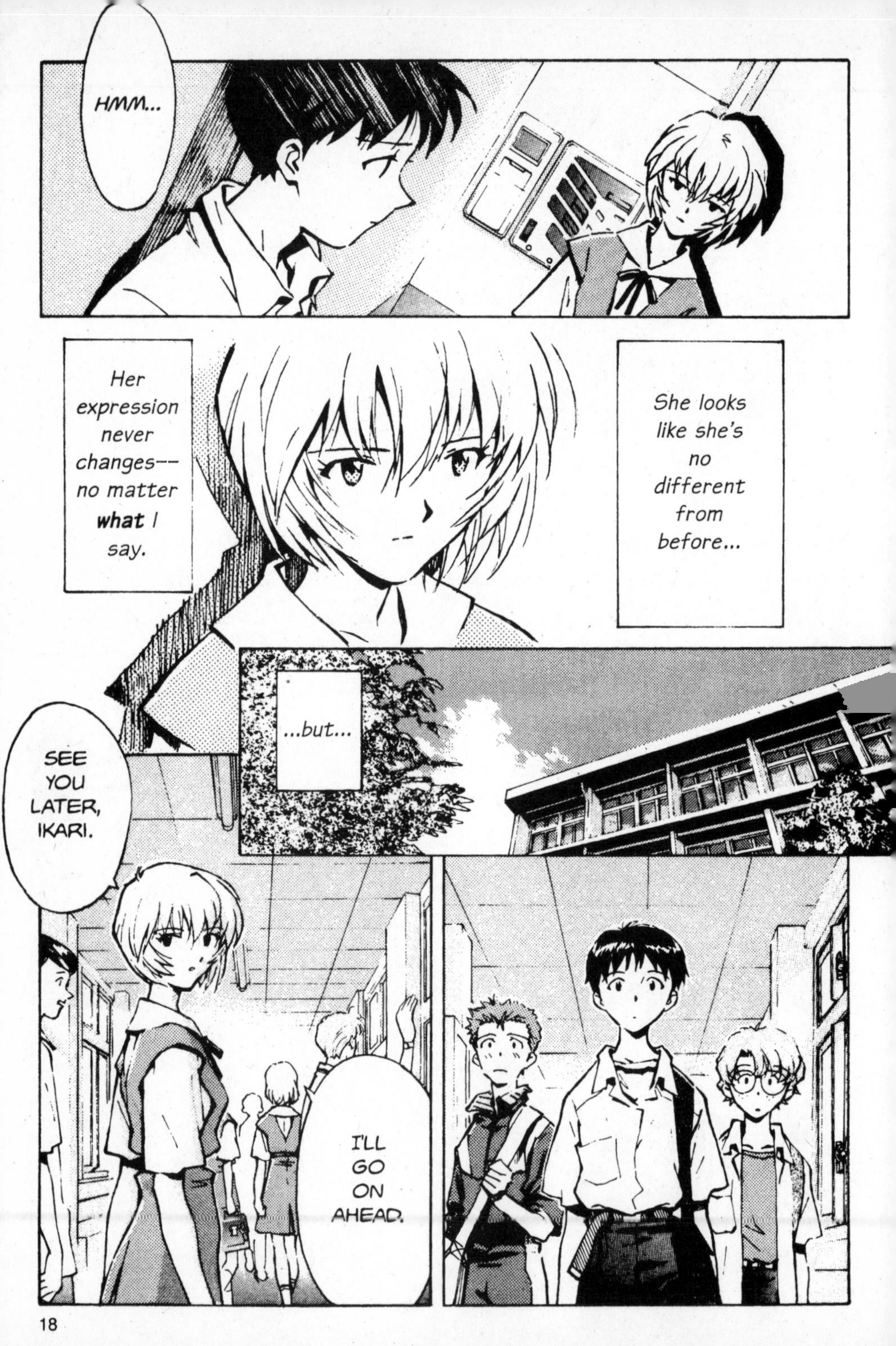
HMM...
Her expression never changes-- no matter **what** I say.
She looks like she's no different from before...
...but...
SEE YOU LATER, IKARI.
I'LL GO ON AHEAD.

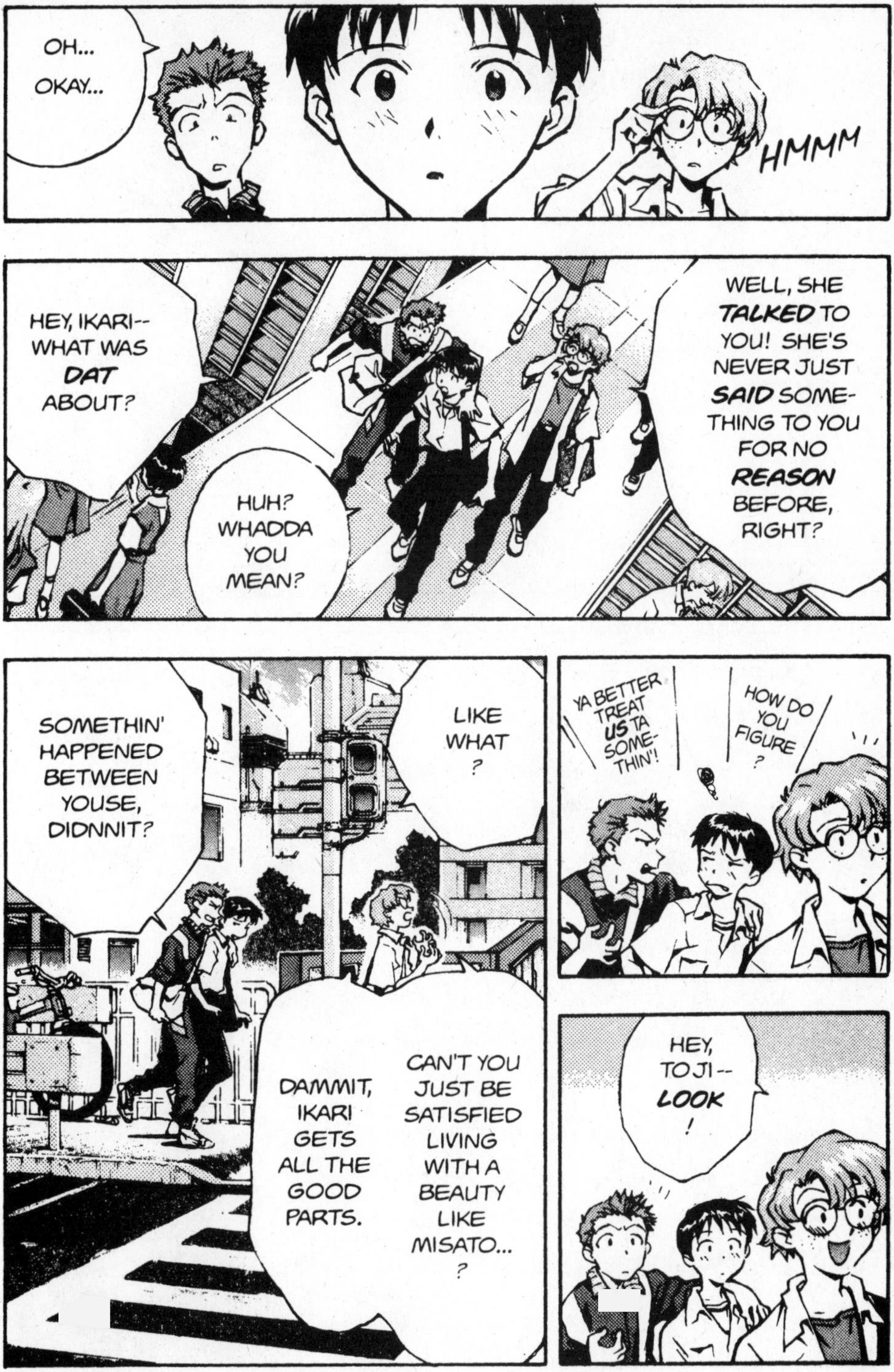
OH... OKAY...
HMMM
HEY, IKARI-- WHAT WAS DAT ABOUT?
HUH? WHADDA YOU MEAN?
WELL, SHE TALKED TO YOU! SHE'S NEVER JUST SAID SOME-THING TO YOU FOR NO REASON BEFORE, RIGHT?
SOMETHIN' HAPPENED BETWEEN YOUSE, DIDNNIT?
LIKE WHAT?
DAMMIT, IKARI GETS ALL THE GOOD PARTS.
CAN'T YOU JUST BE SATISFIED LIVING WITH A BEAUTY LIKE MISATO...?
YA BETTER TREAT US TA SOME-THIN'!
HOW DO YOU FIGURE?
HEY, TOJI-- LOOK!

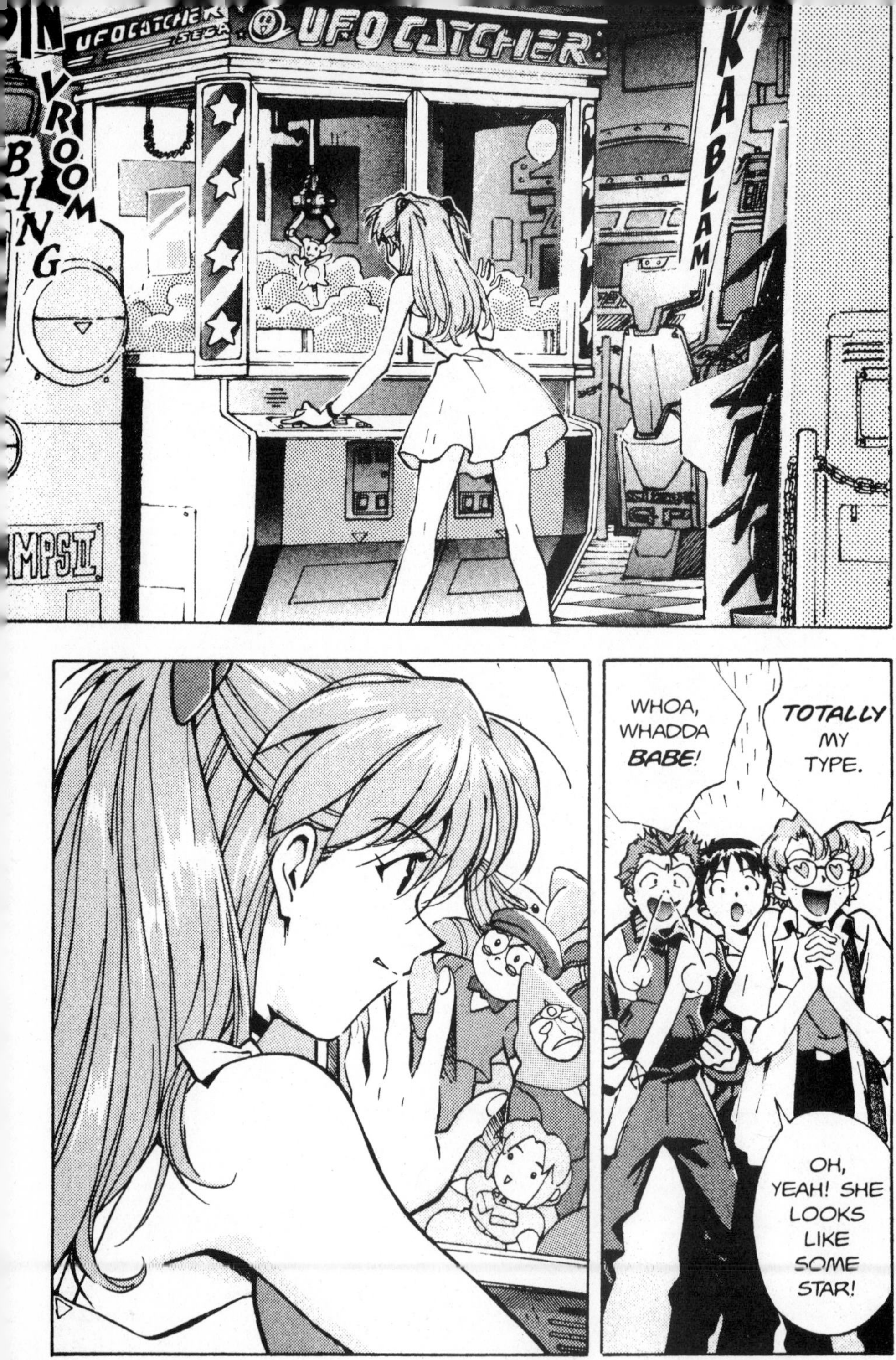
PIN
VROOM
BING
UFO CATCHER
SEGA
UFO CATCHER
KABLAM
MPS II
WHOA, WHADDA ***BABE!***
TOTALLY MY TYPE.
OH, YEAH! SHE LOOKS LIKE SOME STAR!

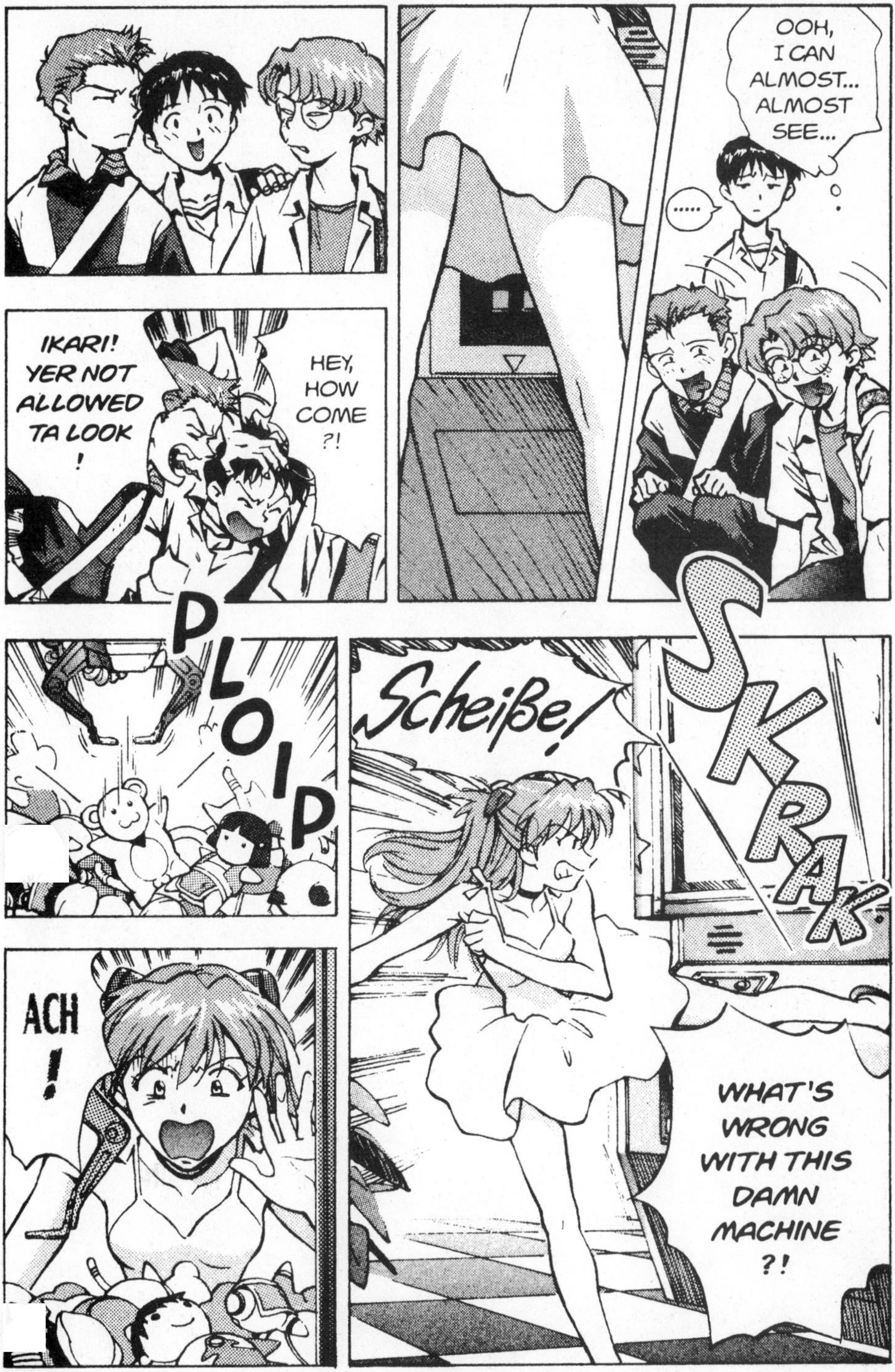
IKARI! YER NOT ALLOWED TA LOOK!
HEY, HOW COME?!
OOH, I CAN ALMOST... ALMOST SEE...
......
PLOIP
ACH!
Scheiße!
SKRAK
WHAT'S WRONG WITH THIS DAMN MACHINE?!

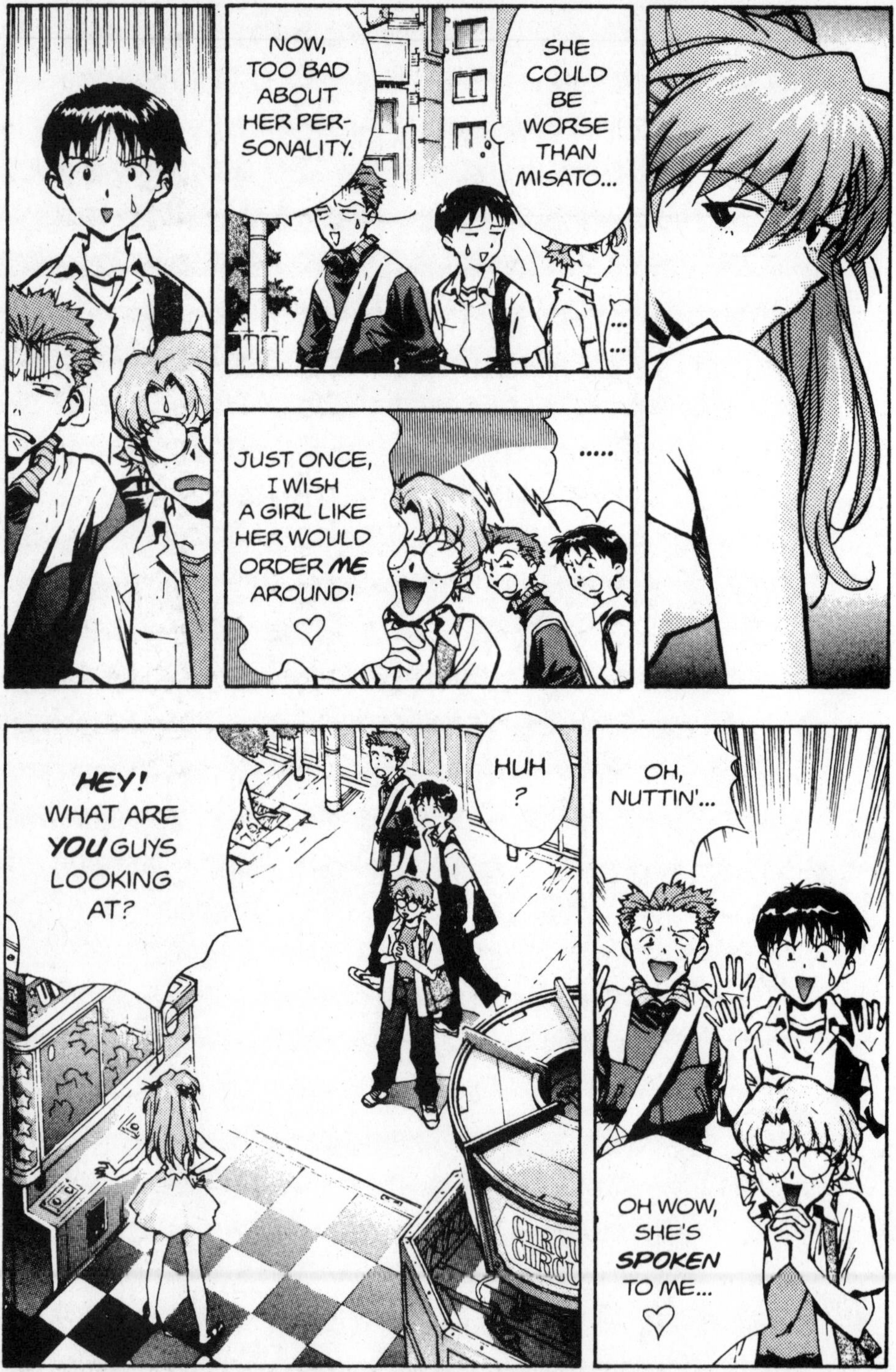
NOW, TOO BAD ABOUT HER PER-SONALITY.
SHE COULD BE WORSE THAN MISATO...
......
JUST ONCE, I WISH A GIRL LIKE HER WOULD ORDER ME AROUND! ♥
.....
HEY! WHAT ARE YOU GUYS LOOKING AT?
HUH ?
OH, NUTTIN'...
OH WOW, SHE'S SPOKEN TO ME... ♥

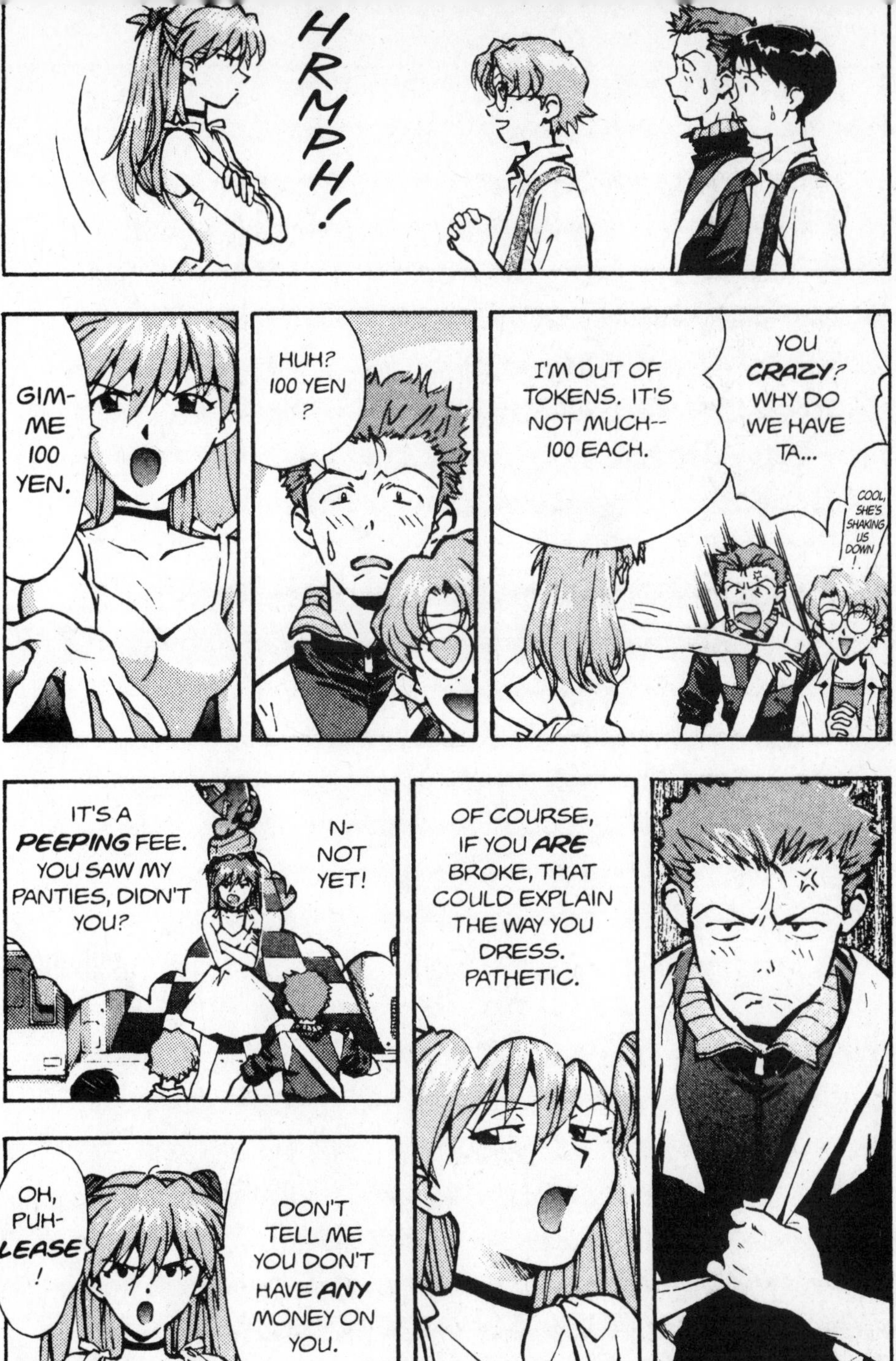
HRMPH!
GIM-ME 100 YEN.
HUH? 100 YEN ?
I'M OUT OF TOKENS. IT'S NOT MUCH-- 100 EACH.
YOU CRAZY? WHY DO WE HAVE TA...
COOL, SHE'S SHAKING US DOWN !
IT'S A PEEPING FEE. YOU SAW MY PANTIES, DIDN'T YOU?
N-NOT YET!
OF COURSE, IF YOU ARE BROKE, THAT COULD EXPLAIN THE WAY YOU DRESS. PATHETIC.
OH, PUH-LEASE !
DON'T TELL ME YOU DON'T HAVE ANY MONEY ON YOU.

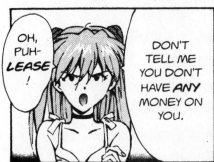

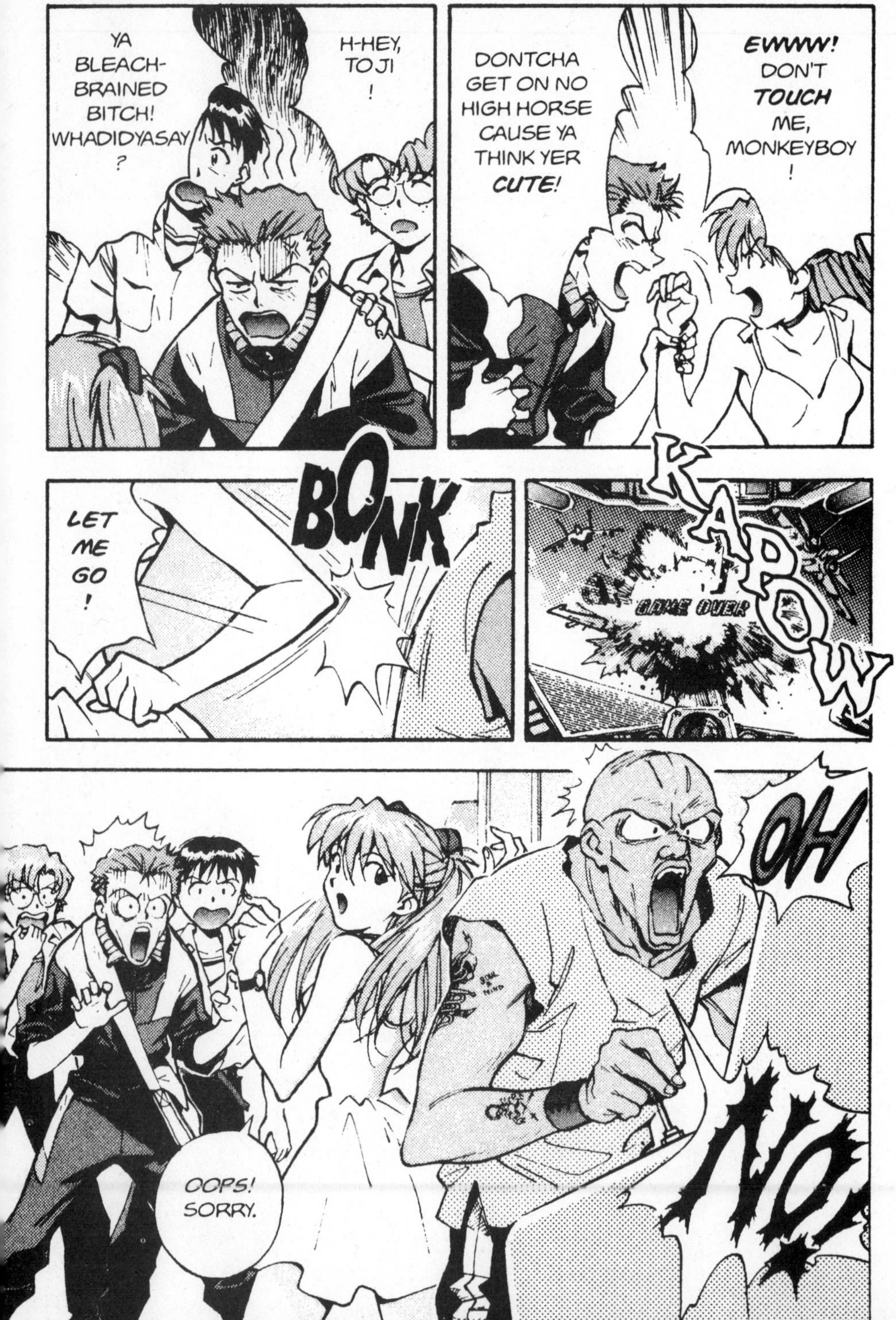
YA BLEACH-BRAINED BITCH! WHADIDYASAY?
H-HEY, TOJI!
DONTCHA GET ON NO HIGH HORSE CAUSE YA THINK YER CUTE!
EWWW! DON'T TOUCH ME, MONKEYBOY!
LET ME GO!
BONK
KAPOW
GAME OVER
OH
NO!
OOPS! SORRY.

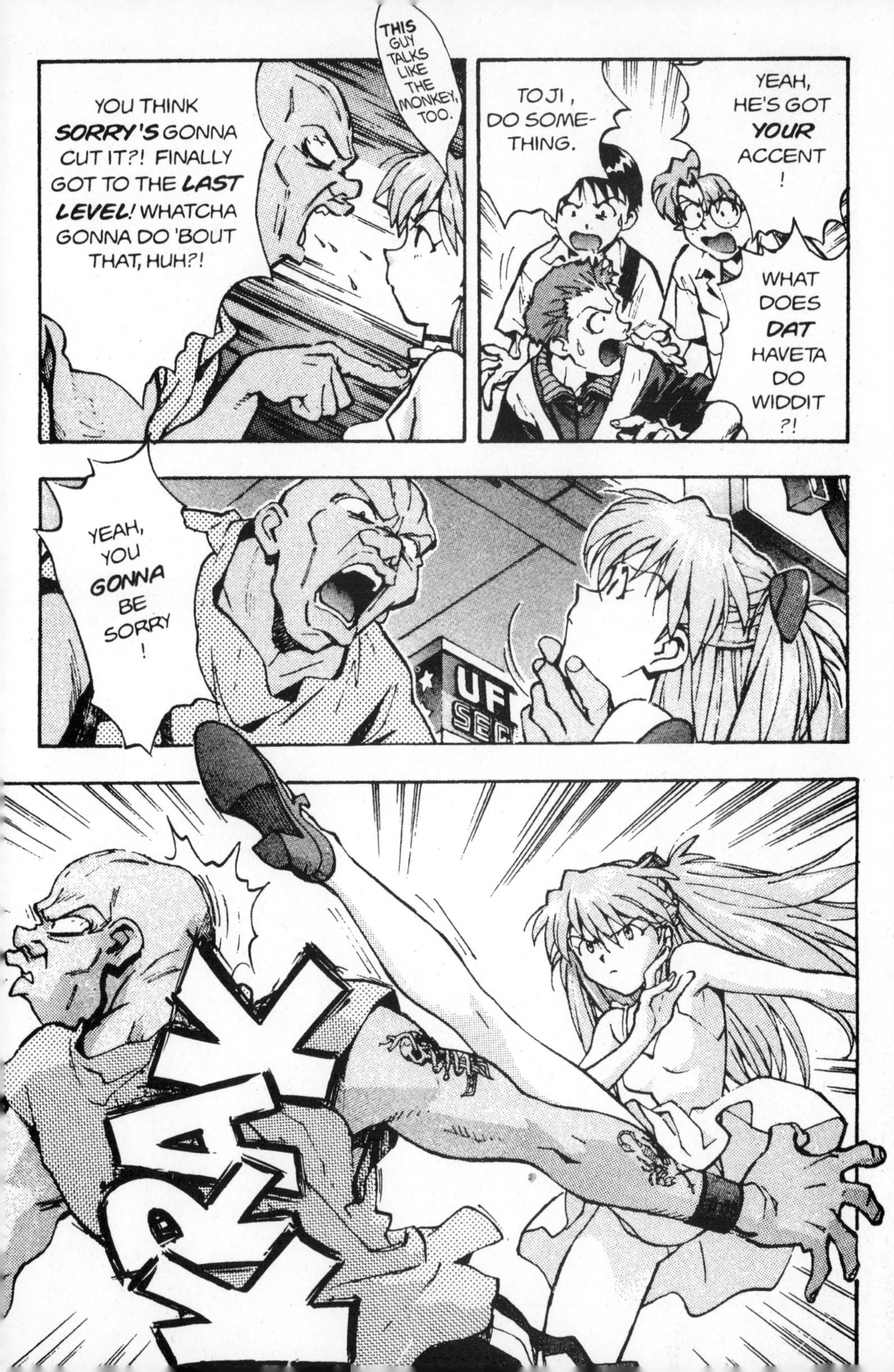
YOU THINK SORRY'S GONNA CUT IT?! FINALLY GOT TO THE LAST LEVEL! WHATCHA GONNA DO 'BOUT THAT, HUH?!
THIS GUY TALKS LIKE THE MONKEY, TOO.
TOJI, DO SOME-THING.
YEAH, HE'S GOT YOUR ACCENT!
WHAT DOES DAT HAVETA DO WIDDIT?!
YEAH, YOU GONNA BE SORRY!

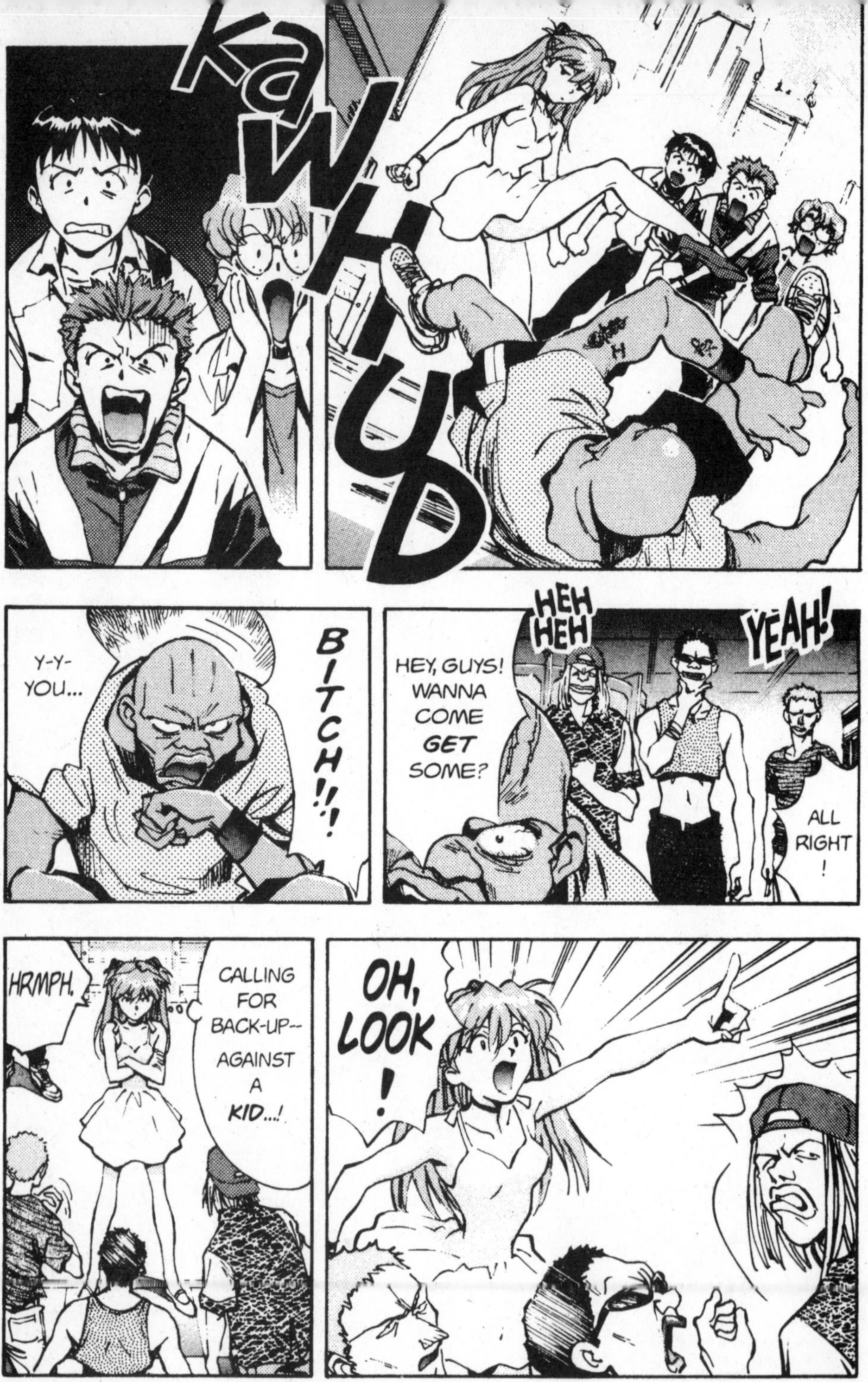
KAWHUD
Y-Y-YOU...
BITCH!!!
HEY, GUYS! WANNA COME GET SOME?
HEH HEH
YEAH!
ALL RIGHT!
HRMPH.
CALLING FOR BACK-UP-- AGAINST A KID...!
OH, LOOK!

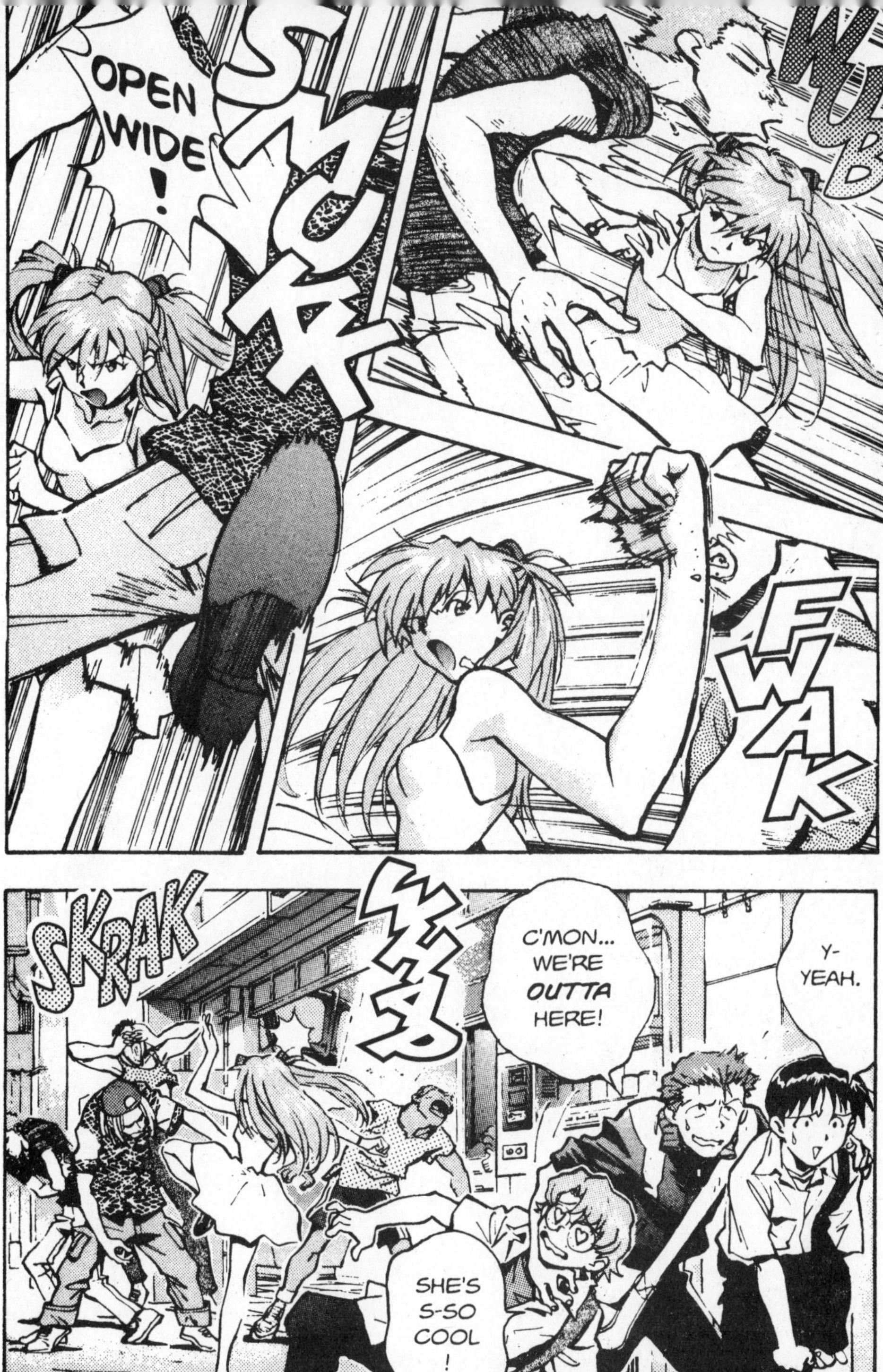
OPEN WIDE !
SMAK
WUB
FWAK
SKRAK
WHAP
C'MON... WE'RE *OUTTA* HERE!
Y- YEAH.
SHE'S S-SO COOL !

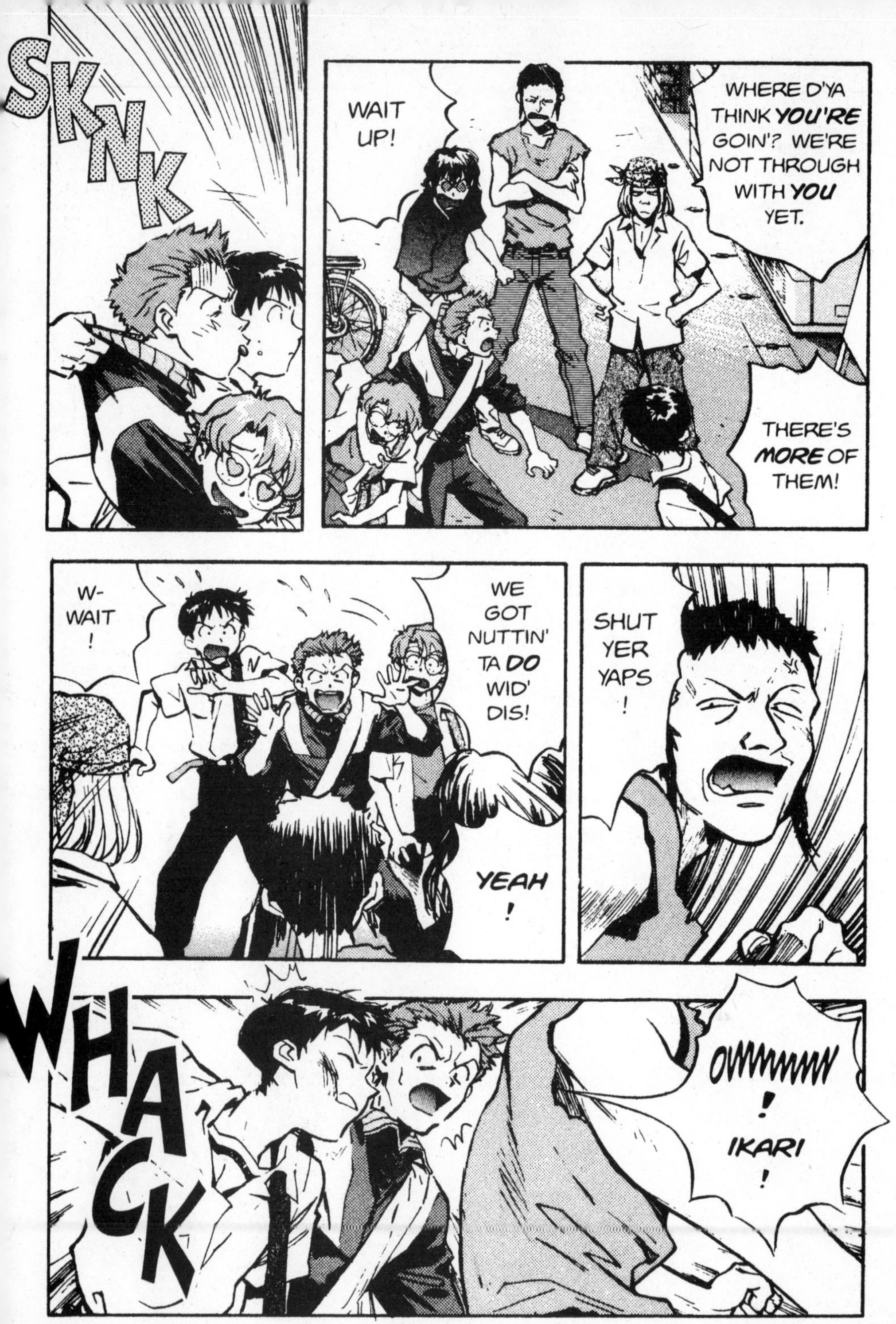
SKNK
WAIT UP!
WHERE D'YA THINK YOU'RE GOIN'? WE'RE NOT THROUGH WITH YOU YET.
THERE'S MORE OF THEM!
W-WAIT!
WE GOT NUTTIN' TA DO WID' DIS!
YEAH!
SHUT YER YAPS!
WHACK
OWWWWW!
IKARI!

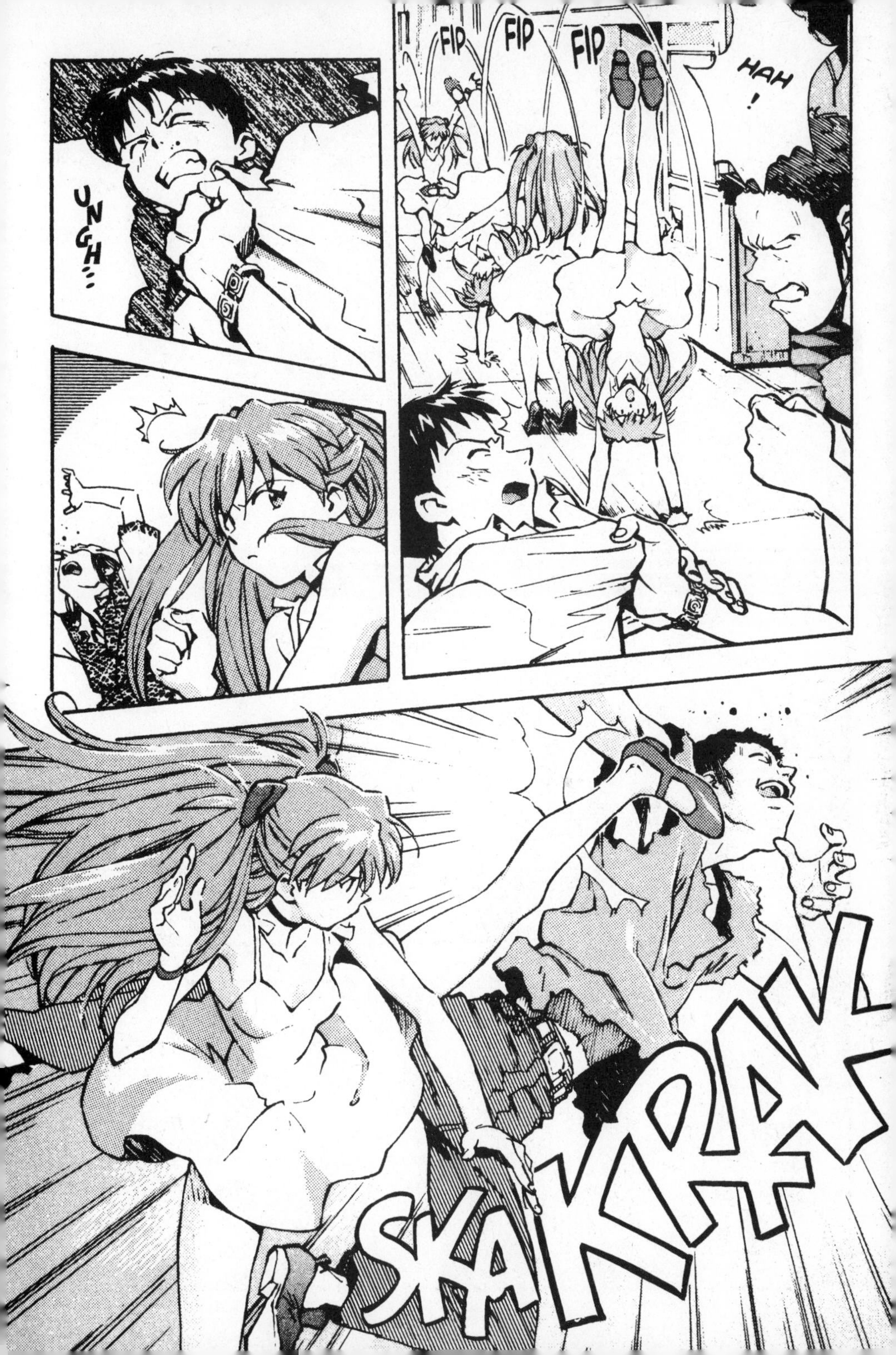
UNGH...
FIP
FIP
FIP
HAH!
SKAKRAK

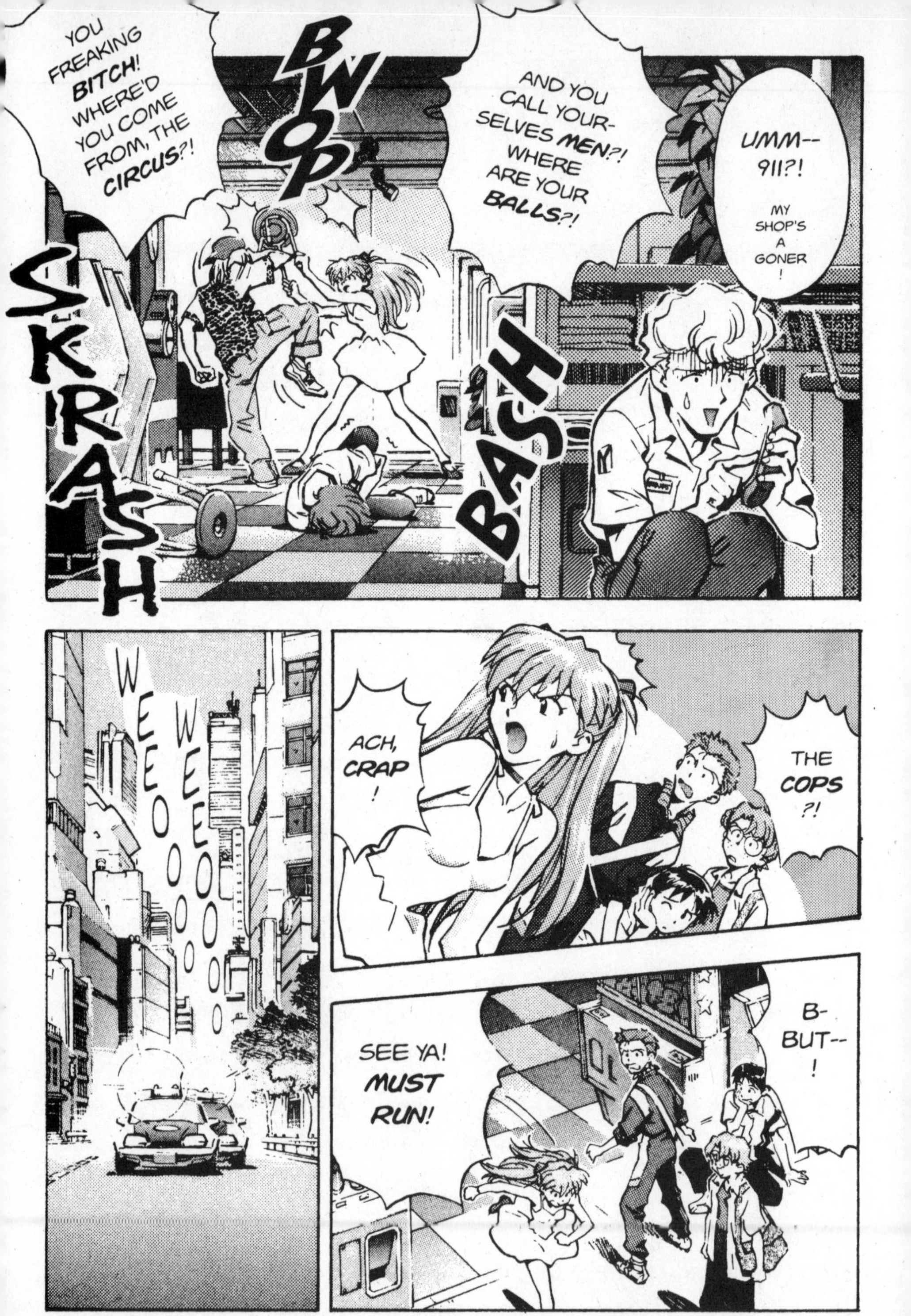
YOU FREAKING BITCH! WHERE'D YOU COME FROM, THE CIRCUS?!
BWOP
AND YOU CALL YOURSELVES MEN?! WHERE ARE YOUR BALLS?!
SKRASH
BASH
UMM--911?!
MY SHOP'S A GONER!
WEEOOOO
WEEOOOO
ACH, CRAP!
THE COPS?!
SEE YA! MUST RUN!
B-BUT--!

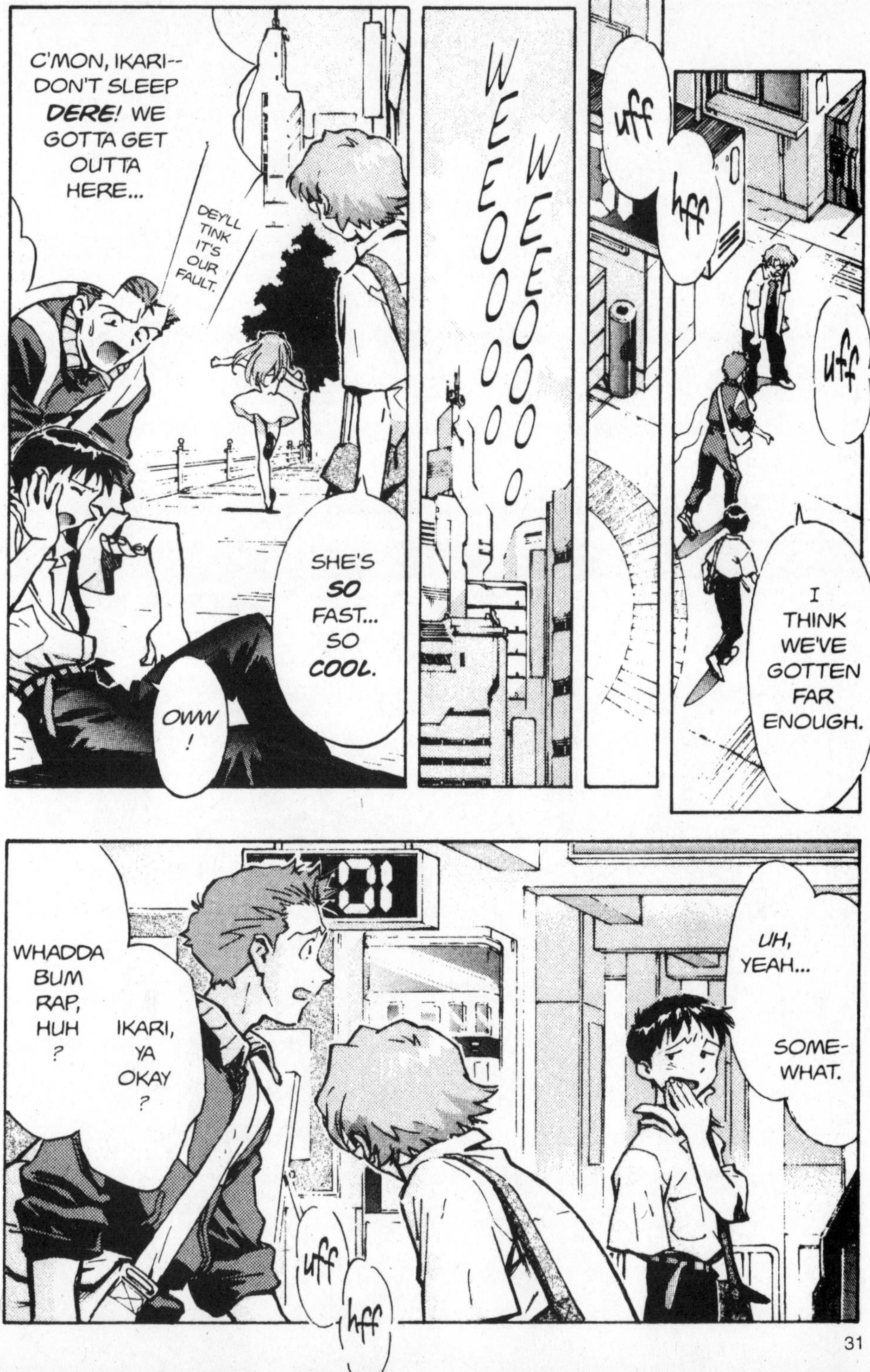
C'MON, IKARI-- DON'T SLEEP DERE! WE GOTTA GET OUTTA HERE...
DEY'LL TINK IT'S OUR FAULT.
SHE'S SO FAST... SO COOL.
OWW!
WEEEOOOO
WEEEOOOOO
uff
hff
uff
I THINK WE'VE GOTTEN FAR ENOUGH.
01
WHADDA BUM RAP, HUH?
IKARI, YA OKAY?
UH, YEAH...
SOME-WHAT.
uff
hff

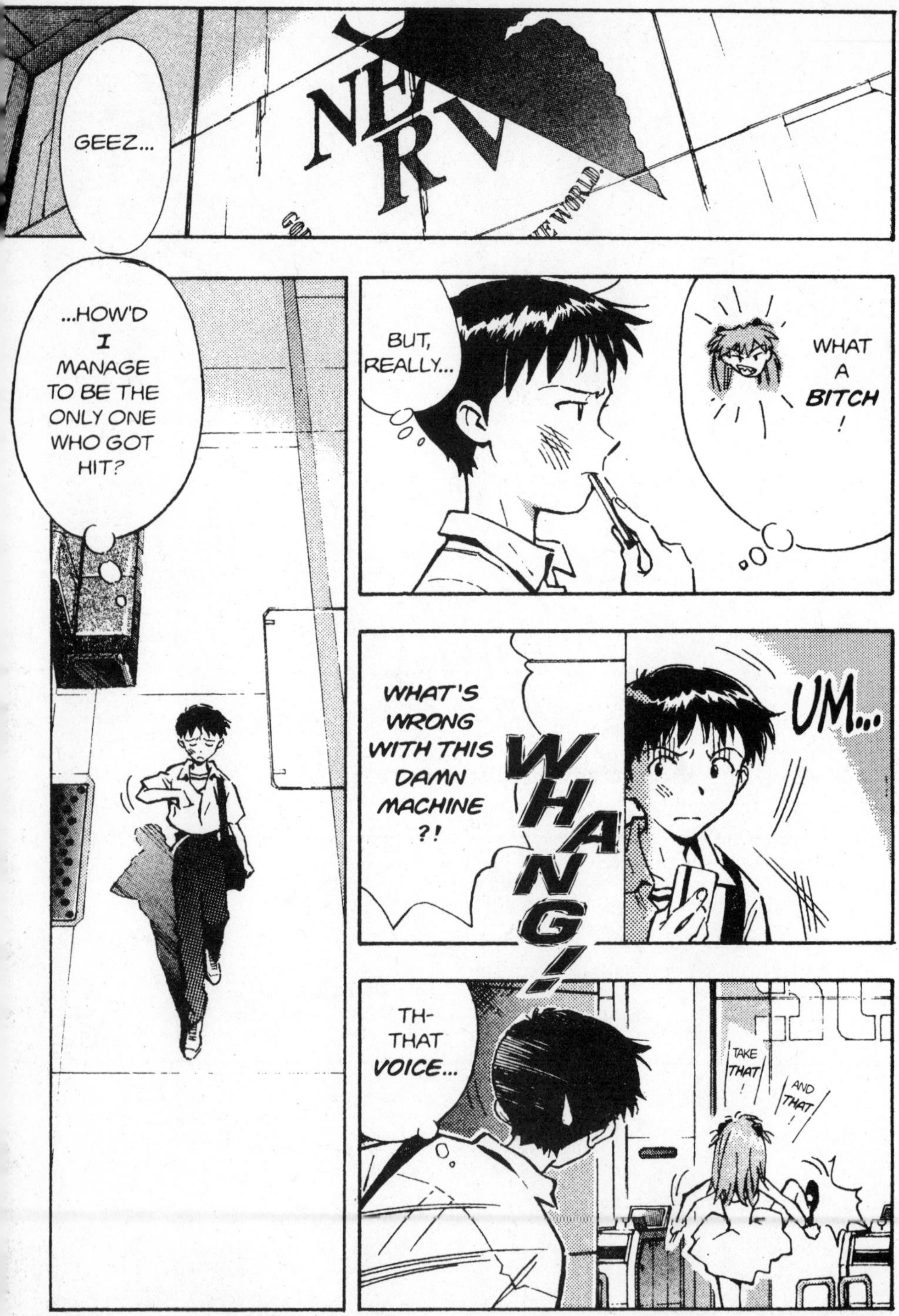
GEEZ...
NERV
...HOW'D I MANAGE TO BE THE ONLY ONE WHO GOT HIT?
BUT, REALLY...
WHAT A BITCH!
WHAT'S WRONG WITH THIS DAMN MACHINE?!
WHANG!
UM...
TH-THAT VOICE...
TAKE THAT!
AND THAT!

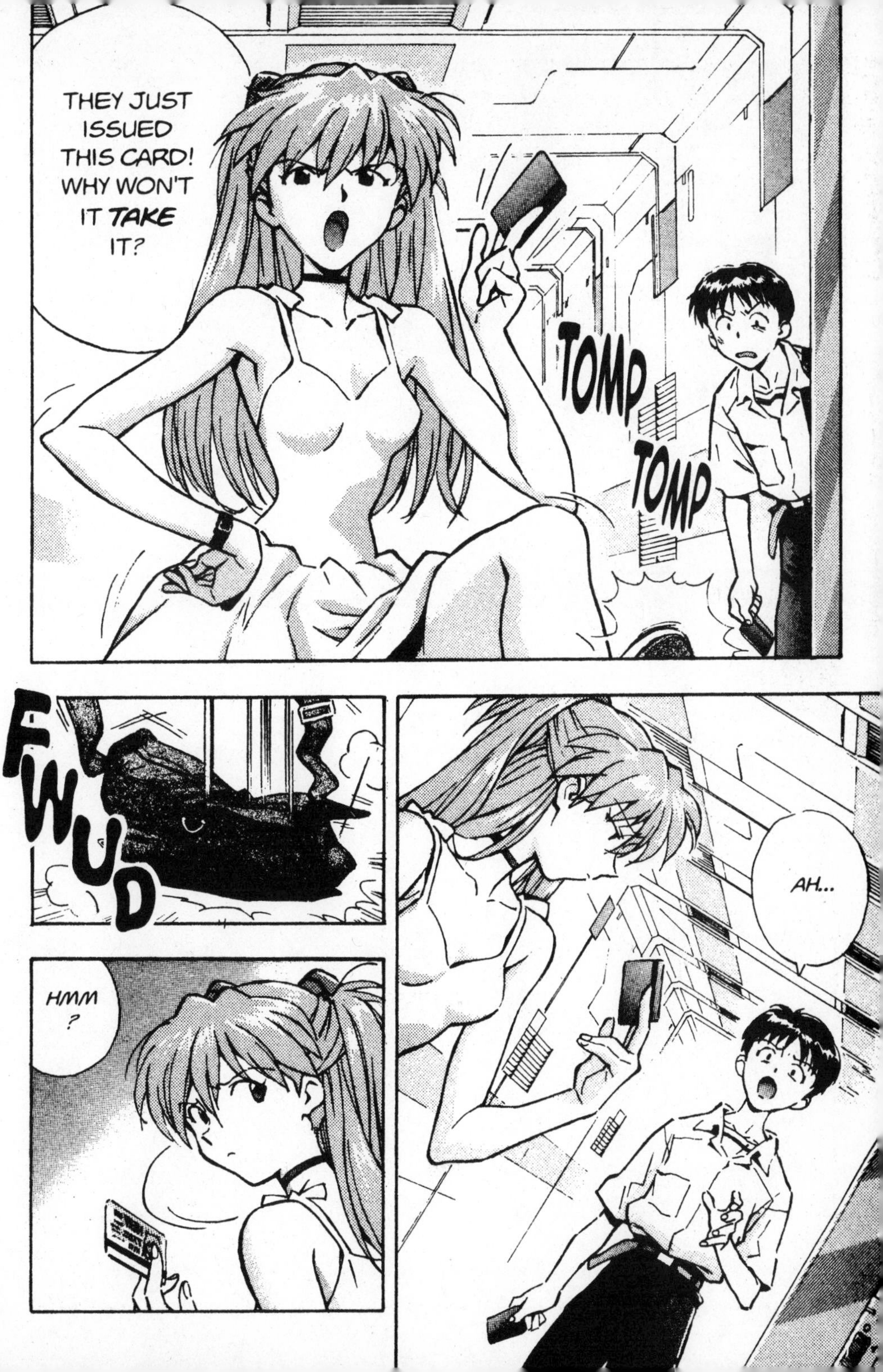
THEY JUST ISSUED THIS CARD! WHY WON'T IT *TAKE* IT?
TOMP
TOMP
FWUD
HMM ?
AH...

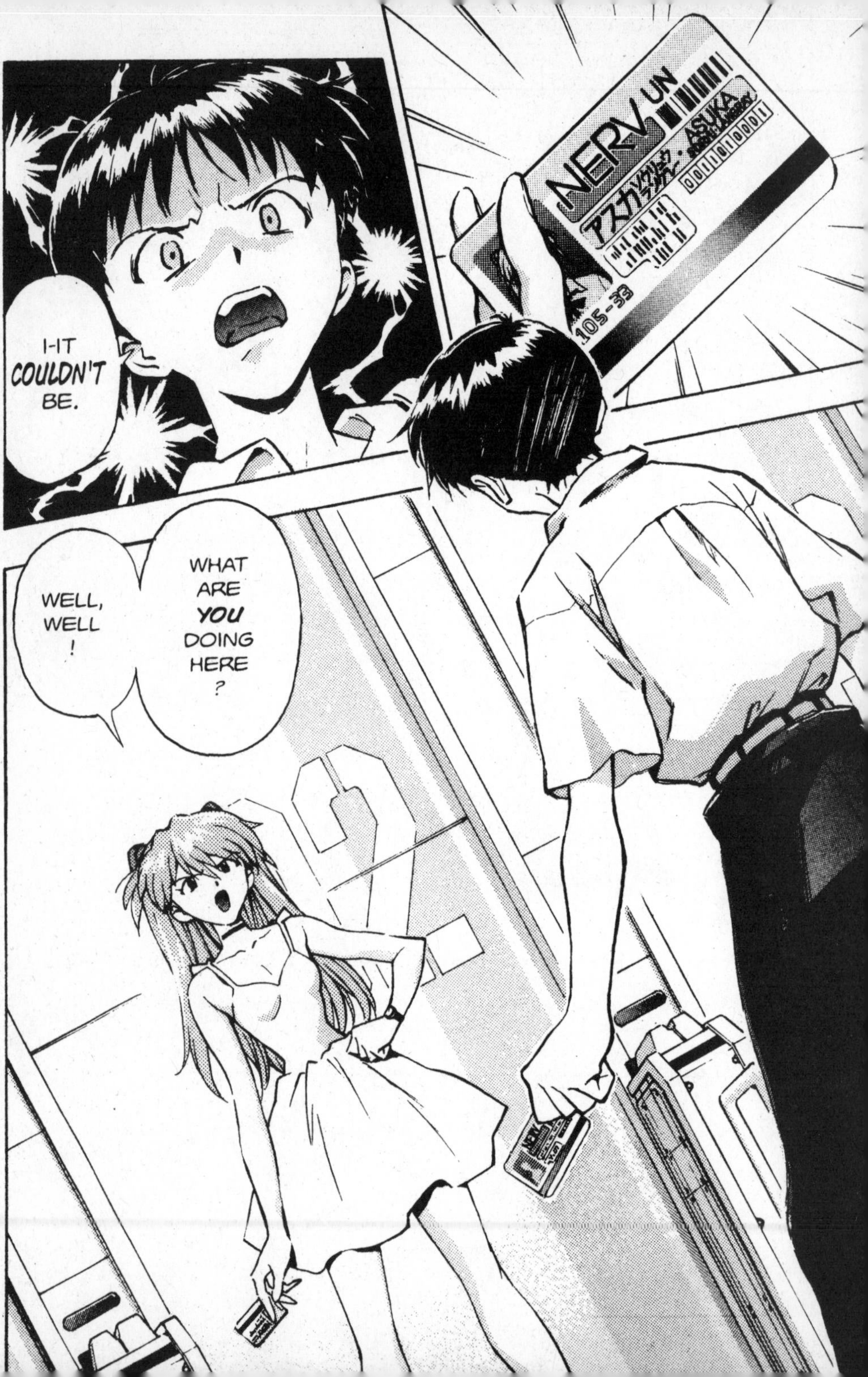
I-IT COULDN'T BE.
NERV
UN
アスカ
ASUKA
105-33
WELL, WELL !
WHAT ARE YOU DOING HERE ?

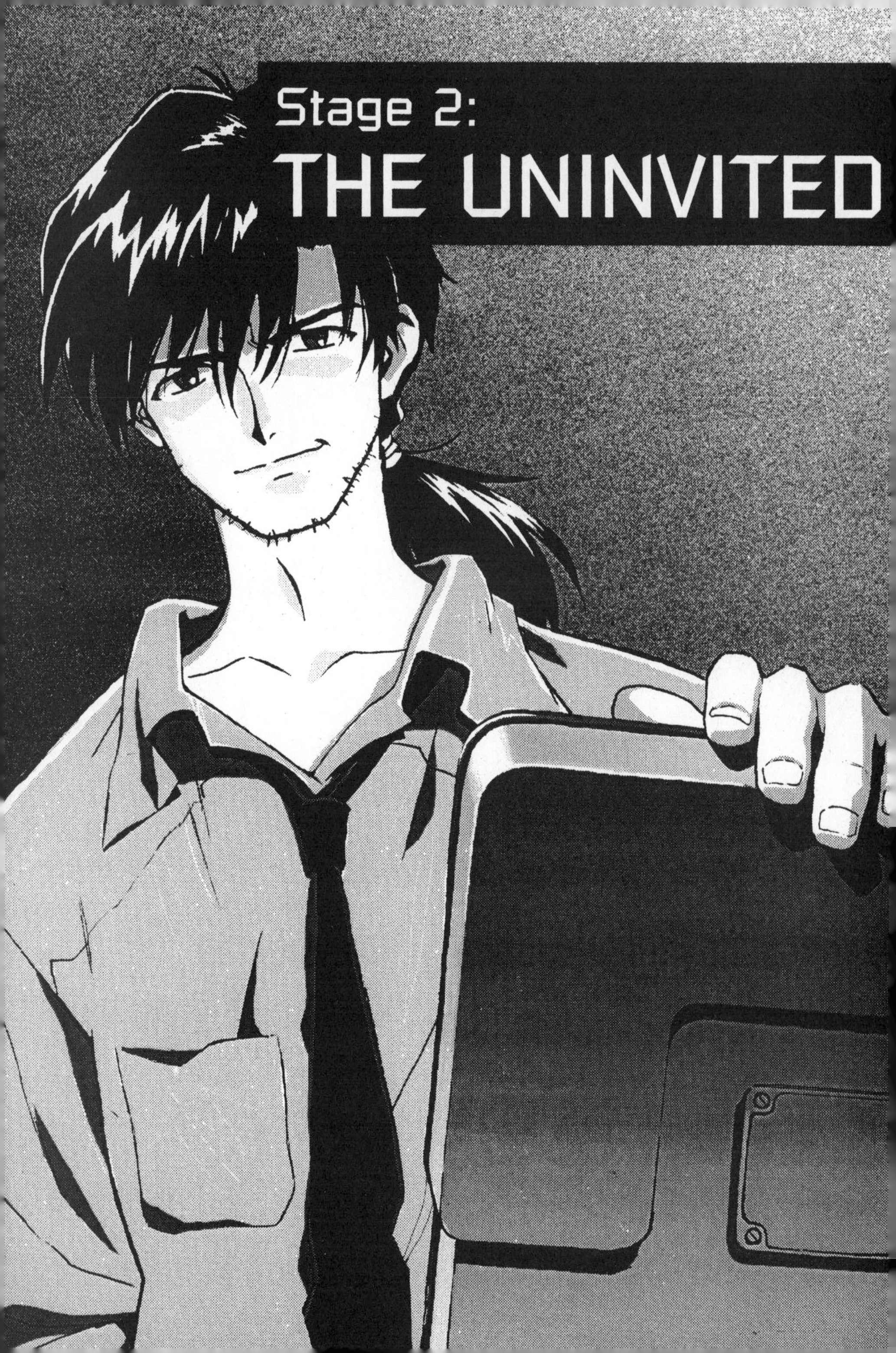
Stage 2:
THE UNINVITED

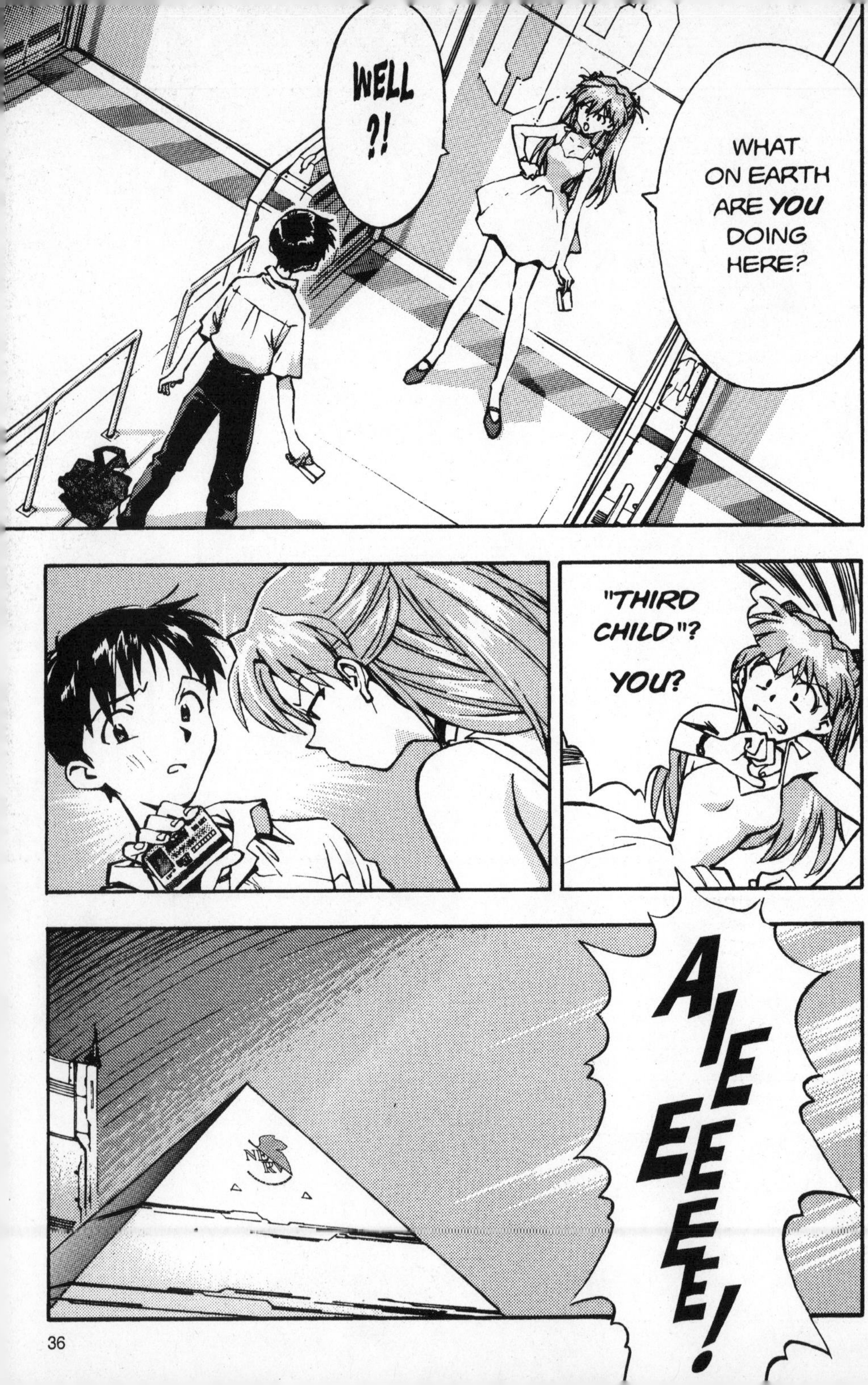
WELL ?!
WHAT ON EARTH ARE YOU DOING HERE?
"THIRD CHILD"? YOU?
AIEEEEEEEE!

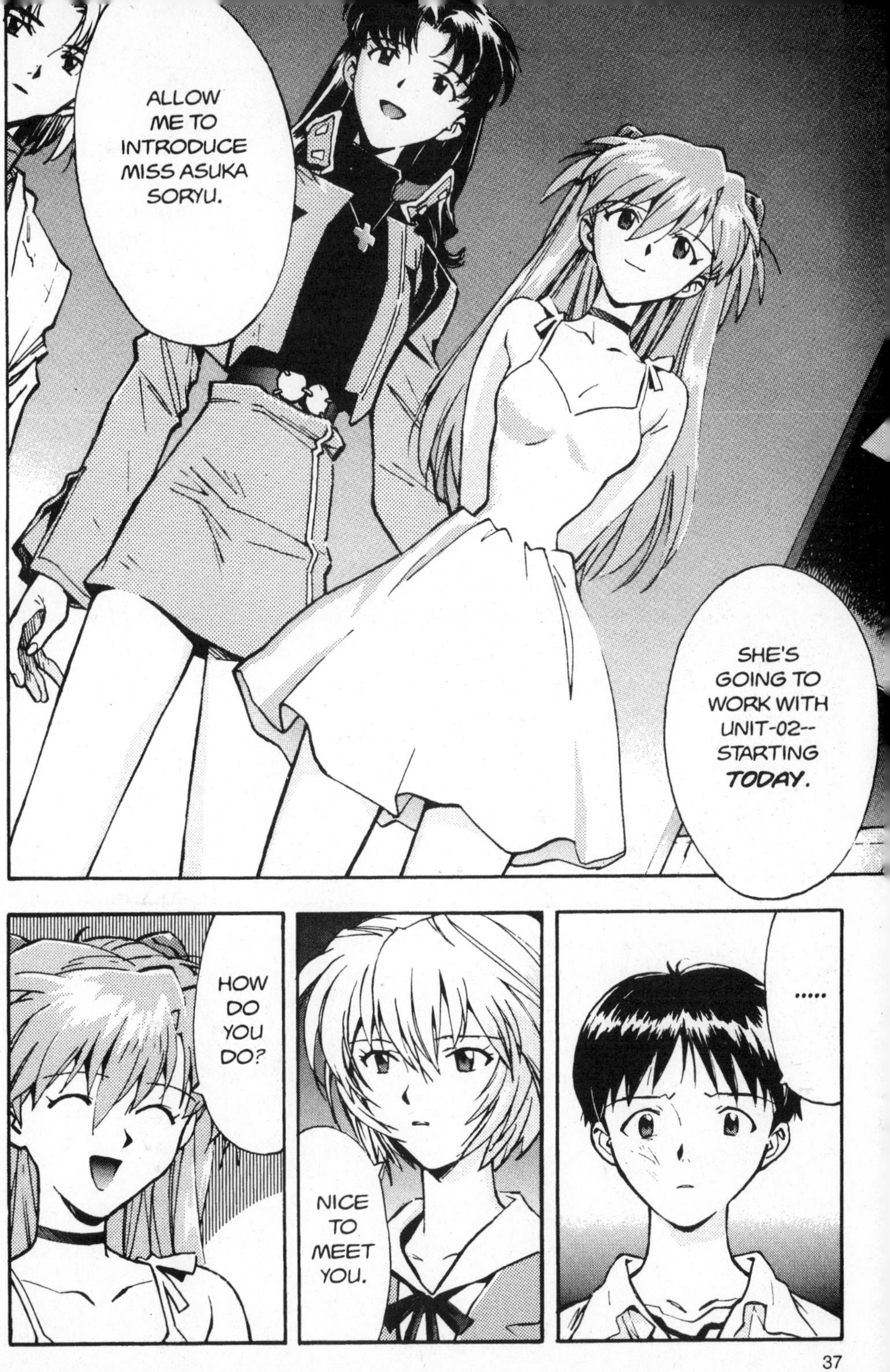
ALLOW ME TO INTRODUCE MISS ASUKA SORYU.
SHE'S GOING TO WORK WITH UNIT-02-- STARTING ***TODAY.***
HOW DO YOU DO?
NICE TO MEET YOU.
.....

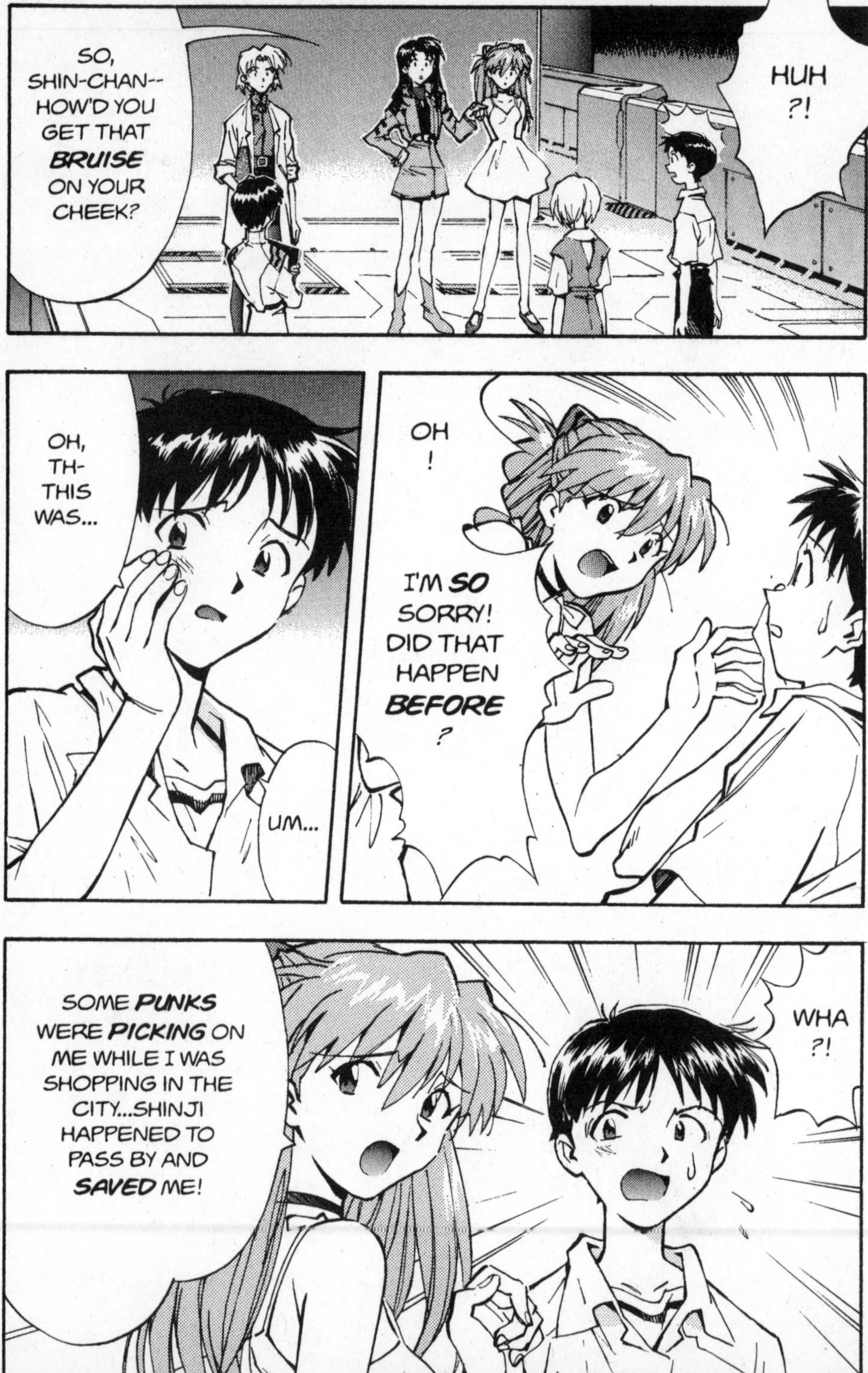
SO, SHIN-CHAN-- HOW'D YOU GET THAT BRUISE ON YOUR CHEEK?
HUH ?!
OH, TH- THIS WAS...
UM...
OH !
I'M SO SORRY! DID THAT HAPPEN BEFORE ?
SOME PUNKS WERE PICKING ON ME WHILE I WAS SHOPPING IN THE CITY...SHINJI HAPPENED TO PASS BY AND SAVED ME!
WHA ?!

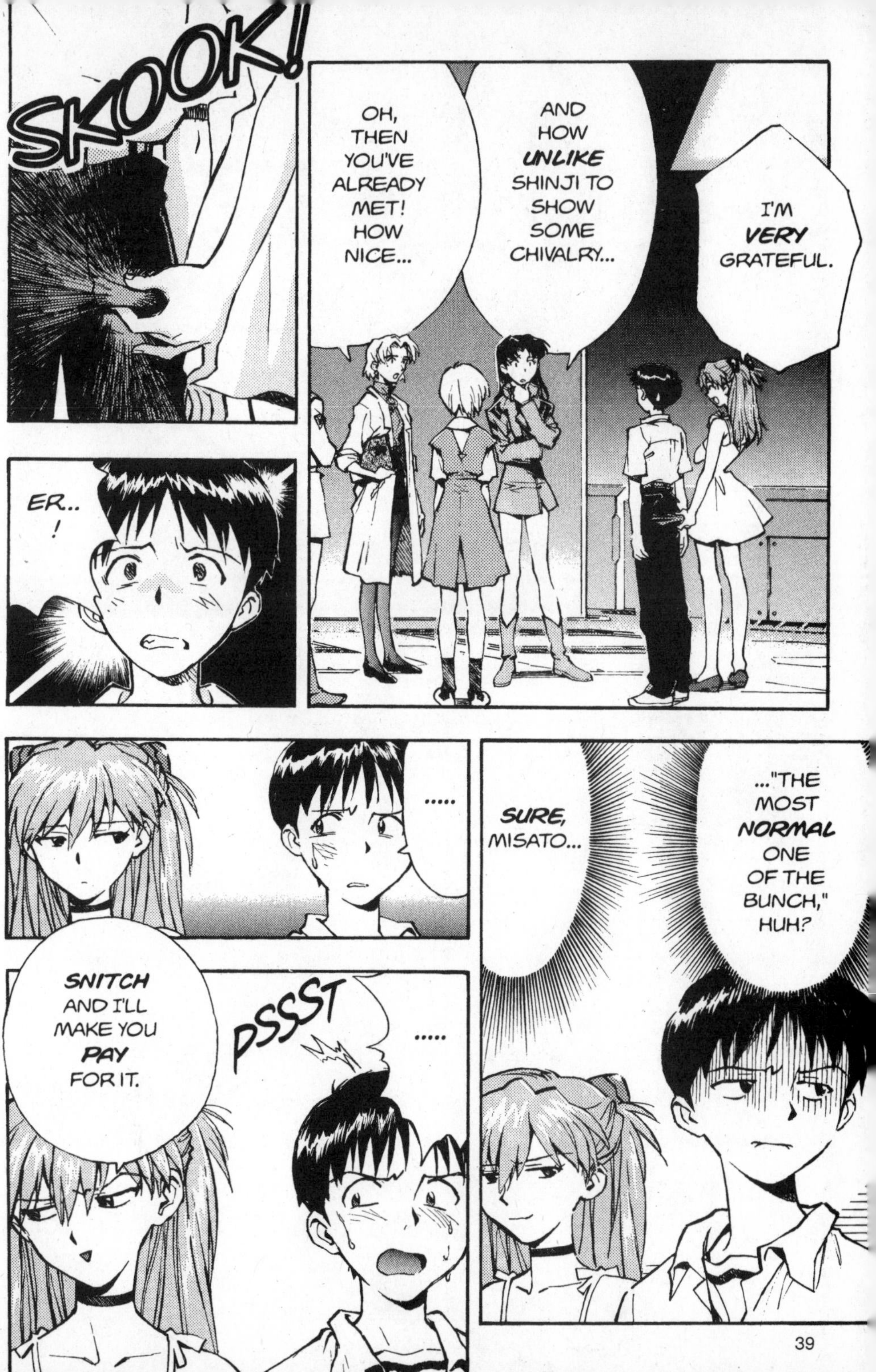
SKOOK!
ER... !
OH, THEN YOU'VE ALREADY MET! HOW NICE...
AND HOW UNLIKE SHINJI TO SHOW SOME CHIVALRY...
I'M VERY GRATEFUL.
.....
SNITCH AND I'LL MAKE YOU PAY FOR IT.
PSSST
.....
SURE, MISATO...
..."THE MOST NORMAL ONE OF THE BUNCH," HUH?

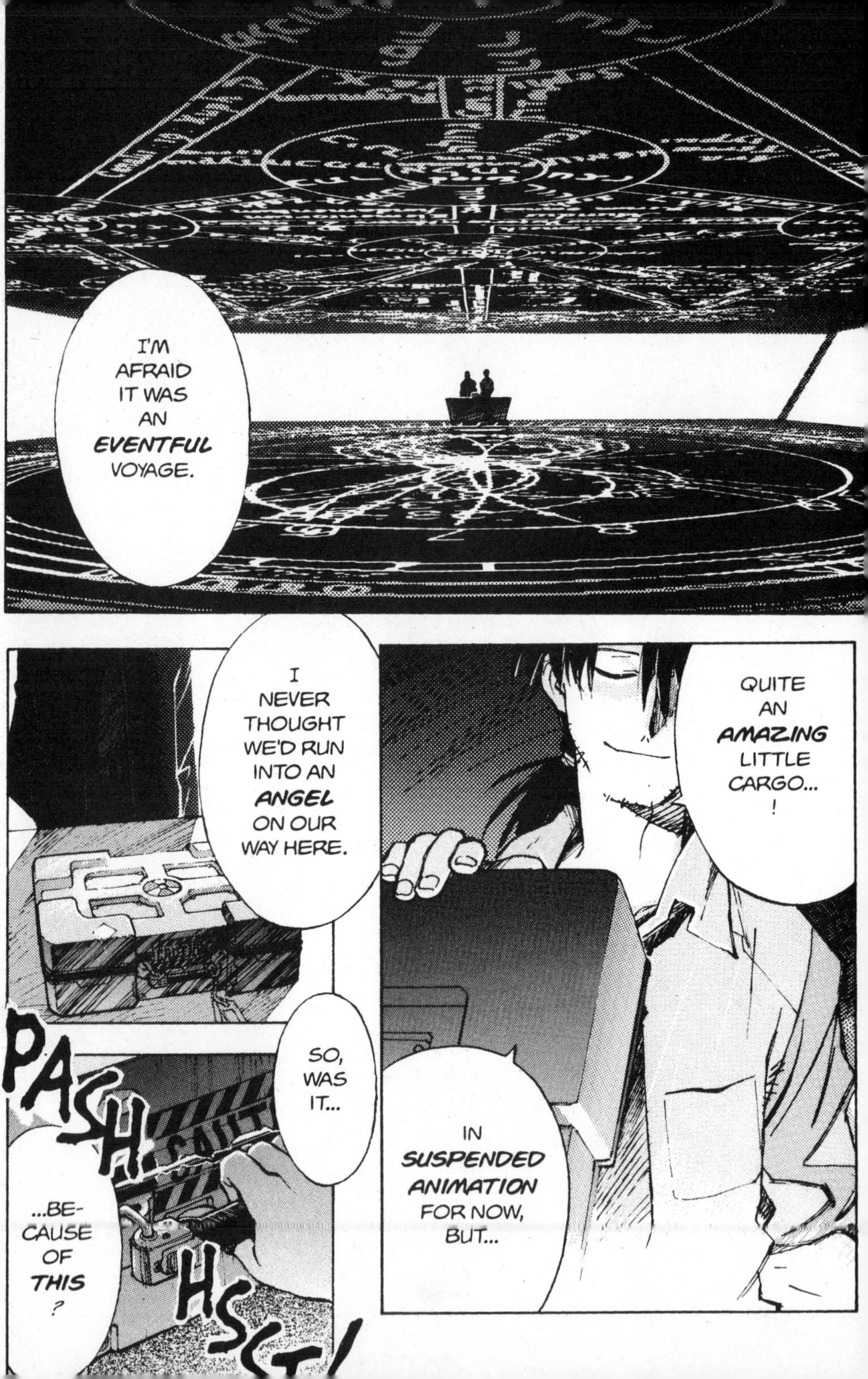

I'M AFRAID IT WAS AN EVENTFUL VOYAGE.
I NEVER THOUGHT WE'D RUN INTO AN ANGEL ON OUR WAY HERE.
PASH
SO, WAS IT...
...BE-CAUSE OF THIS?
HSST!
QUITE AN AMAZING LITTLE CARGO...!
IN SUSPENDED ANIMATION FOR NOW, BUT...

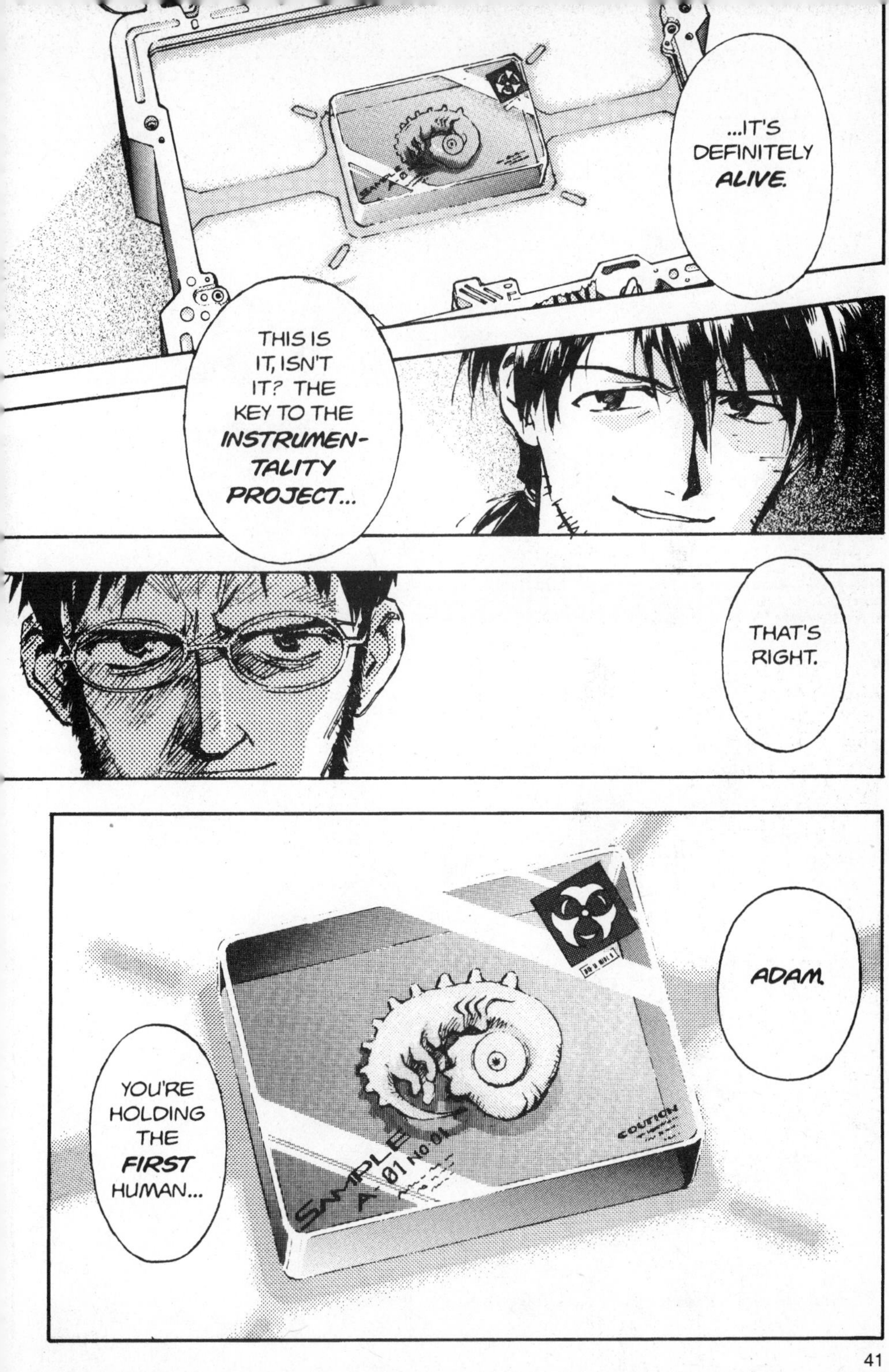
...IT'S DEFINITELY ALIVE.
THIS IS IT, ISN'T IT? THE KEY TO THE INSTRUMENTALITY PROJECT...
THAT'S RIGHT.
ADAM.
YOU'RE HOLDING THE FIRST HUMAN...
SAMPLE

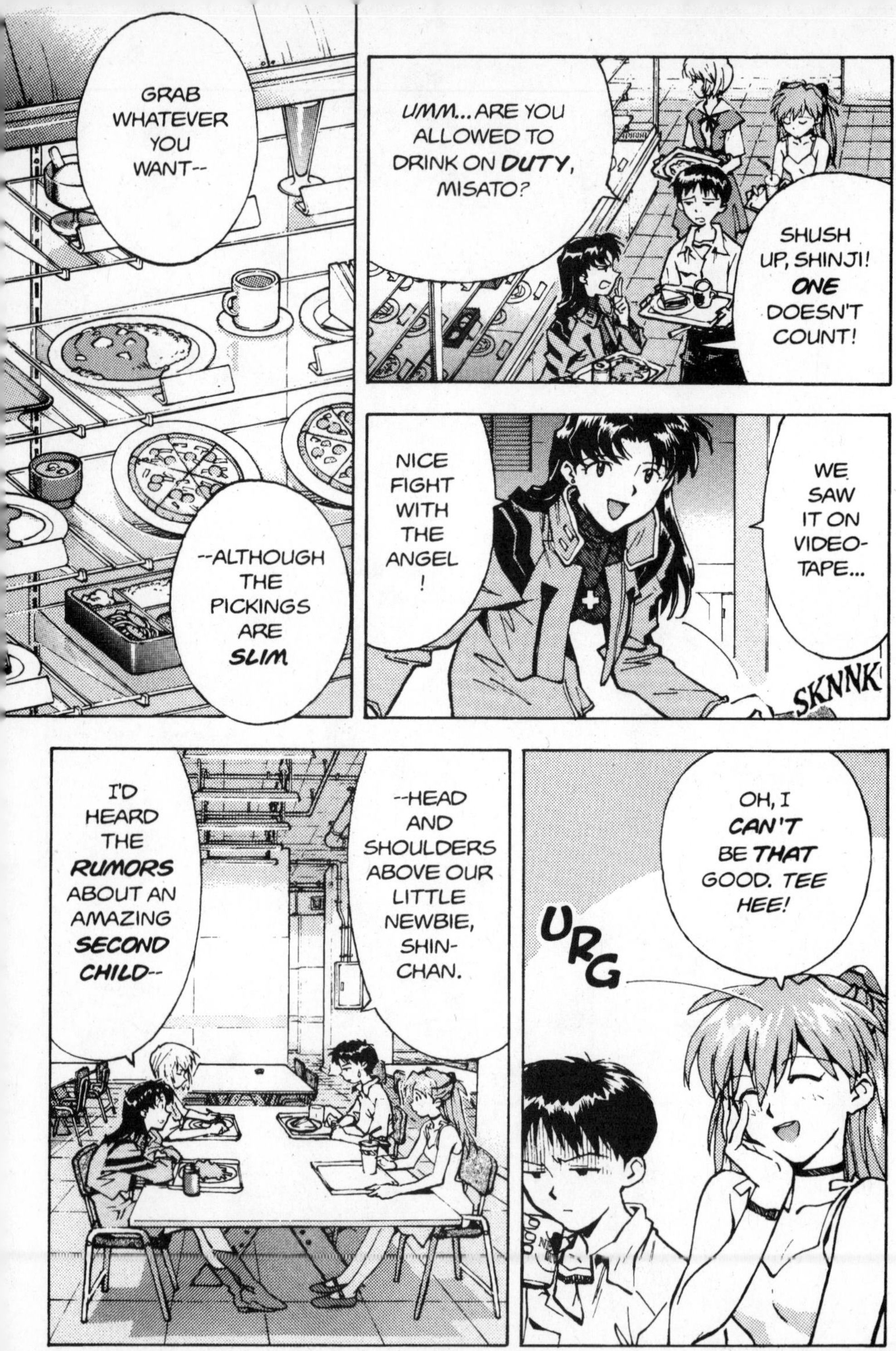
GRAB WHATEVER YOU WANT--
--ALTHOUGH THE PICKINGS ARE SLIM
UMM... ARE YOU ALLOWED TO DRINK ON DUTY, MISATO?
SHUSH UP, SHINJI! ONE DOESN'T COUNT!
NICE FIGHT WITH THE ANGEL!
WE SAW IT ON VIDEO-TAPE...
SKNNK
I'D HEARD THE RUMORS ABOUT AN AMAZING SECOND CHILD--
--HEAD AND SHOULDERS ABOVE OUR LITTLE NEWBIE, SHIN-CHAN.
OH, I CAN'T BE THAT GOOD. TEE HEE!
URG

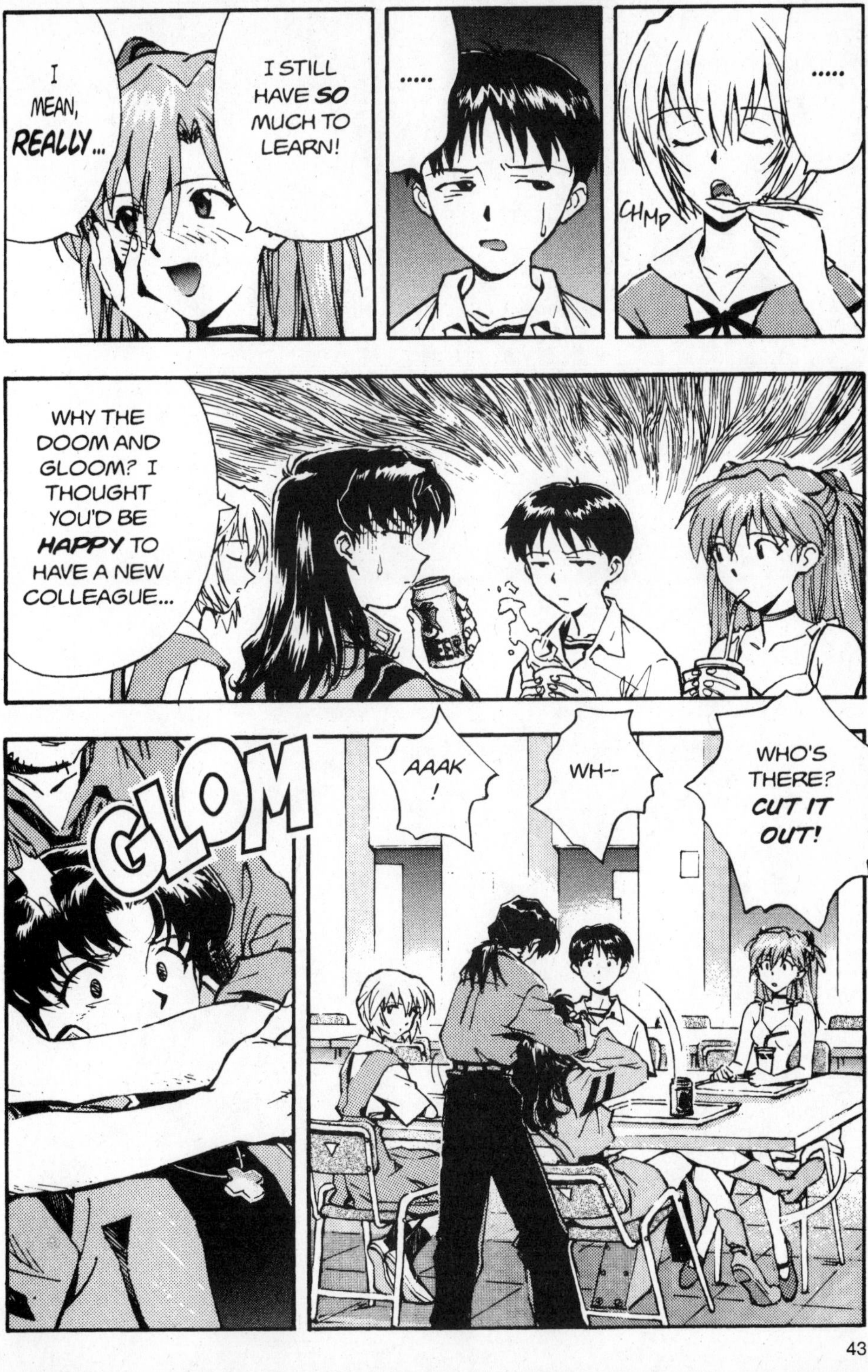
I MEAN, REALLY...
I STILL HAVE SO MUCH TO LEARN!
.....
.....
CHMP
WHY THE DOOM AND GLOOM? I THOUGHT YOU'D BE HAPPY TO HAVE A NEW COLLEAGUE...
GLOM
AAAK!
WH--
WHO'S THERE? CUT IT OUT!

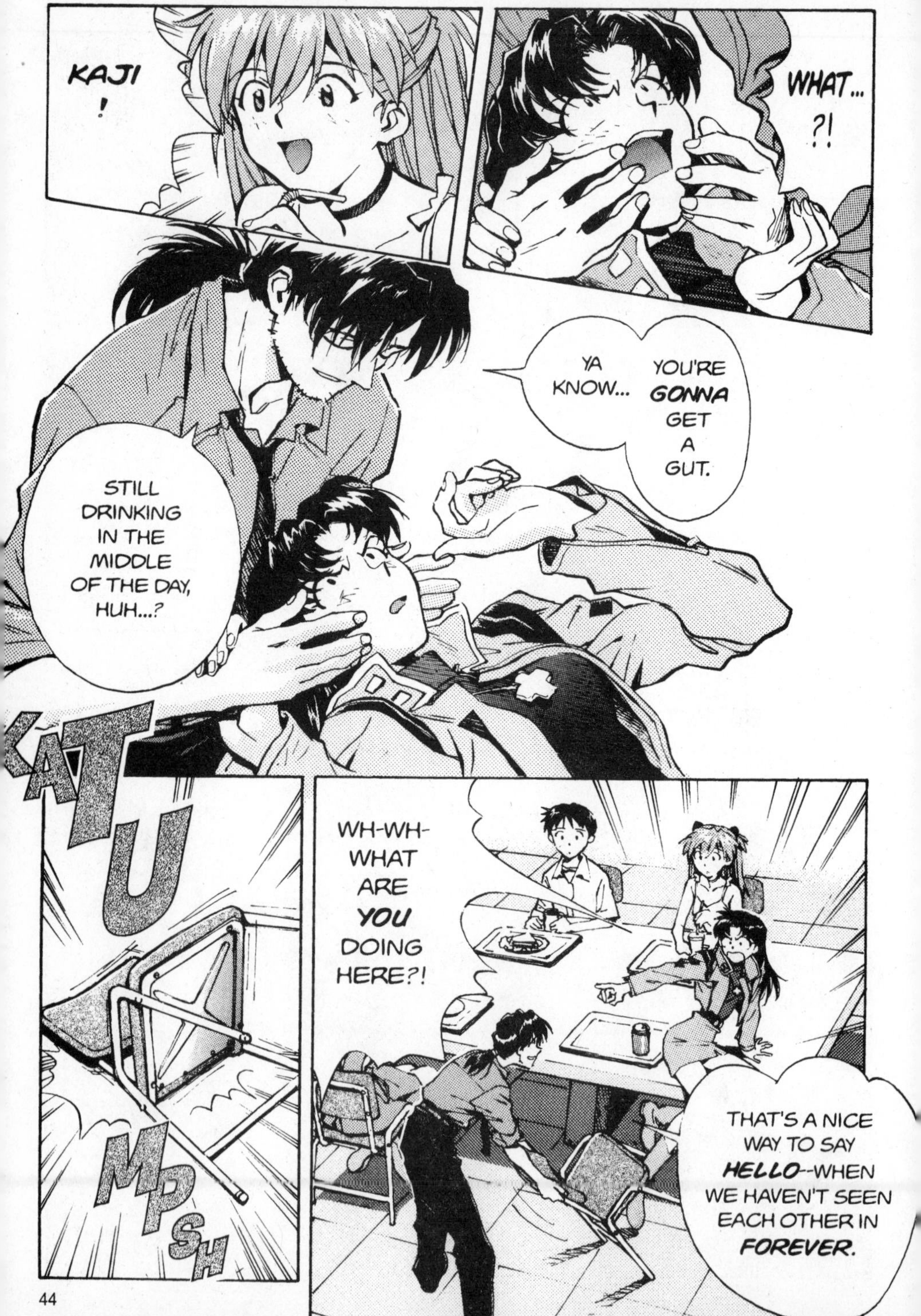
KAJI!
WHAT...?!
STILL DRINKING IN THE MIDDLE OF THE DAY, HUH...?
YA KNOW...
YOU'RE GONNA GET A GUT.
KATUMPSH
WH-WH-WHAT ARE YOU DOING HERE?!
THAT'S A NICE WAY TO SAY HELLO--WHEN WE HAVEN'T SEEN EACH OTHER IN FOREVER.

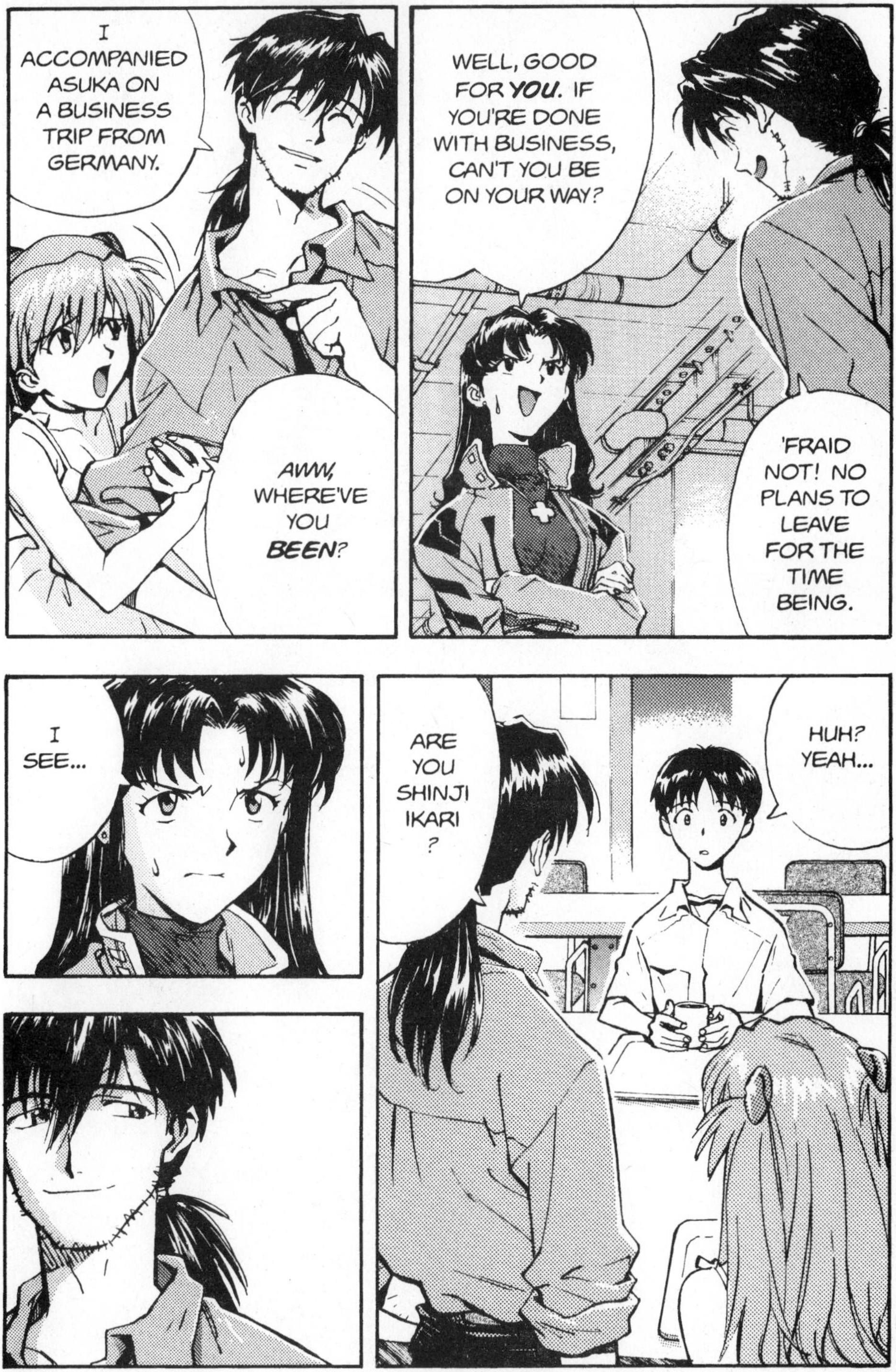
I ACCOMPANIED ASUKA ON A BUSINESS TRIP FROM GERMANY.
AWW, WHERE'VE YOU BEEN?
WELL, GOOD FOR YOU. IF YOU'RE DONE WITH BUSINESS, CAN'T YOU BE ON YOUR WAY?
'FRAID NOT! NO PLANS TO LEAVE FOR THE TIME BEING.
I SEE...
ARE YOU SHINJI IKARI?
HUH? YEAH...

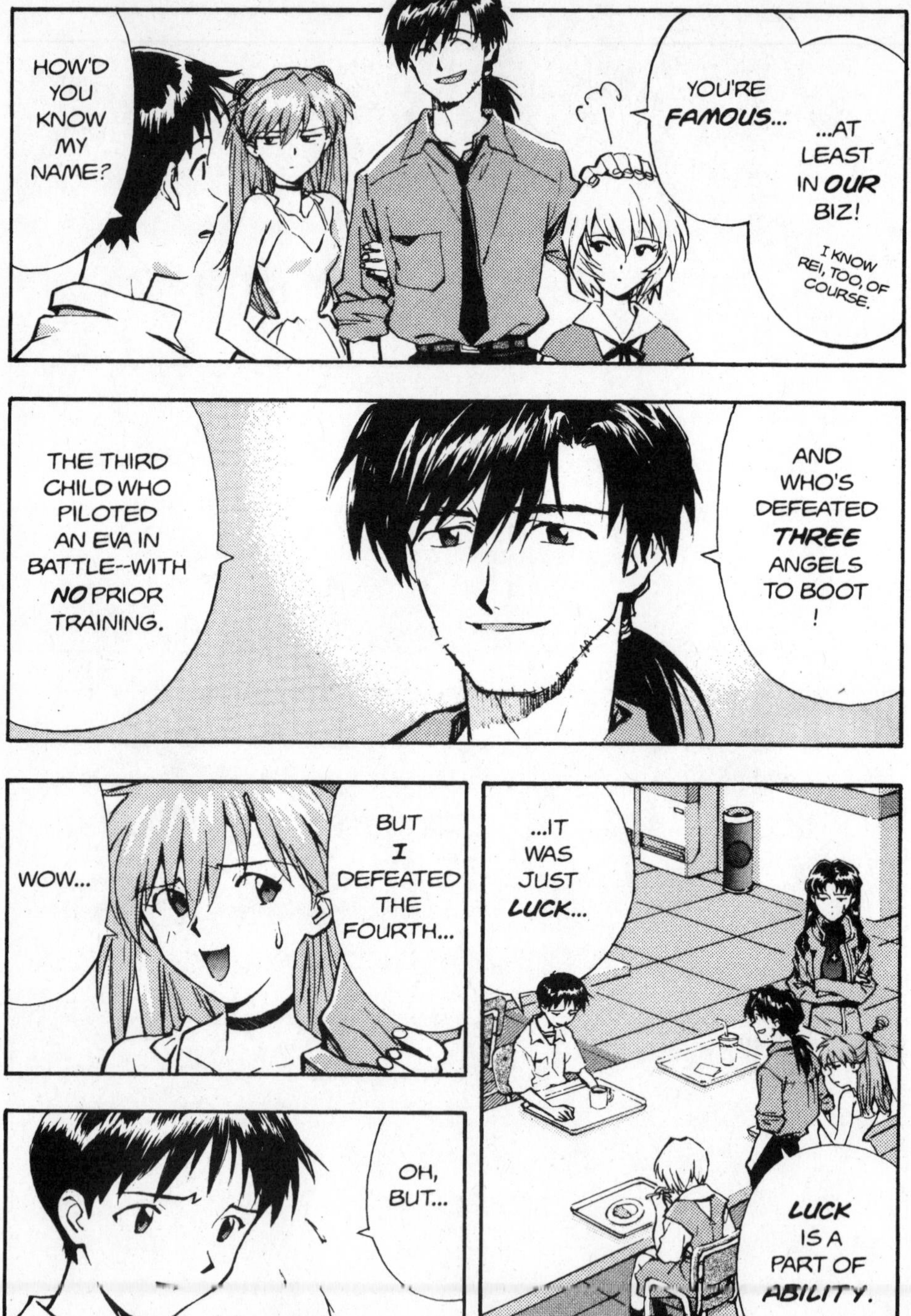
HOW'D YOU KNOW MY NAME?
YOU'RE **FAMOUS**...
...AT LEAST IN **OUR** BIZ!
I KNOW REI, TOO, OF COURSE.
THE THIRD CHILD WHO PILOTED AN EVA IN BATTLE--WITH **NO** PRIOR TRAINING.
AND WHO'S DEFEATED **THREE** ANGELS TO BOOT!
WOW...
BUT **I** DEFEATED THE FOURTH...
OH, BUT...
...IT WAS JUST **LUCK**...
LUCK IS A PART OF **ABILITY**.

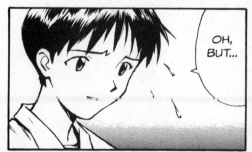

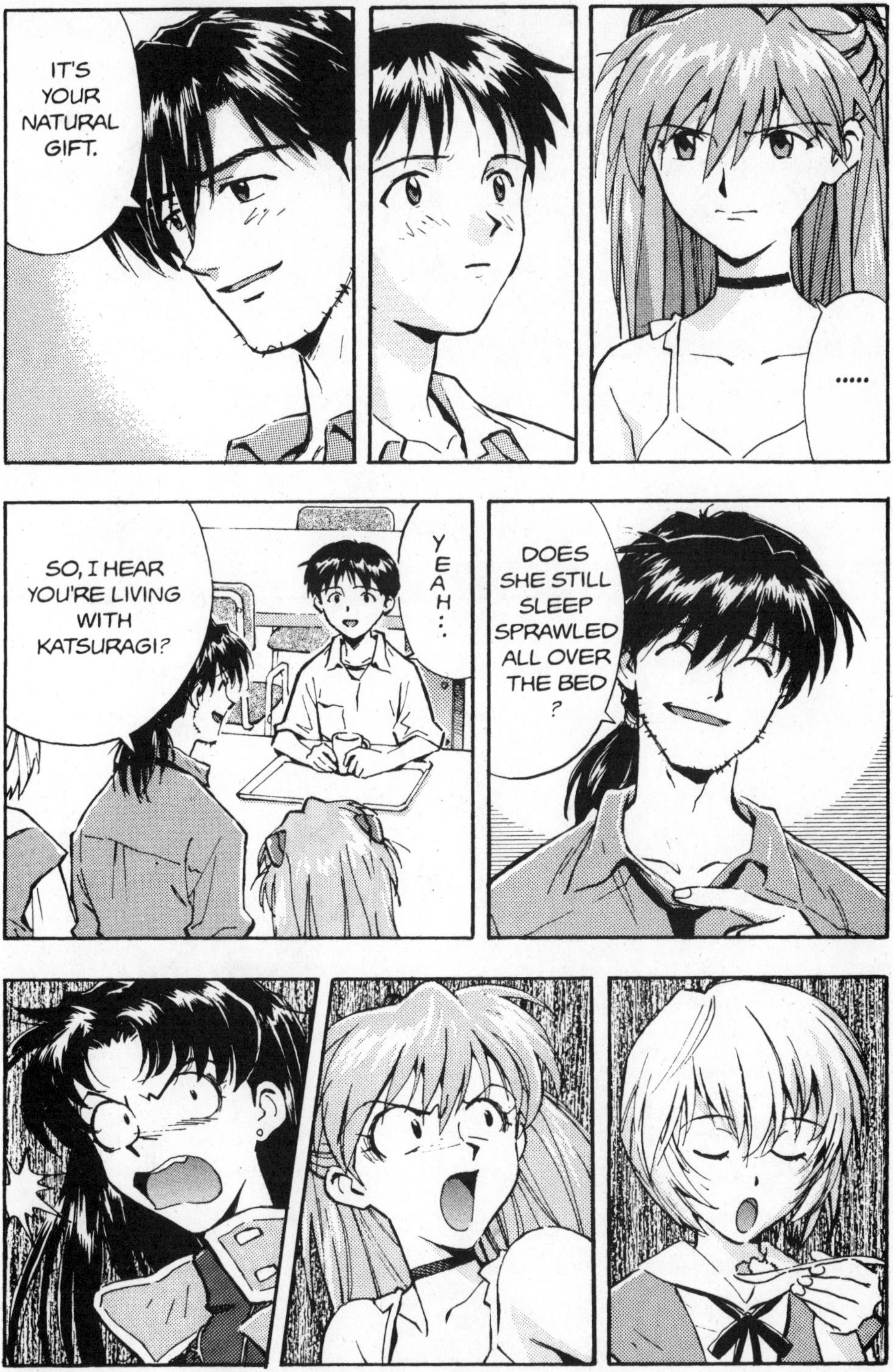
IT'S YOUR NATURAL GIFT.
.....
SO, I HEAR YOU'RE LIVING WITH KATSURAGI?
YEAH...
DOES SHE STILL SLEEP SPRAWLED ALL OVER THE BED ?

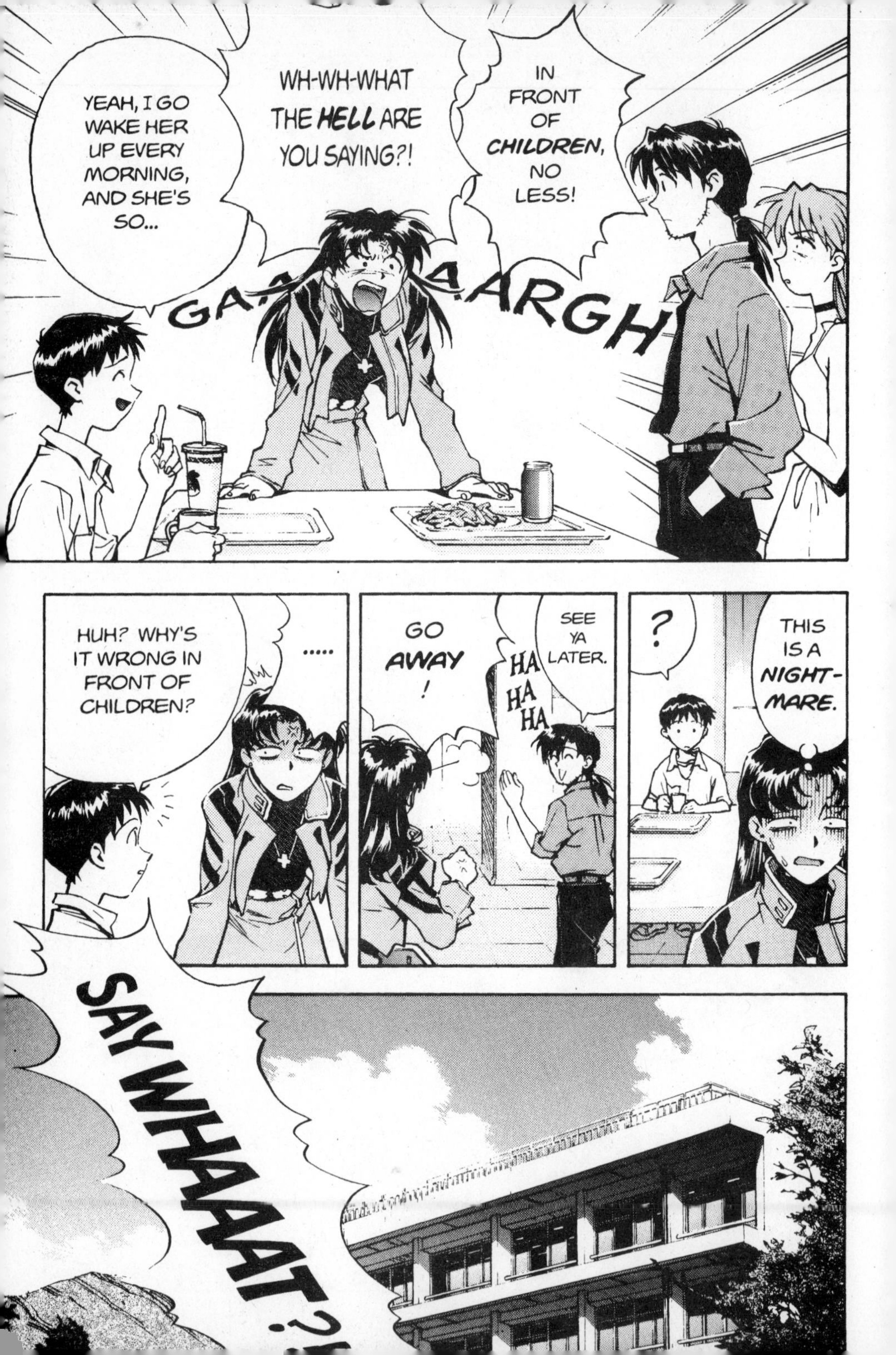
YEAH, I GO WAKE HER UP EVERY MORNING, AND SHE'S SO...
WH-WH-WHAT THE HELL ARE YOU SAYING?!
IN FRONT OF CHILDREN, NO LESS!
GAAAARGH
HUH? WHY'S IT WRONG IN FRONT OF CHILDREN?
.....
GO AWAY!
HA HA HA
SEE YA LATER.
?
THIS IS A NIGHT-MARE.
SAY WHAAAT?!

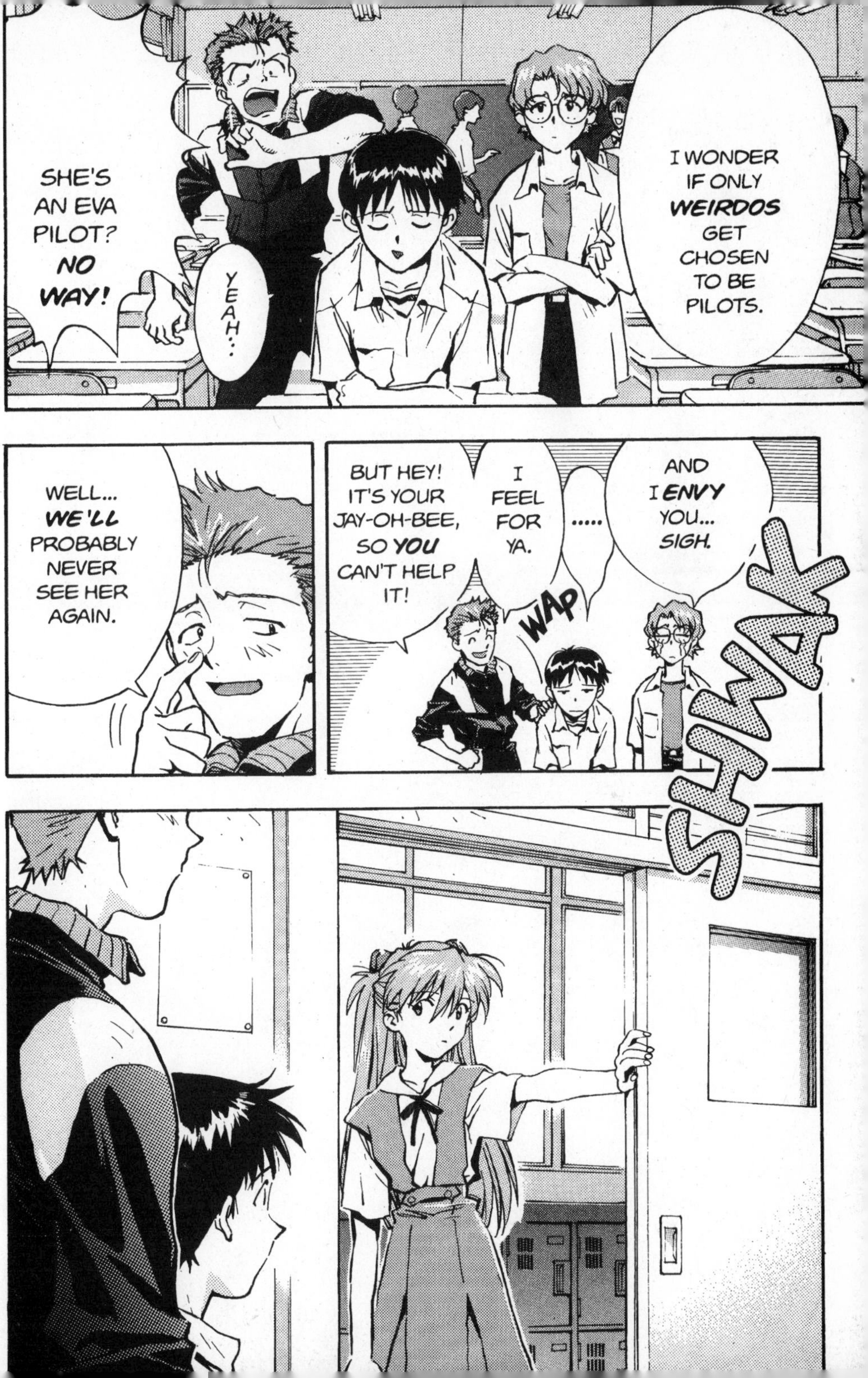
SHE'S AN EVA PILOT? NO WAY!
YEAH...
I WONDER IF ONLY WEIRDOS GET CHOSEN TO BE PILOTS.
WELL... WE'LL PROBABLY NEVER SEE HER AGAIN.
BUT HEY! IT'S YOUR JAY-OH-BEE, SO YOU CAN'T HELP IT!
I FEEL FOR YA.
.....
AND I ENVY YOU... SIGH.
WAP
SHWAK

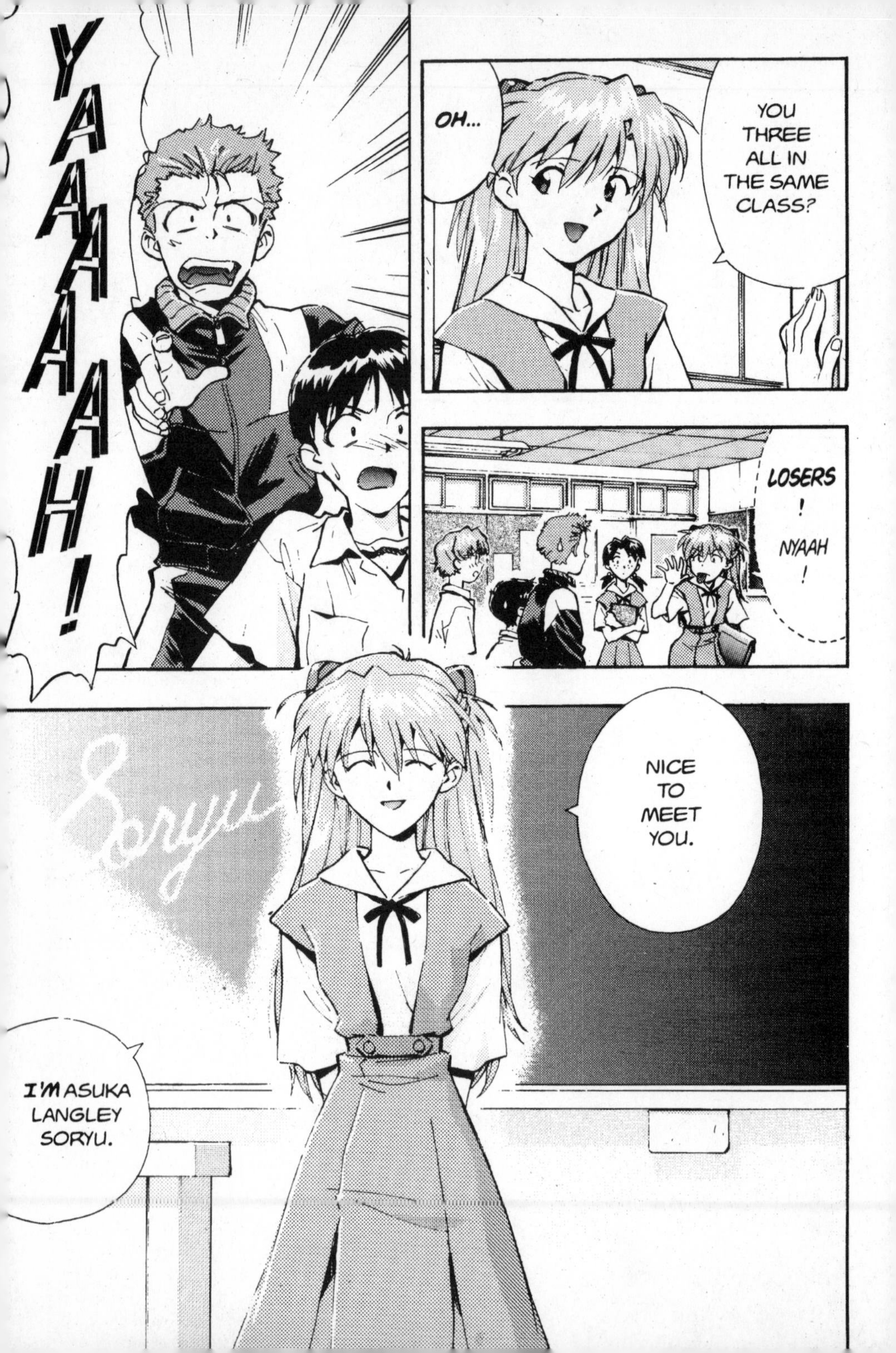
YAAAAAH!!
OH...
YOU THREE ALL IN THE SAME CLASS?
LOSERS! NYAAH!
Soryu
NICE TO MEET YOU.
I'M ASUKA LANGLEY SORYU.

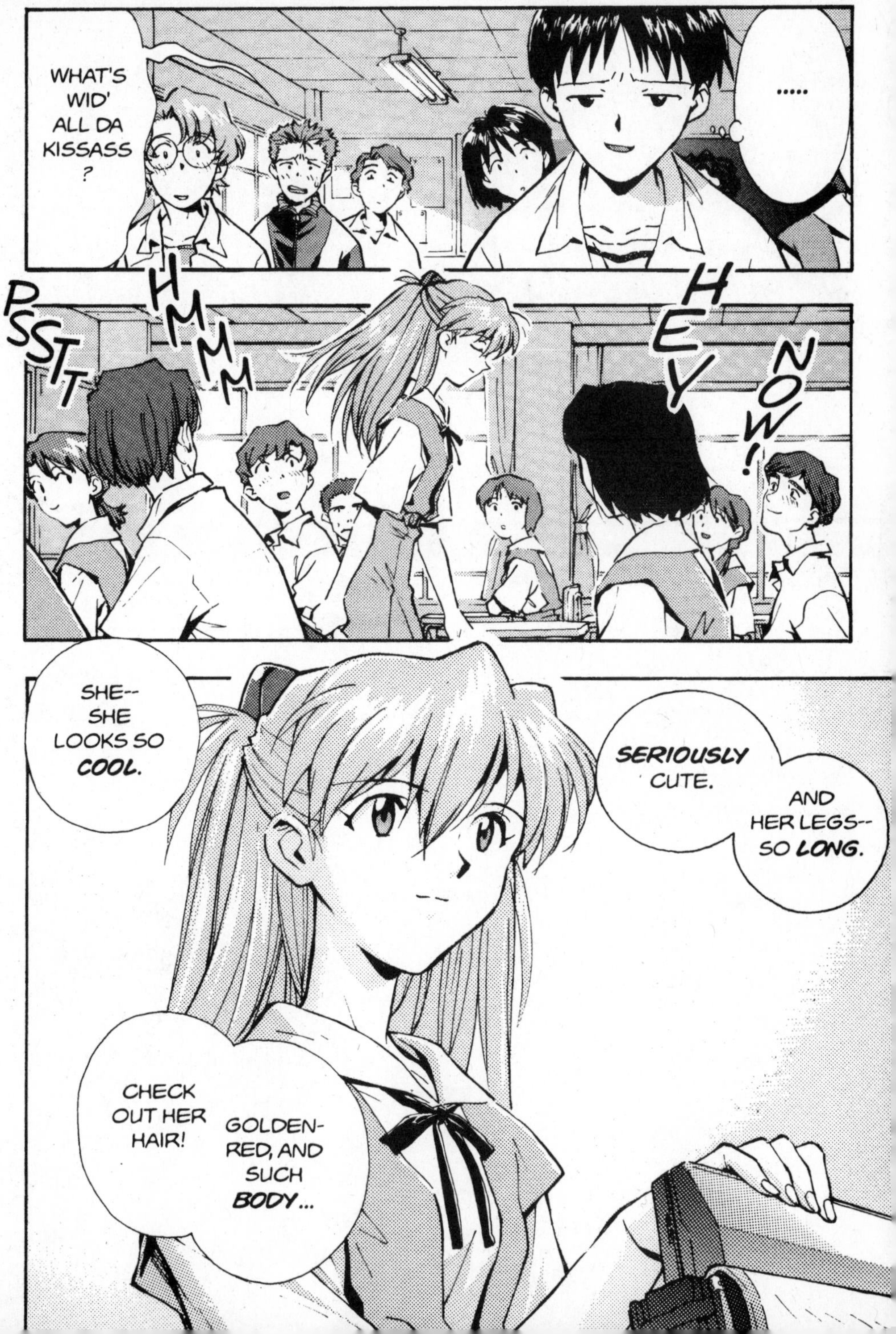
.....
WHAT'S WID' ALL DA KISSASS ?
HEY NOW!
HMMM
PSSTT
SERIOUSLY CUTE.
AND HER LEGS-- SO LONG.
SHE-- SHE LOOKS SO COOL.
CHECK OUT HER HAIR!
GOLDEN-RED, AND SUCH BODY...

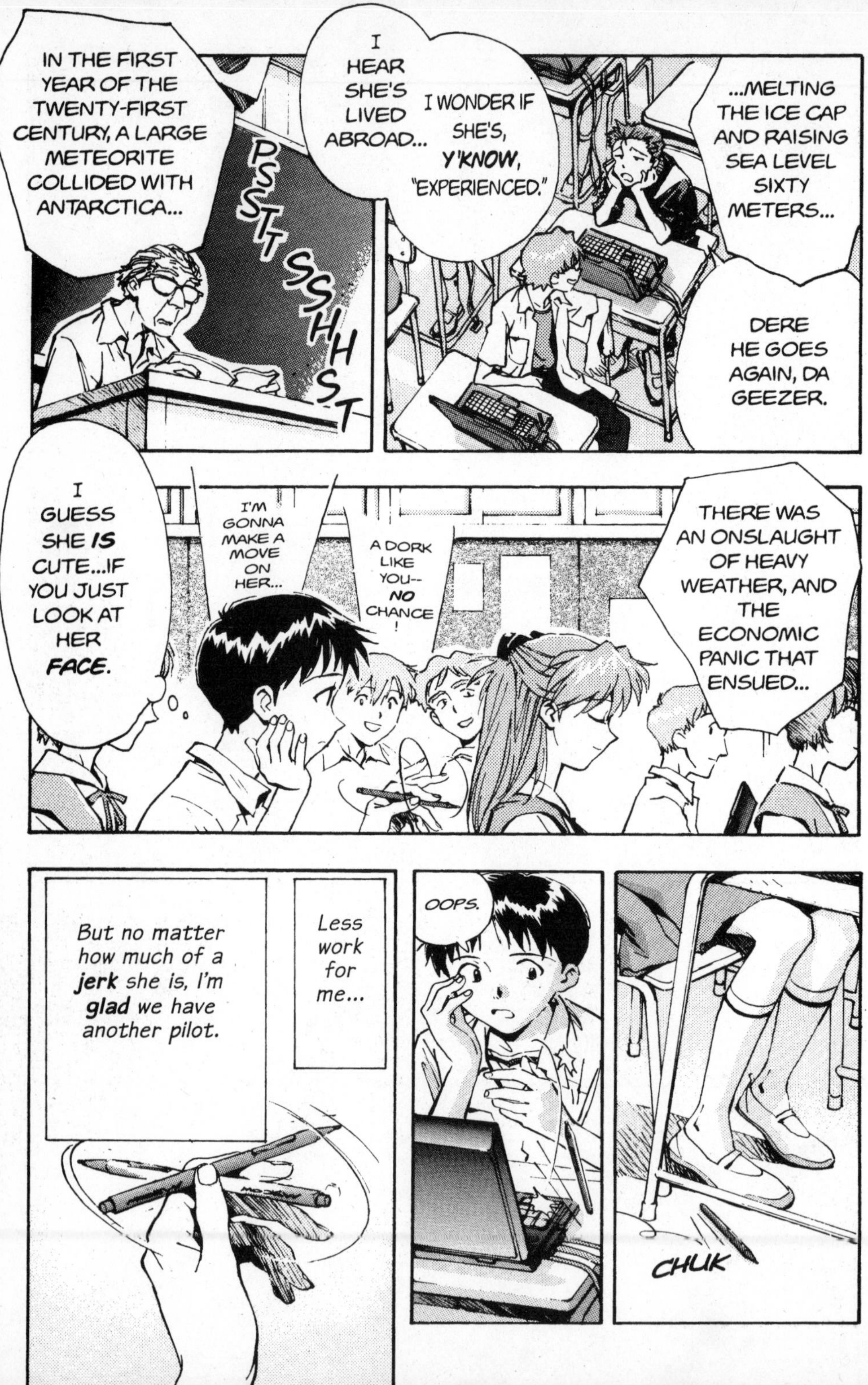
IN THE FIRST YEAR OF THE TWENTY-FIRST CENTURY, A LARGE METEORITE COLLIDED WITH ANTARCTICA...
PSSTT SSHHST
I HEAR SHE'S LIVED ABROAD...
I WONDER IF SHE'S, **Y'KNOW**, "EXPERIENCED."
...MELTING THE ICE CAP AND RAISING SEA LEVEL SIXTY METERS...
DERE HE GOES AGAIN, DA GEEZER.
I GUESS SHE ***IS*** CUTE...IF YOU JUST LOOK AT HER ***FACE***.
I'M GONNA MAKE A MOVE ON HER...
A DORK LIKE YOU-- ***NO*** CHANCE!
THERE WAS AN ONSLAUGHT OF HEAVY WEATHER, AND THE ECONOMIC PANIC THAT ENSUED...
But no matter how much of a ***jerk*** *she is, I'm* ***glad*** *we have another pilot.*
Less work for me...
OOPS.
CHUK

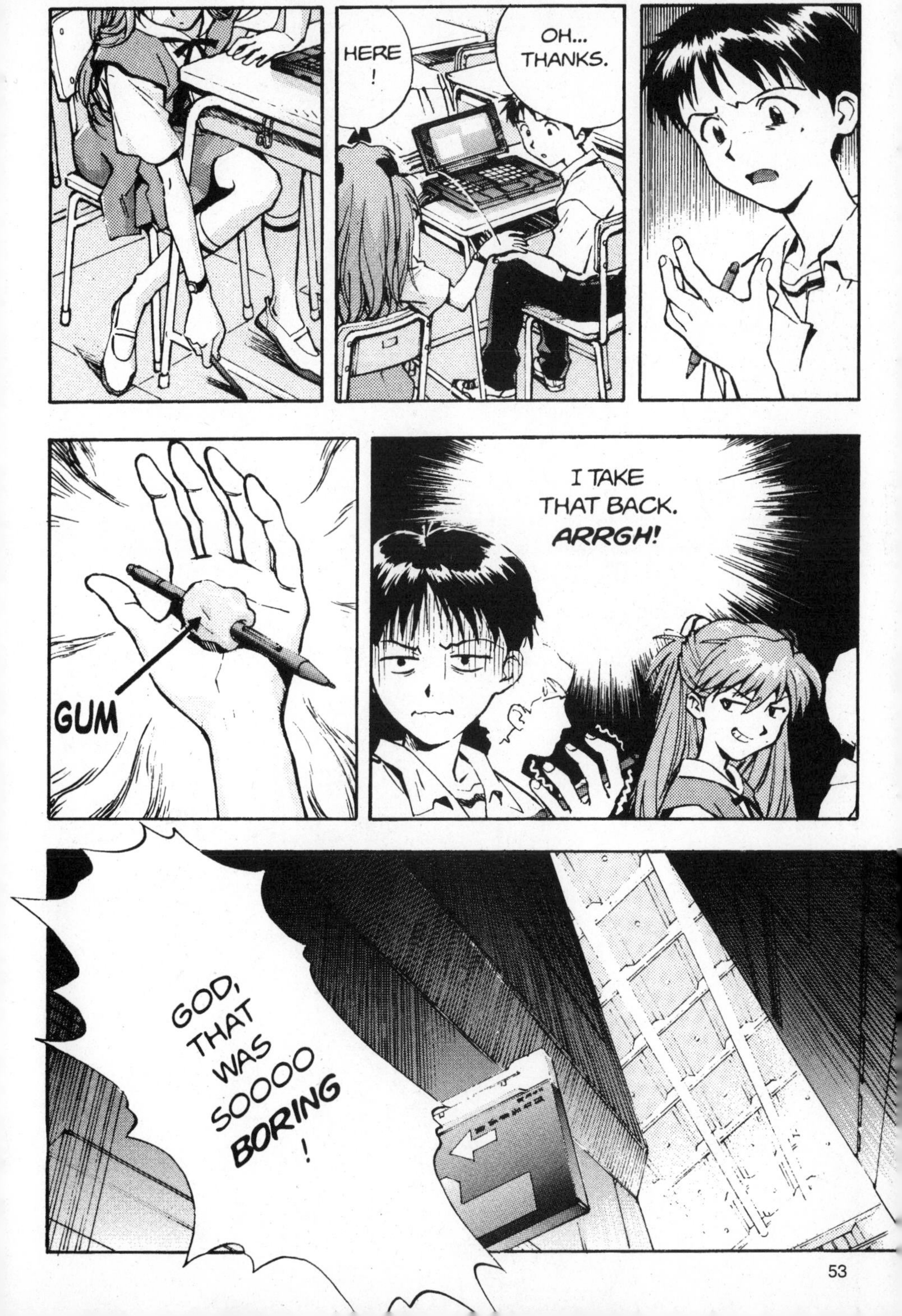
HERE !
OH... THANKS.
GUM
I TAKE THAT BACK. ARRGH!
GOD, THAT WAS SOOOO BORING !

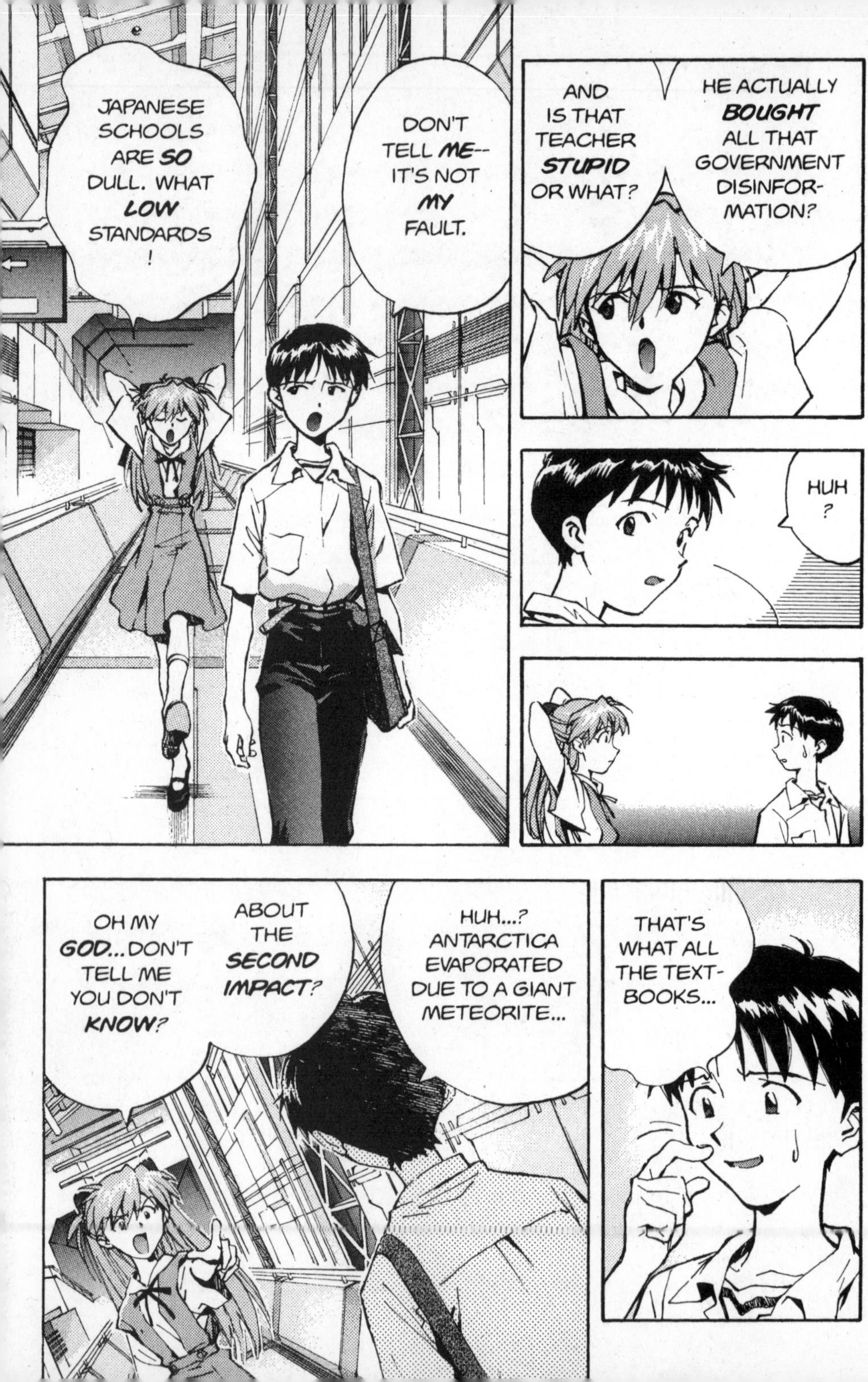
JAPANESE SCHOOLS ARE SO DULL. WHAT LOW STANDARDS!
DON'T TELL ME-- IT'S NOT MY FAULT.
AND IS THAT TEACHER STUPID OR WHAT?
HE ACTUALLY BOUGHT ALL THAT GOVERNMENT DISINFORMATION?
HUH?
OH MY GOD...DON'T TELL ME YOU DON'T KNOW?
ABOUT THE SECOND IMPACT?
HUH...? ANTARCTICA EVAPORATED DUE TO A GIANT METEORITE...
THAT'S WHAT ALL THE TEXT-BOOKS...

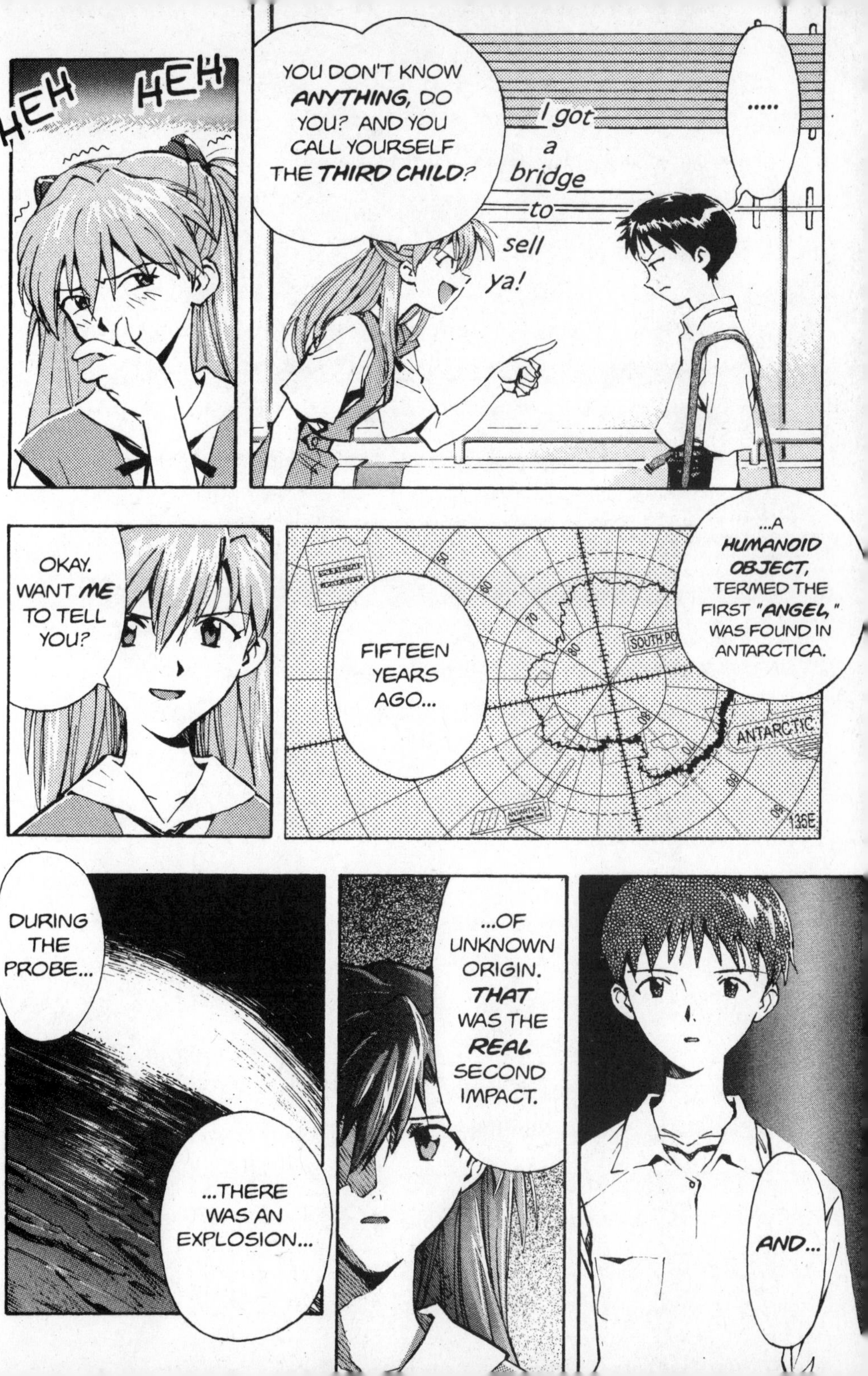
HEH HEH
YOU DON'T KNOW ANYTHING, DO YOU? AND YOU CALL YOURSELF THE THIRD CHILD?
I got a bridge to sell ya!
.....
OKAY. WANT ME TO TELL YOU?
FIFTEEN YEARS AGO...
...A HUMANOID OBJECT, TERMED THE FIRST "ANGEL," WAS FOUND IN ANTARCTICA.
SOUTH PO
ANTARCTIC
135E
DURING THE PROBE...
...THERE WAS AN EXPLOSION...
...OF UNKNOWN ORIGIN. THAT WAS THE REAL SECOND IMPACT.
AND...

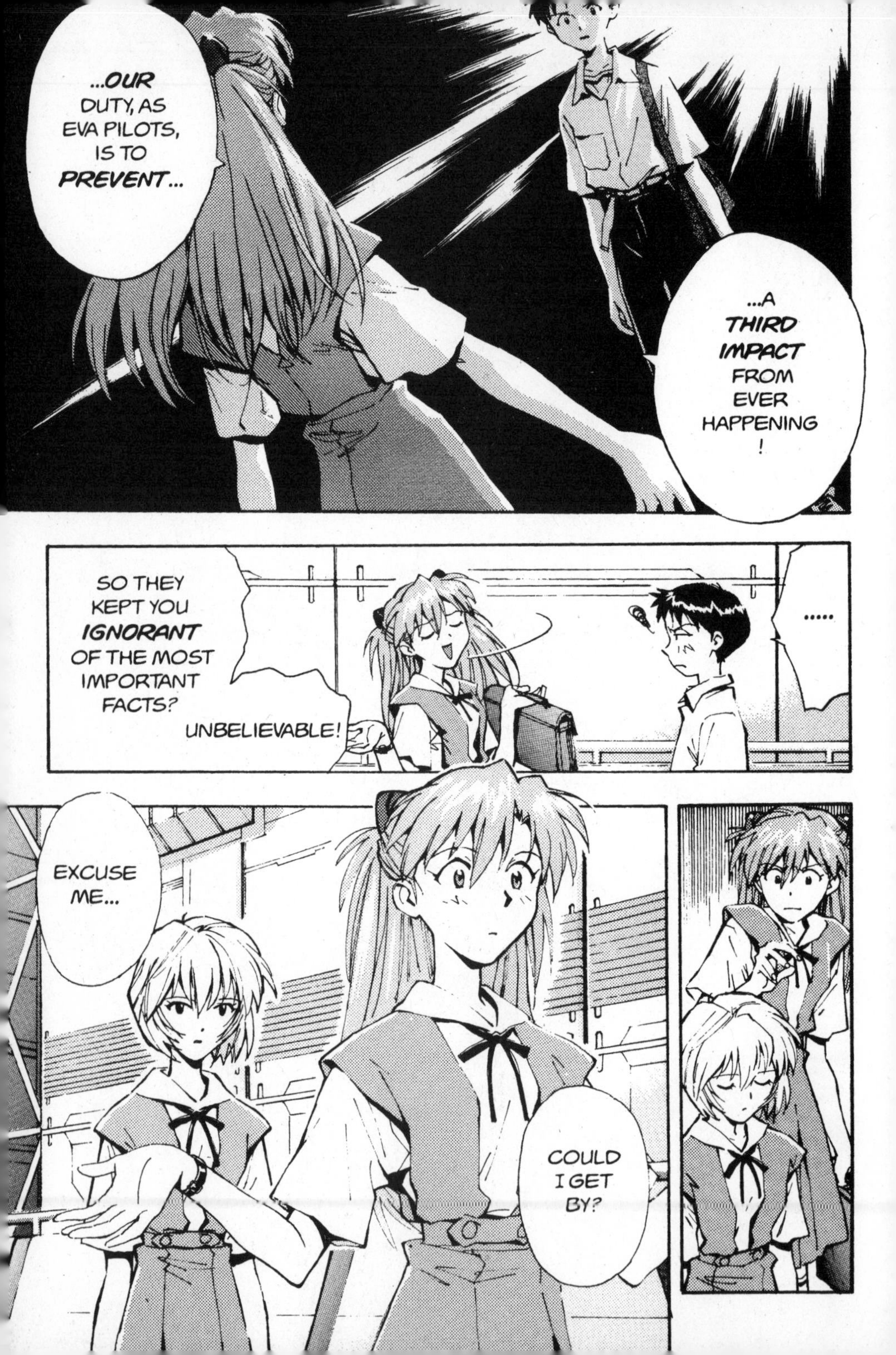
...OUR DUTY, AS EVA PILOTS, IS TO PREVENT...
...A THIRD IMPACT FROM EVER HAPPENING!
SO THEY KEPT YOU IGNORANT OF THE MOST IMPORTANT FACTS?
UNBELIEVABLE!
.....
EXCUSE ME...
COULD I GET BY?

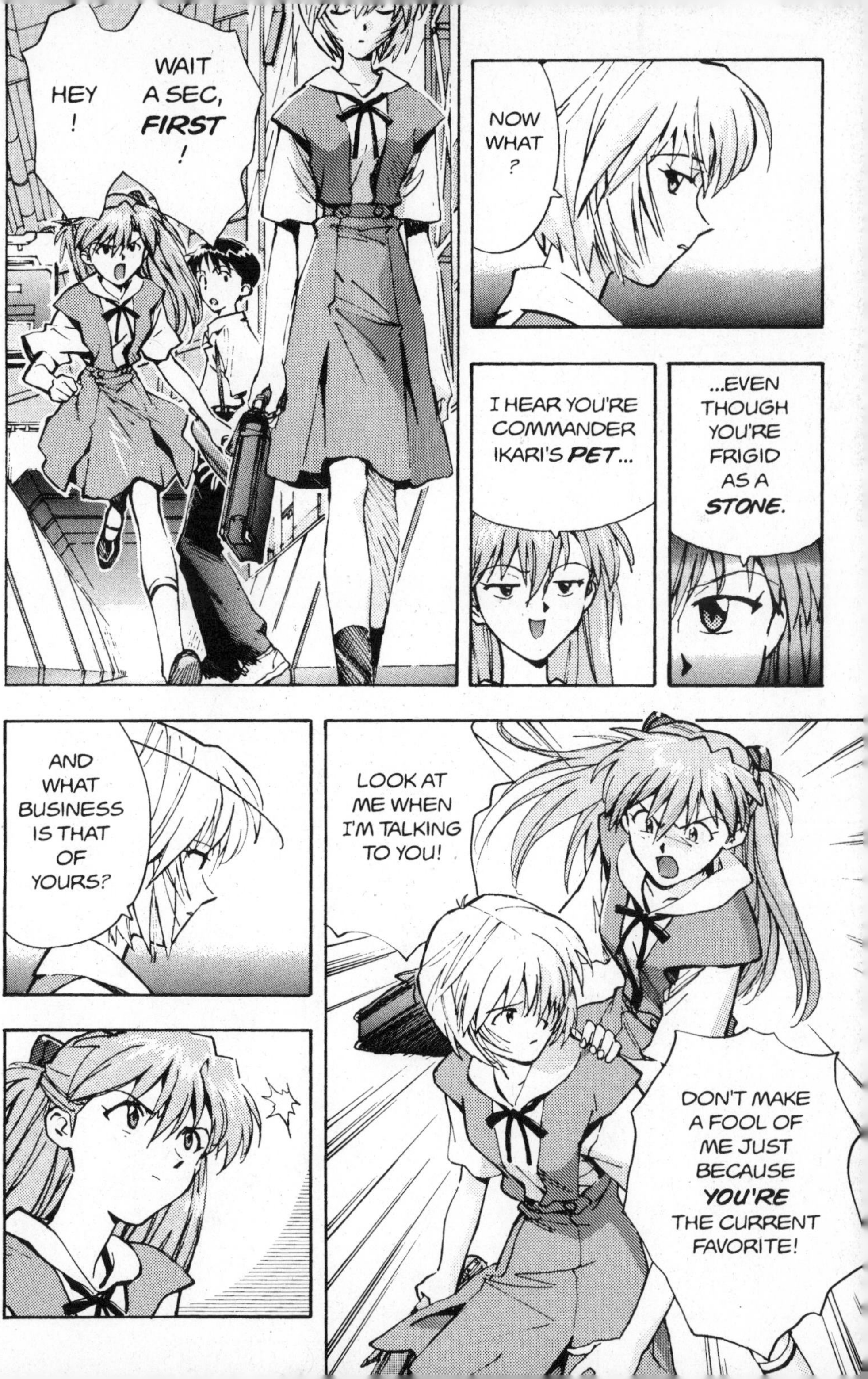
HEY!
WAIT A SEC, FIRST!
NOW WHAT?
I HEAR YOU'RE COMMANDER IKARI'S PET...
...EVEN THOUGH YOU'RE FRIGID AS A STONE.
AND WHAT BUSINESS IS THAT OF YOURS?
LOOK AT ME WHEN I'M TALKING TO YOU!
DON'T MAKE A FOOL OF ME JUST BECAUSE YOU'RE THE CURRENT FAVORITE!

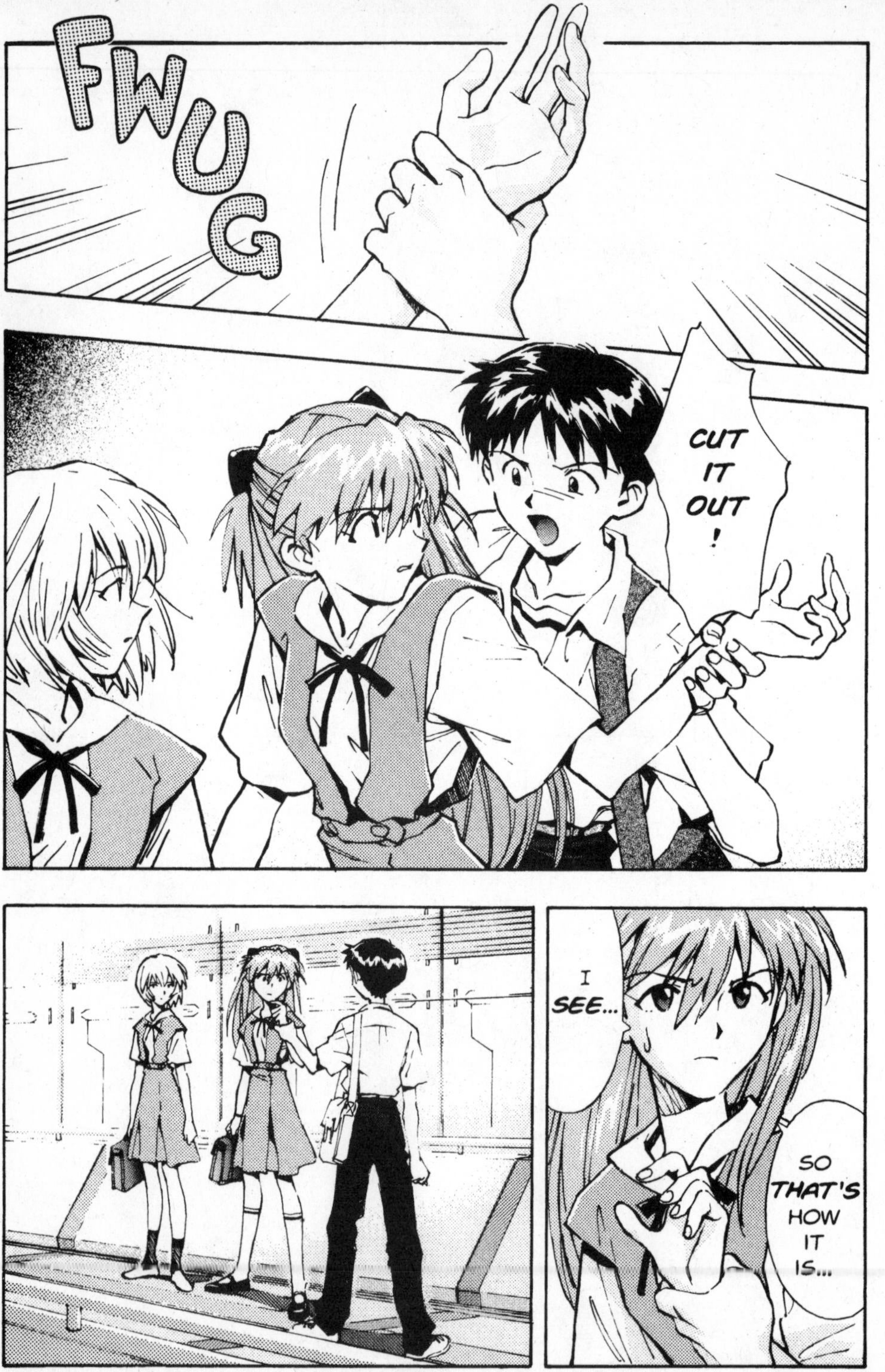
FWUG
CUT IT OUT!
I SEE...
SO THAT'S HOW IT IS...

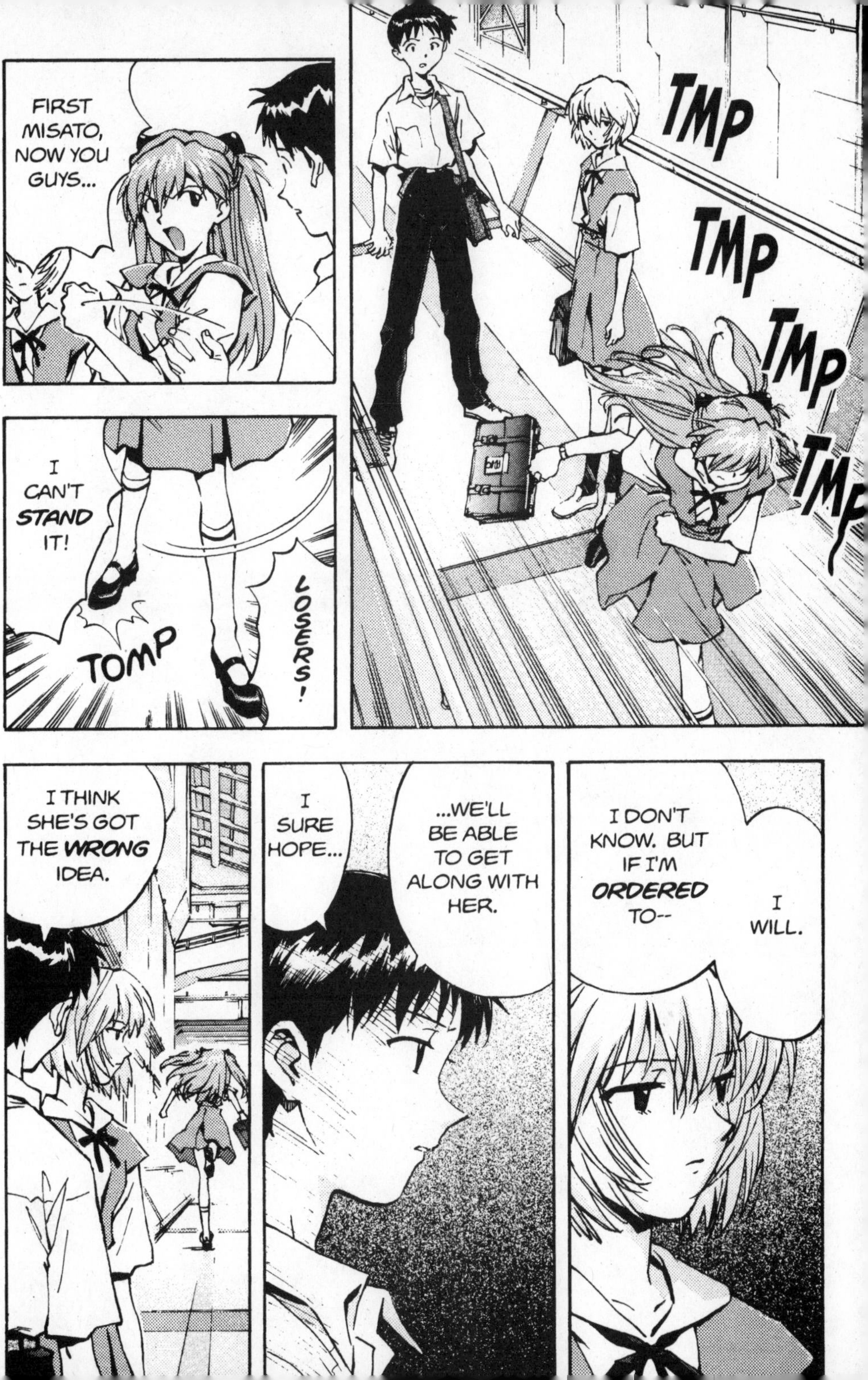
FIRST MISATO, NOW YOU GUYS...
I CAN'T STAND IT!
TOMP
LOSERS!
TMP TMP TMP TMP
I THINK SHE'S GOT THE WRONG IDEA.
I SURE HOPE...
...WE'LL BE ABLE TO GET ALONG WITH HER.
I DON'T KNOW. BUT IF I'M ORDERED TO--
I WILL.

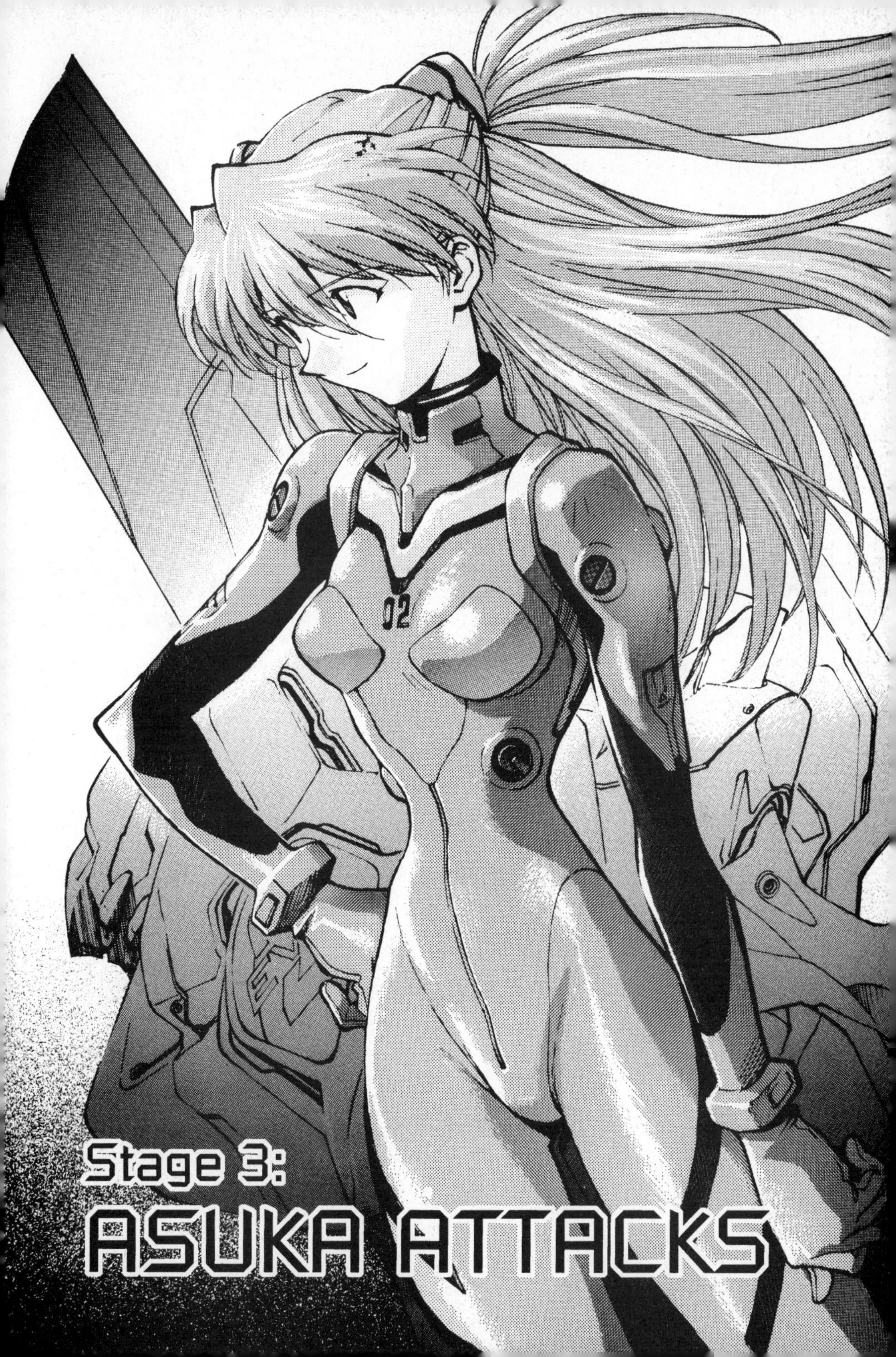
02
Stage 3:
ASUKA ATTACKS

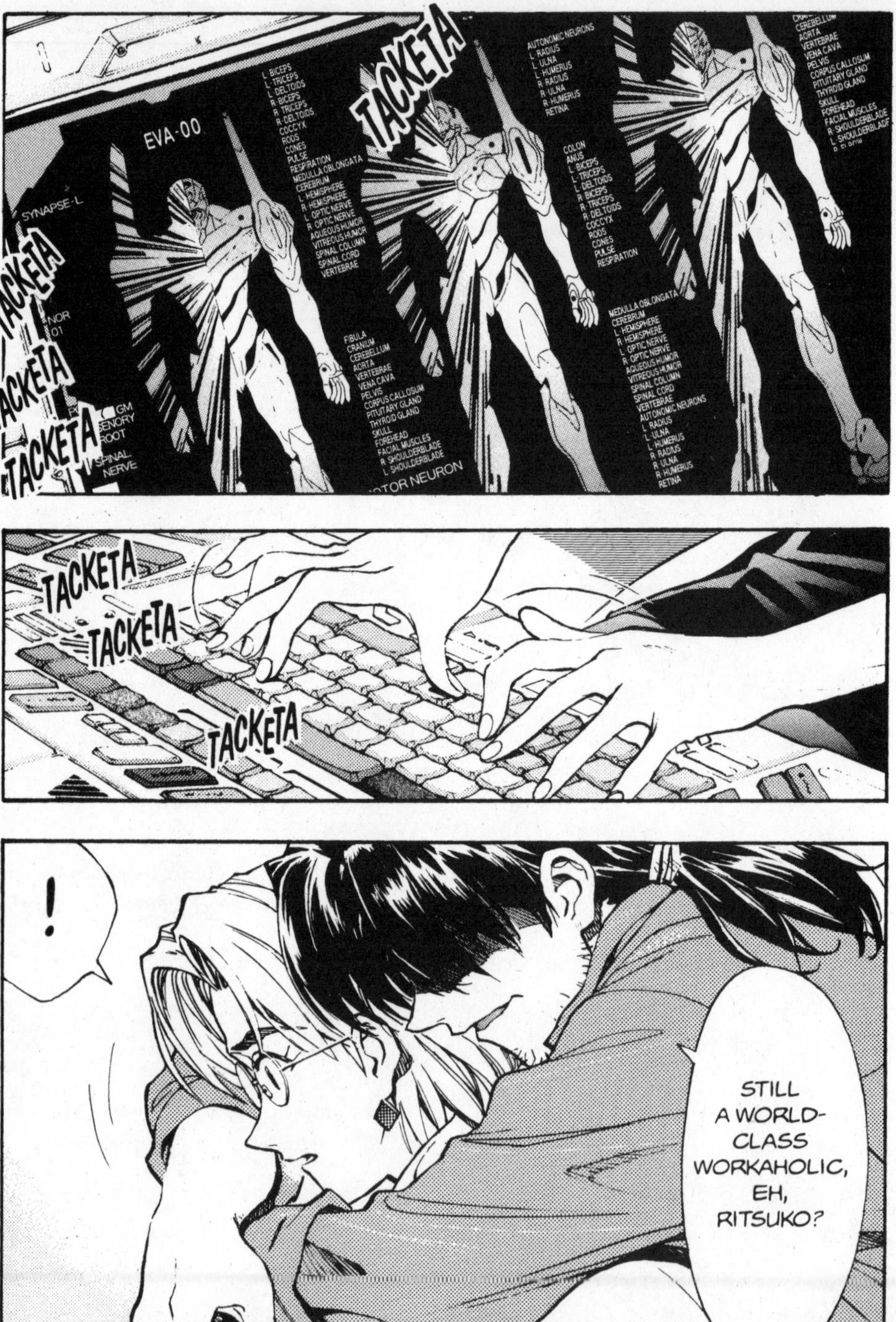
TACKETA
TACKETA
TACKETA
SYNAPSE-L
SPINAL NERVE
EVA-00
L·BICEPS
L·TRICEPS
L·DELTOIDS
R·BICEPS
R·TRICEPS
R·DELTOIDS
COCCYX
RODS
CONES
PULSE
RESPIRATION
MEDULLA OBLONGATA
CEREBRUM
L·HEMISPHERE
R·HEMISPHERE
L·OPTIC NERVE
AQUEOUS HUMOR
VITREOUS HUMOR
SPINAL COLUMN
SPINAL CORD
VERTEBRAE
FIBULA
CRANIUM
CEREBELLUM
AORTA
VERTEBRAE
VENA CAVA
PELVIS
CORPUS CALLOSUM
PITUITARY GLAND
THYROID GLAND
SKULL
FOREHEAD
FACIAL MUSCLES
R·SHOULDERBLADE
L·SHOULDERBLADE
TACKETA
AUTONOMIC NEURONS
L·RADIUS
L·ULNA
L·HUMERUS
R·RADIUS
R·ULNA
R·HUMERUS
RETINA
COLON
ANUS
L·BICEPS
L·TRICEPS
L·DELTOIDS
R·BICEPS
R·TRICEPS
R·DELTOIDS
COCCYX
RODS
CONES
PULSE
RESPIRATION
MEDULLA OBLONGATA
CEREBRUM
L·HEMISPHERE
R·HEMISPHERE
L·OPTIC NERVE
R·OPTIC NERVE
AQUEOUS HUMOR
VITREOUS HUMOR
SPINAL COLUMN
SPINAL CORD
VERTEBRAE
AUTONOMIC NEURONS
L·RADIUS
L·ULNA
L·HUMERUS
R·RADIUS
R·ULNA
R·HUMERUS
RETINA
CEREBELLUM
AORTA
VERTEBRAE
VENA CAVA
PELVIS
CORPUS CALLOSUM
PITUITARY GLAND
THYROID GLAND
SKULL
FOREHEAD
FACIAL MUSCLES
R·SHOULDERBLADE
L·SHOULDERBLADE
TACKETA
TACKETA
TACKETA
!
STILL A WORLD-CLASS WORKAHOLIC, EH, RITSUKO?

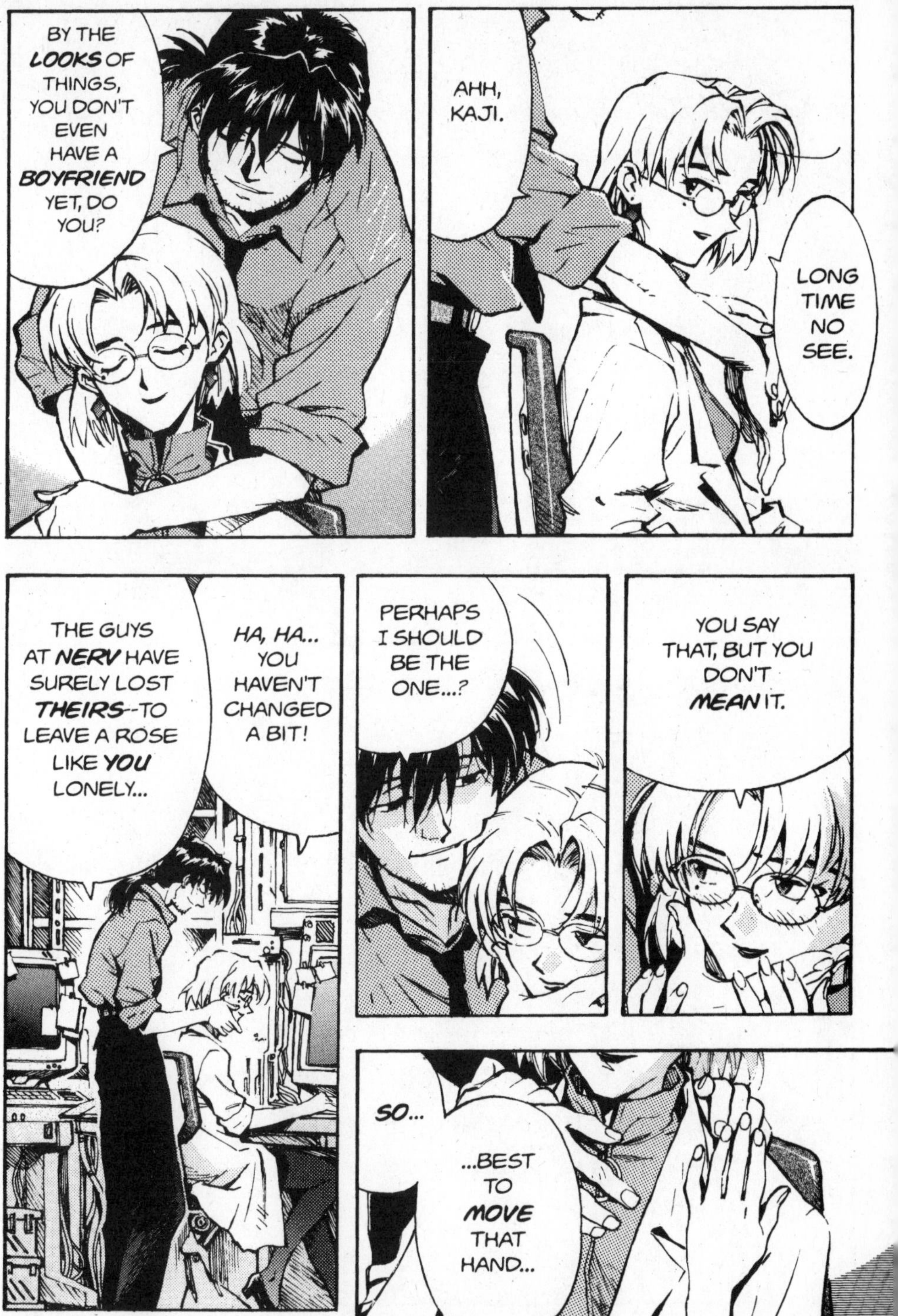
BY THE LOOKS OF THINGS, YOU DON'T EVEN HAVE A BOYFRIEND YET, DO YOU?
AHH, KAJI.
LONG TIME NO SEE.
THE GUYS AT NERV HAVE SURELY LOST THEIRS--TO LEAVE A ROSE LIKE YOU LONELY...
HA, HA... YOU HAVEN'T CHANGED A BIT!
PERHAPS I SHOULD BE THE ONE...?
YOU SAY THAT, BUT YOU DON'T MEAN IT.
SO...
...BEST TO MOVE THAT HAND...

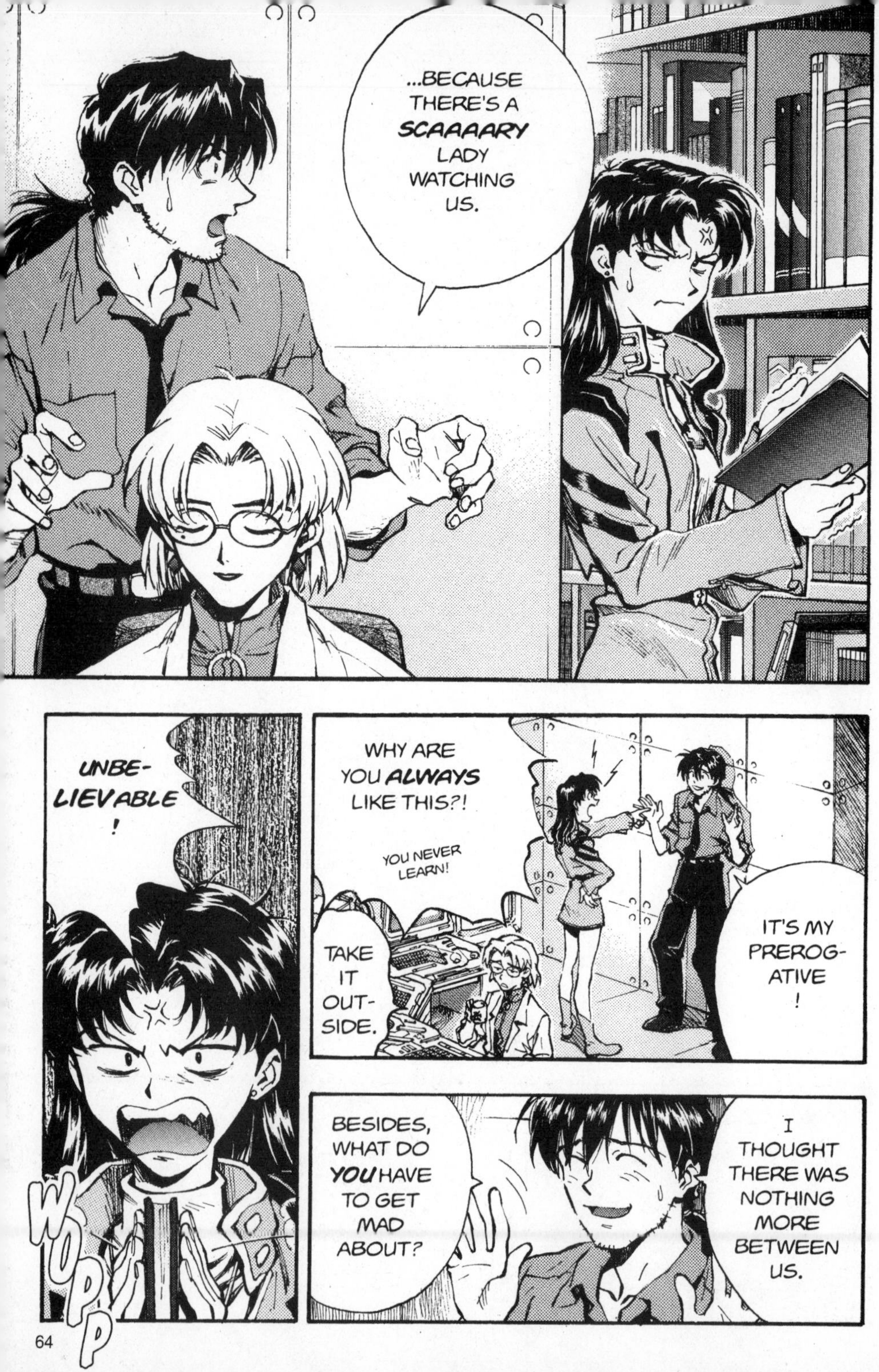
...BECAUSE THERE'S A SCAAAARY LADY WATCHING US.
UNBE-LIEVABLE!
WOPP
WHY ARE YOU ALWAYS LIKE THIS?!
YOU NEVER LEARN!
TAKE IT OUT-SIDE.
IT'S MY PREROG-ATIVE!
BESIDES, WHAT DO YOU HAVE TO GET MAD ABOUT?
I THOUGHT THERE WAS NOTHING MORE BETWEEN US.

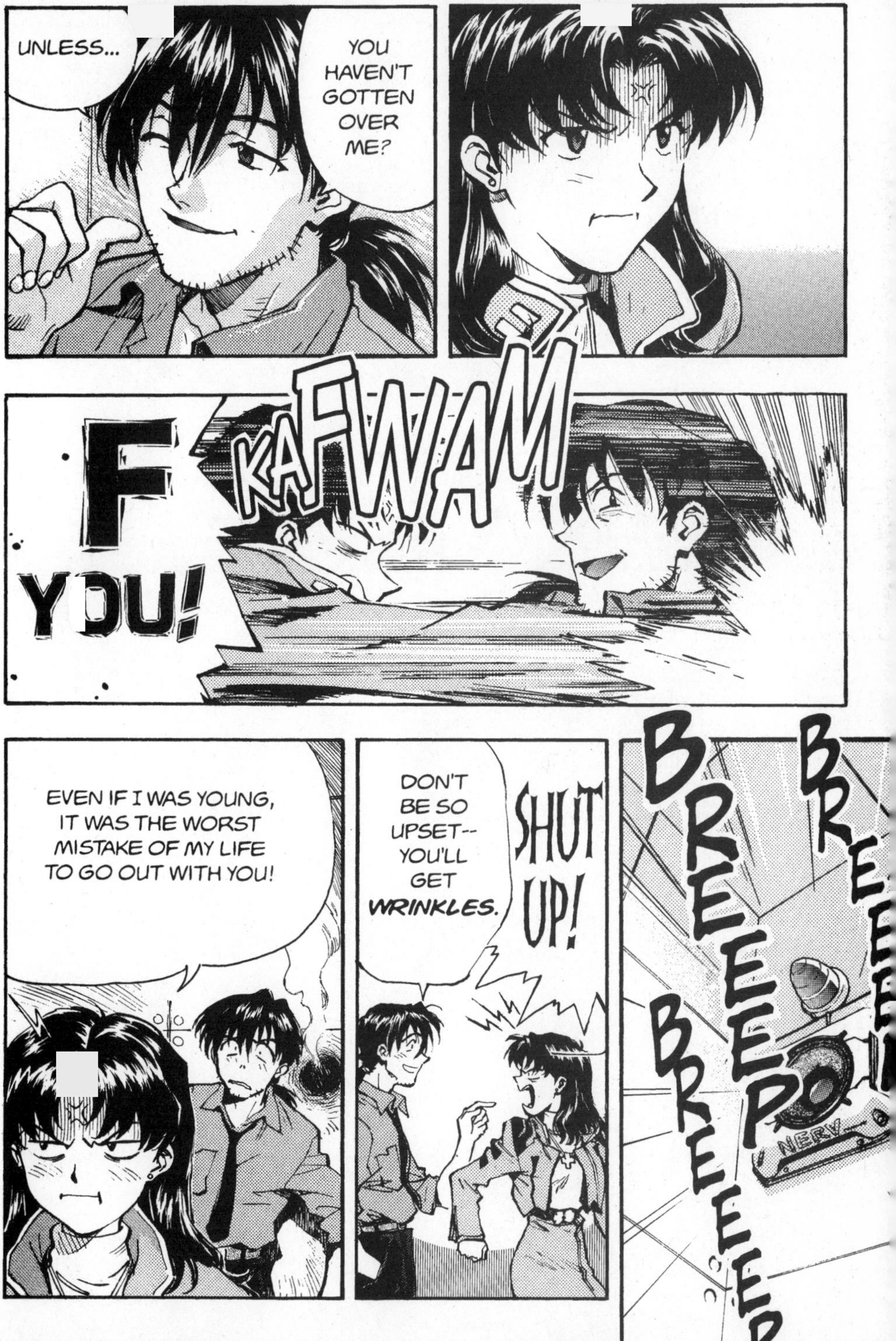
UNLESS...
YOU HAVEN'T GOTTEN OVER ME?
KAFWAM
F YOU!
EVEN IF I WAS YOUNG, IT WAS THE WORST MISTAKE OF MY LIFE TO GO OUT WITH YOU!
DON'T BE SO UPSET-- YOU'LL GET WRINKLES.
SHUT UP!
BREEEP
BREEEEEP
BREEE
NERV

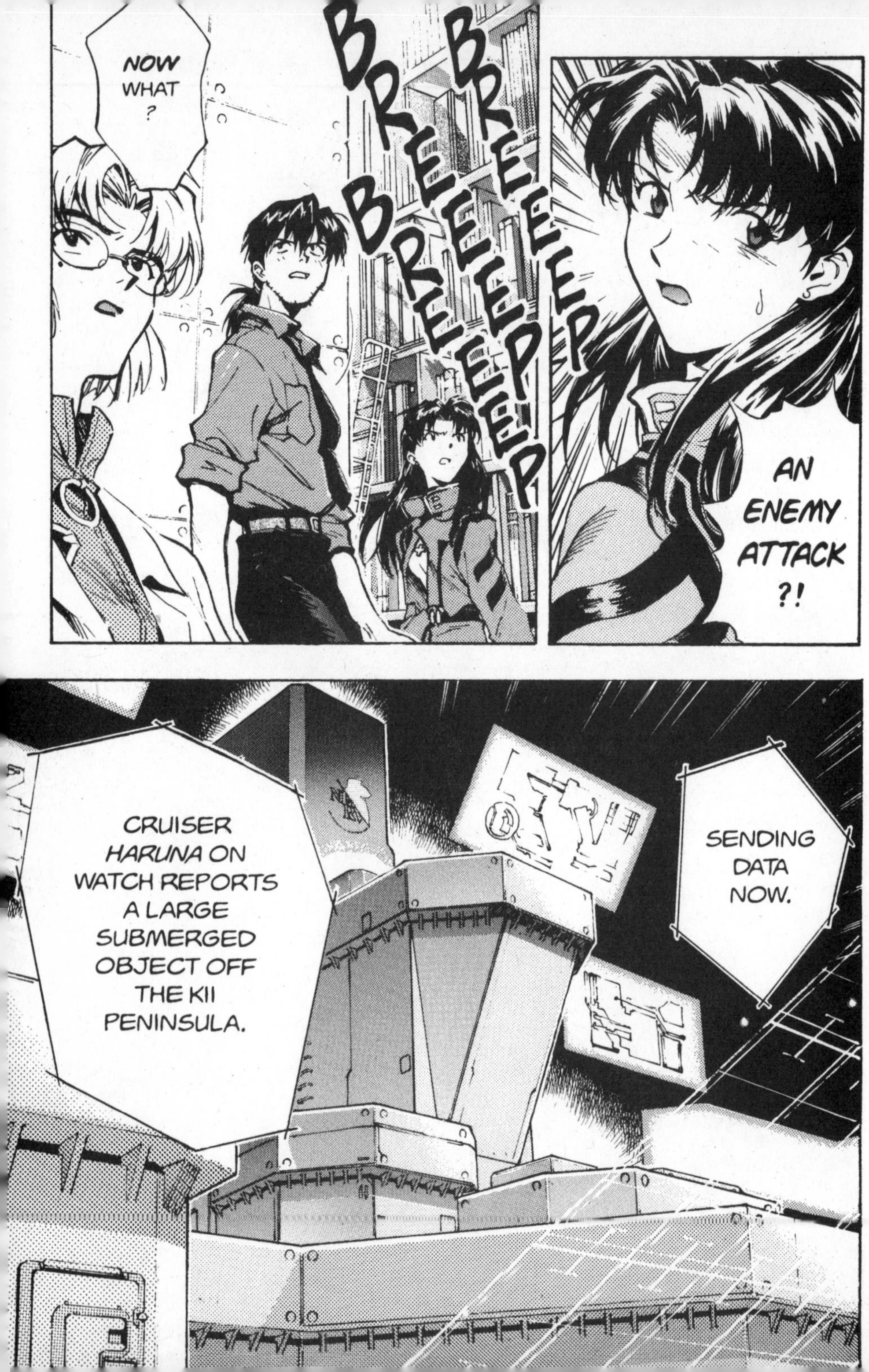
NOW WHAT ?
BREEEEP
BREEEEP
BREEEP
AN ENEMY ATTACK ?!
CRUISER HARUNA ON WATCH REPORTS A LARGE SUBMERGED OBJECT OFF THE KII PENINSULA.
SENDING DATA NOW.

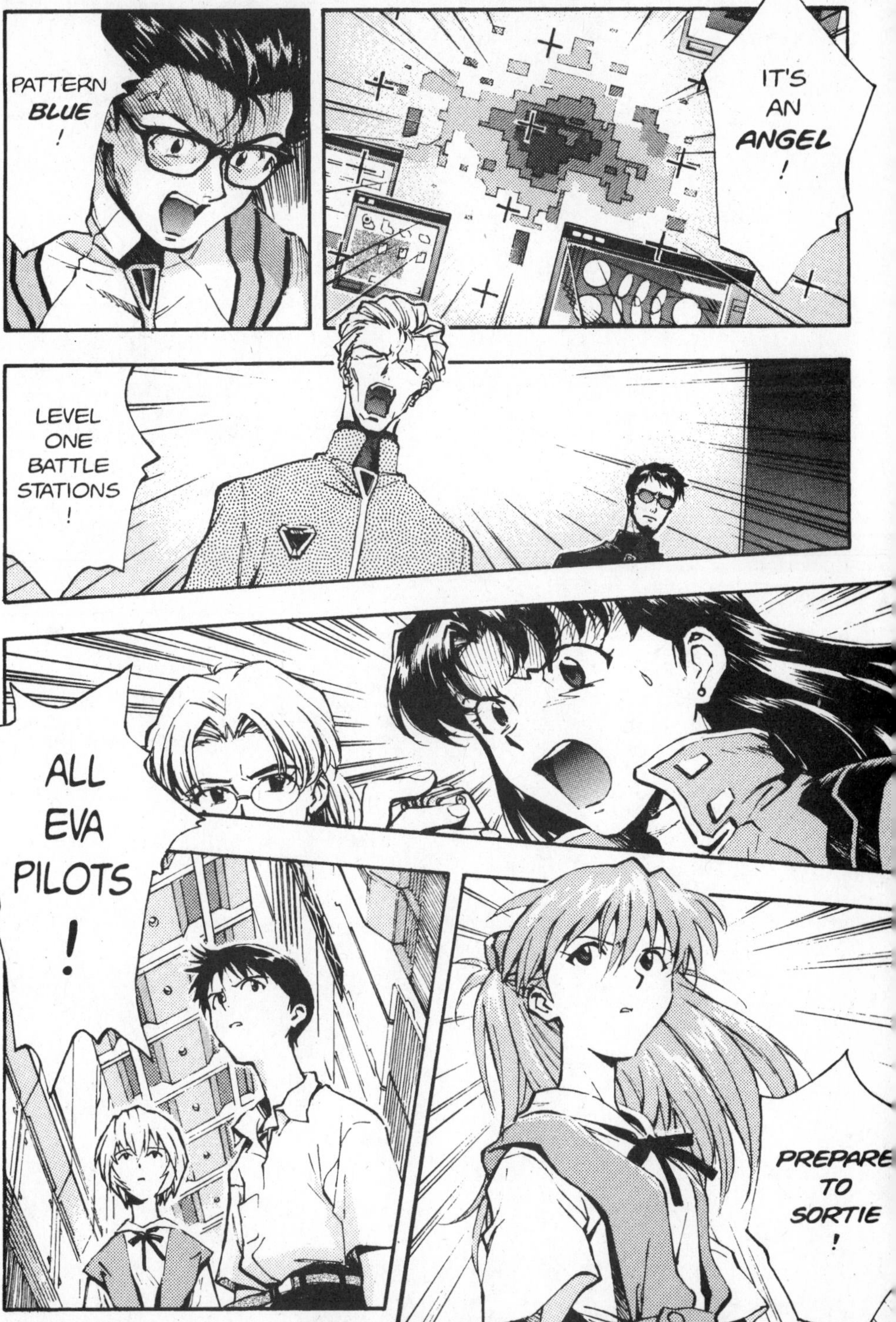
PATTERN BLUE!
IT'S AN ANGEL!
LEVEL ONE BATTLE STATIONS!
ALL EVA PILOTS!
PREPARE TO SORTIE!

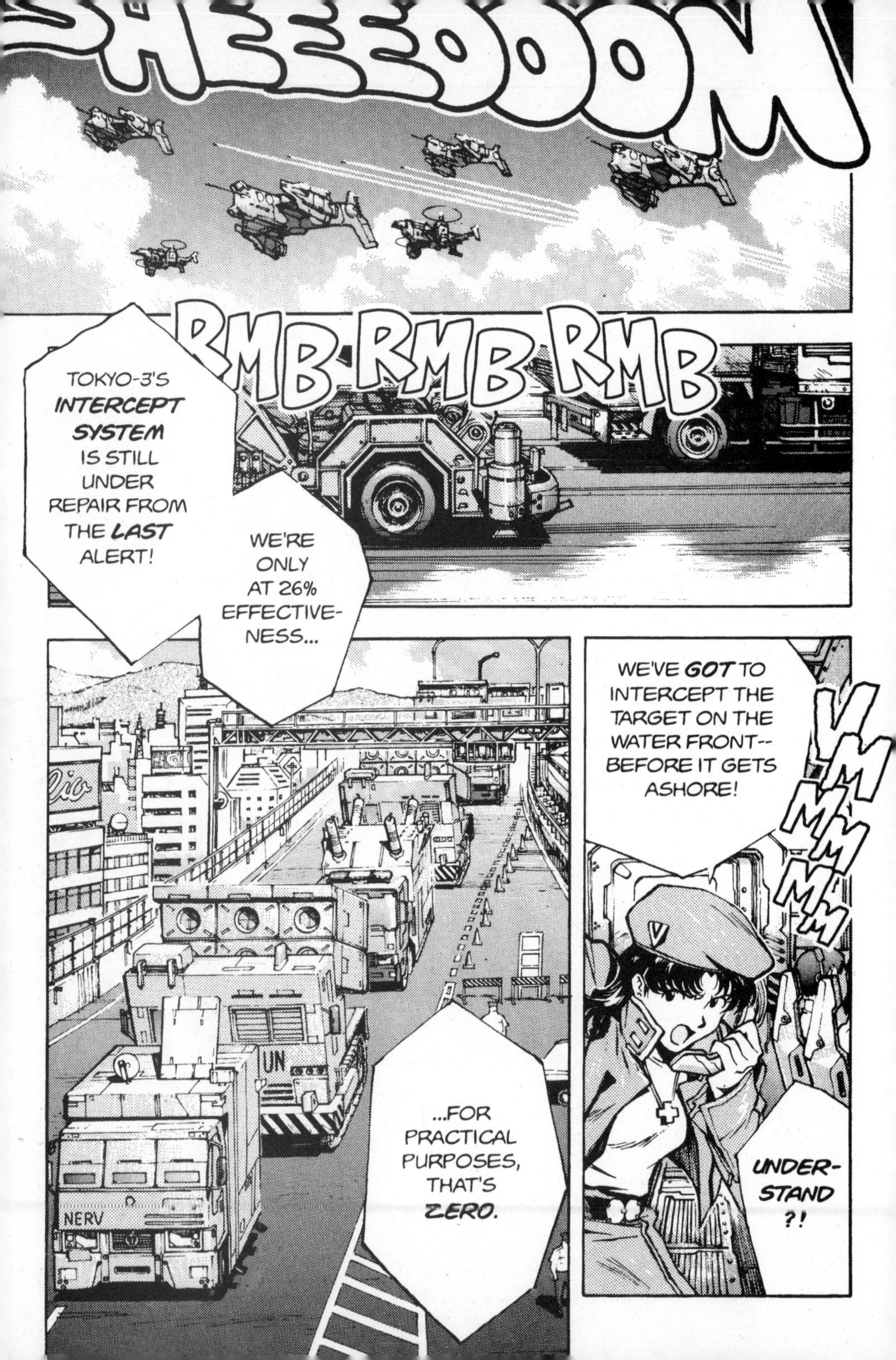
RMB RMB RMB
TOKYO-3'S **INTERCEPT SYSTEM** IS STILL UNDER REPAIR FROM THE **LAST** ALERT!
WE'RE ONLY AT 26% EFFECTIVE-NESS...
...FOR PRACTICAL PURPOSES, THAT'S **ZERO**.
WE'VE **GOT** TO INTERCEPT THE TARGET ON THE WATER FRONT-- BEFORE IT GETS ASHORE!
VMMMMMMM
UNDER-STAND ?!

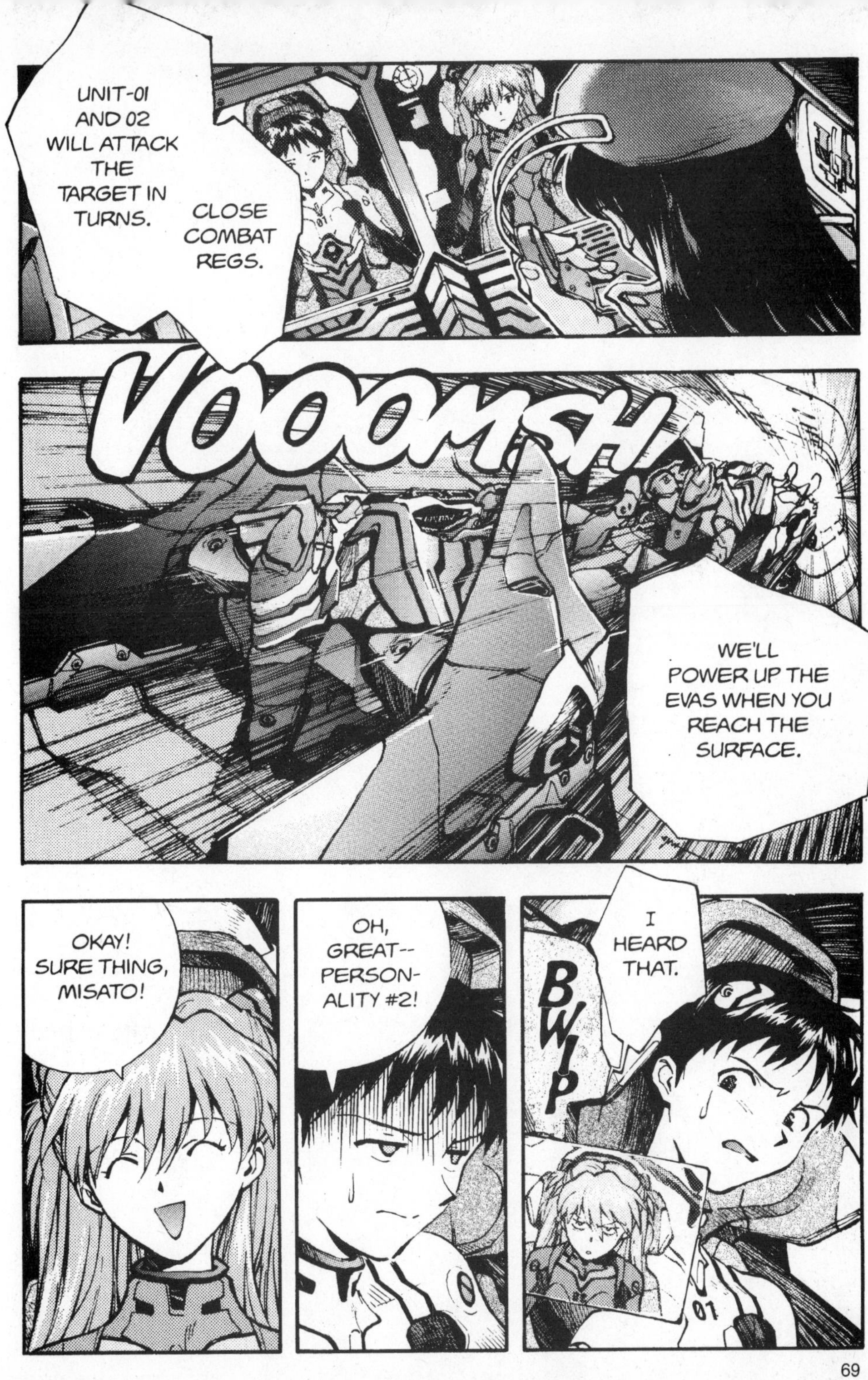
UNIT-01 AND 02 WILL ATTACK THE TARGET IN TURNS.
CLOSE COMBAT REGS.
VOOOMSH
WE'LL POWER UP THE EVAS WHEN YOU REACH THE SURFACE.
OKAY! SURE THING, MISATO!
OH, GREAT-- PERSON-ALITY #2!
I HEARD THAT.
BWIP

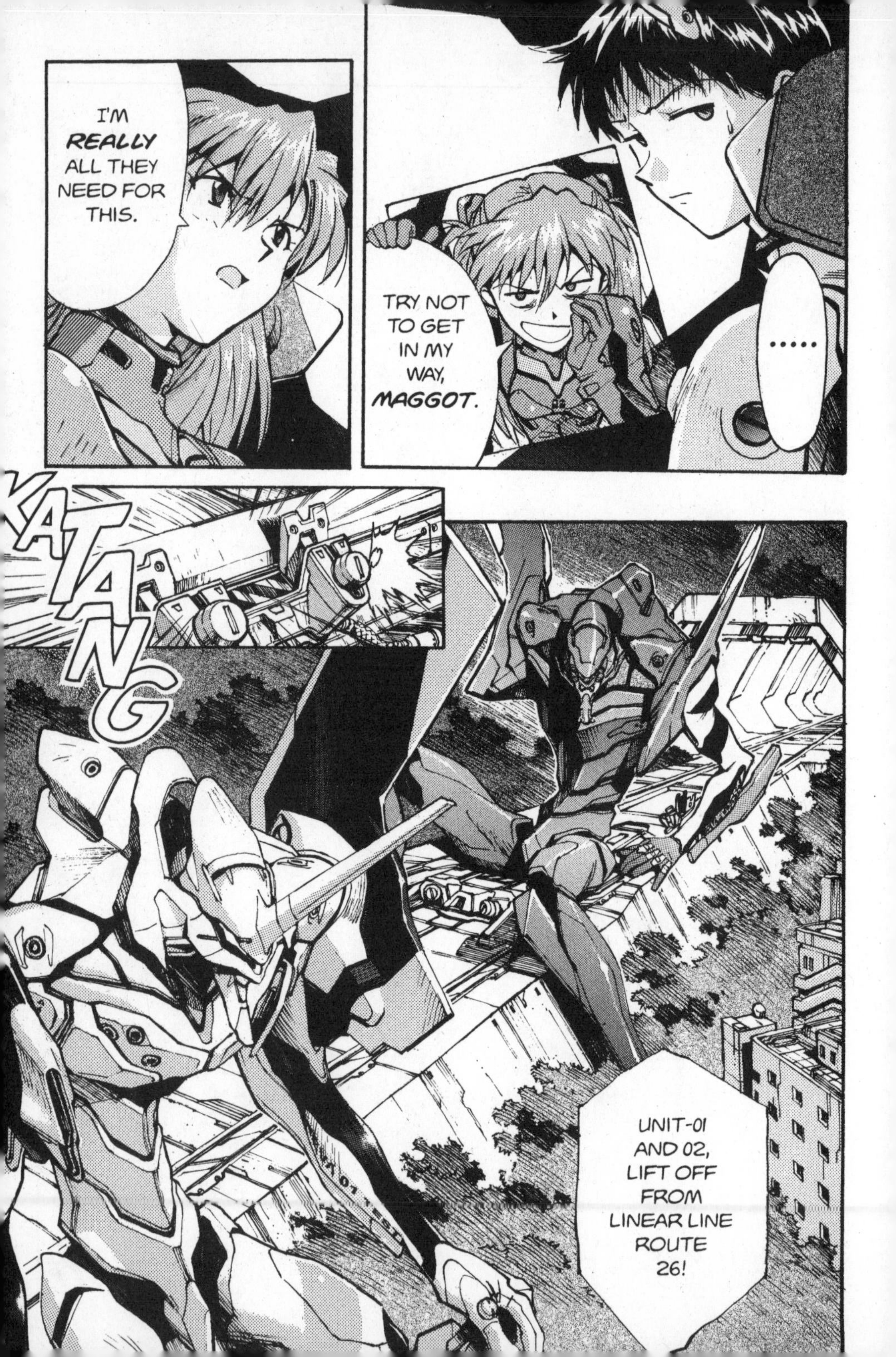
I'M **REALLY** ALL THEY NEED FOR THIS.
TRY NOT TO GET IN MY WAY, **MAGGOT**.
.....
KATANG
UNIT-01 AND 02, LIFT OFF FROM LINEAR LINE ROUTE 26!

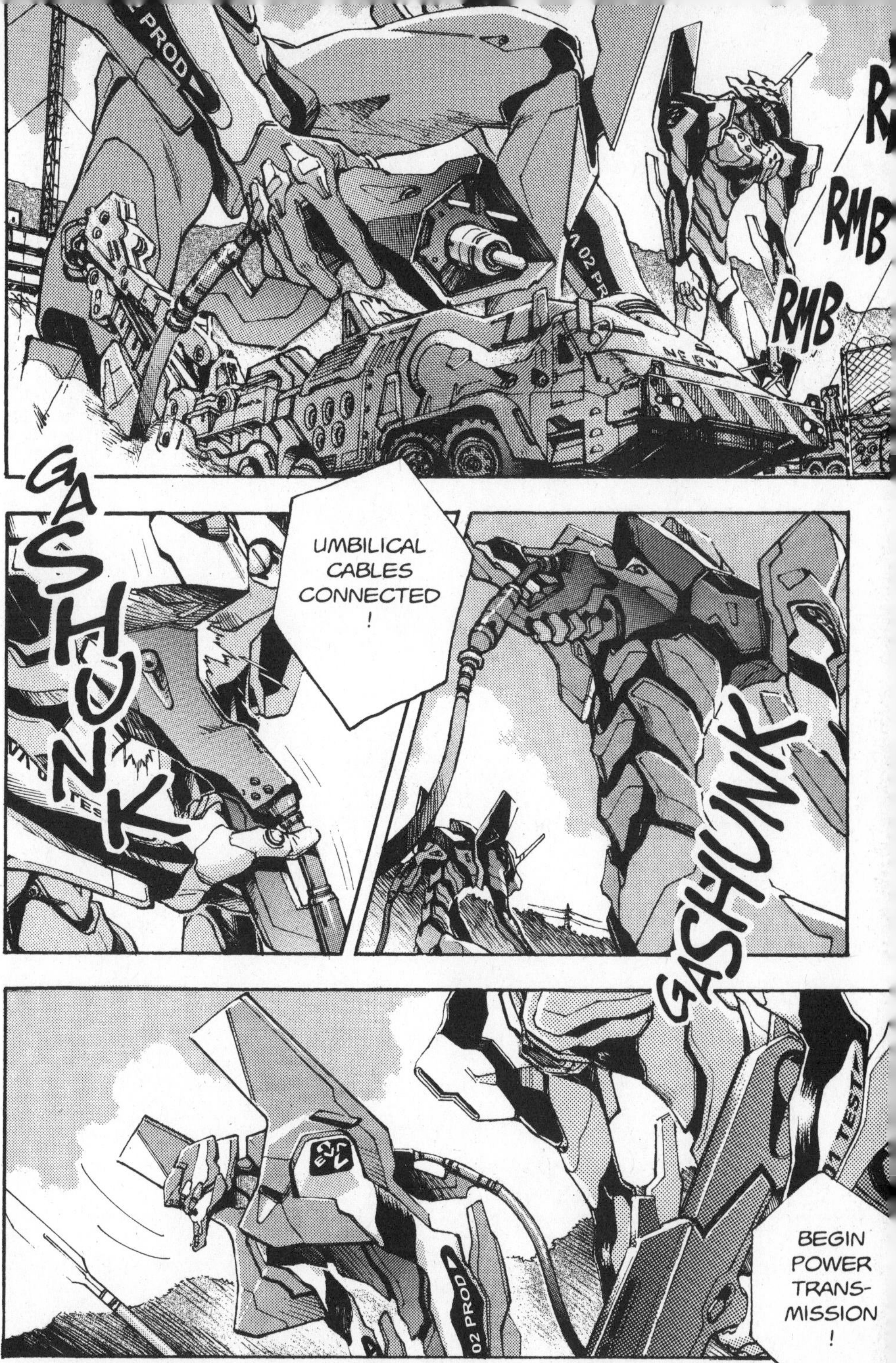
RMB
RMB
GASHUNK
UMBILICAL CABLES CONNECTED!
GASHUNK
BEGIN POWER TRANS-MISSION!

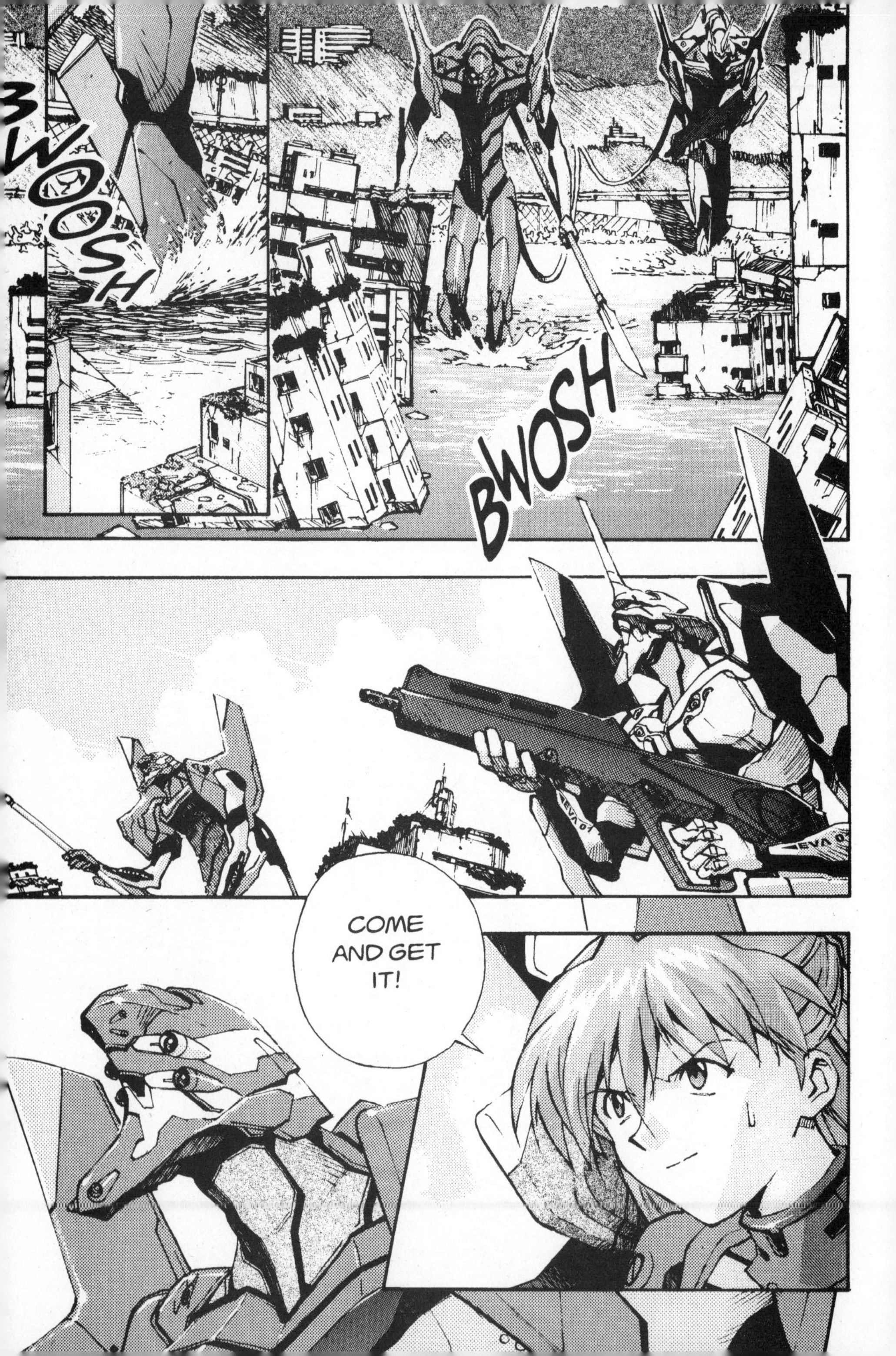
WOOSH
BWOSH
COME AND GET IT!

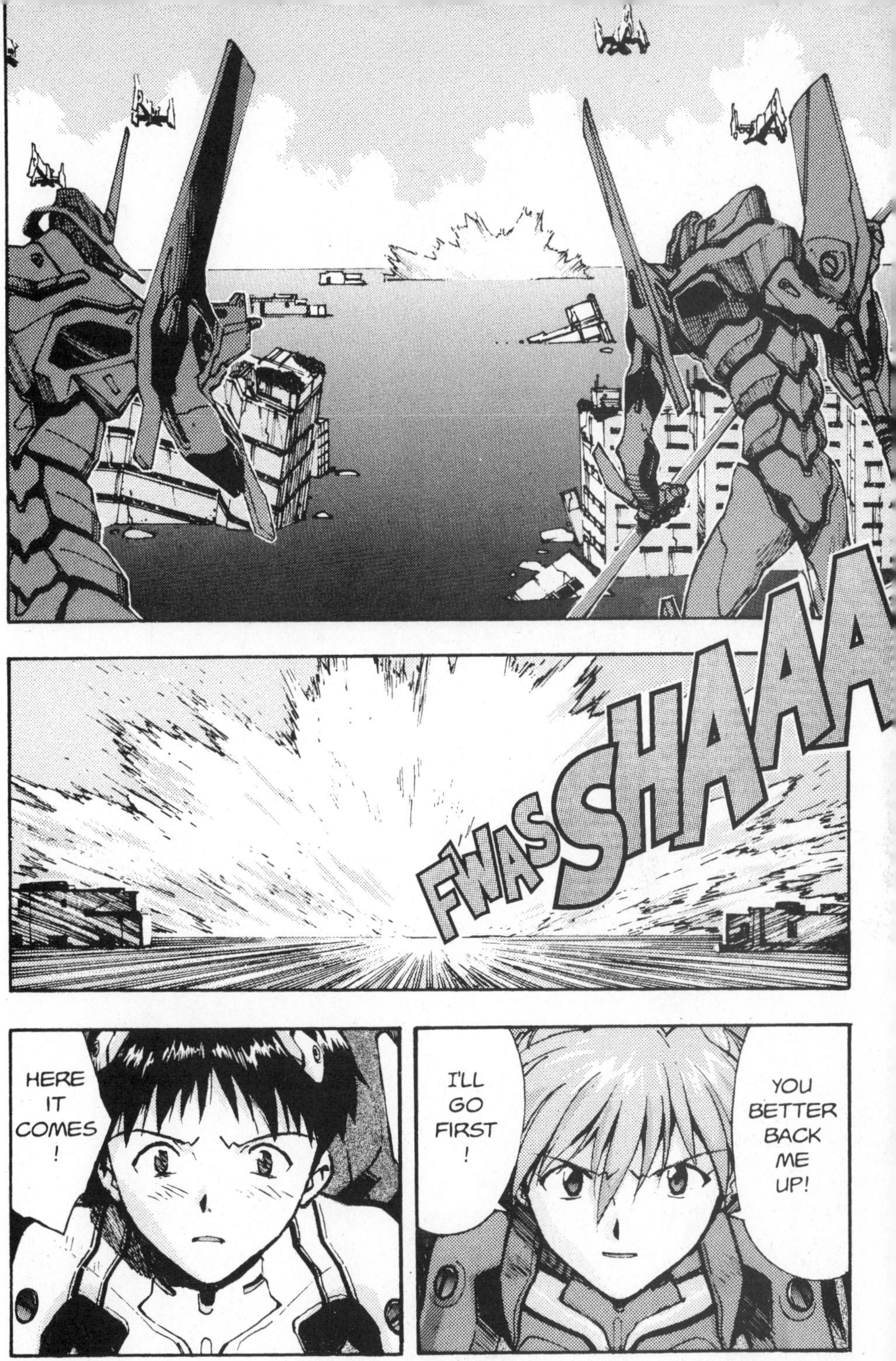
F'WASSHAAA
HERE IT COMES!
I'LL GO FIRST!
YOU BETTER BACK ME UP!

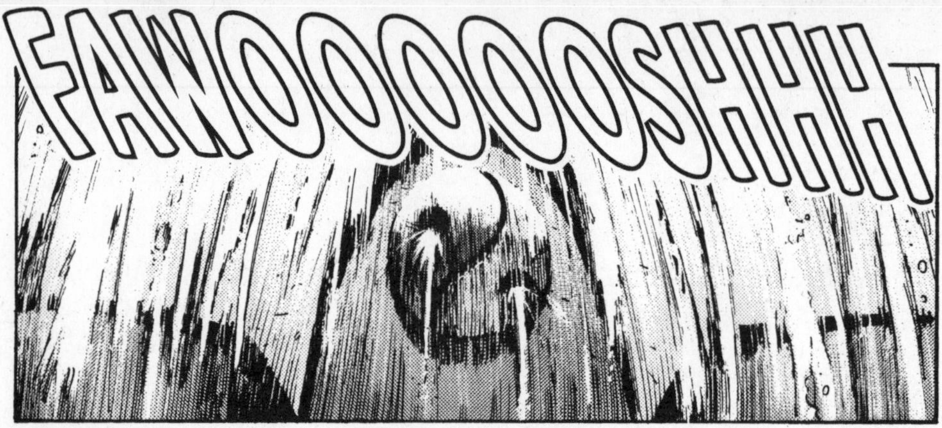
FAWOOOOOOSHHHH
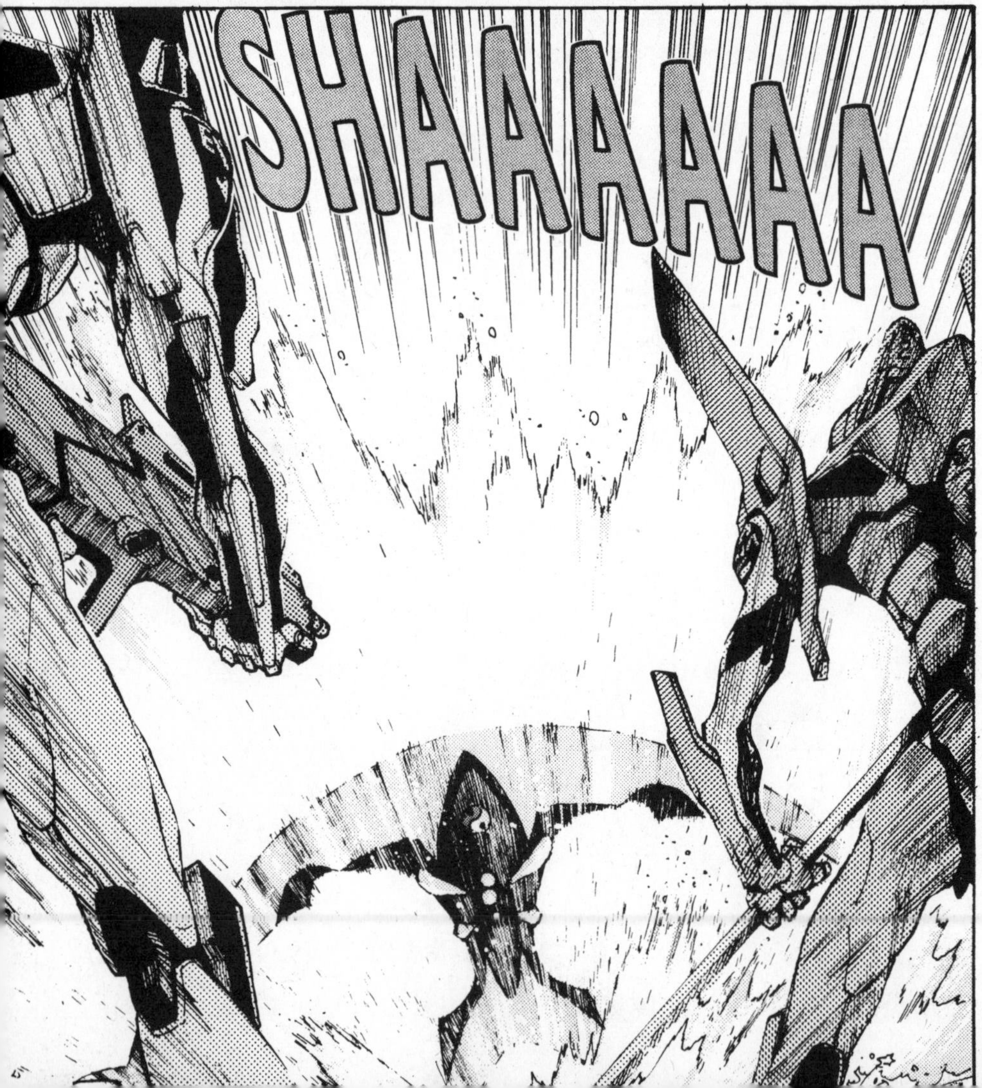
SHAAAAAAA

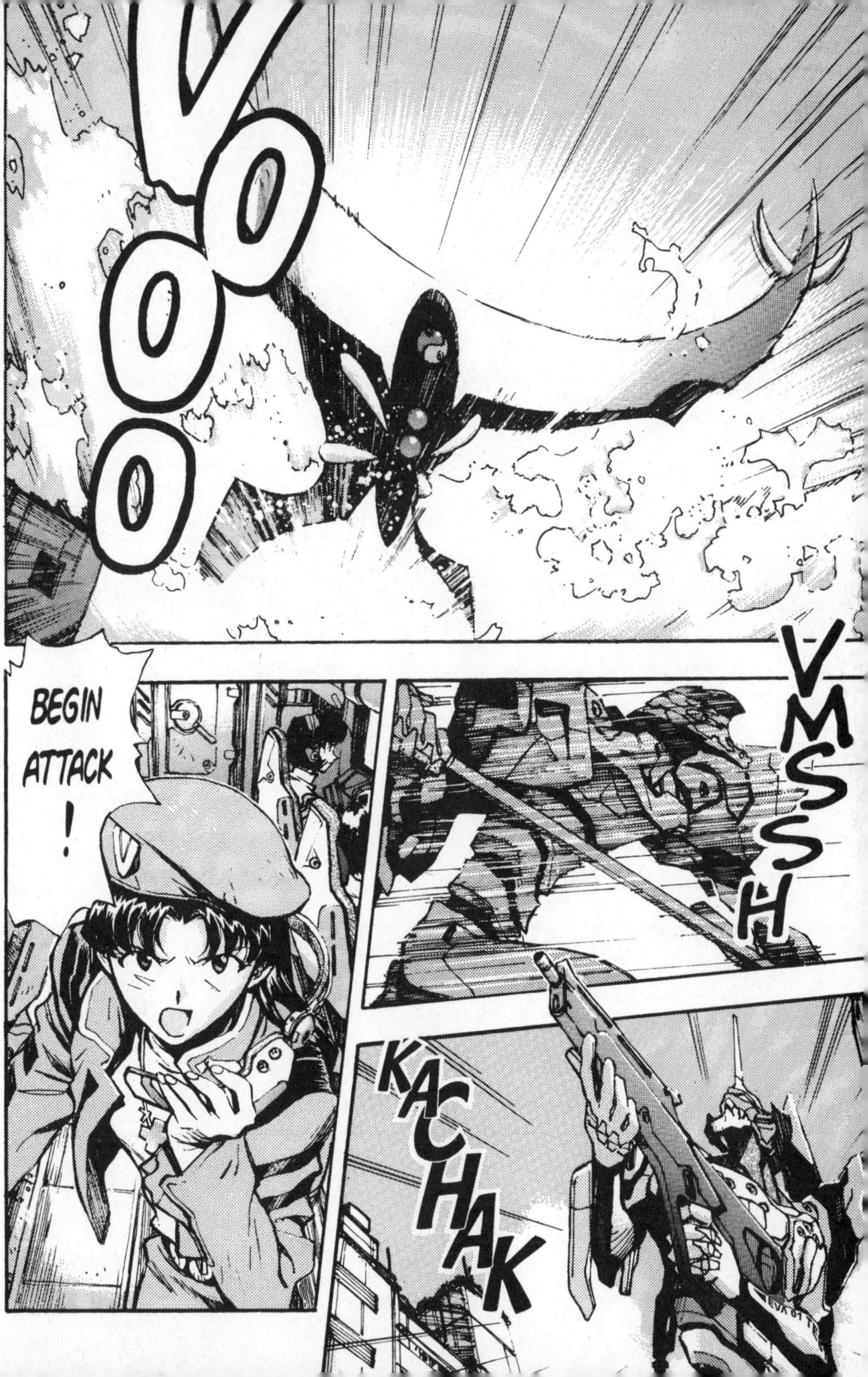
VOOO
BEGIN ATTACK!
VMSSH
KACHAK

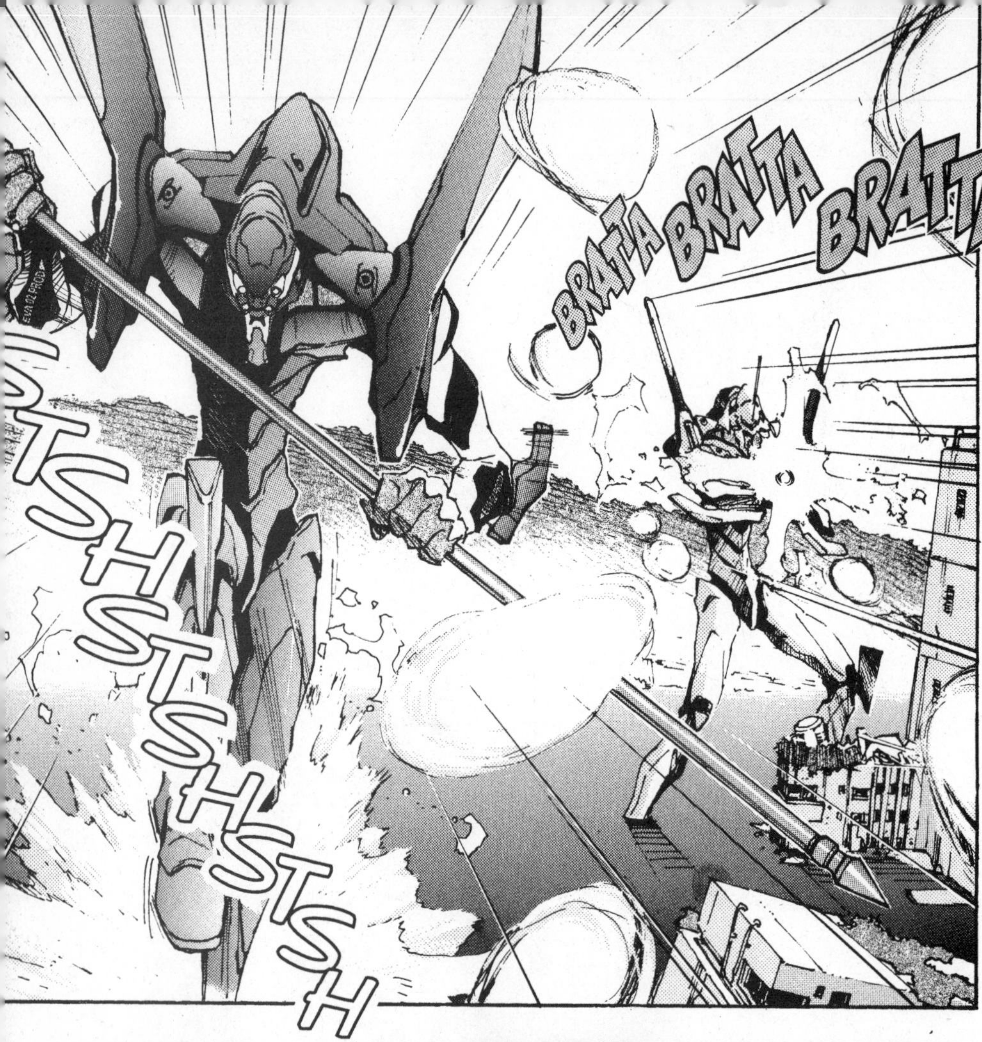
EVA 02 PROD
STSHSTSHSTSH
BRATTA BRATTA BRATTA

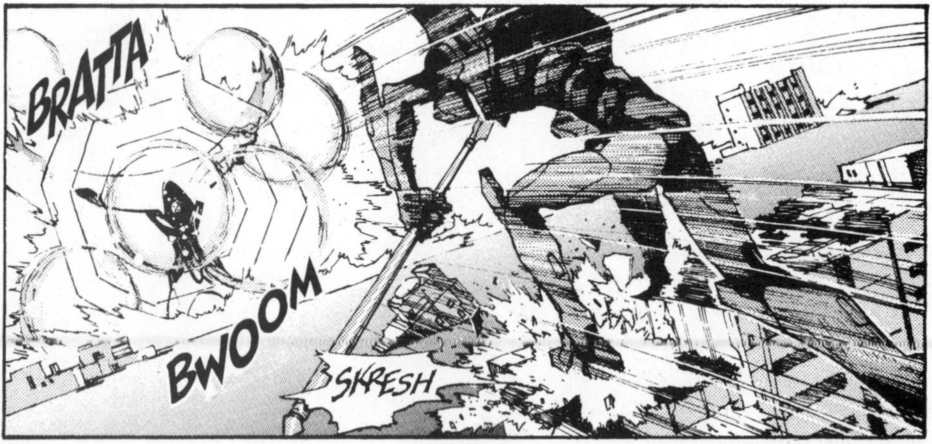
BRATTA
BWOOM
SKRESH

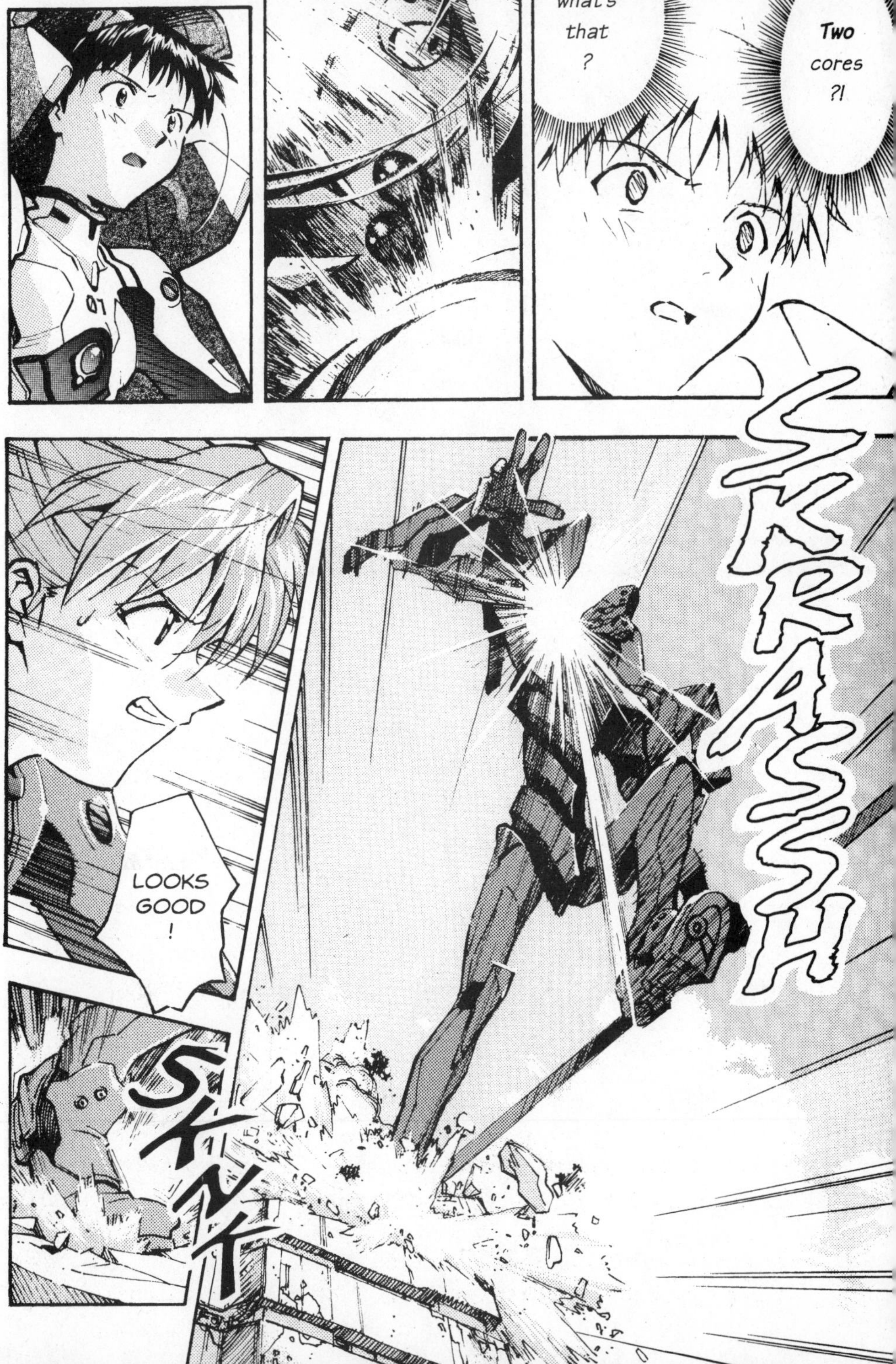
Wh- what's that ?
Two cores ?!
LOOKS GOOD !
SKRASSH
SKNK

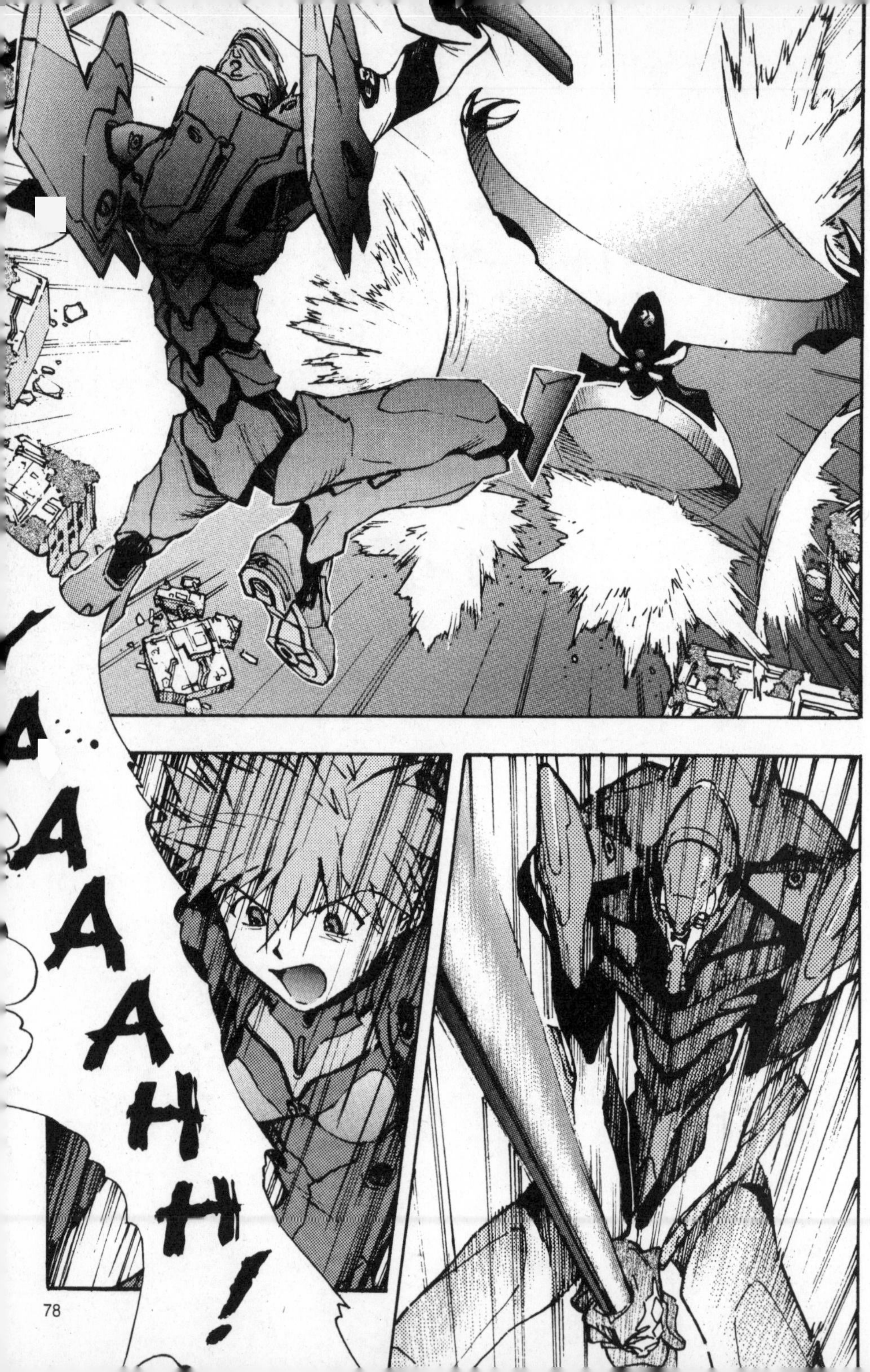
A···AAAHH!

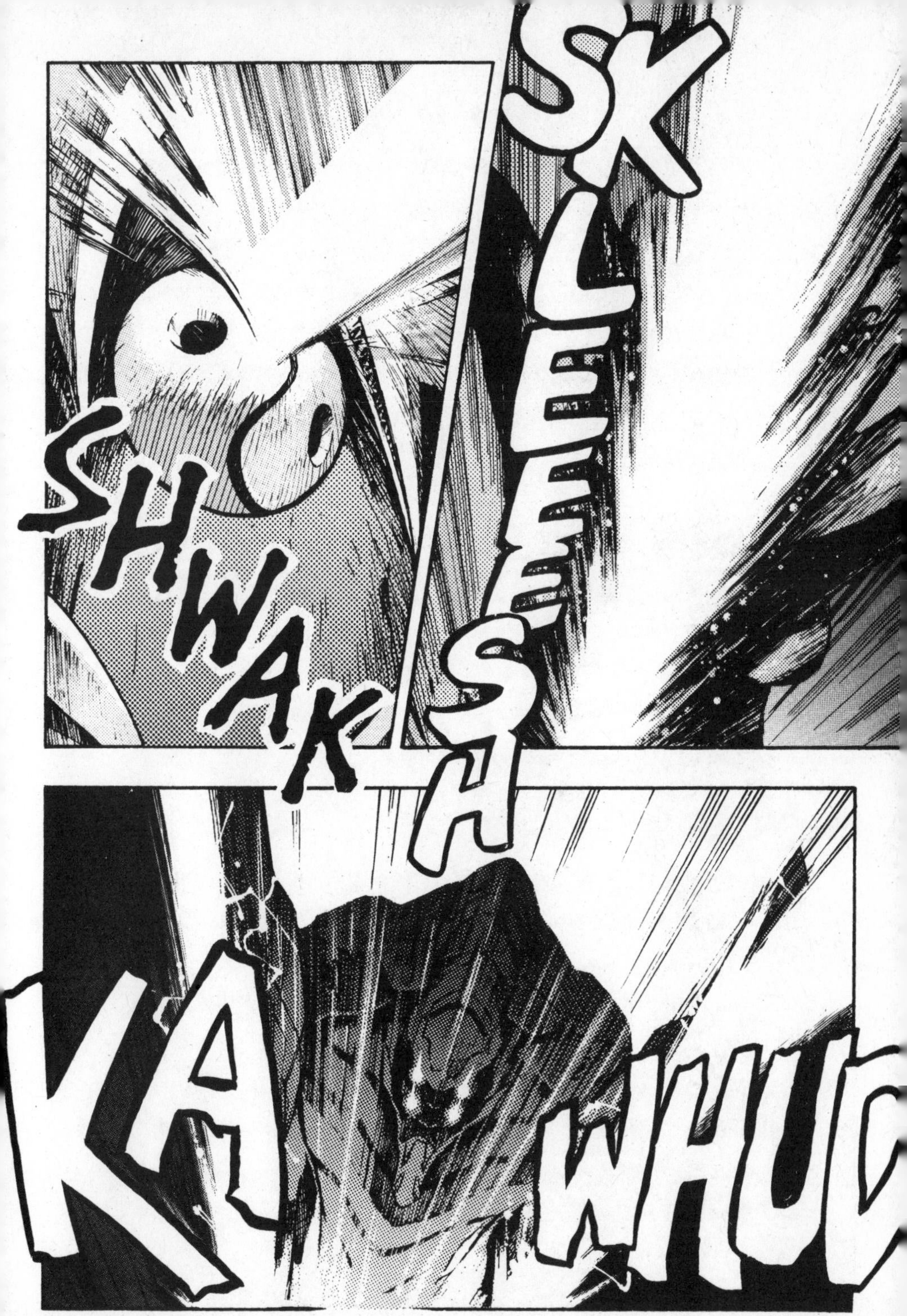
SHWAK
SKLEEESH
KA
WHU

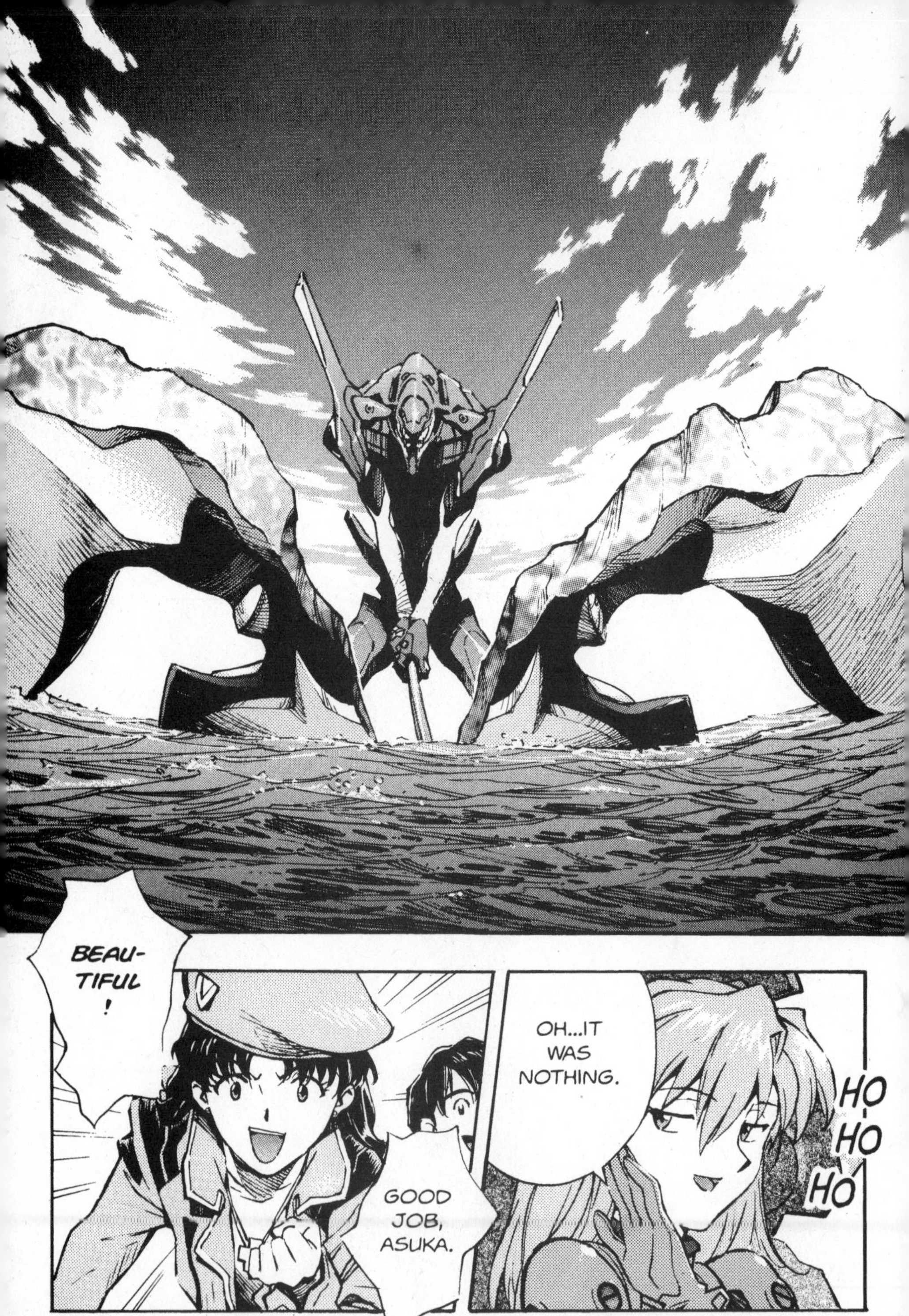
BEAU-
TIFUL
!
GOOD
JOB,
ASUKA.
OH...IT
WAS
NOTHING.
HO
HO
HO

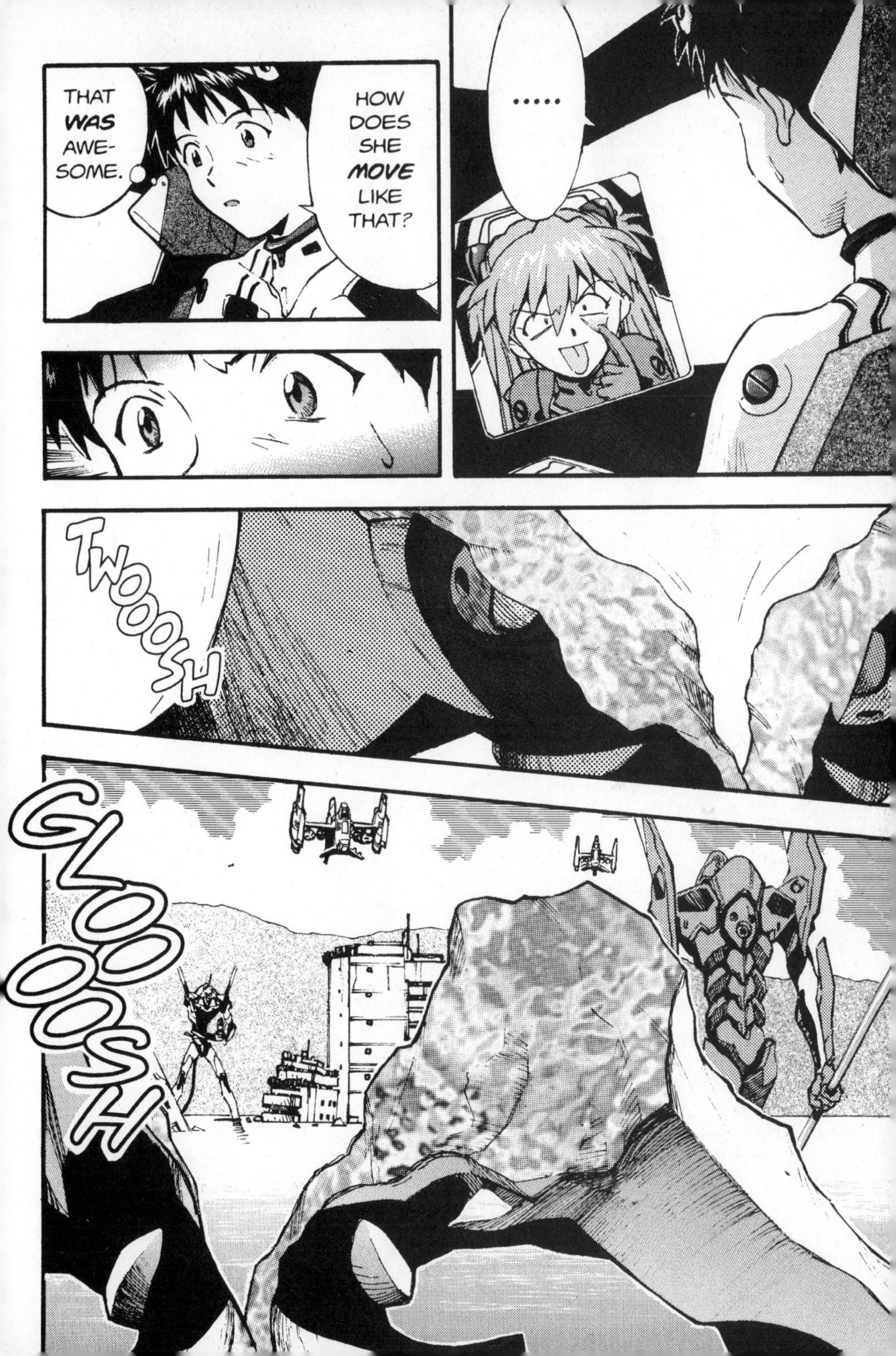

THAT **WAS** AWE-SOME.
HOW DOES SHE ***MOVE*** LIKE THAT?
.....
TWOOOSH
GLOOOOOSH

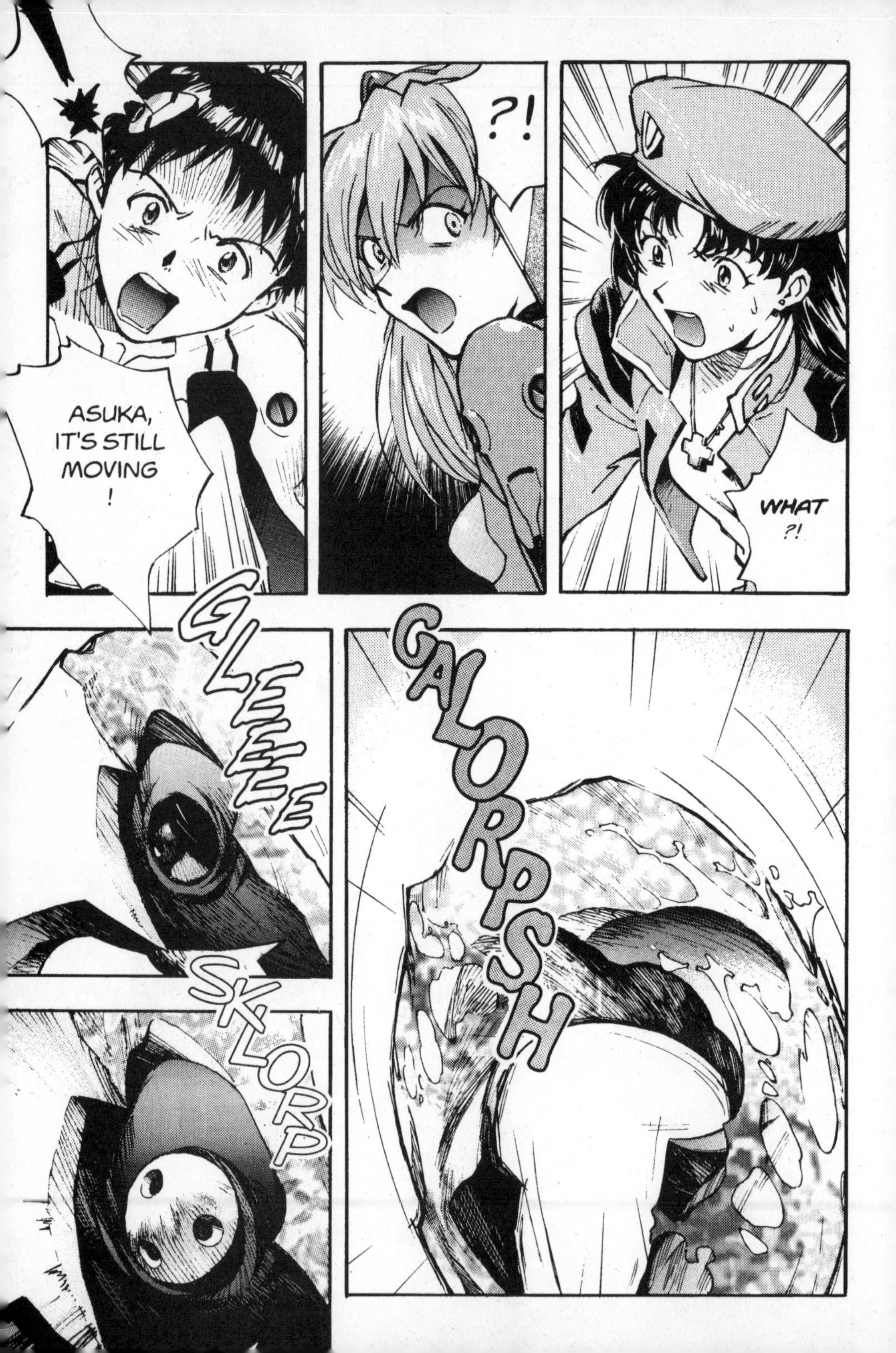
ASUKA, IT'S STILL MOVING !
?!
WHAT ?!
GLEEEEE
SKLORP
GALORPSH

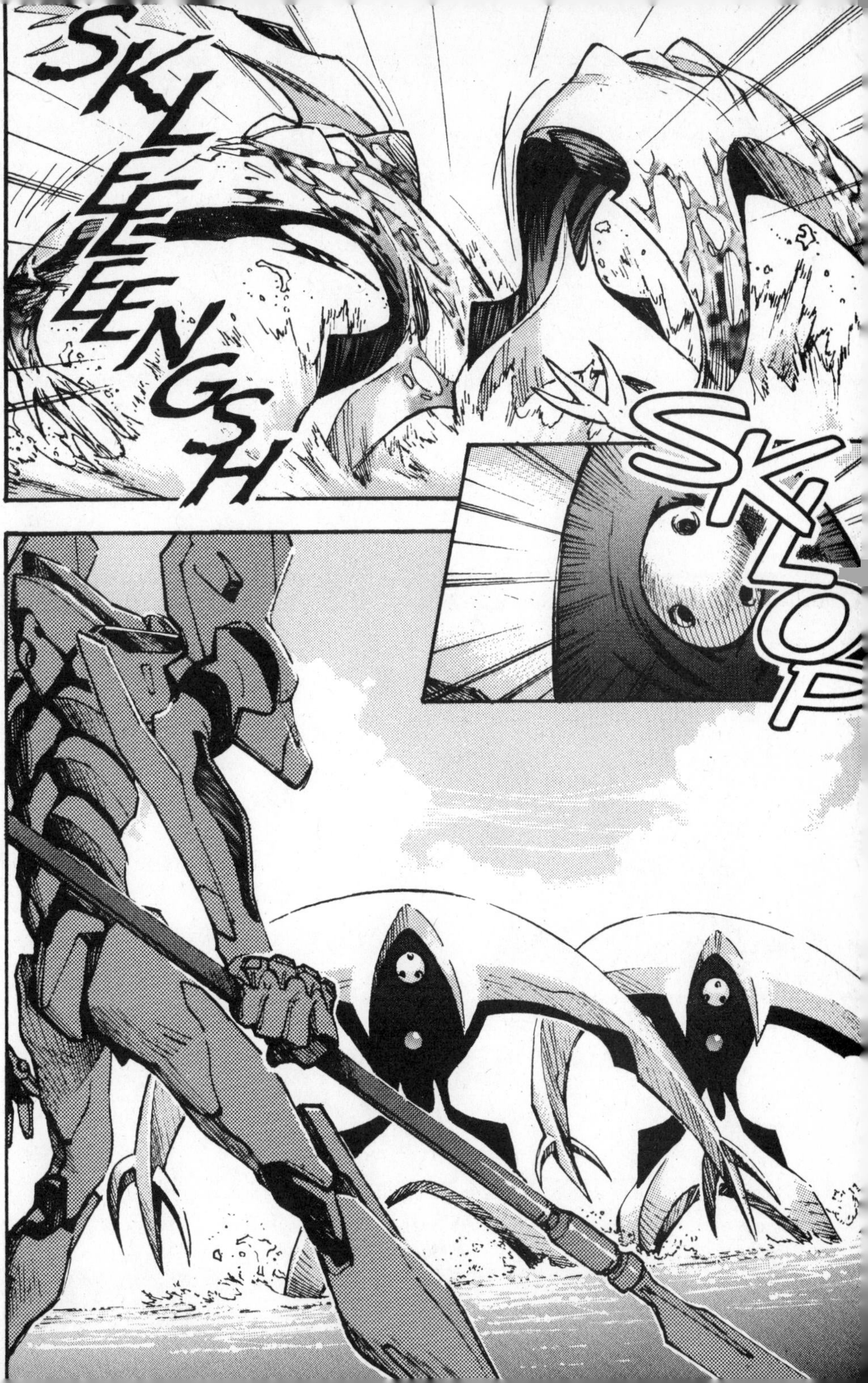
SKLEEEEENGSH
SKLOP

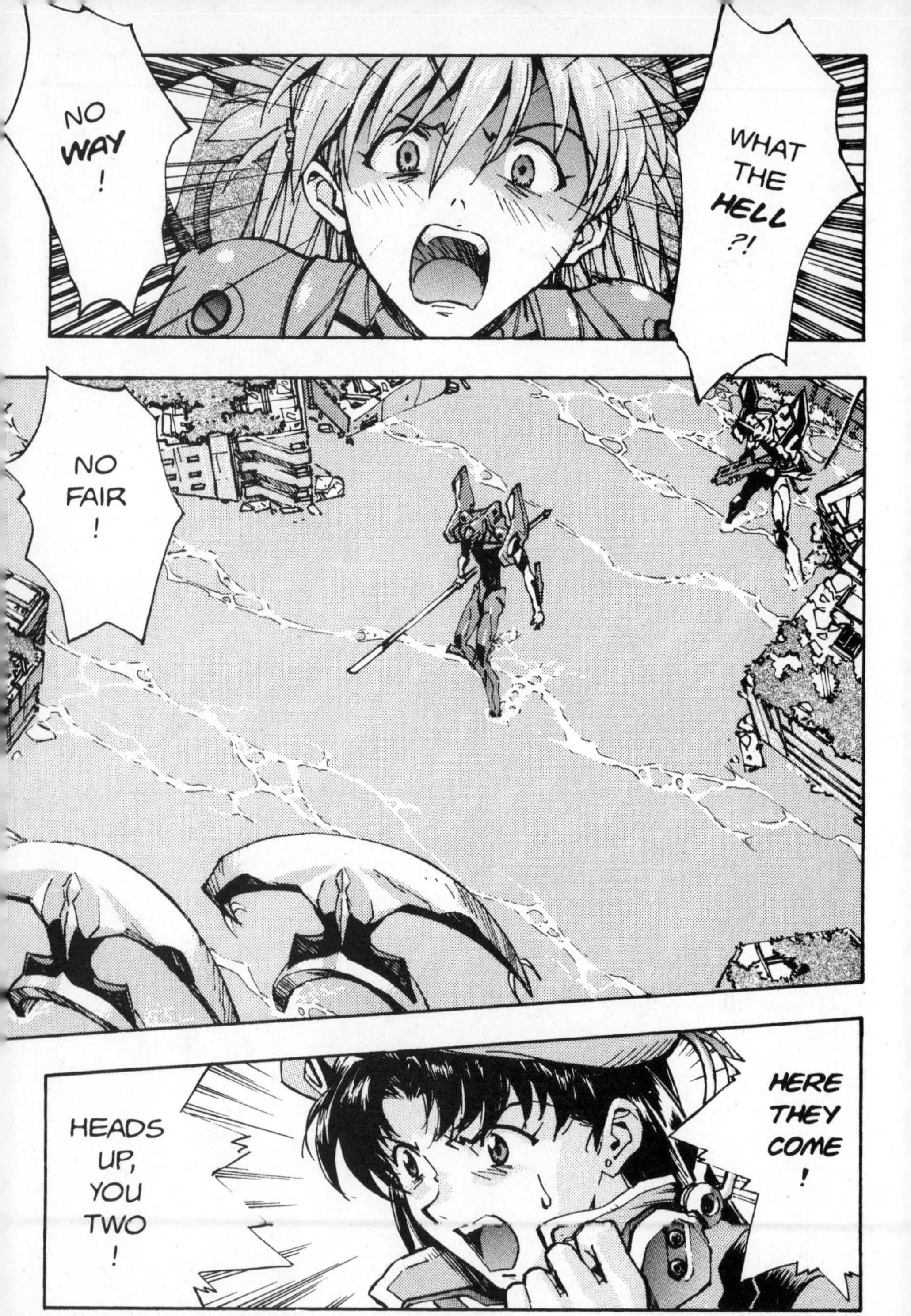
NO WAY !
WHAT THE HELL ?!
NO FAIR !
HEADS UP, YOU TWO !
HERE THEY COME !

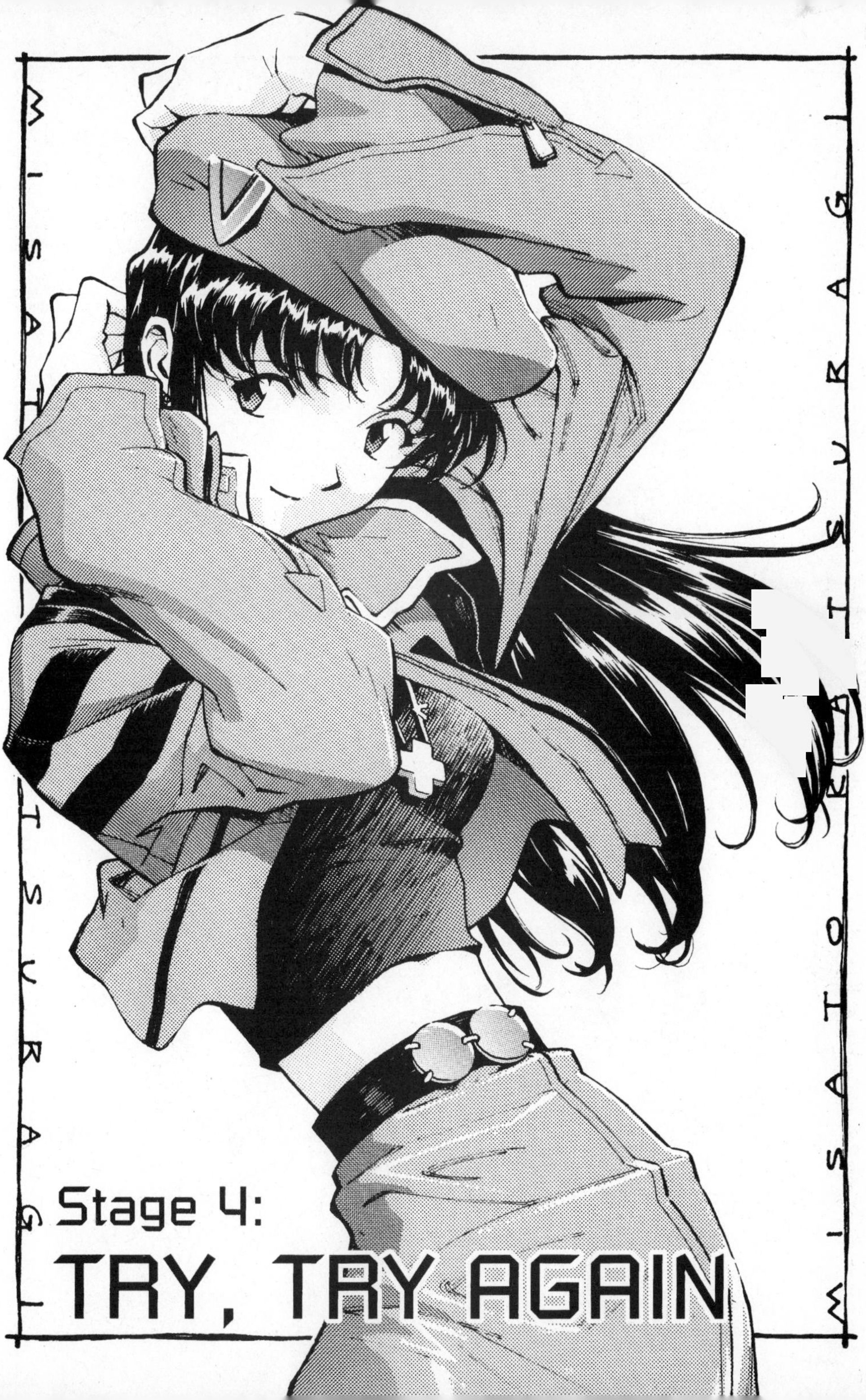
Stage 4:
TRY, TRY AGAIN

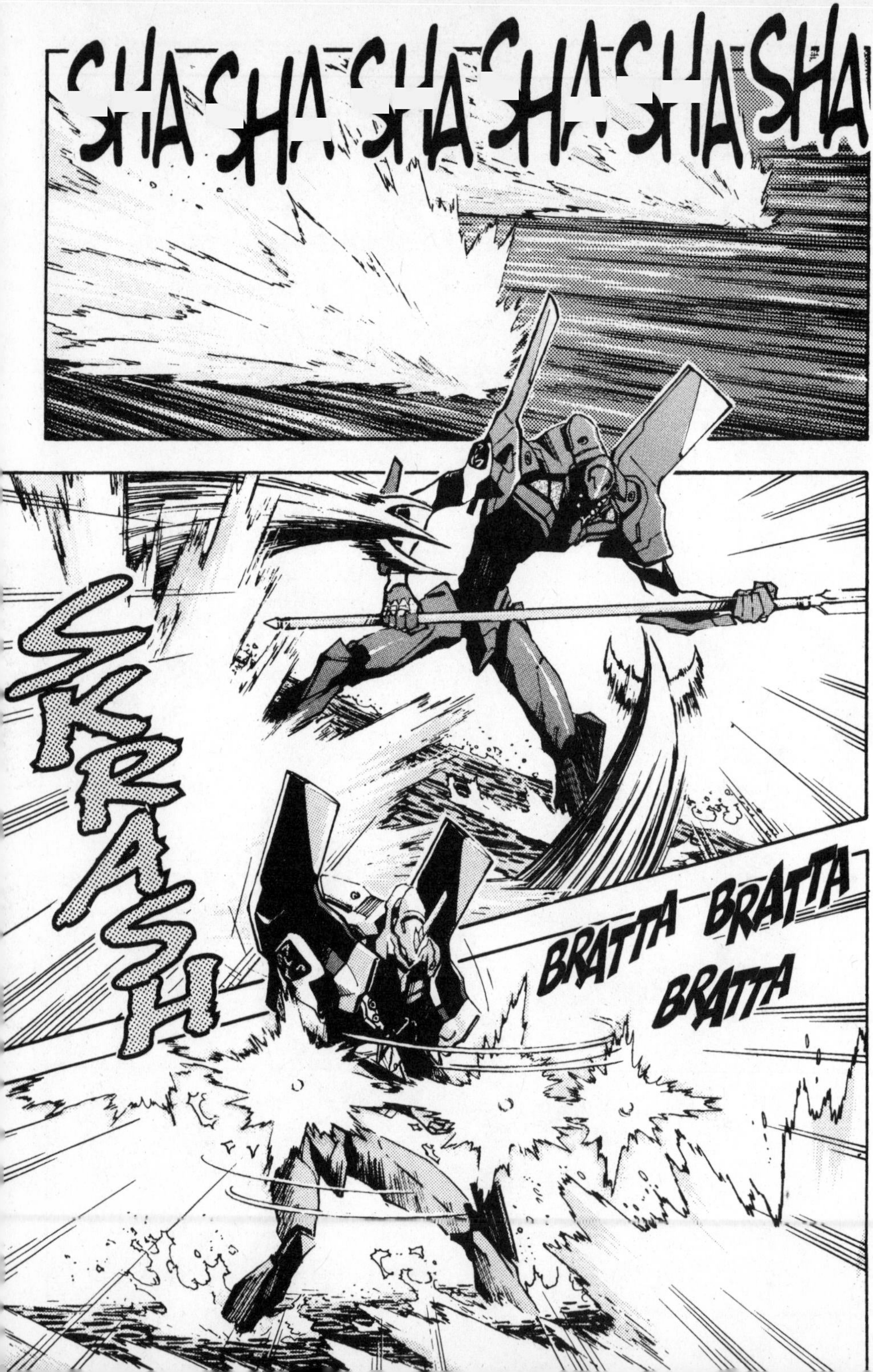
SHA SHA SHA SHA SHA SHA
SKRASH
BRATTA BRATTA
BRATTA

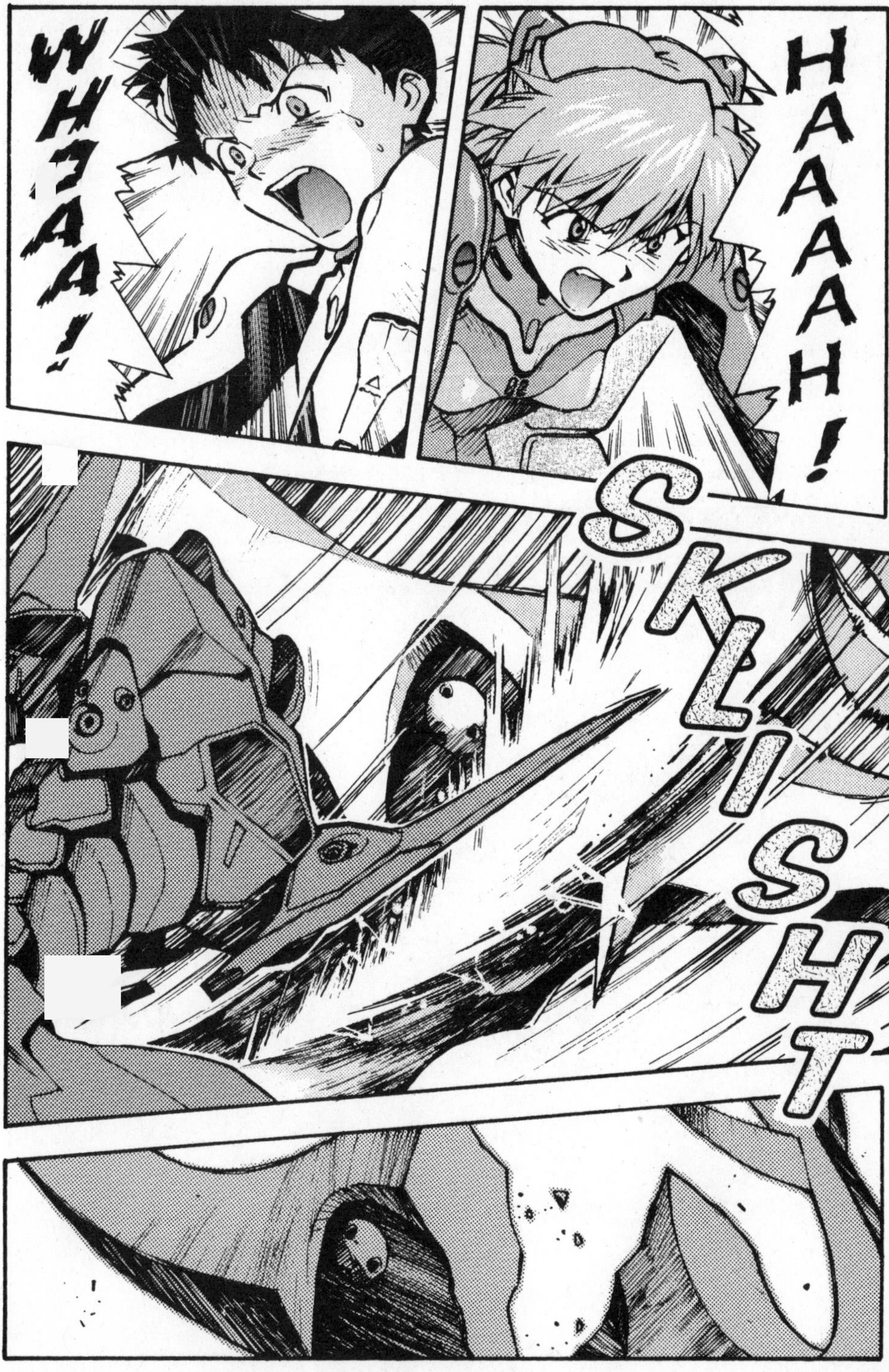
WHOAA!
HAAAAH!
SKLISHT

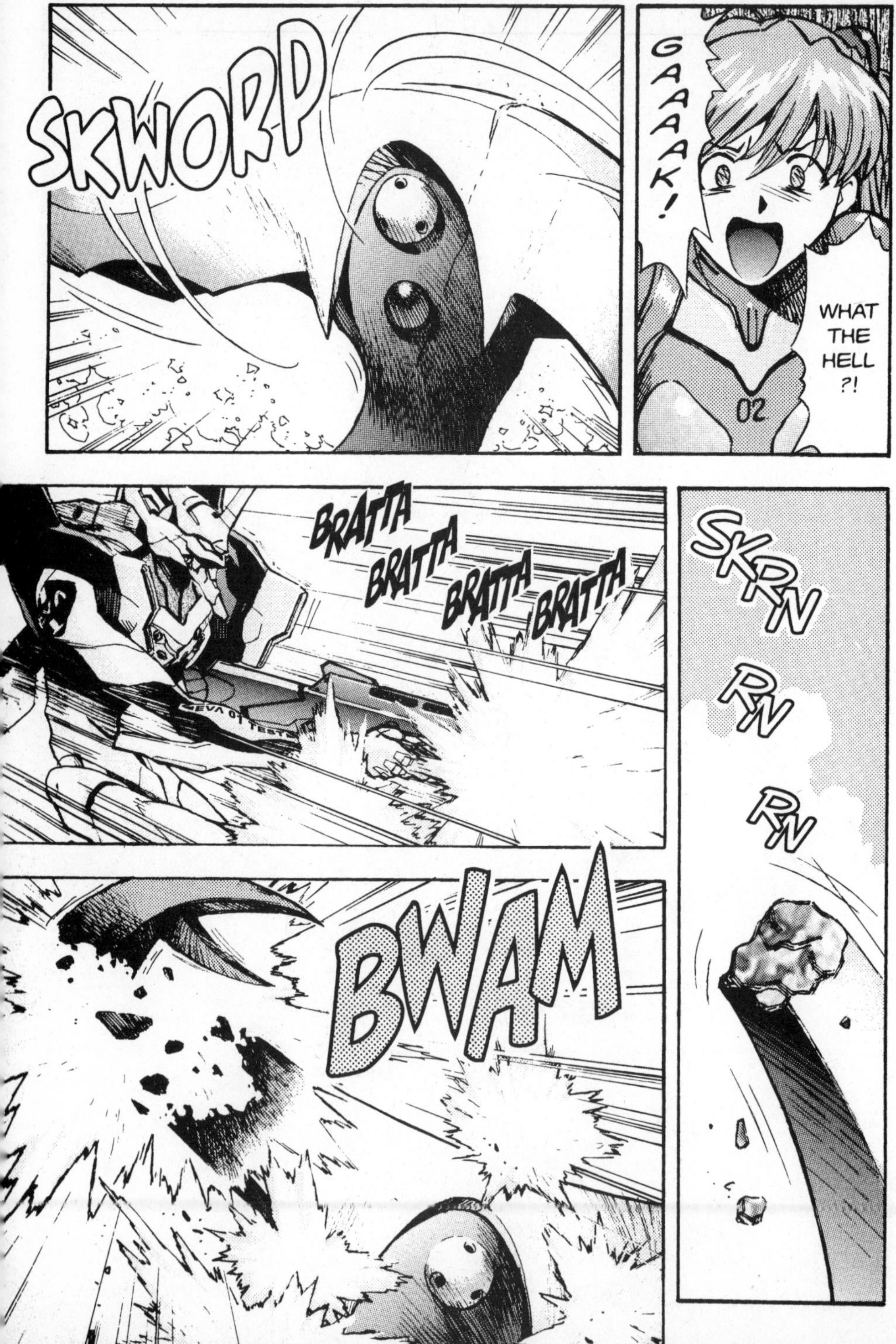
SKWORP
GAAAAK!
02
WHAT THE HELL ?!
BRATTA BRATTA BRATTA BRATTA
BWAM
SKRN RN RN

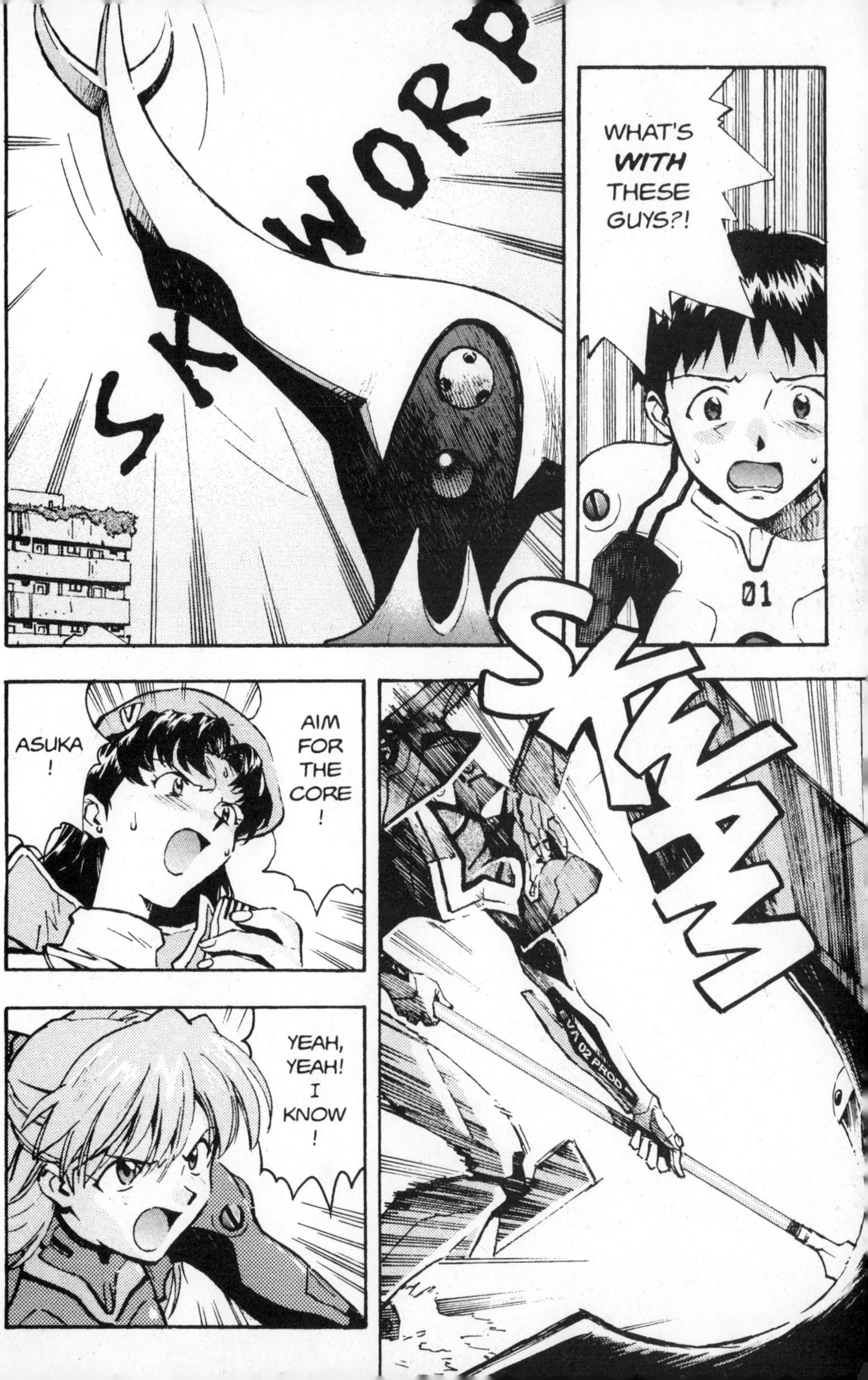
SKWORP
WHAT'S *WITH* THESE GUYS?!
ASUKA!
AIM FOR THE CORE!
YEAH, YEAH! I KNOW!
SKWAM
EVA 02 PROD

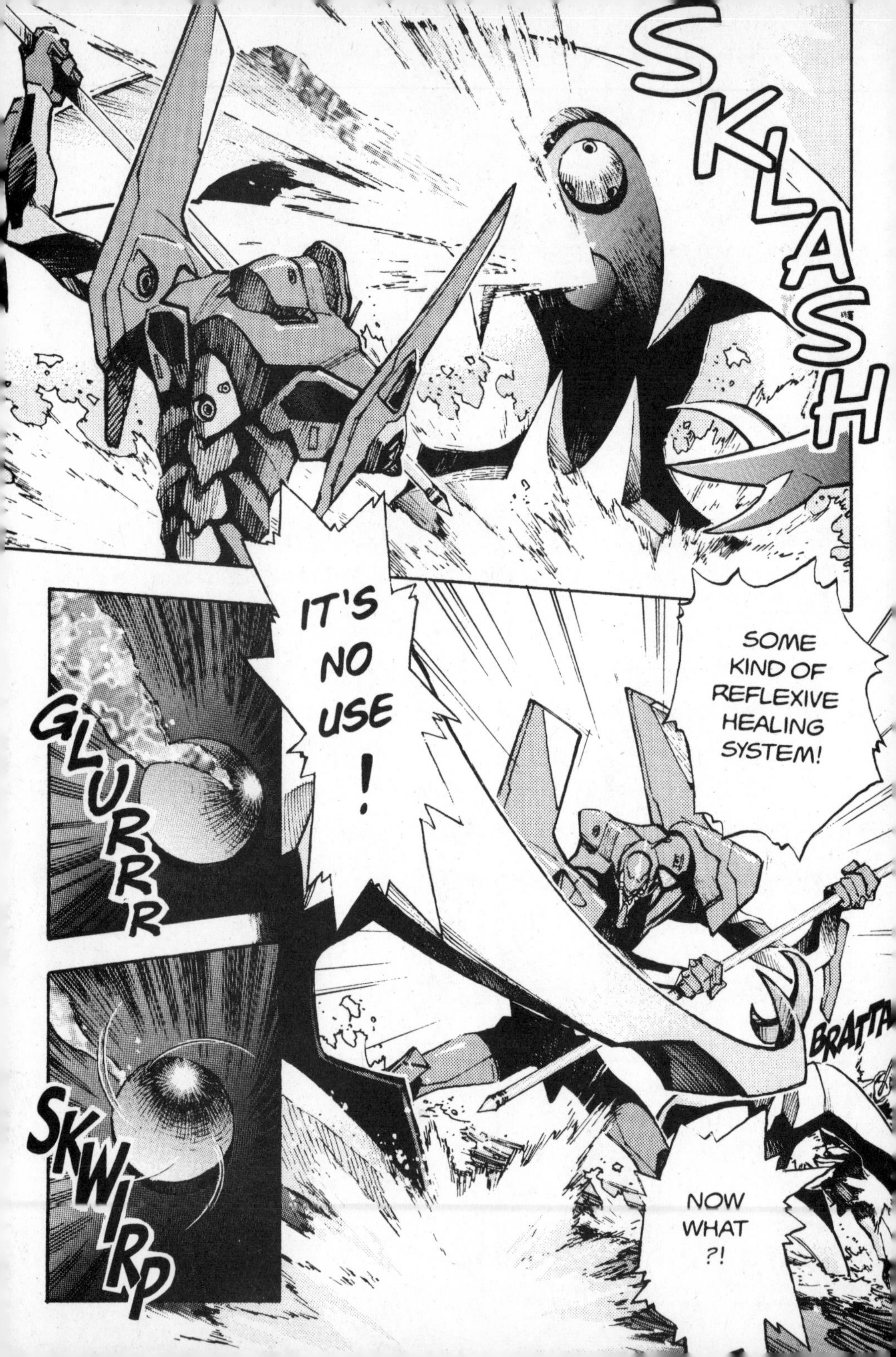
SKLASH
GLURRR
SKWIRP
IT'S NO USE!
SOME KIND OF REFLEXIVE HEALING SYSTEM!
BRATTA
NOW WHAT?!

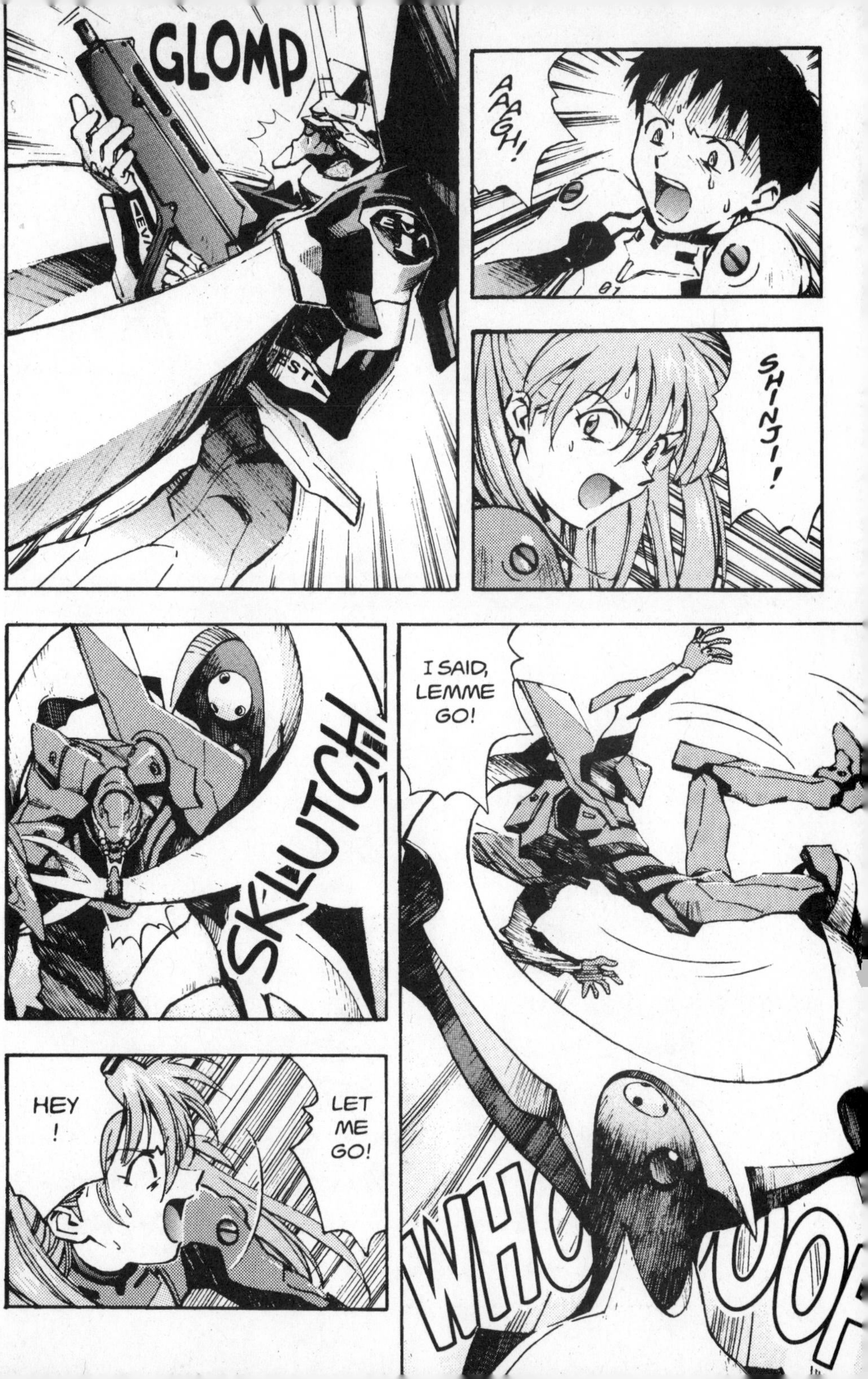
GLOMP
AAAGH!
SHINJI!!
SKLUTCH
HEY!
LET ME GO!
I SAID, LEMME GO!
WHO OOF

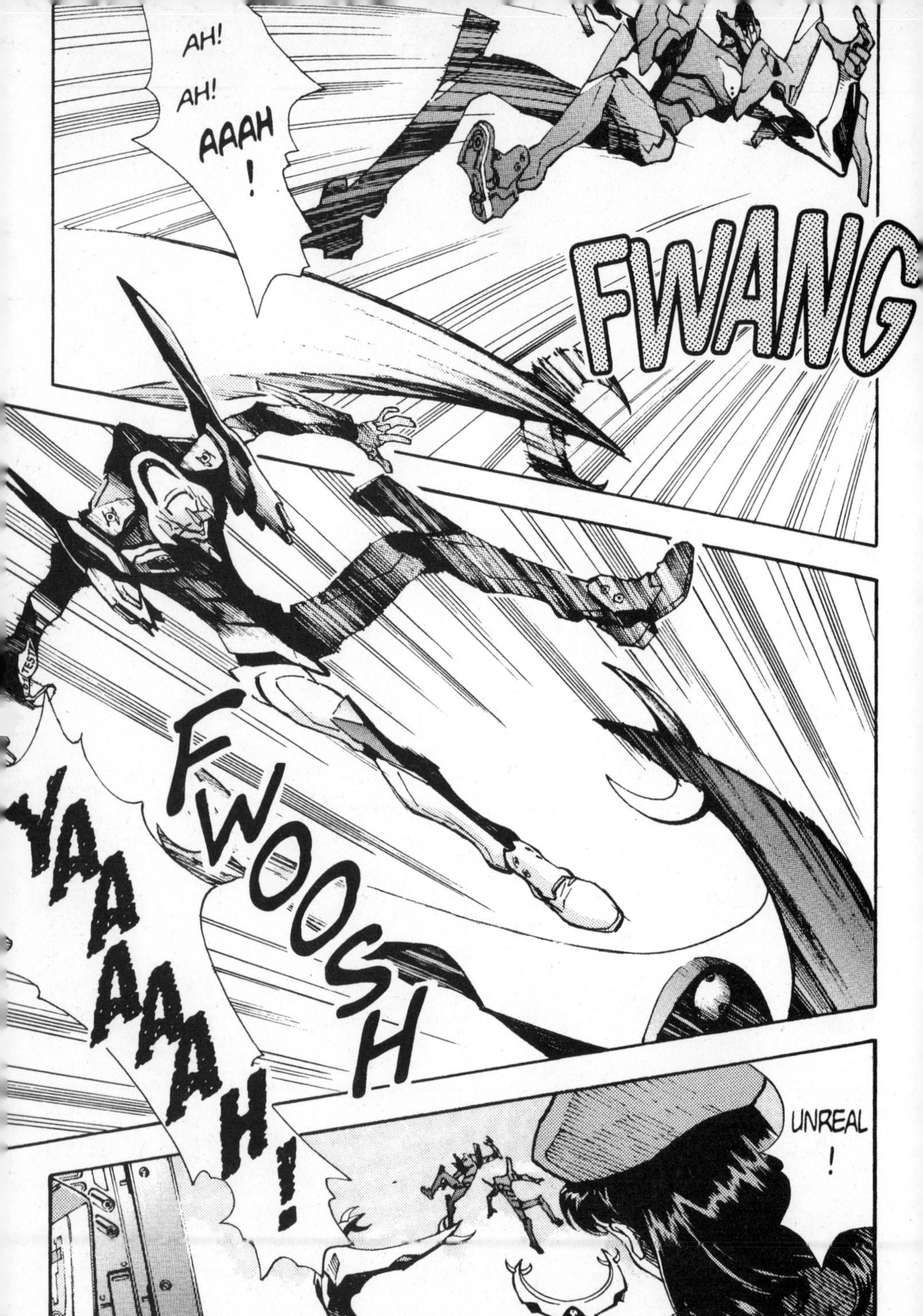
AH! AH! AAAH!
FWANG
FWOOSH
YAAAAAH!
UNREAL!
TEST

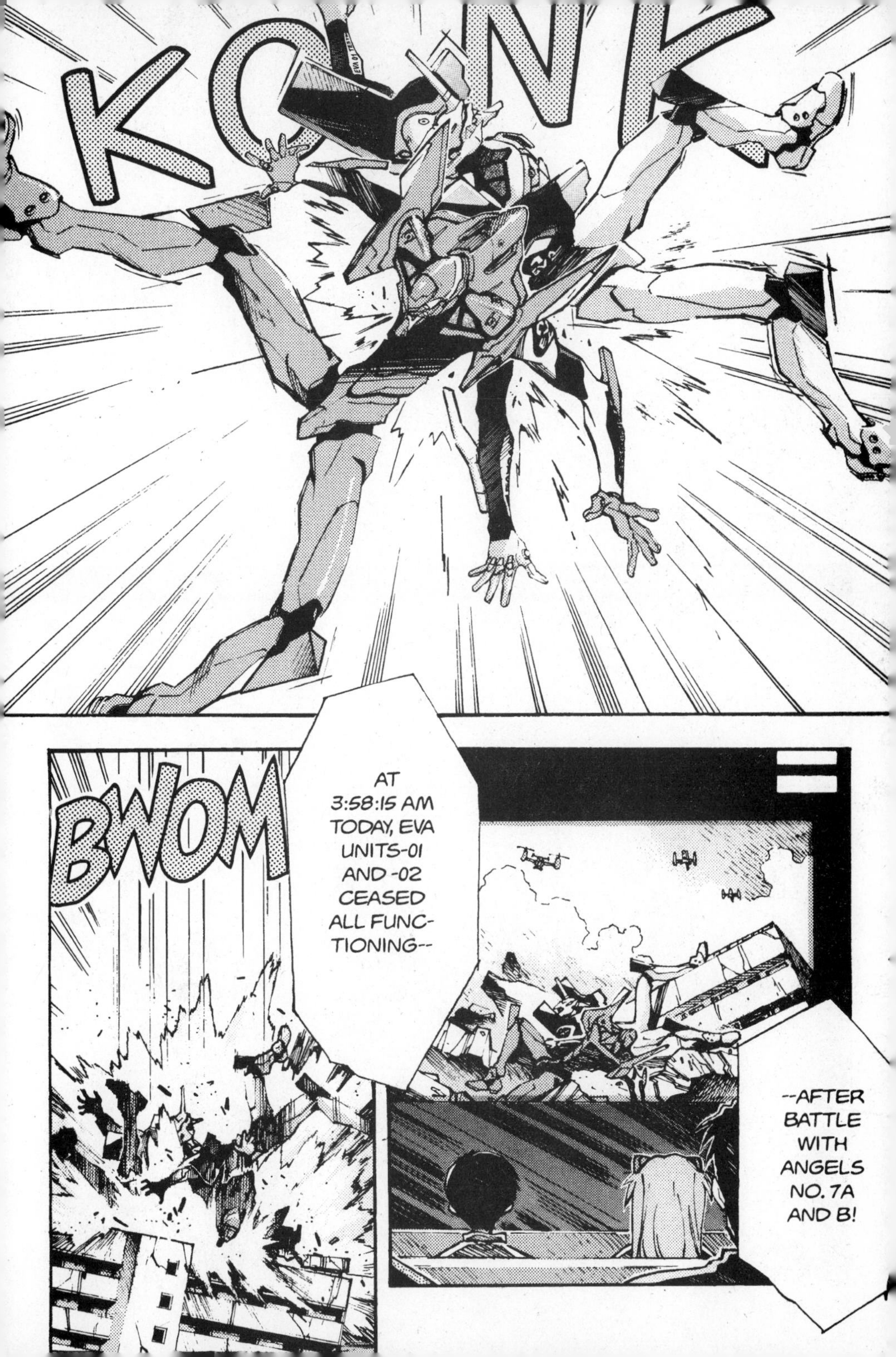
KONK
BWOM
AT 3:58:15 AM TODAY, EVA UNITS-01 AND -02 CEASED ALL FUNCTIONING--
--AFTER BATTLE WITH ANGELS NO. 7A AND B!

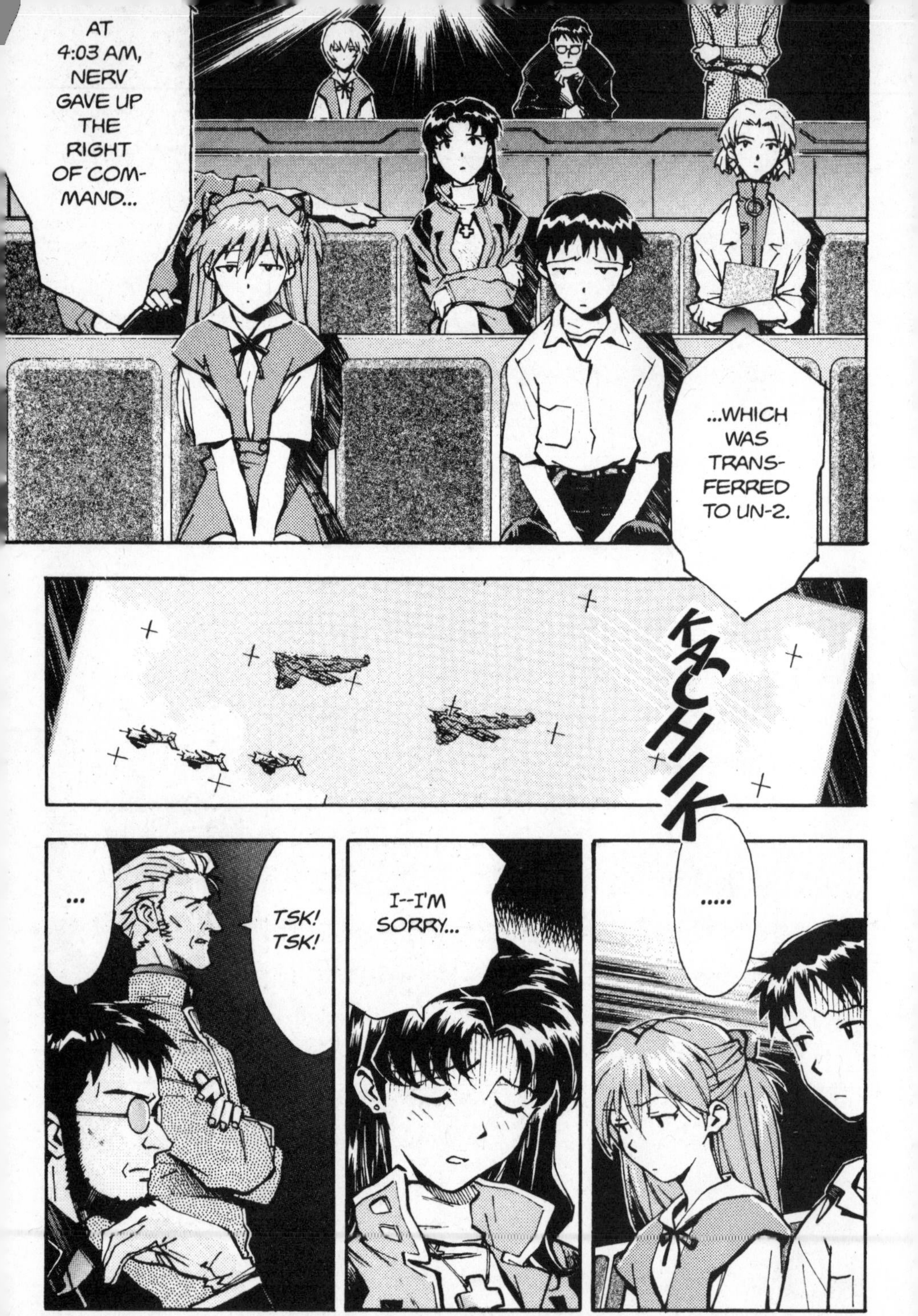

AT 4:03 AM, NERV GAVE UP THE RIGHT OF COM-MAND...
...WHICH WAS TRANS-FERRED TO UN-2.
KACHIK
...
TSK! TSK!
I--I'M SORRY...
.....

I didn't want dad to see me like that... even on tape.

AT 4:05, THE TARGET IS ATTACKED WITH A NEW N^2 BOMB...

KACHIK

KACHIK

KACHIK

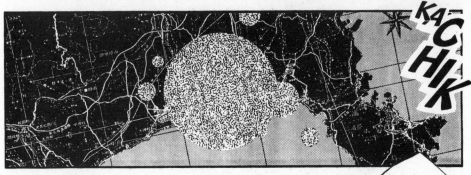

YOU KNOW WHAT THIS MEANS, DON'T YOU? WE'LL HAVE TO REDRAW THE MAP AGAIN...

...RESULTING IN A TWENTY-EIGHT PERCENT INCINERATION OF THE TARGET.

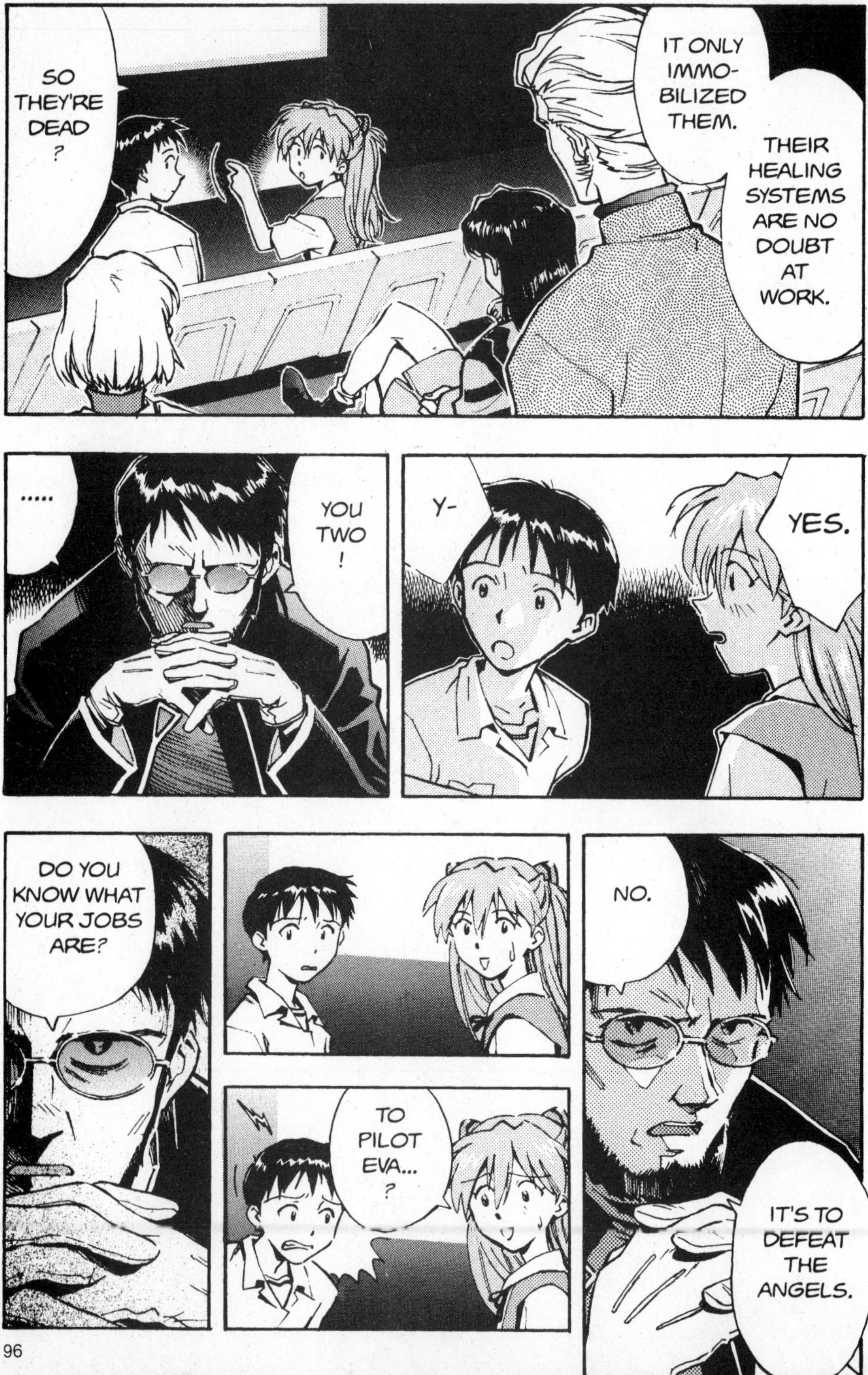
SO THEY'RE DEAD ?
IT ONLY IMMOBILIZED THEM.
THEIR HEALING SYSTEMS ARE NO DOUBT AT WORK.
.....
YOU TWO !
Y-
YES.
DO YOU KNOW WHAT YOUR JOBS ARE?
TO PILOT EVA... ?
NO.
IT'S TO DEFEAT THE ANGELS.

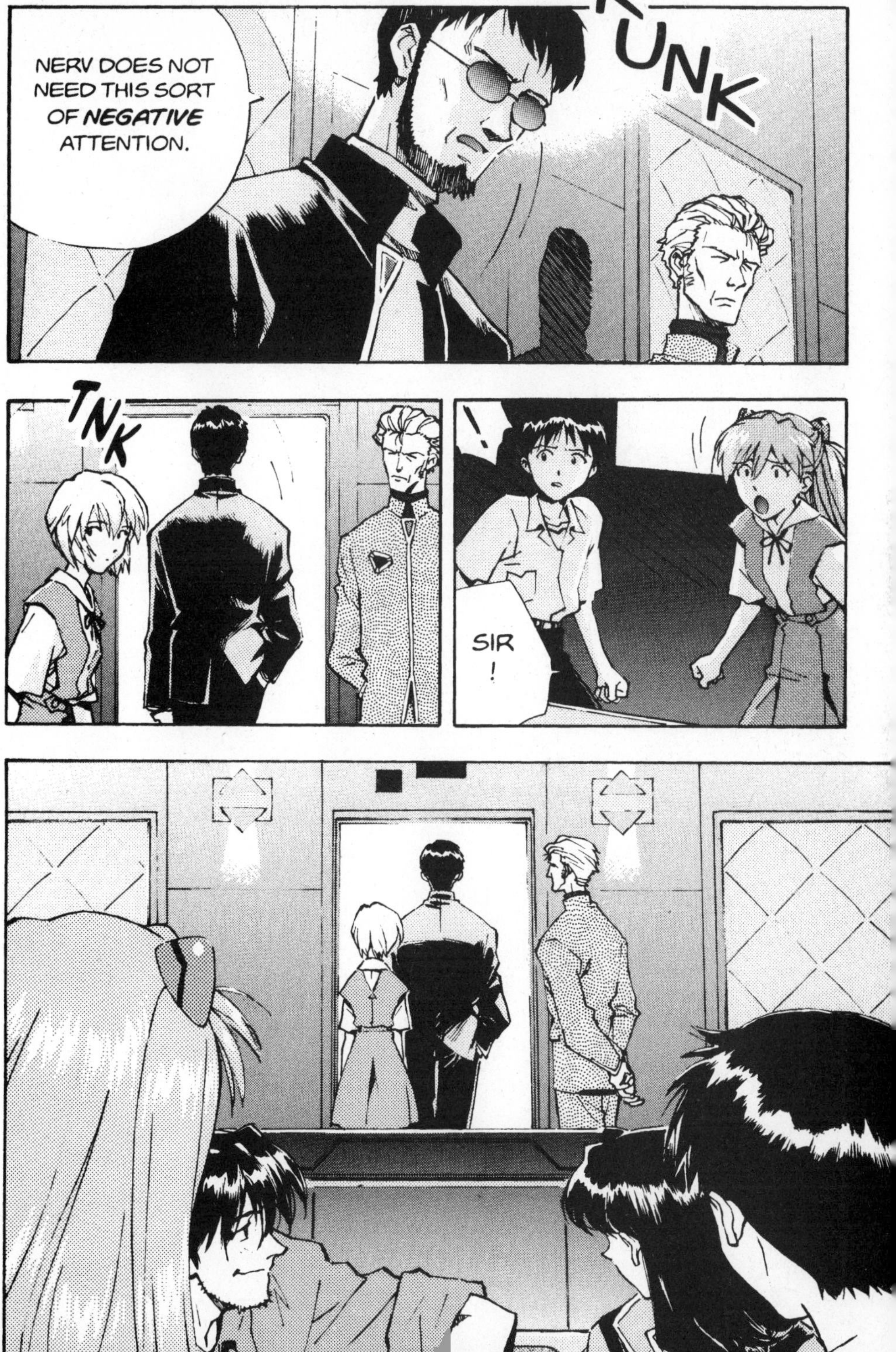
NERV DOES NOT NEED THIS SORT OF *NEGATIVE* ATTENTION.
KUNK
TNK
!
SIR !

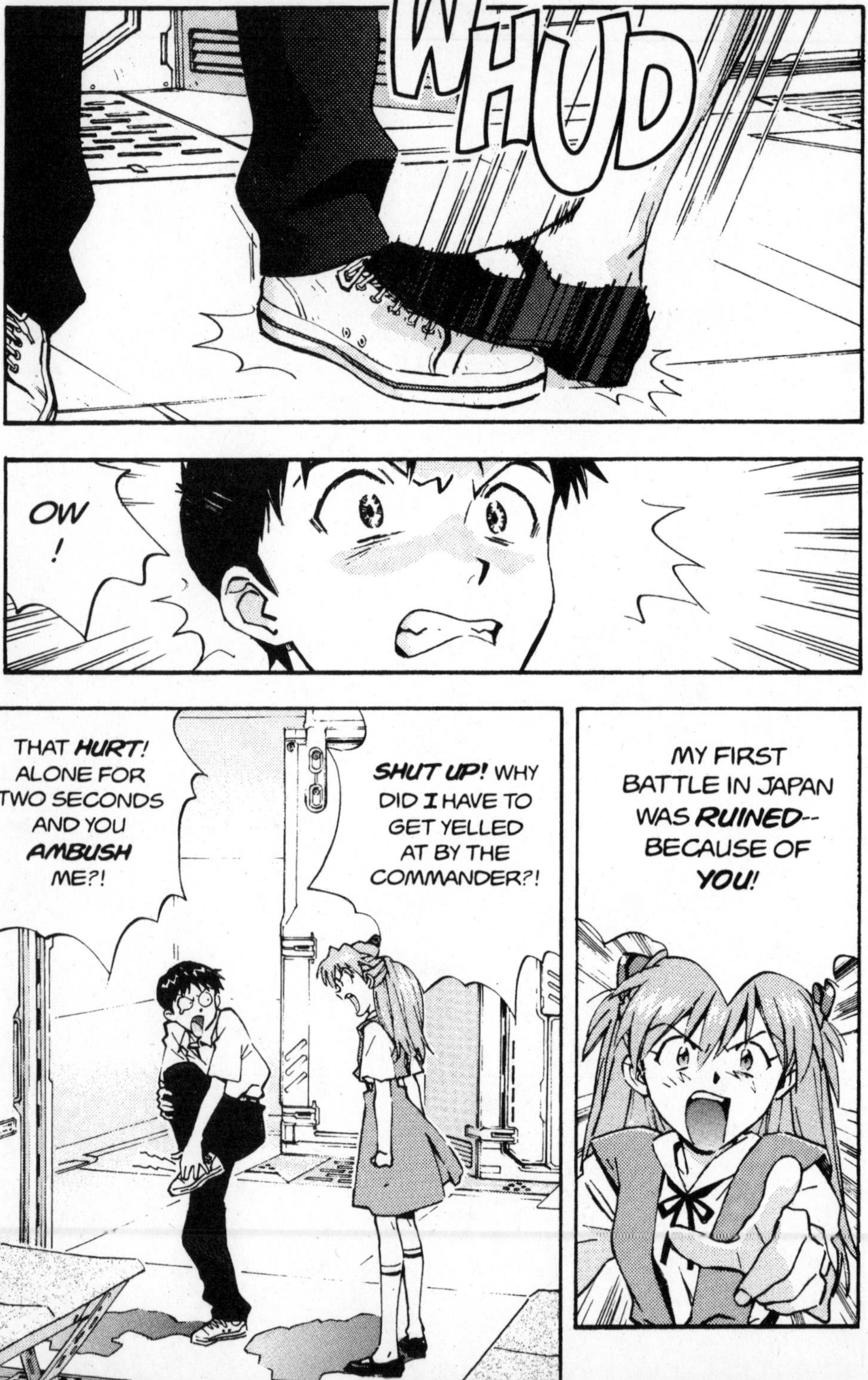
WHUD
OW!
THAT HURT! ALONE FOR TWO SECONDS AND YOU AMBUSH ME?!
SHUT UP! WHY DID I HAVE TO GET YELLED AT BY THE COMMANDER?!
MY FIRST BATTLE IN JAPAN WAS RUINED-- BECAUSE OF YOU!

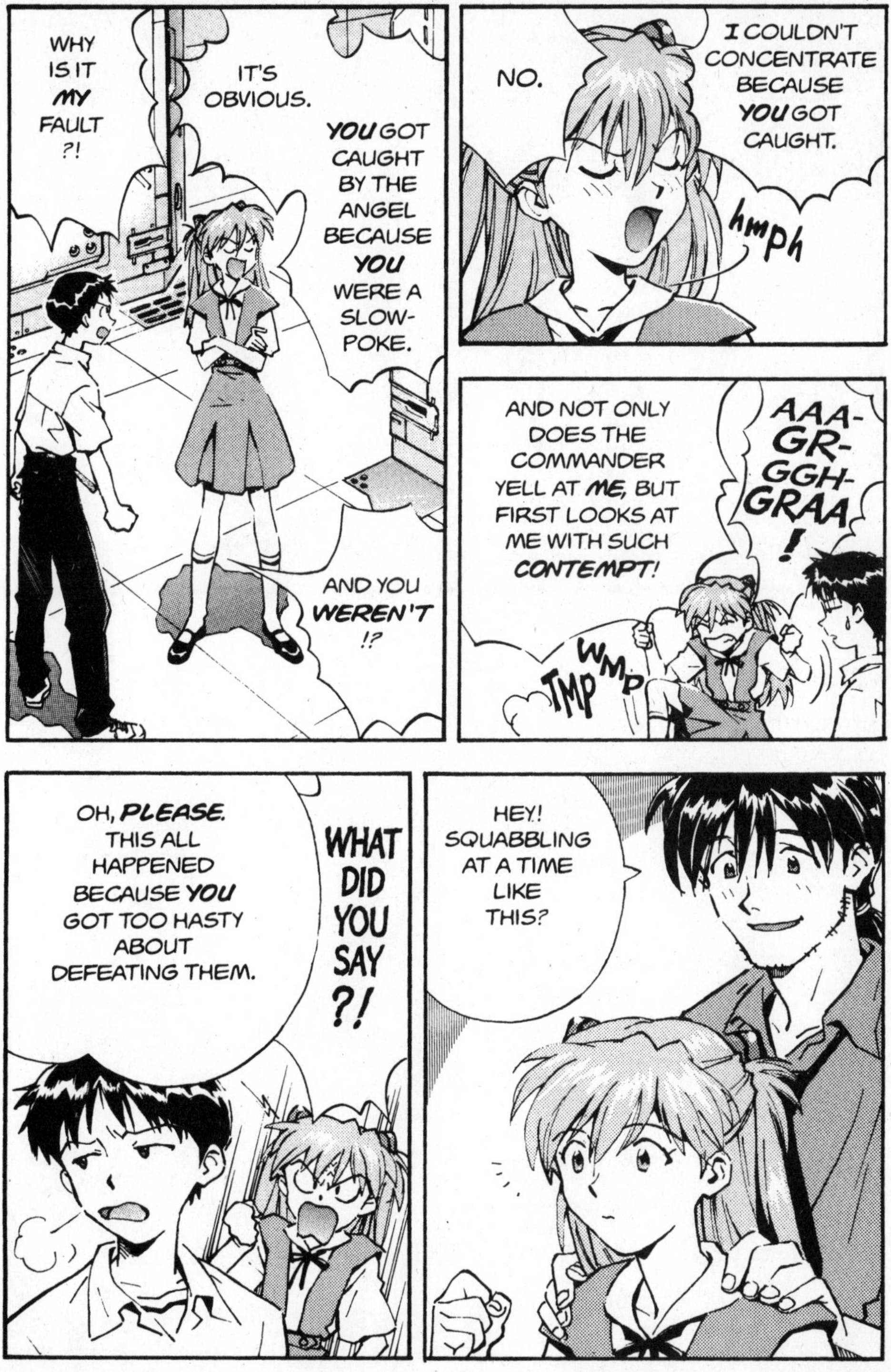
WHY IS IT MY FAULT ?!
IT'S OBVIOUS.
YOU GOT CAUGHT BY THE ANGEL BECAUSE YOU WERE A SLOW-POKE.
AND YOU WEREN'T !?
NO.
I COULDN'T CONCENTRATE BECAUSE YOU GOT CAUGHT.
hmph
AND NOT ONLY DOES THE COMMANDER YELL AT ME, BUT FIRST LOOKS AT ME WITH SUCH CONTEMPT!
AAA-GR-GGH-GRAA!
TMP WMP
OH, PLEASE. THIS ALL HAPPENED BECAUSE YOU GOT TOO HASTY ABOUT DEFEATING THEM.
WHAT DID YOU SAY ?!
HEY! SQUABBLING AT A TIME LIKE THIS?

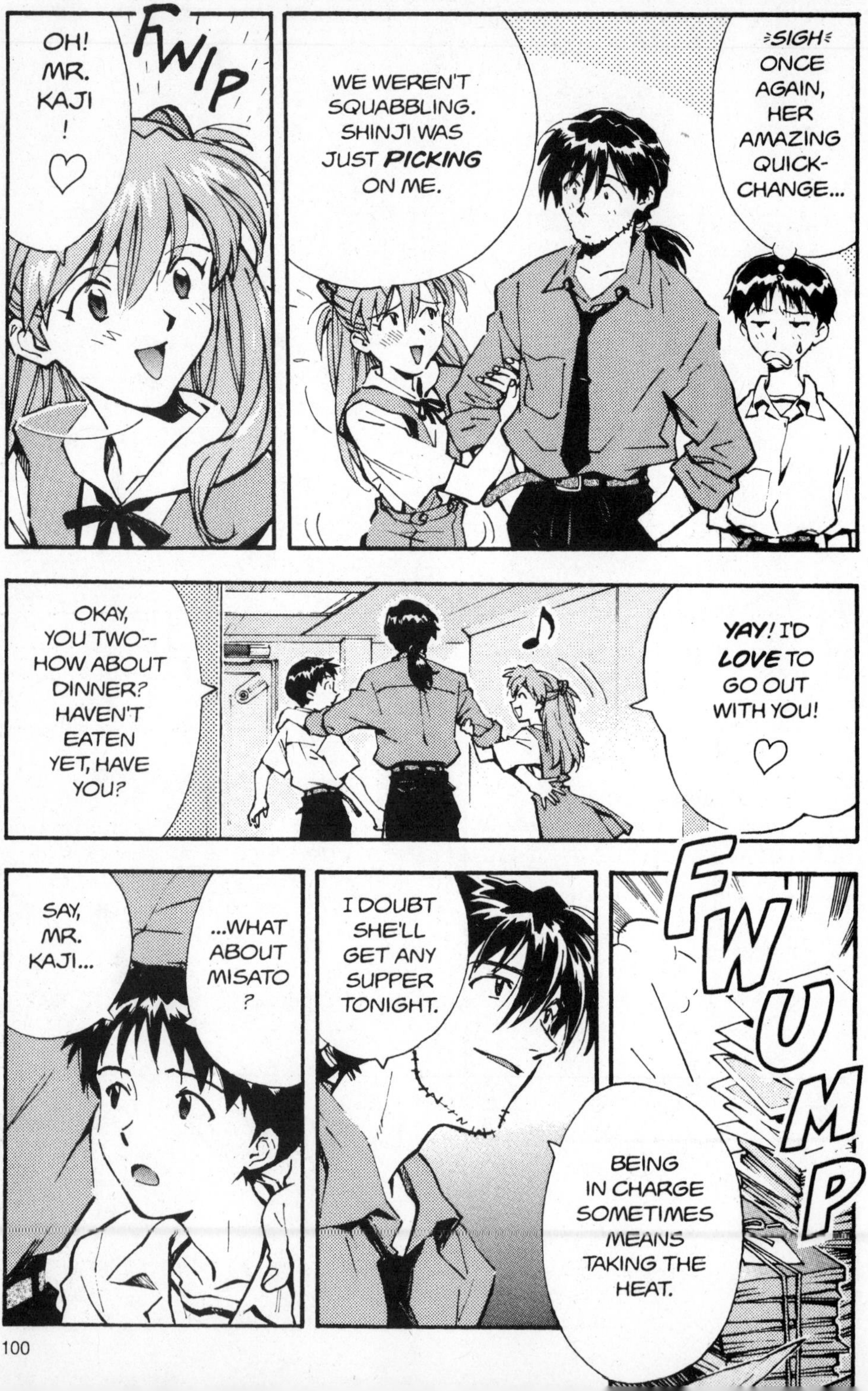
FWIP
OH! MR. KAJI! ♡
WE WEREN'T SQUABBLING. SHINJI WAS JUST **PICKING** ON ME.
SIGH ONCE AGAIN, HER AMAZING QUICK-CHANGE...
OKAY, YOU TWO--HOW ABOUT DINNER? HAVEN'T EATEN YET, HAVE YOU?
YAY! I'D **LOVE** TO GO OUT WITH YOU! ♡
SAY, MR. KAJI...
...WHAT ABOUT MISATO?
I DOUBT SHE'LL GET ANY SUPPER TONIGHT.
FWUMP
BEING IN CHARGE SOMETIMES MEANS TAKING THE HEAT.

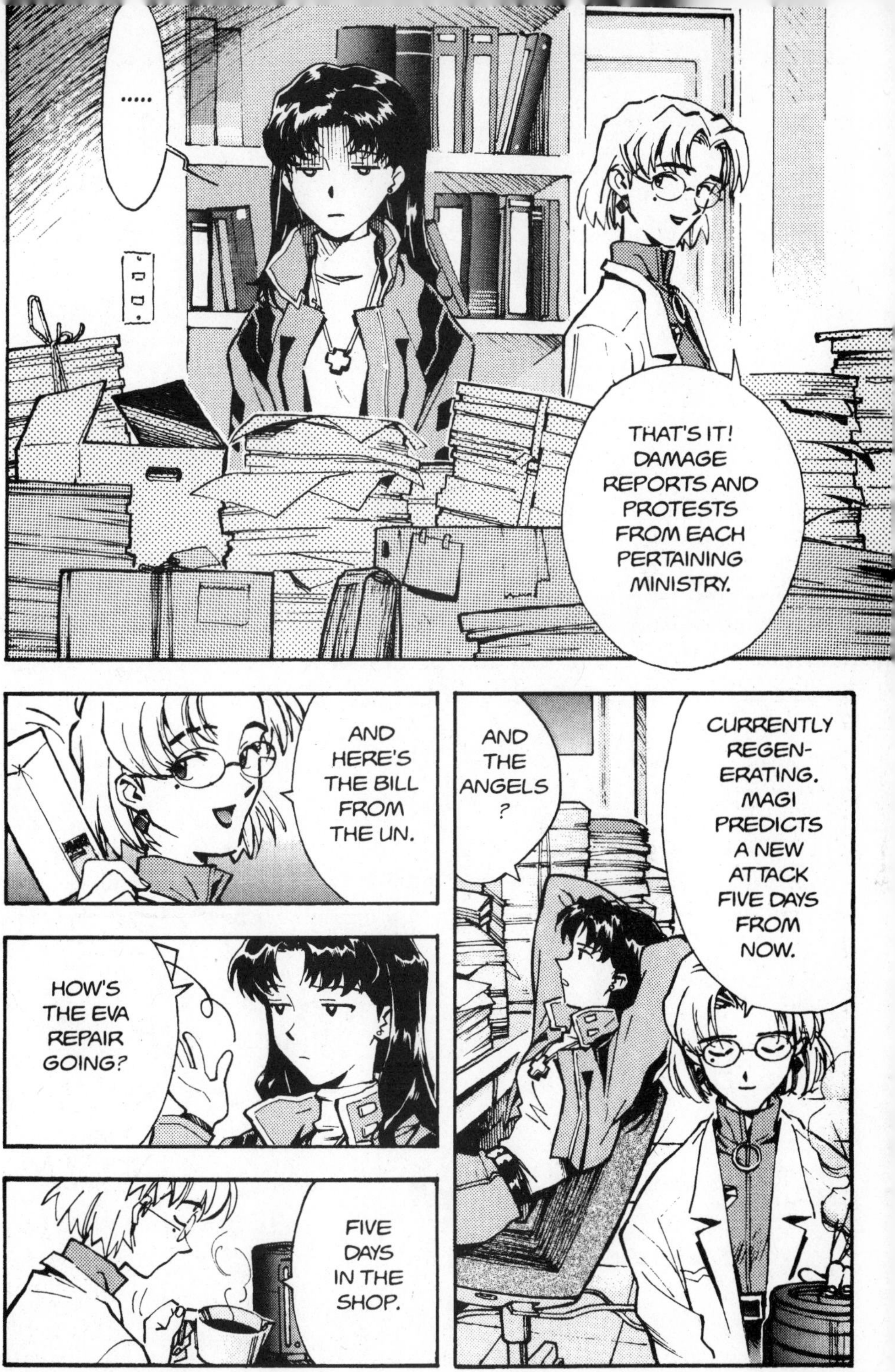
.....
THAT'S IT! DAMAGE REPORTS AND PROTESTS FROM EACH PERTAINING MINISTRY.
AND HERE'S THE BILL FROM THE UN.
HOW'S THE EVA REPAIR GOING?
FIVE DAYS IN THE SHOP.
AND THE ANGELS?
CURRENTLY REGEN-ERATING. MAGI PREDICTS A NEW ATTACK FIVE DAYS FROM NOW.

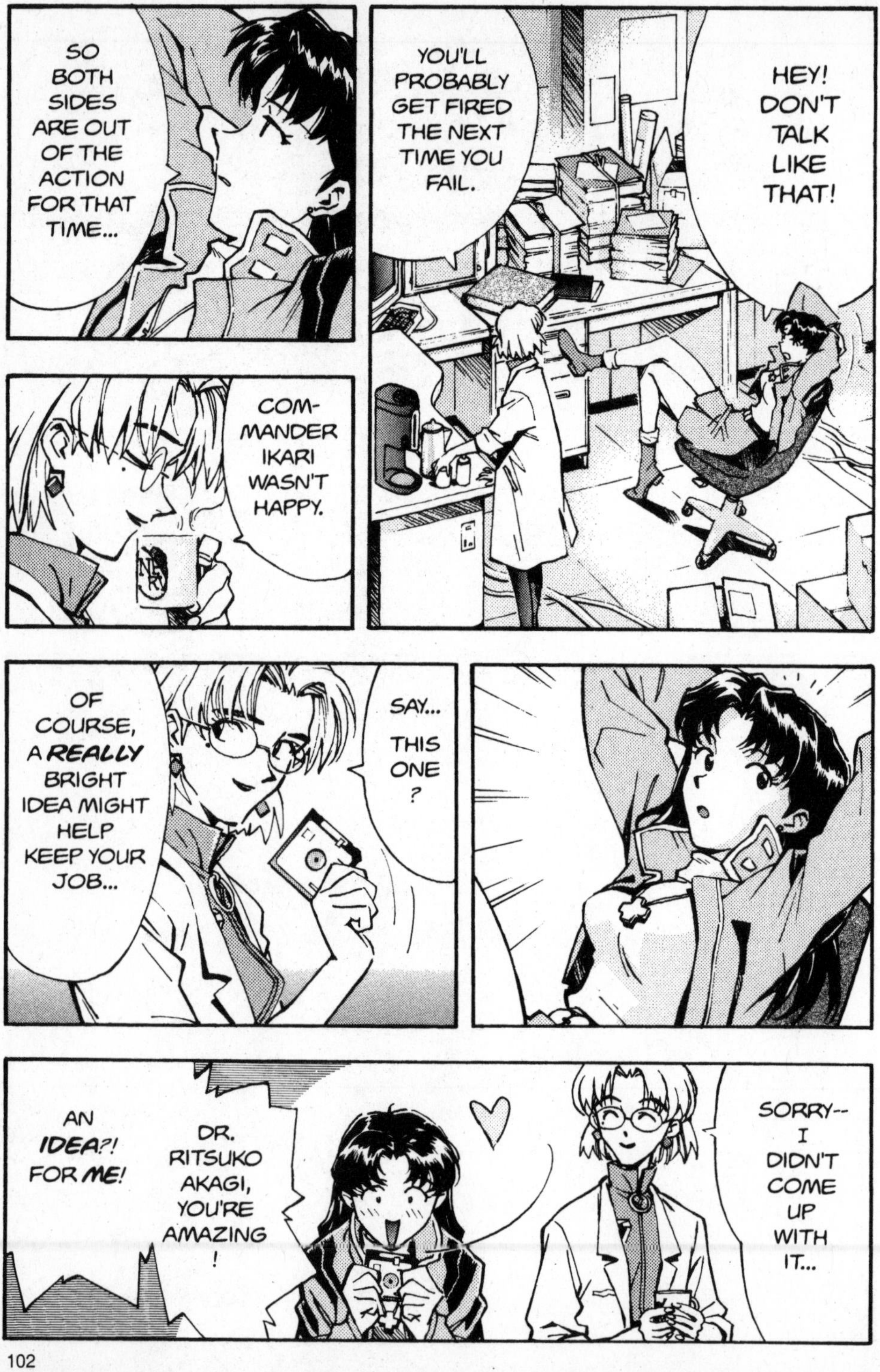
SO BOTH SIDES ARE OUT OF THE ACTION FOR THAT TIME...
COMMANDER IKARI WASN'T HAPPY.
YOU'LL PROBABLY GET FIRED THE NEXT TIME YOU FAIL.
HEY! DON'T TALK LIKE THAT!
OF COURSE, A **REALLY** BRIGHT IDEA MIGHT HELP KEEP YOUR JOB...
SAY... THIS ONE?
AN ***IDEA***?! FOR ***ME***!
DR. RITSUKO AKAGI, YOU'RE AMAZING!
SORRY-- I DIDN'T COME UP WITH IT...

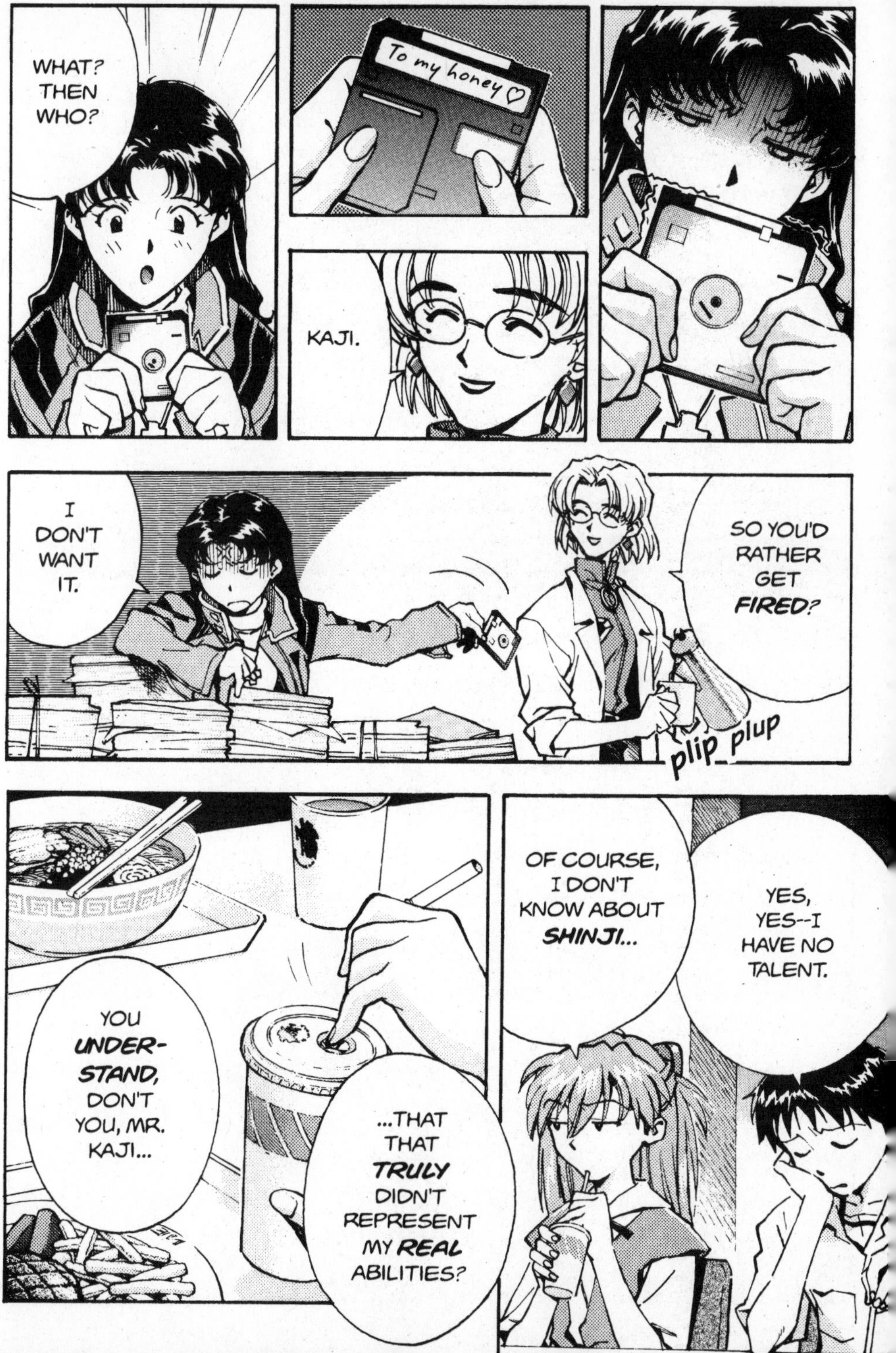
WHAT? THEN WHO?
To my honey ♡
KAJI.
I DON'T WANT IT.
SO YOU'D RATHER GET FIRED?
plip plup
YOU UNDER-STAND, DON'T YOU, MR. KAJI...
...THAT THAT TRULY DIDN'T REPRESENT MY REAL ABILITIES?
OF COURSE, I DON'T KNOW ABOUT SHINJI...
YES, YES--I HAVE NO TALENT.

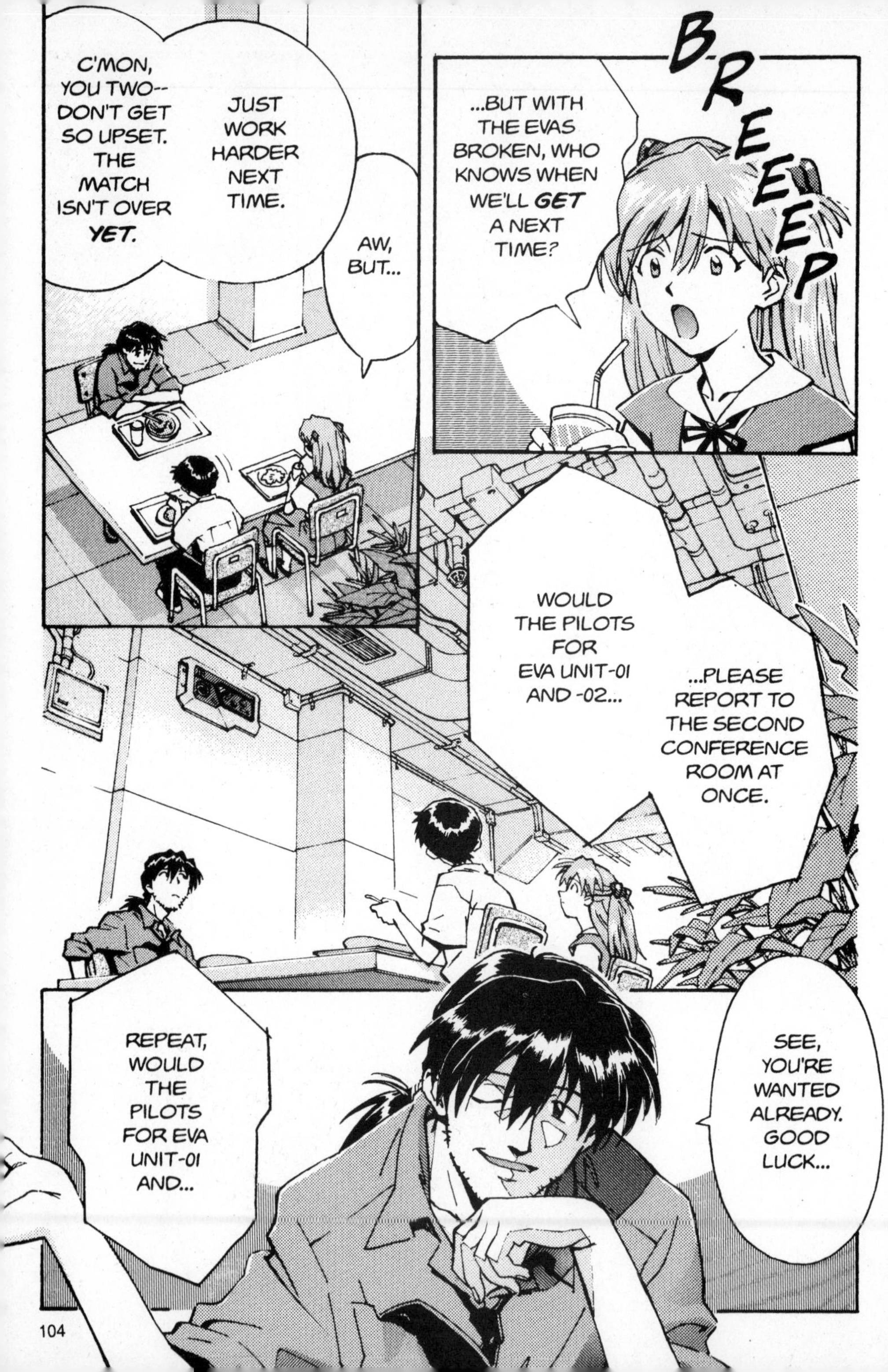

C'MON, YOU TWO-- DON'T GET SO UPSET. THE MATCH ISN'T OVER **YET**.
JUST WORK HARDER NEXT TIME.
AW, BUT...
B-REEEP
...BUT WITH THE EVAS BROKEN, WHO KNOWS WHEN WE'LL **GET** A NEXT TIME?
WOULD THE PILOTS FOR EVA UNIT-01 AND -02...
...PLEASE REPORT TO THE SECOND CONFERENCE ROOM AT ONCE.
REPEAT, WOULD THE PILOTS FOR EVA UNIT-01 AND...
SEE, YOU'RE WANTED ALREADY. GOOD LUCK...

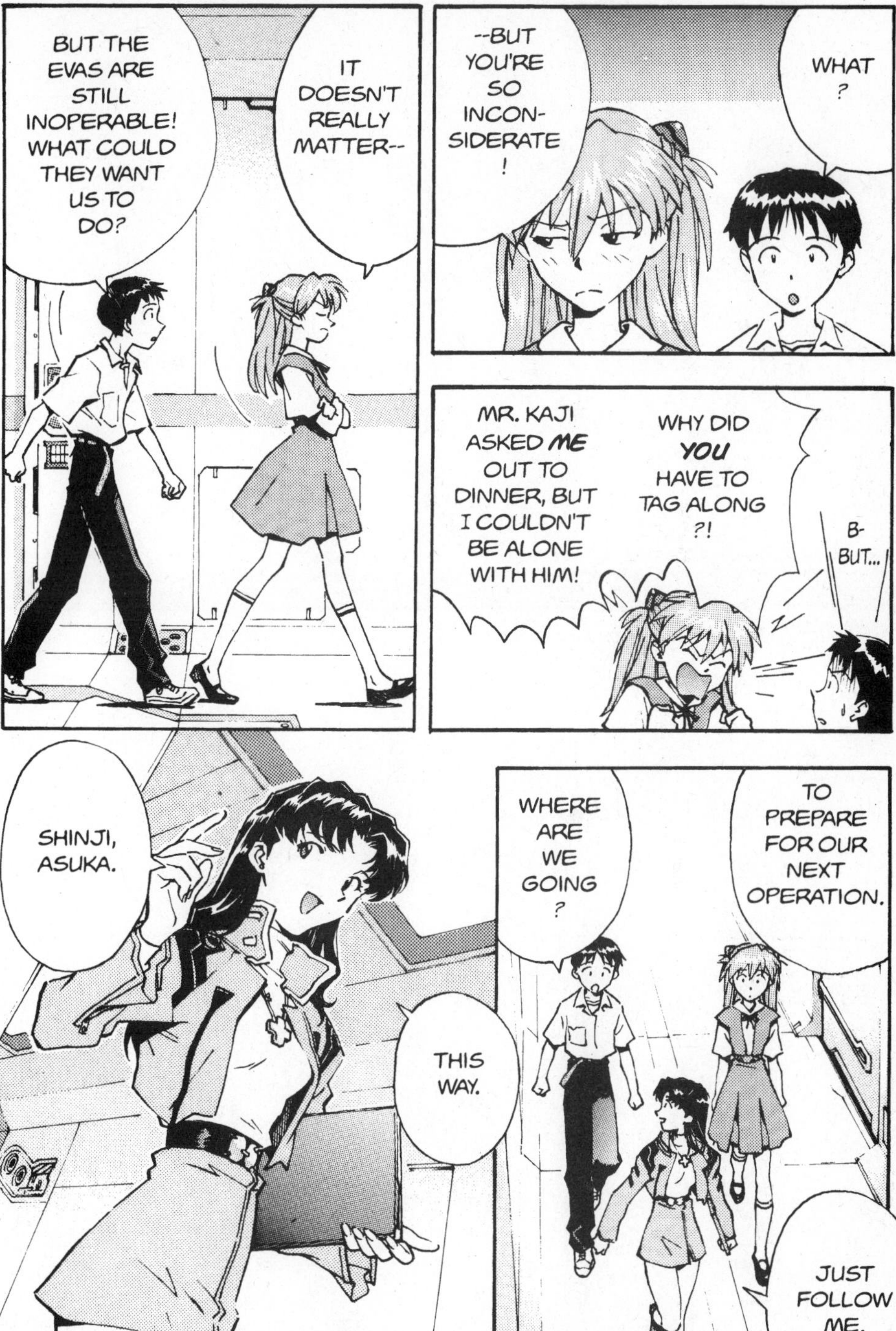
BUT THE EVAS ARE STILL INOPERABLE! WHAT COULD THEY WANT US TO DO?
IT DOESN'T REALLY MATTER--
--BUT YOU'RE SO INCONSIDERATE!
WHAT?
MR. KAJI ASKED *ME* OUT TO DINNER, BUT I COULDN'T BE ALONE WITH HIM!
WHY DID *YOU* HAVE TO TAG ALONG?!
B-BUT...
SHINJI, ASUKA.
THIS WAY.
WHERE ARE WE GOING?
TO PREPARE FOR OUR NEXT OPERATION.
JUST FOLLOW ME.

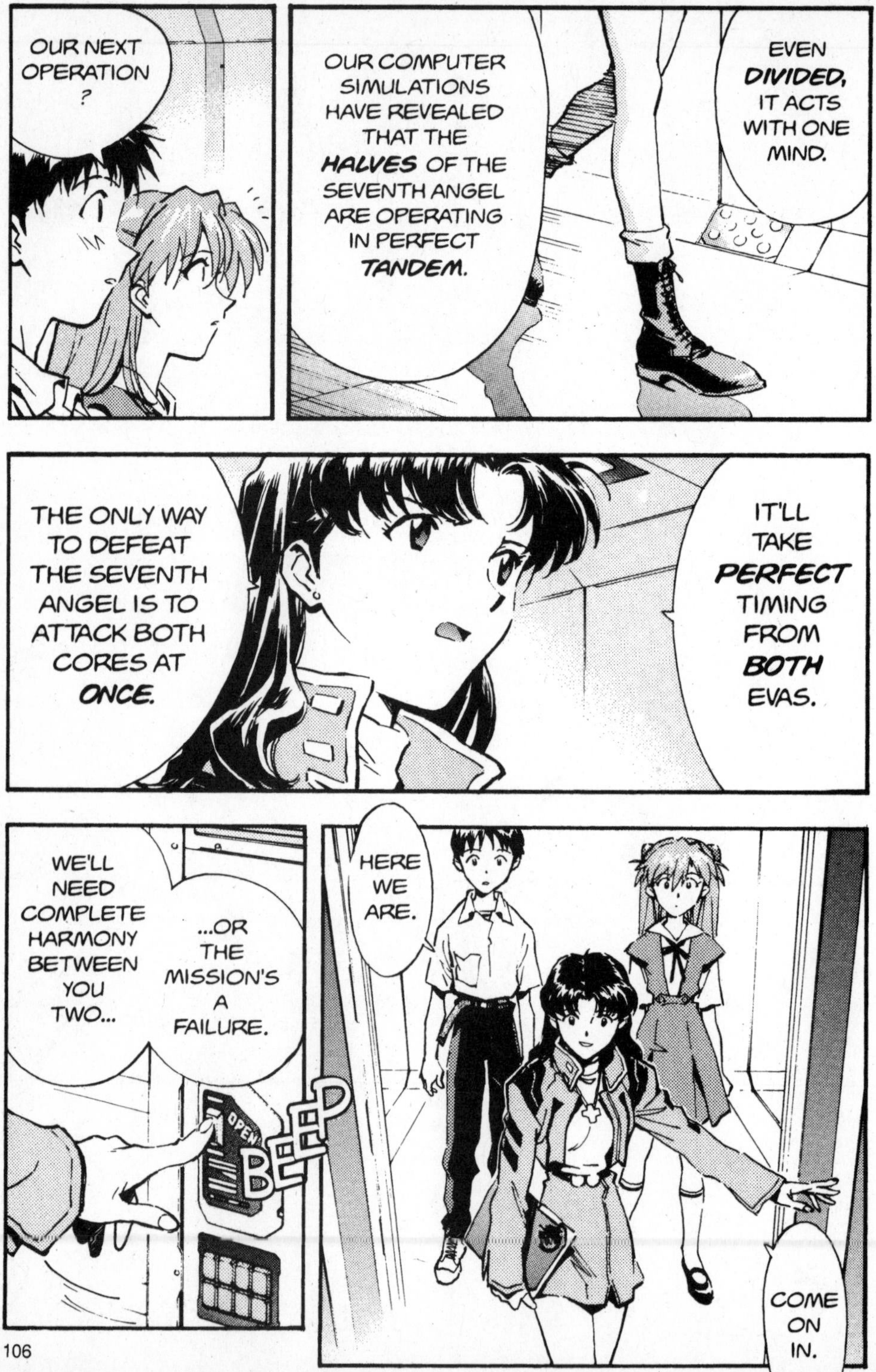
OUR NEXT OPERATION ?
OUR COMPUTER SIMULATIONS HAVE REVEALED THAT THE HALVES OF THE SEVENTH ANGEL ARE OPERATING IN PERFECT TANDEM.
EVEN DIVIDED, IT ACTS WITH ONE MIND.
THE ONLY WAY TO DEFEAT THE SEVENTH ANGEL IS TO ATTACK BOTH CORES AT ONCE.
IT'LL TAKE PERFECT TIMING FROM BOTH EVAS.
WE'LL NEED COMPLETE HARMONY BETWEEN YOU TWO...
...OR THE MISSION'S A FAILURE.
OPEN
BEEP
HERE WE ARE.
COME ON IN.

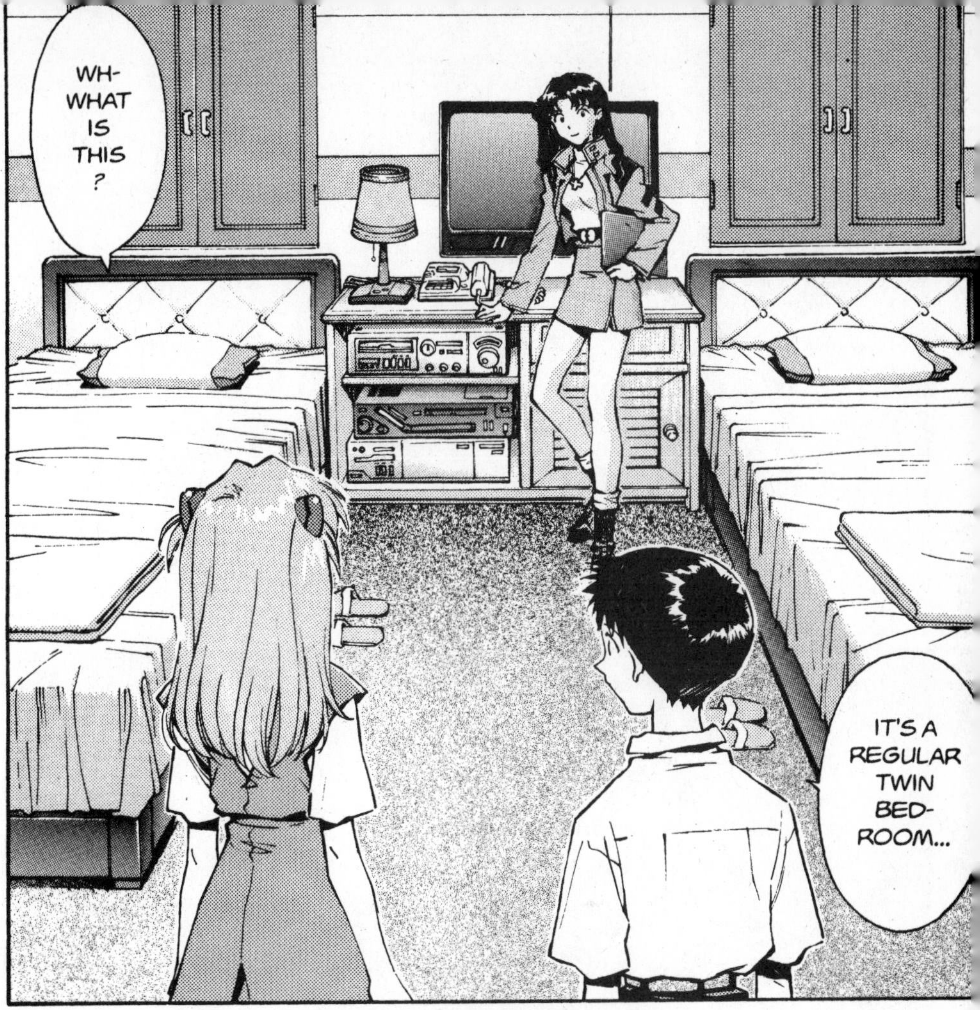
WH- WHAT IS THIS ?
IT'S A REGULAR TWIN BED- ROOM...

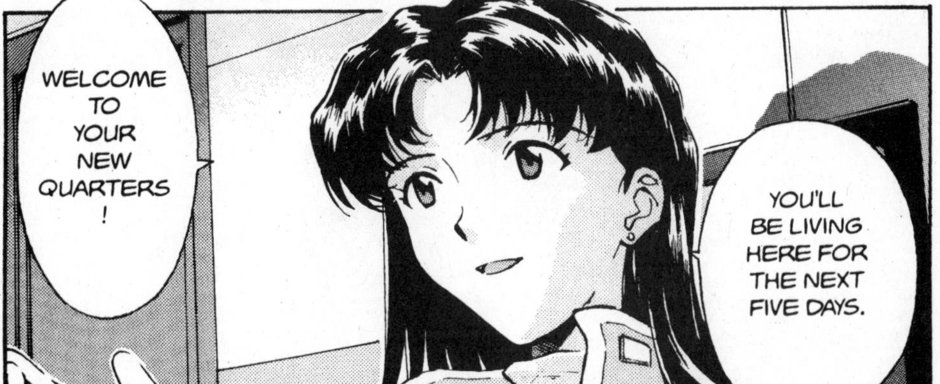
WELCOME TO YOUR NEW QUARTERS !
YOU'LL BE LIVING HERE FOR THE NEXT FIVE DAYS.

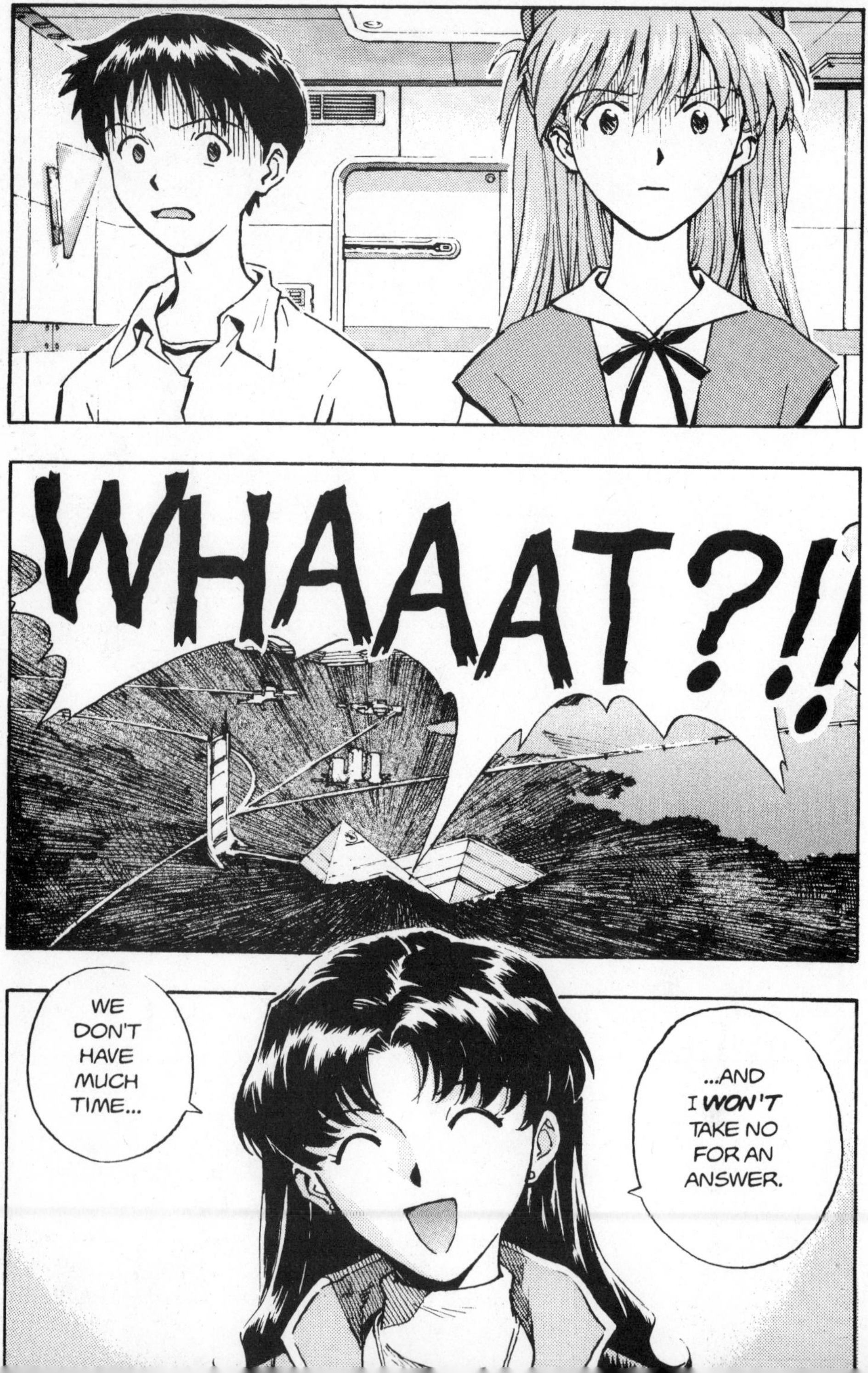
WHAAAT?!!
WE DON'T HAVE MUCH TIME...
...AND I WON'T TAKE NO FOR AN ANSWER.

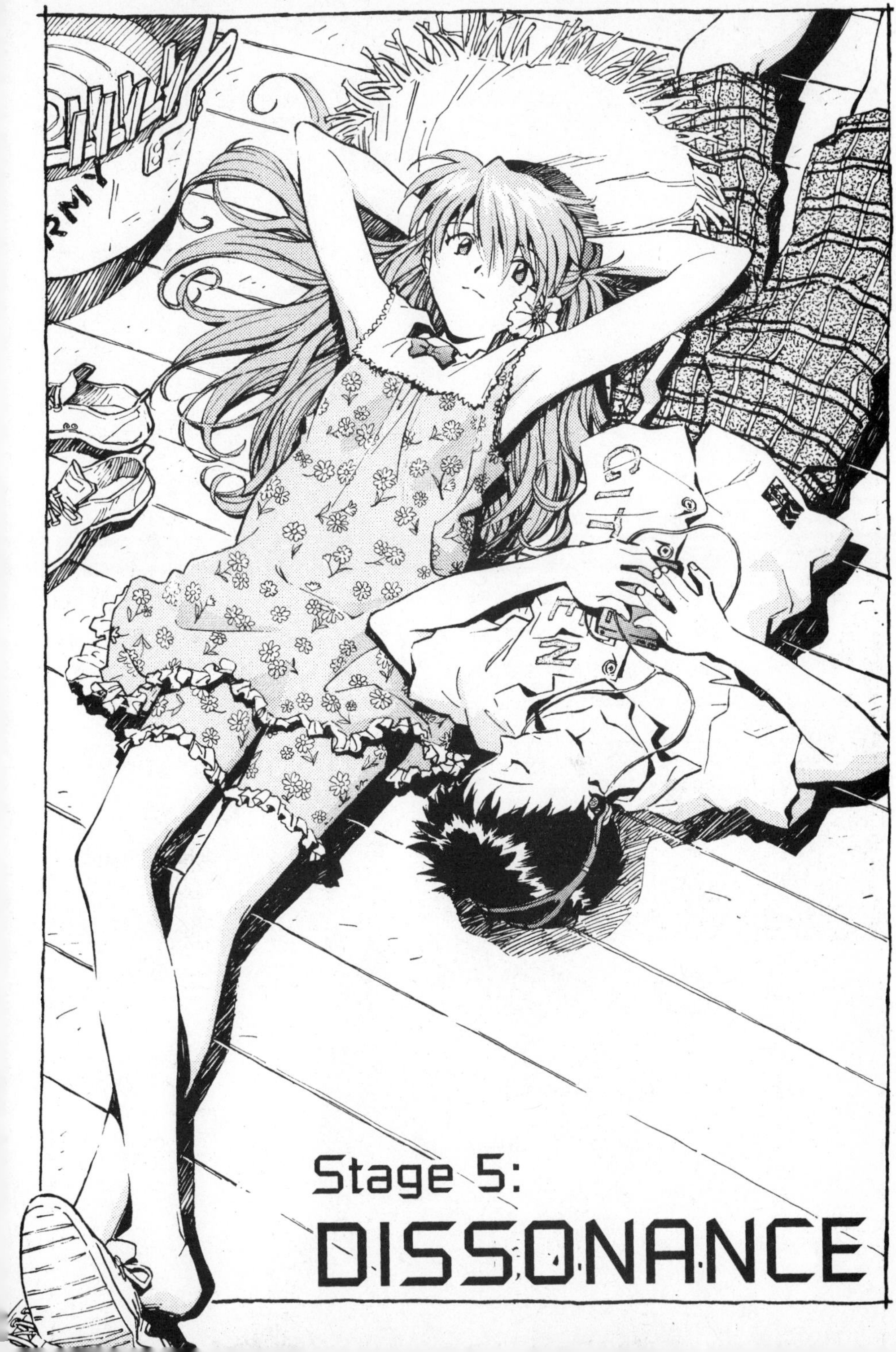
Stage 5:
DISSONANCE

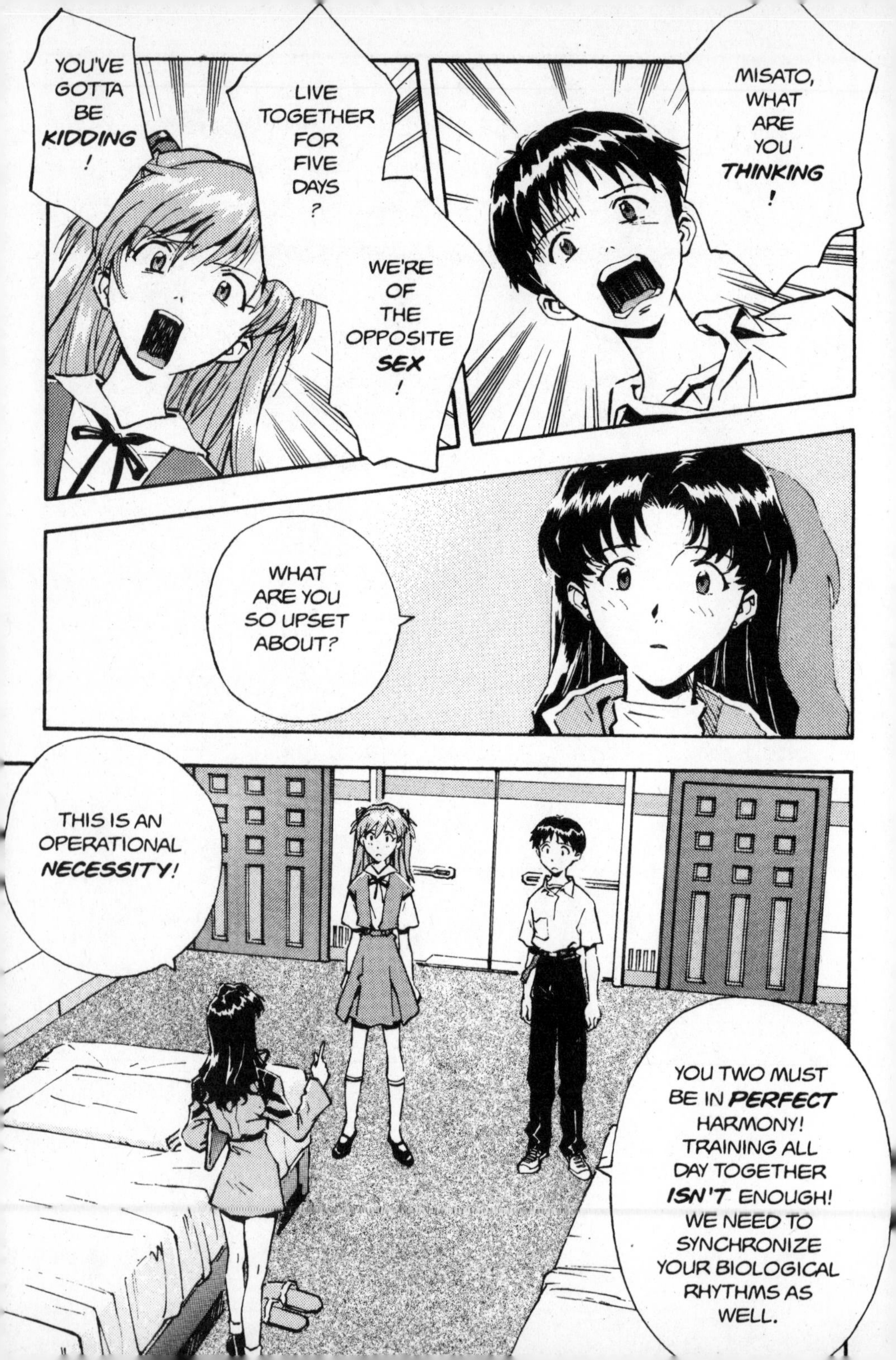
YOU'VE GOTTA BE KIDDING!
LIVE TOGETHER FOR FIVE DAYS?
WE'RE OF THE OPPOSITE SEX!
MISATO, WHAT ARE YOU THINKING!
WHAT ARE YOU SO UPSET ABOUT?
THIS IS AN OPERATIONAL NECESSITY!
YOU TWO MUST BE IN PERFECT HARMONY! TRAINING ALL DAY TOGETHER ISN'T ENOUGH! WE NEED TO SYNCHRONIZE YOUR BIOLOGICAL RHYTHMS AS WELL.

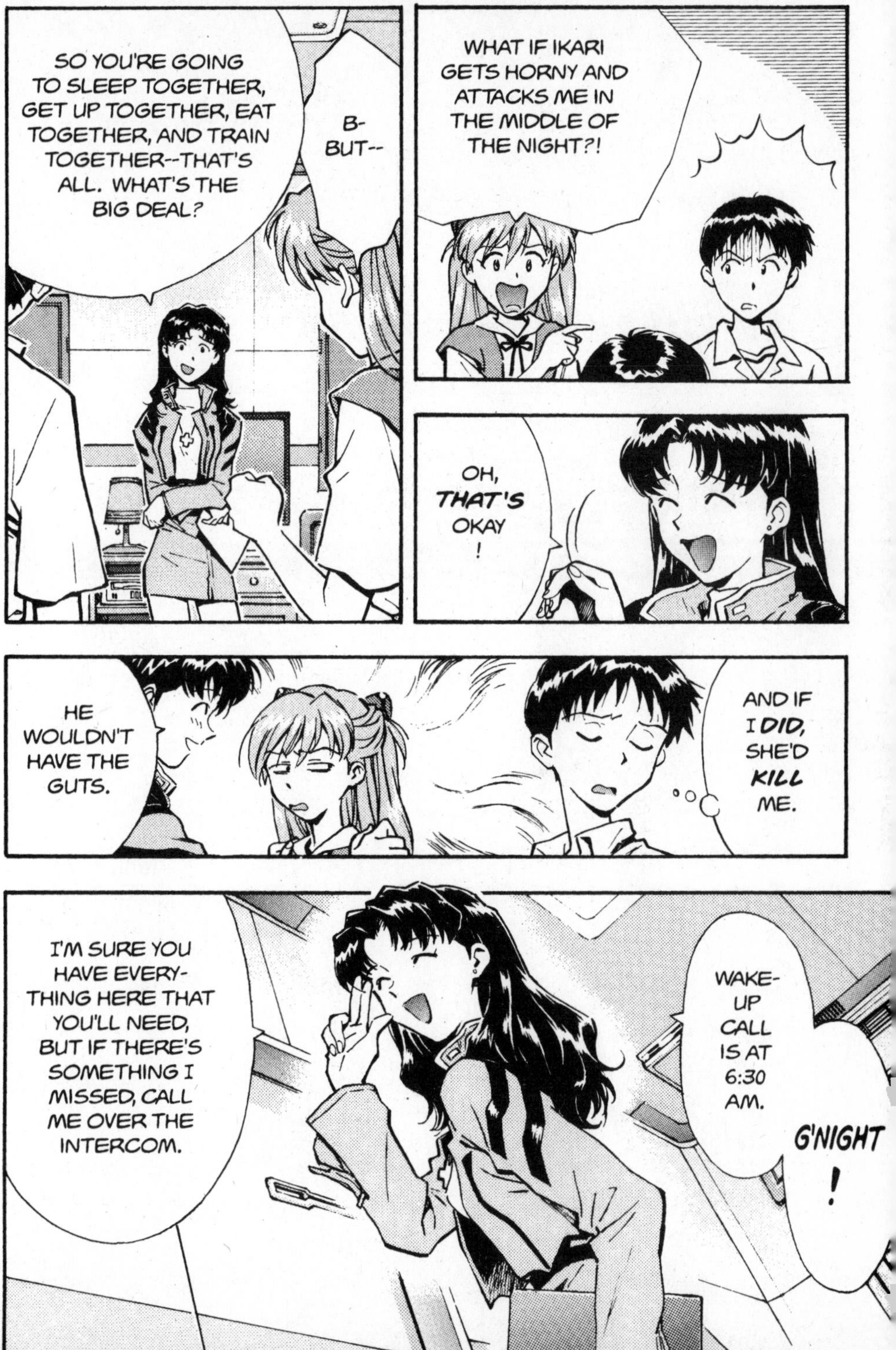
SO YOU'RE GOING TO SLEEP TOGETHER, GET UP TOGETHER, EAT TOGETHER, AND TRAIN TOGETHER--THAT'S ALL. WHAT'S THE BIG DEAL?
B- BUT--
WHAT IF IKARI GETS HORNY AND ATTACKS ME IN THE MIDDLE OF THE NIGHT?!
OH, *THAT'S* OKAY!
HE WOULDN'T HAVE THE GUTS.
AND IF I *DID*, SHE'D *KILL* ME.
I'M SURE YOU HAVE EVERYTHING HERE THAT YOU'LL NEED, BUT IF THERE'S SOMETHING I MISSED, CALL ME OVER THE INTERCOM.
WAKE-UP CALL IS AT 6:30 AM.
G'NIGHT!

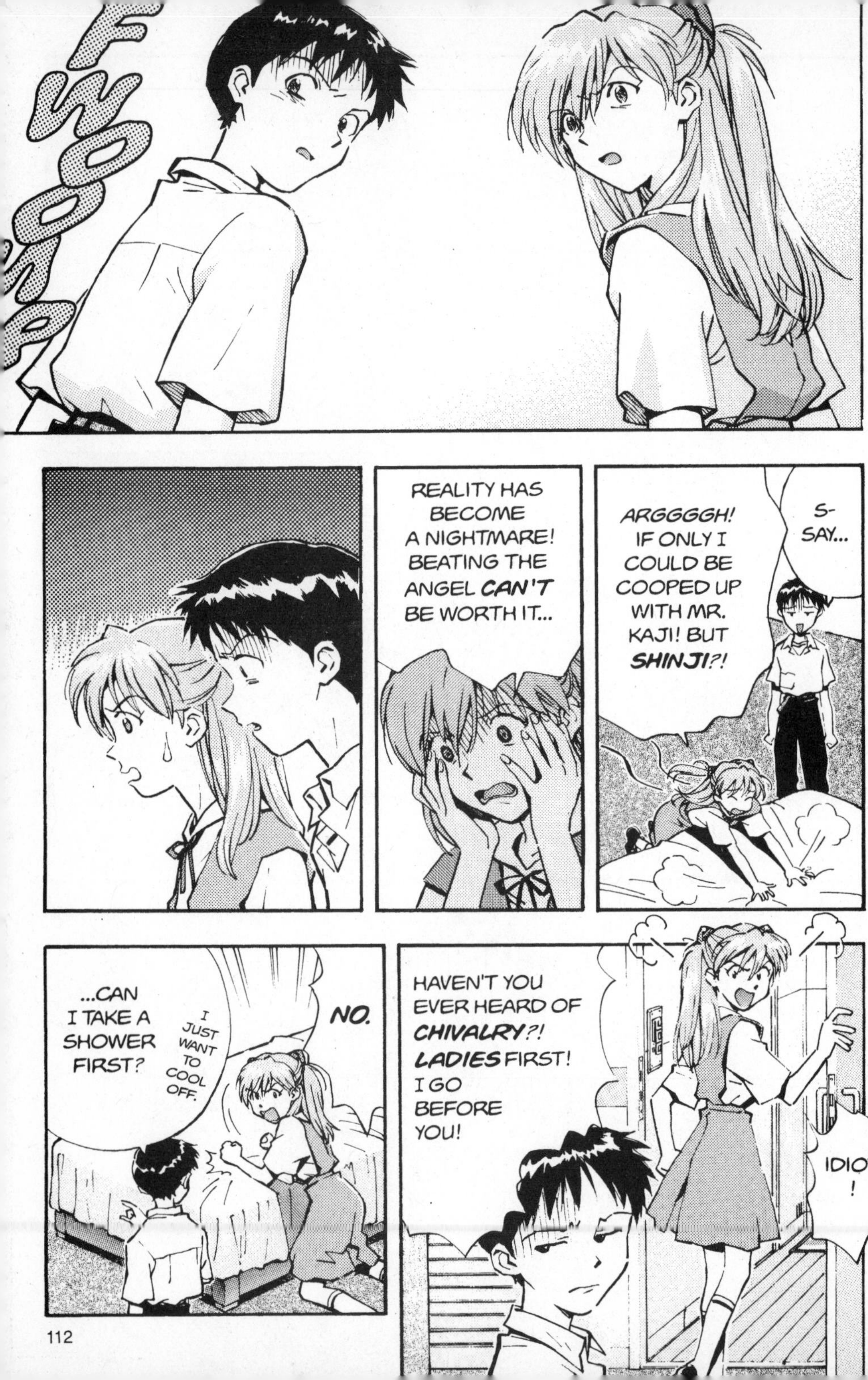
FWOO
REALITY HAS BECOME A NIGHTMARE! BEATING THE ANGEL ***CAN'T*** BE WORTH IT...
ARGGGGH! IF ONLY I COULD BE COOPED UP WITH MR. KAJI! BUT ***SHINJI***?!
S-SAY...
...CAN I TAKE A SHOWER FIRST?
I JUST WANT TO COOL OFF.
NO.
HAVEN'T YOU EVER HEARD OF ***CHIVALRY***?! ***LADIES*** FIRST! I GO BEFORE YOU!
IDIOT!

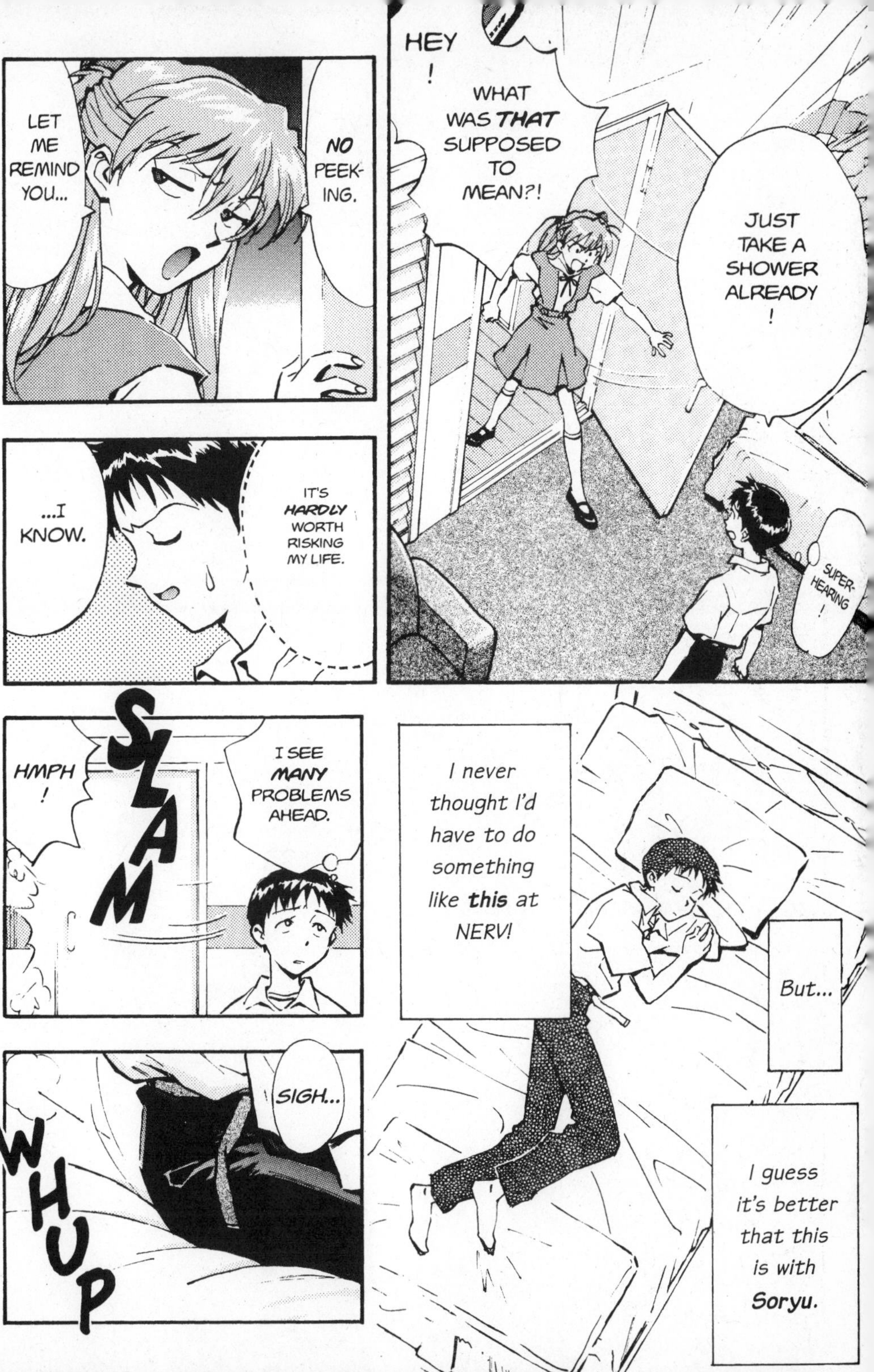
LET ME REMIND YOU...
NO PEEKING.
...I KNOW.
IT'S HARDLY WORTH RISKING MY LIFE.
HEY!
WHAT WAS THAT SUPPOSED TO MEAN?!
JUST TAKE A SHOWER ALREADY!
SUPER-HEARING!
HMPH!
SLAM
I SEE MANY PROBLEMS AHEAD.
WHUP
SIGH...
I never thought I'd have to do something like this at NERV!
But...
I guess it's better that this is with Soryu.

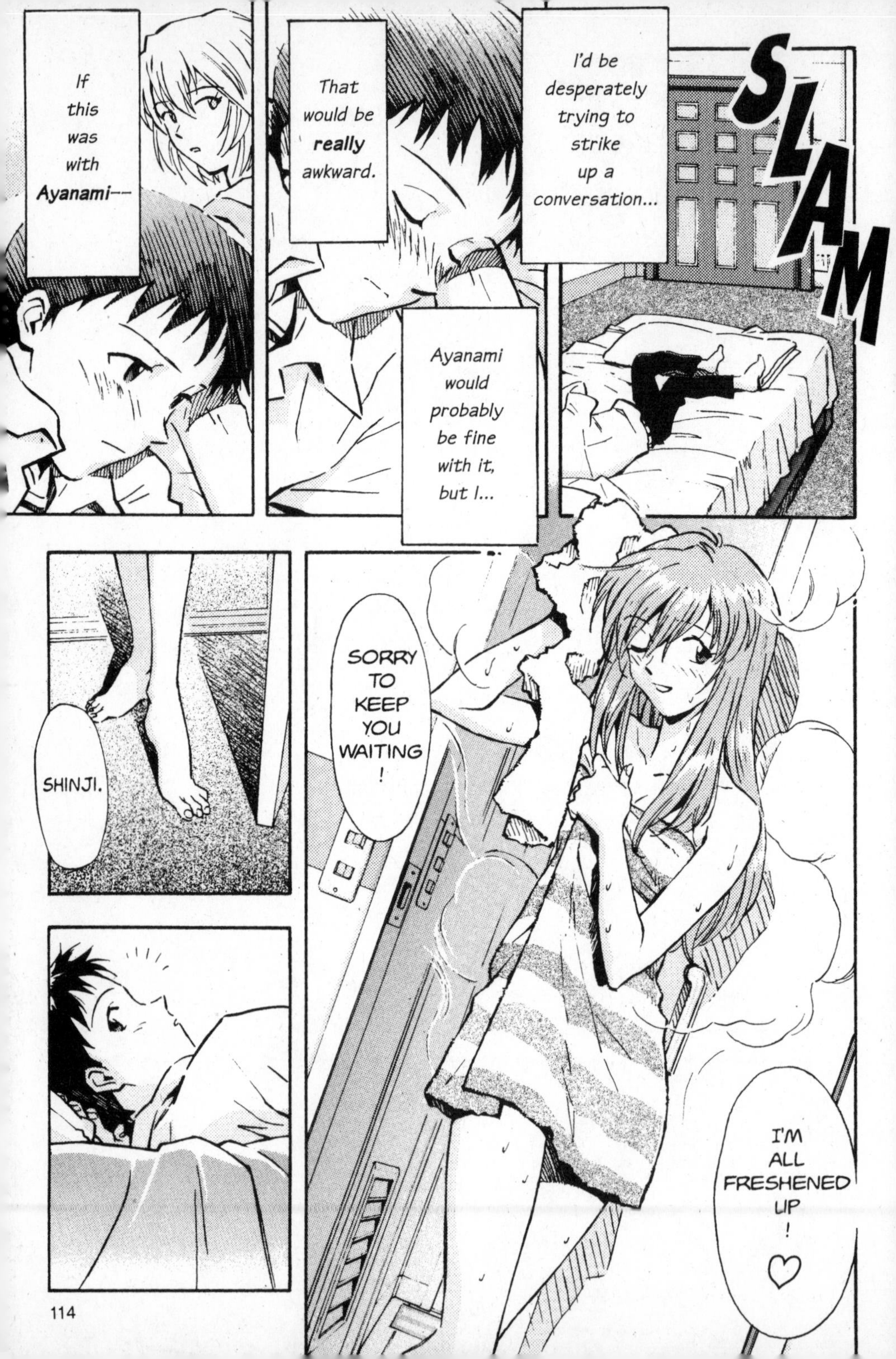
If this was with Ayanami--
That would be really awkward.
I'd be desperately trying to strike up a conversation...
Ayanami would probably be fine with it, but I...
SLAM
SHINJI.
SORRY TO KEEP YOU WAITING!
I'M ALL FRESHENED UP! ♡

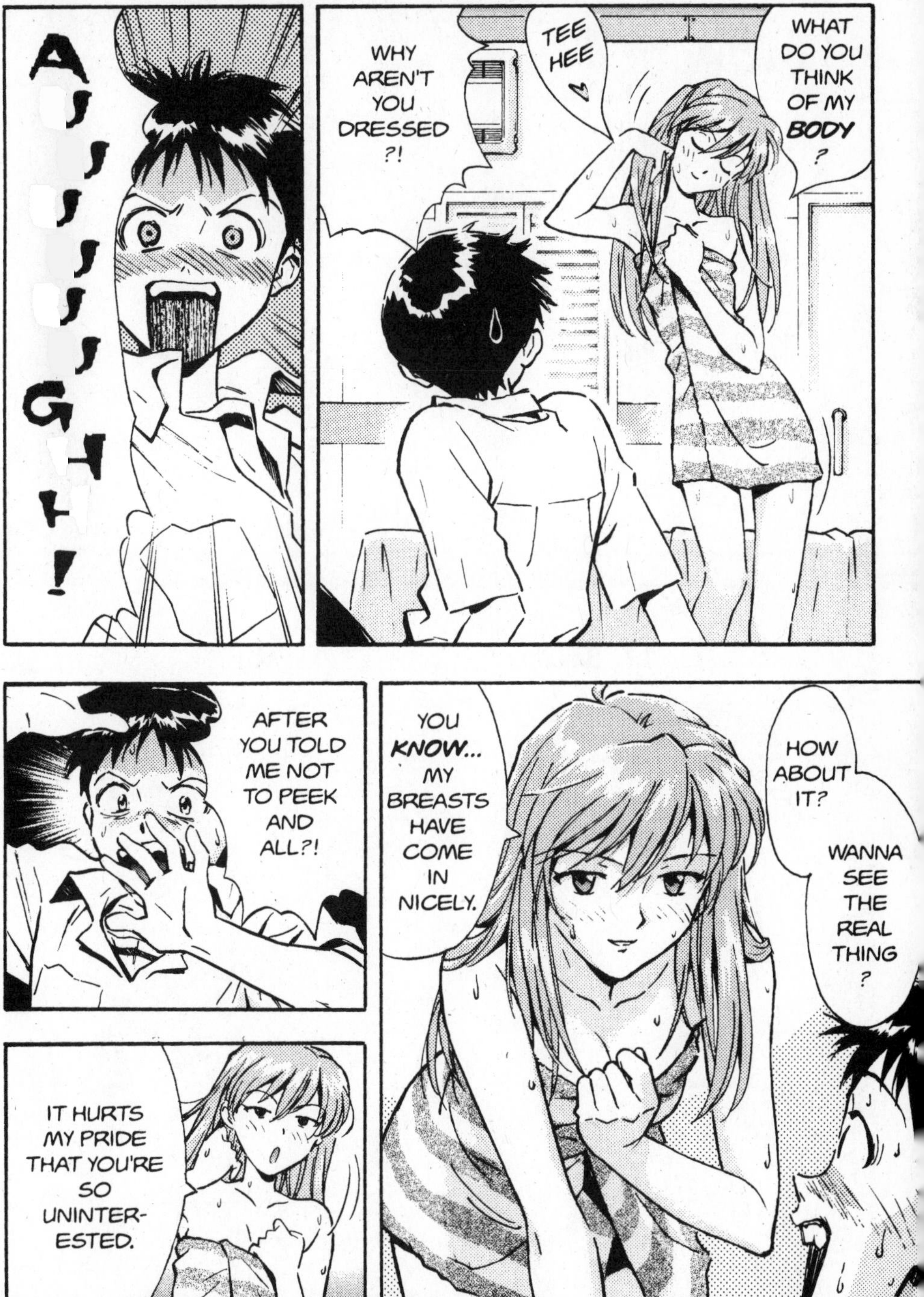
AUUUUUUGHH!
WHY AREN'T YOU DRESSED ?!
TEE HEE ♥
WHAT DO YOU THINK OF MY **BODY** ?
AFTER YOU TOLD ME NOT TO PEEK AND ALL?!
IT HURTS MY PRIDE THAT YOU'RE SO UNINTER-ESTED.
YOU **KNOW**... MY BREASTS HAVE COME IN NICELY.
HOW ABOUT IT?
WANNA SEE THE REAL THING ?

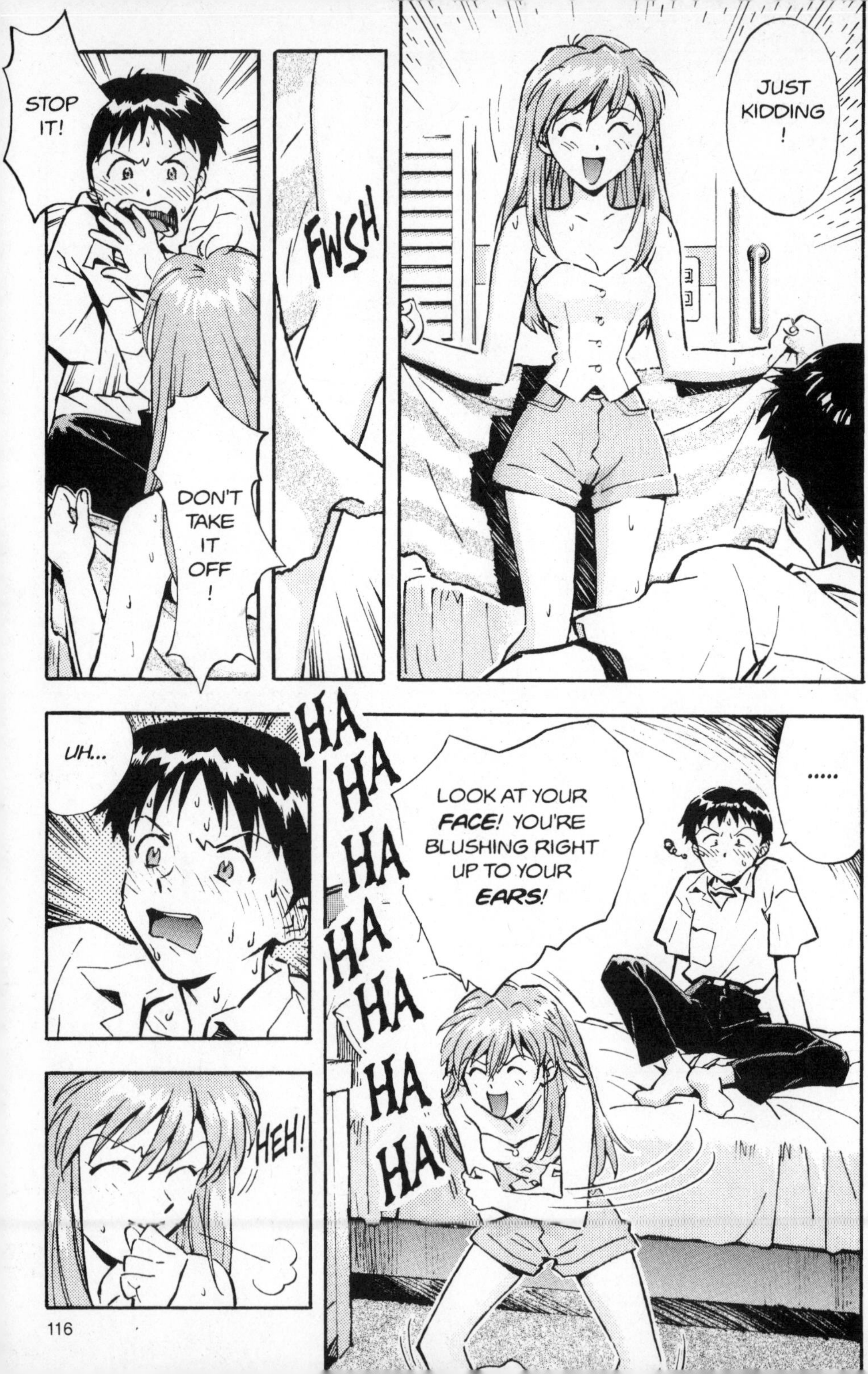
STOP IT!
DON'T TAKE IT OFF!
FWSH
JUST KIDDING!
UH...
HEH!
HA HA HA HA HA HA HA HA HA HA
LOOK AT YOUR FACE! YOU'RE BLUSHING RIGHT UP TO YOUR EARS!
.....

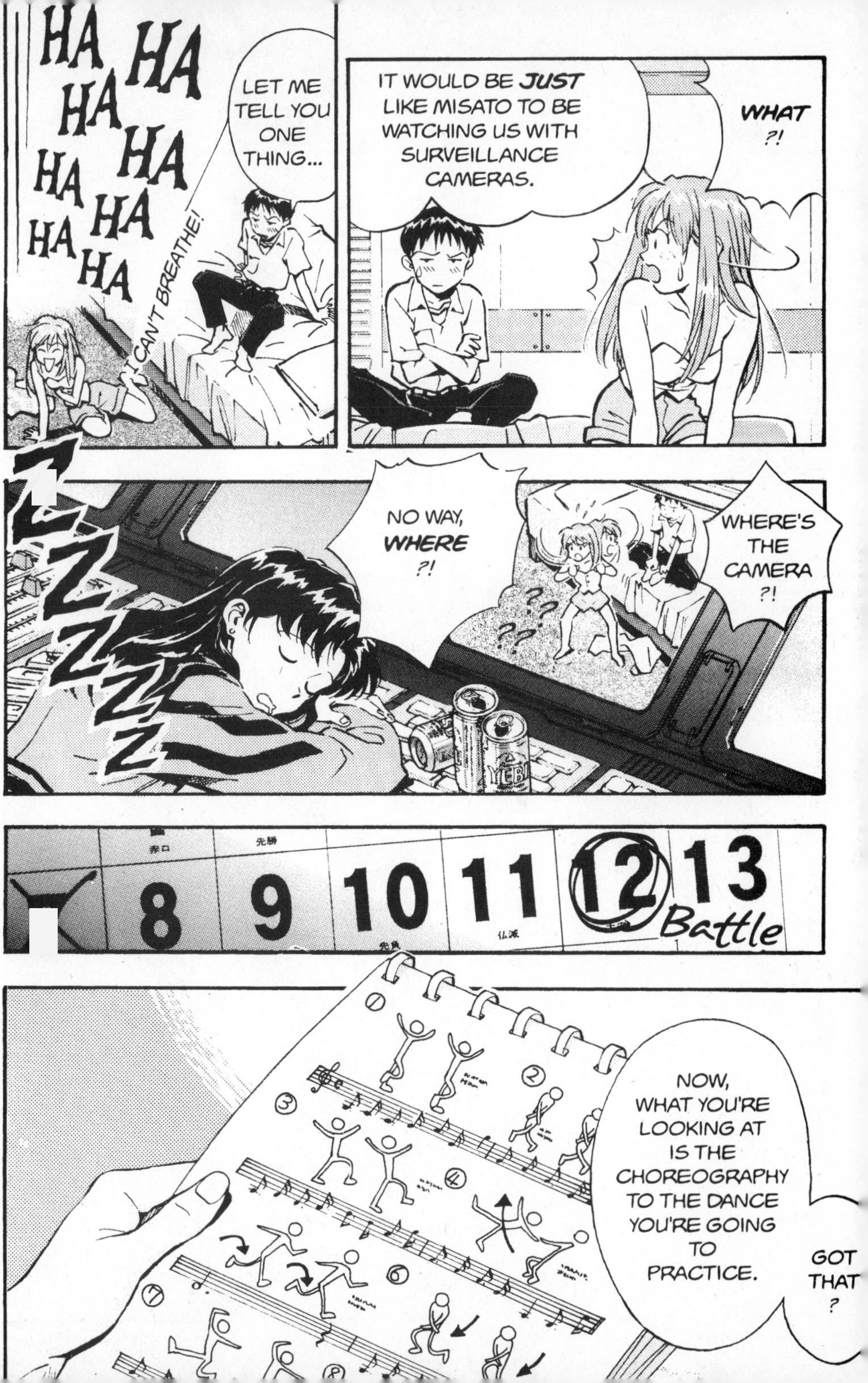
HA HA HA HA HA HA HA HA HA
I CAN'T BREATHE!
LET ME TELL YOU ONE THING...
IT WOULD BE JUST LIKE MISATO TO BE WATCHING US WITH SURVEILLANCE CAMERAS.
WHAT ?!
ZZZZZZZ
NO WAY, WHERE ?!
WHERE'S THE CAMERA ?!
赤口
先勝
8 9 10 11 12 13
先負
仏滅
Battle
NOW, WHAT YOU'RE LOOKING AT IS THE CHOREOGRAPHY TO THE DANCE YOU'RE GOING TO PRACTICE.
GOT THAT ?

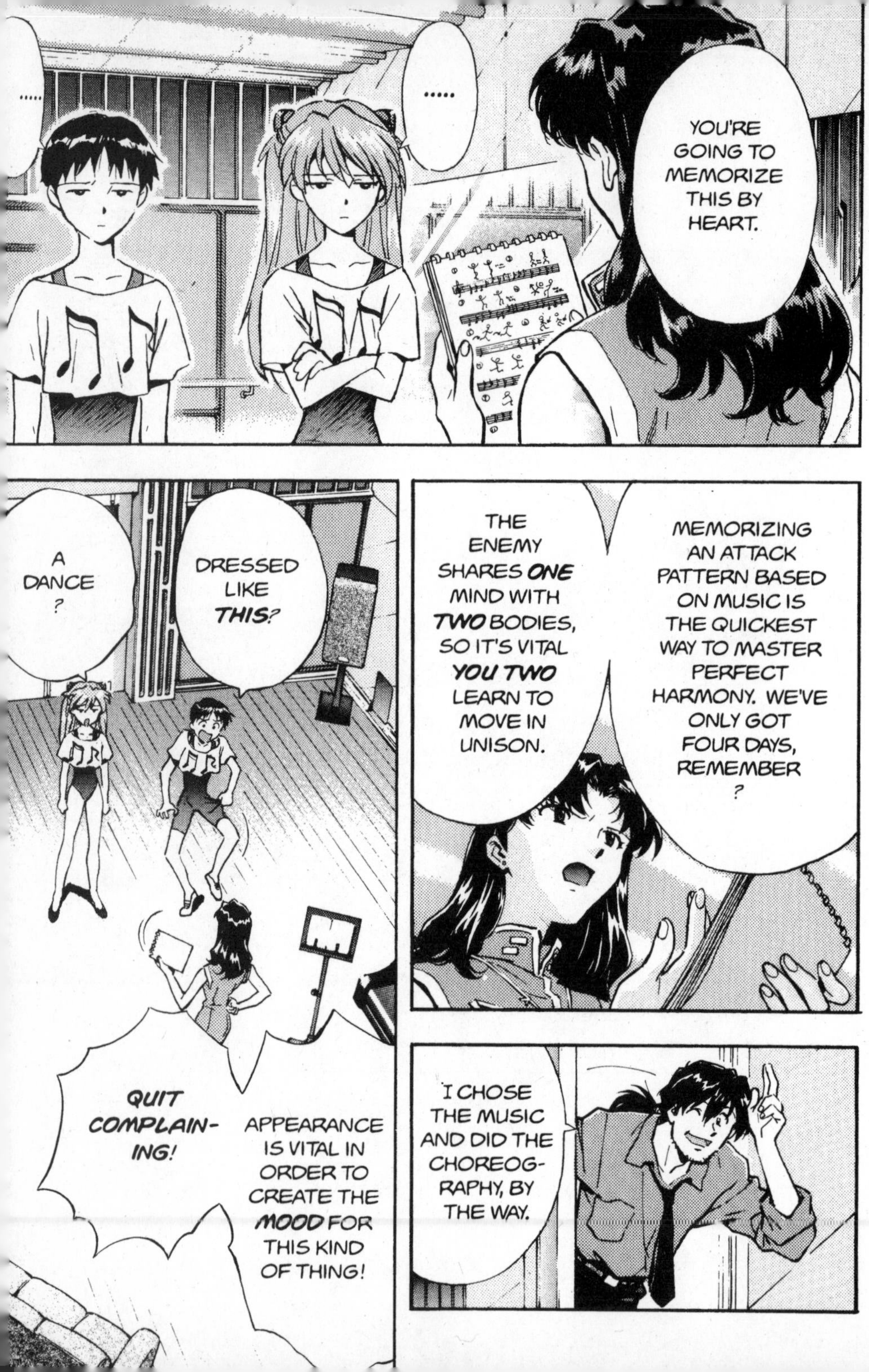

......
......
YOU'RE GOING TO MEMORIZE THIS BY HEART.
A DANCE?
DRESSED LIKE *THIS*?
QUIT COMPLAIN-ING!
APPEARANCE IS VITAL IN ORDER TO CREATE THE *MOOD* FOR THIS KIND OF THING!
THE ENEMY SHARES *ONE* MIND WITH *TWO* BODIES, SO IT'S VITAL *YOU TWO* LEARN TO MOVE IN UNISON.
MEMORIZING AN ATTACK PATTERN BASED ON MUSIC IS THE QUICKEST WAY TO MASTER PERFECT HARMONY. WE'VE ONLY GOT FOUR DAYS, REMEMBER?
I CHOSE THE MUSIC AND DID THE CHOREOG-RAPHY, BY THE WAY.

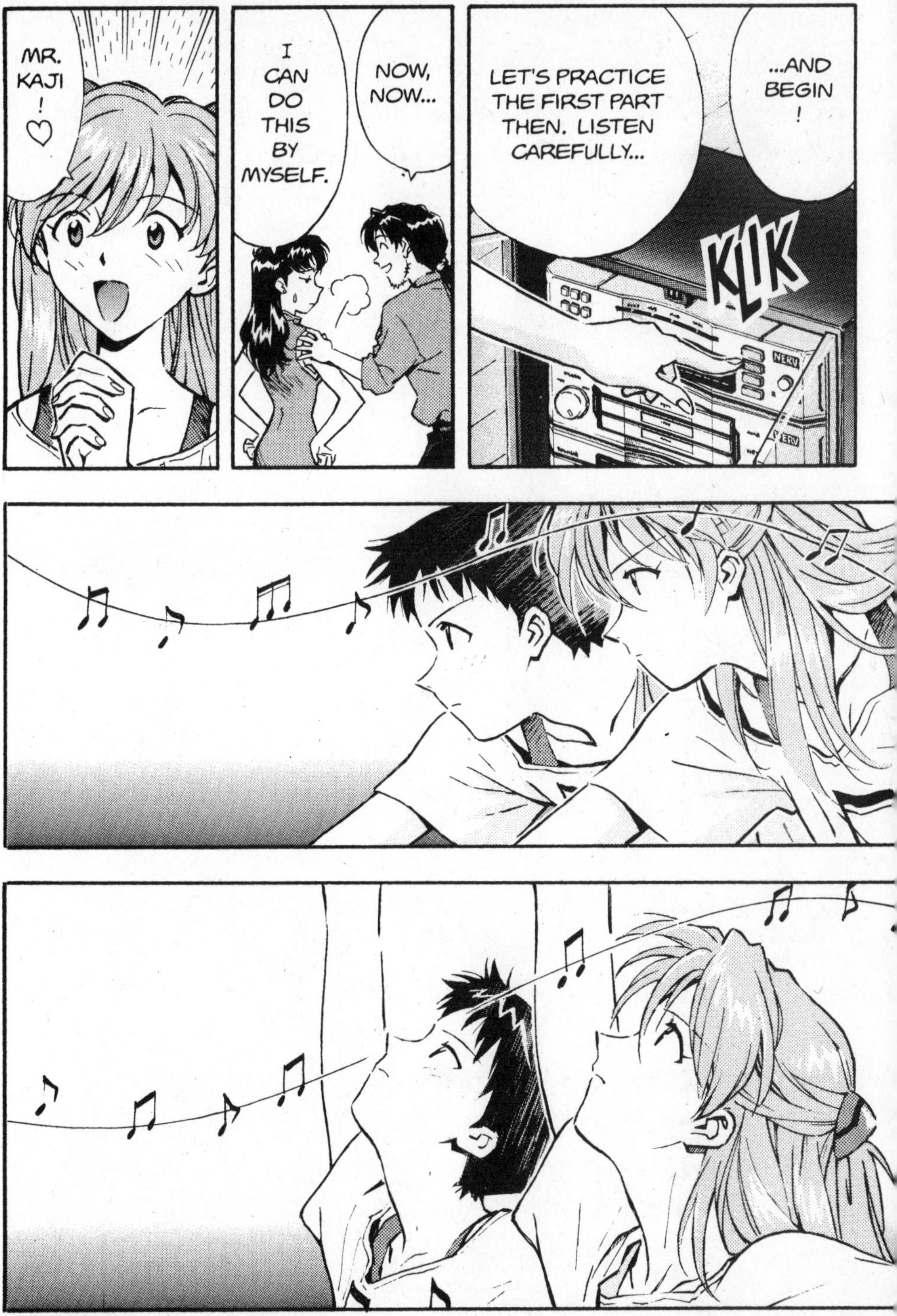
MR. KAJI ! ♡
I CAN DO THIS BY MYSELF.
NOW, NOW...
LET'S PRACTICE THE FIRST PART THEN. LISTEN CAREFULLY...
...AND BEGIN !
KLIK

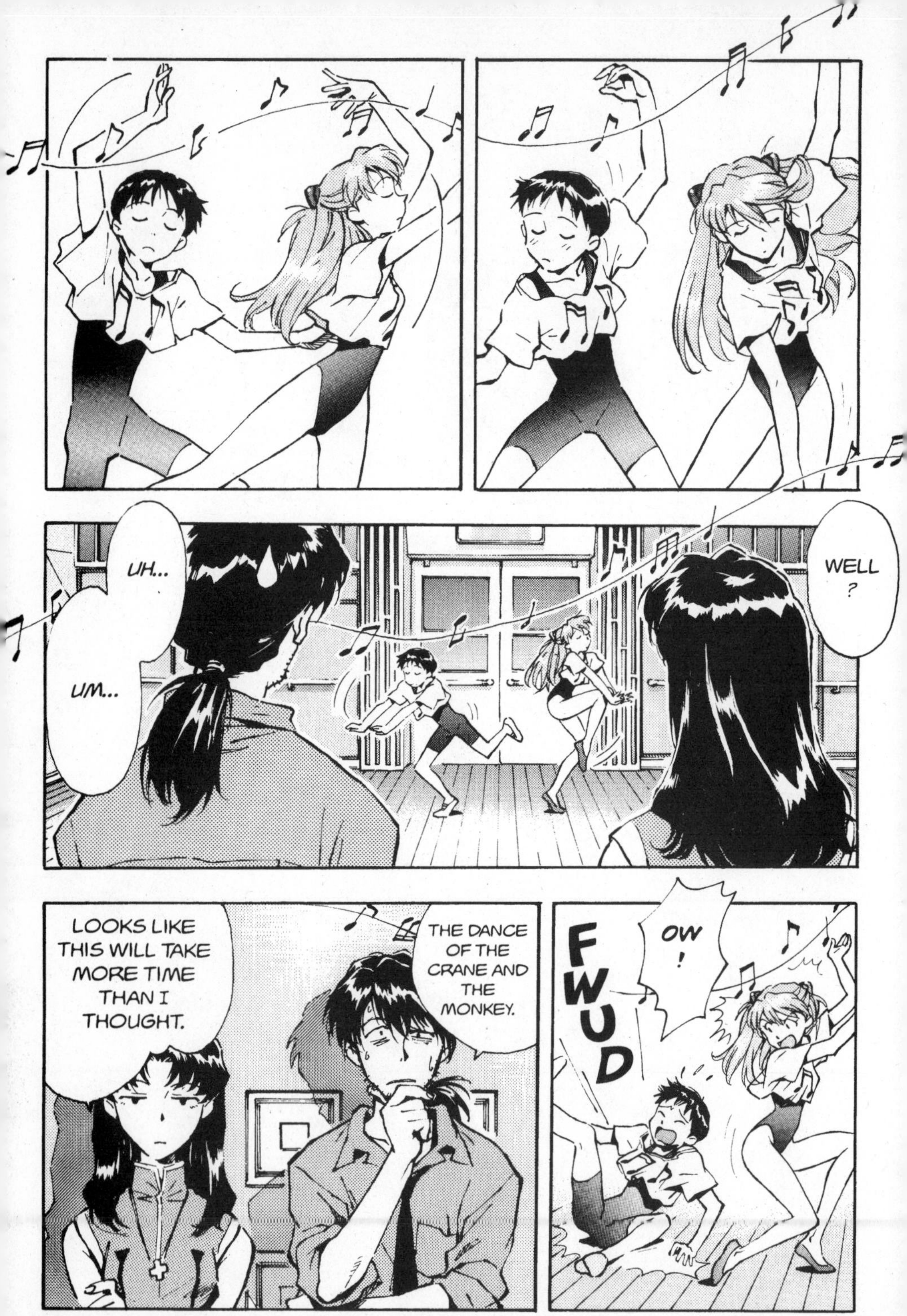
UH...
UM...
WELL?
LOOKS LIKE THIS WILL TAKE MORE TIME THAN I THOUGHT.
THE DANCE OF THE CRANE AND THE MONKEY.
FWUD
OW!

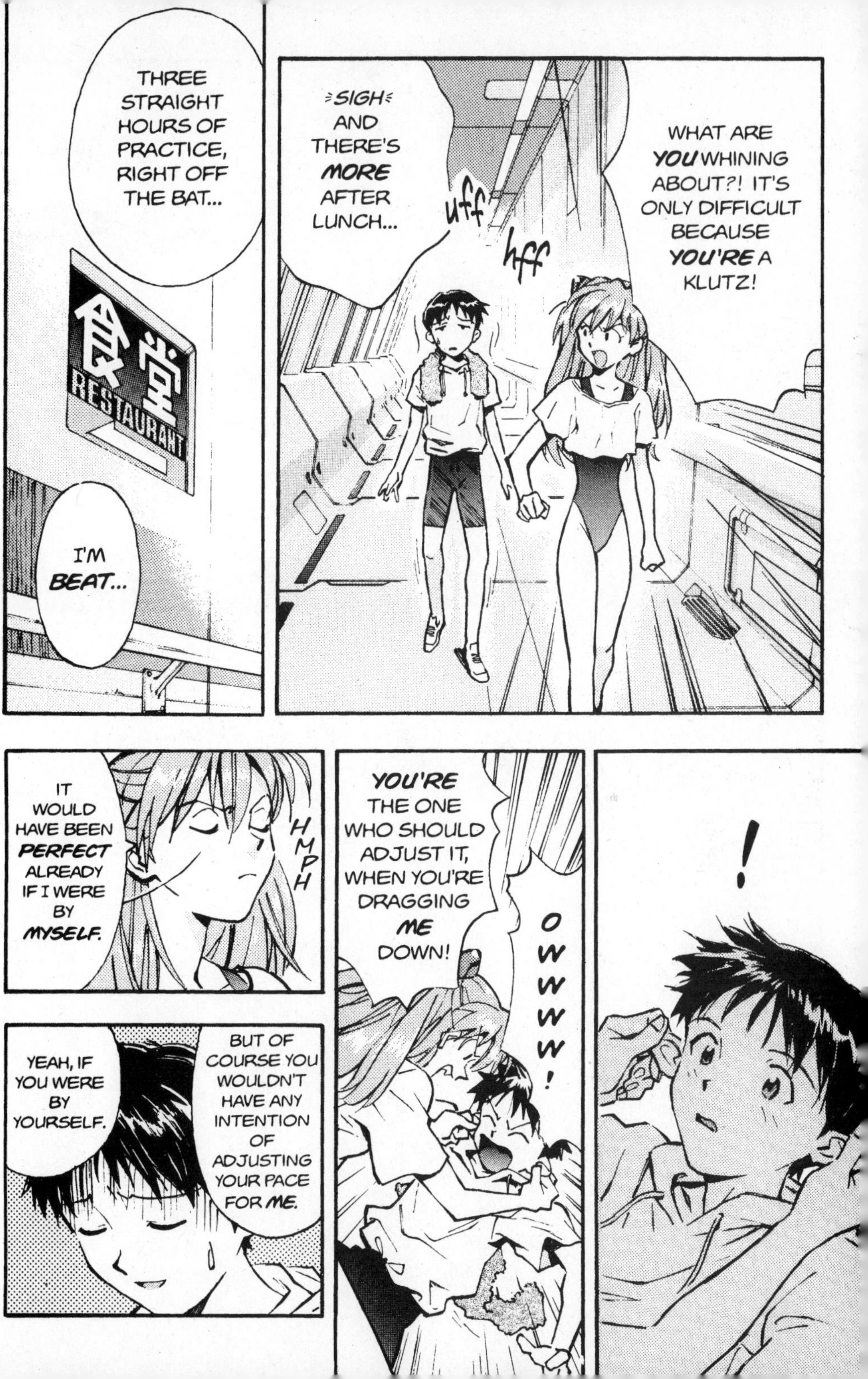
THREE STRAIGHT HOURS OF PRACTICE, RIGHT OFF THE BAT...
食堂
RESTAURANT
I'M BEAT...
SIGH AND THERE'S MORE AFTER LUNCH...
uff
hff
WHAT ARE YOU WHINING ABOUT?! IT'S ONLY DIFFICULT BECAUSE YOU'RE A KLUTZ!
IT WOULD HAVE BEEN PERFECT ALREADY IF I WERE BY MYSELF.
HMPH
YEAH, IF YOU WERE BY YOURSELF.
BUT OF COURSE YOU WOULDN'T HAVE ANY INTENTION OF ADJUSTING YOUR PACE FOR ME.
YOU'RE THE ONE WHO SHOULD ADJUST IT, WHEN YOU'RE DRAGGING ME DOWN!
OWWWWW!
!

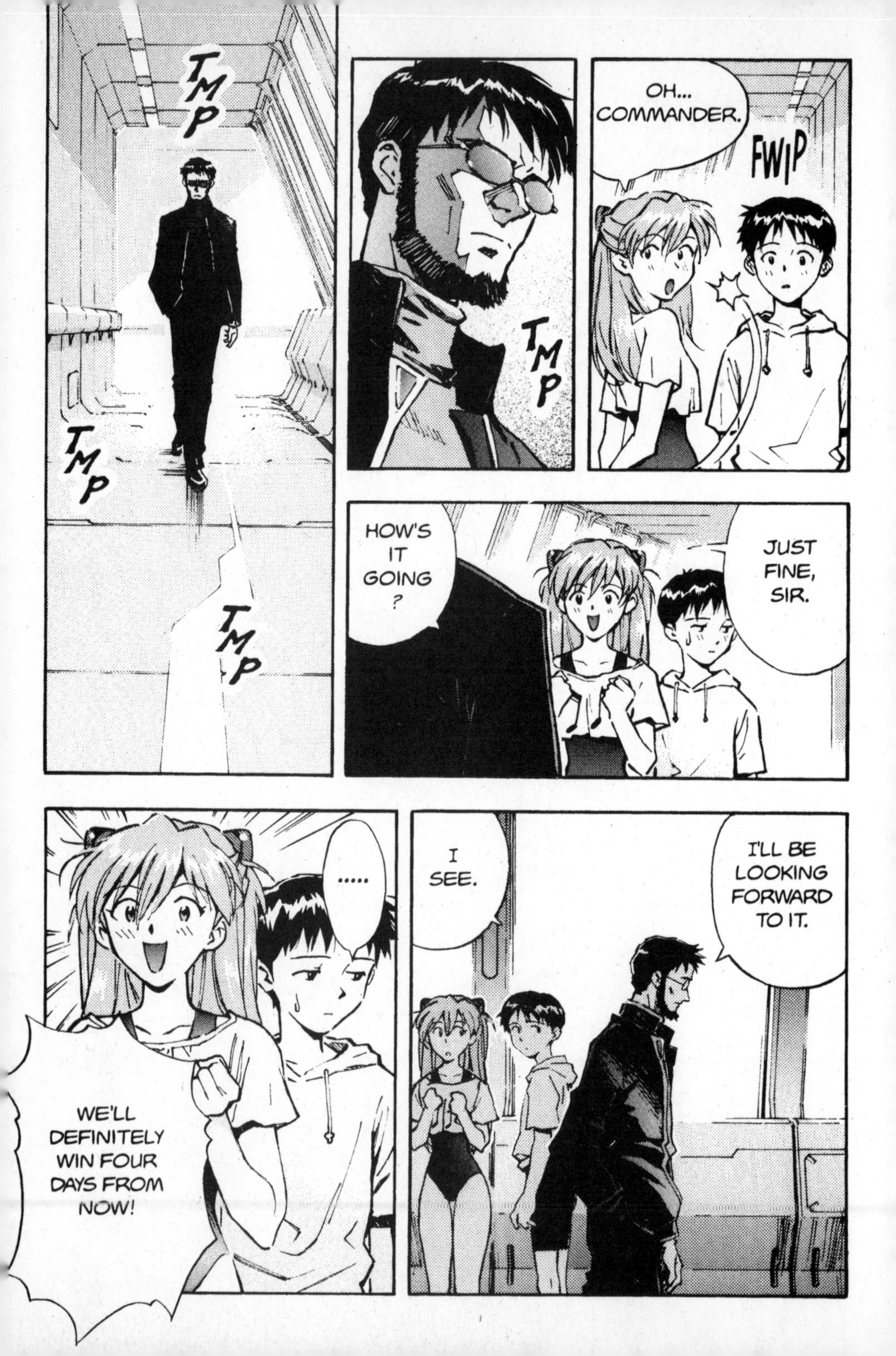
TMP
TMP
TMP
TMP
OH... COMMANDER.
FWIP
HOW'S IT GOING ?
JUST FINE, SIR.
.....
WE'LL DEFINITELY WIN FOUR DAYS FROM NOW!
I SEE.
I'LL BE LOOKING FORWARD TO IT.

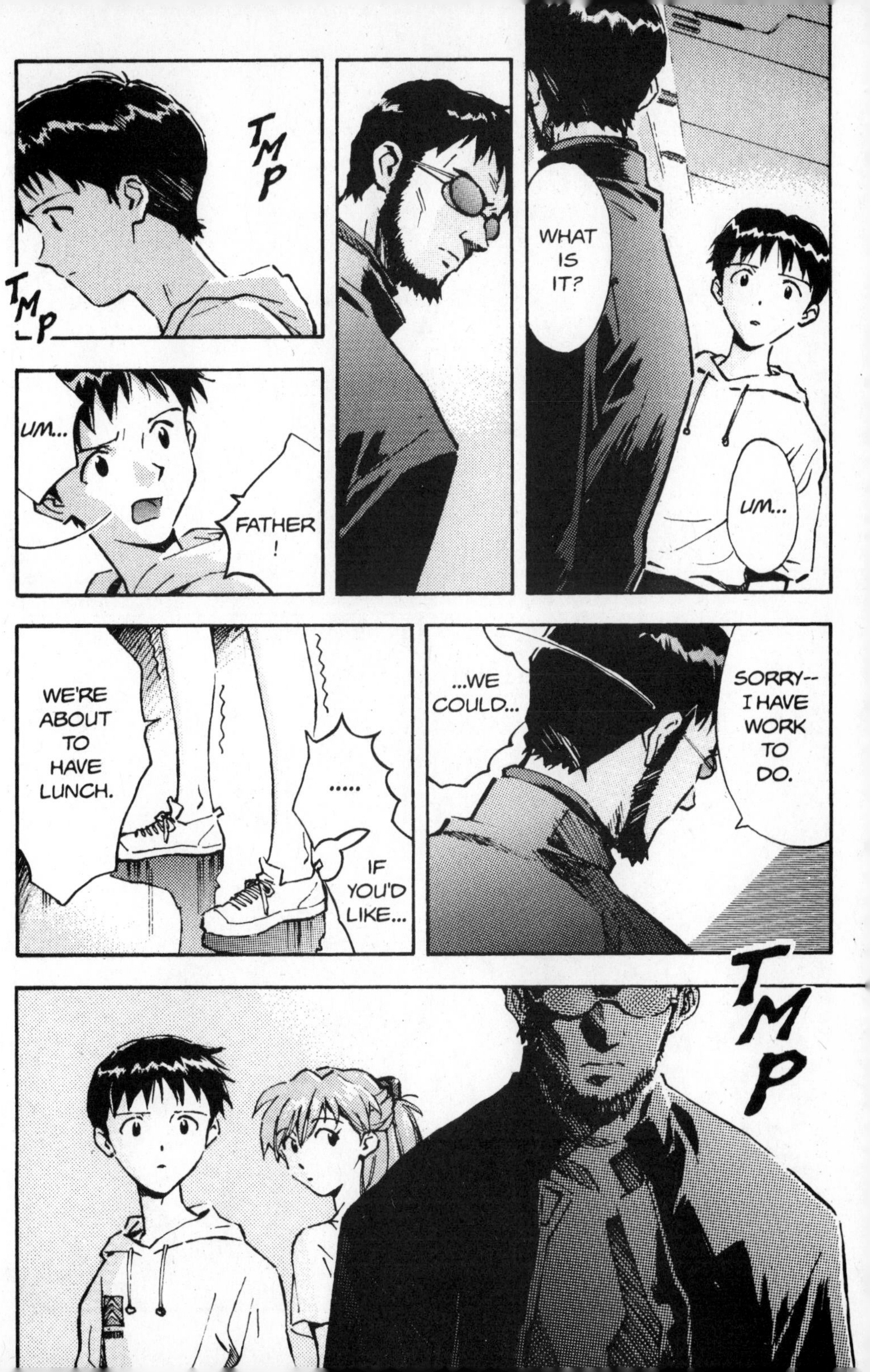
TMP
TMP
UM...
FATHER!
WHAT IS IT?
UM...
WE'RE ABOUT TO HAVE LUNCH.
.....
IF YOU'D LIKE...
...WE COULD...
SORRY-- I HAVE WORK TO DO.
TMP

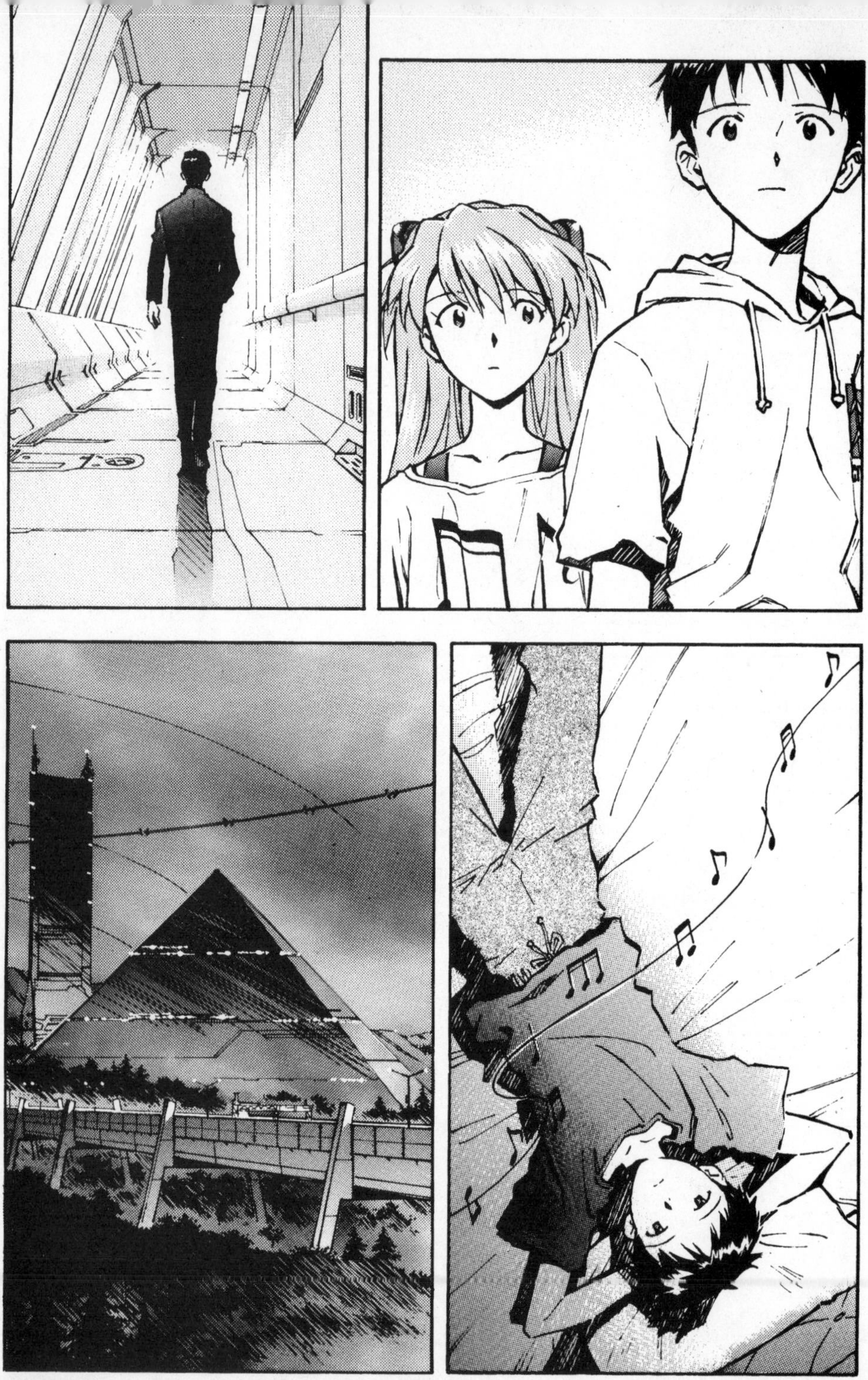

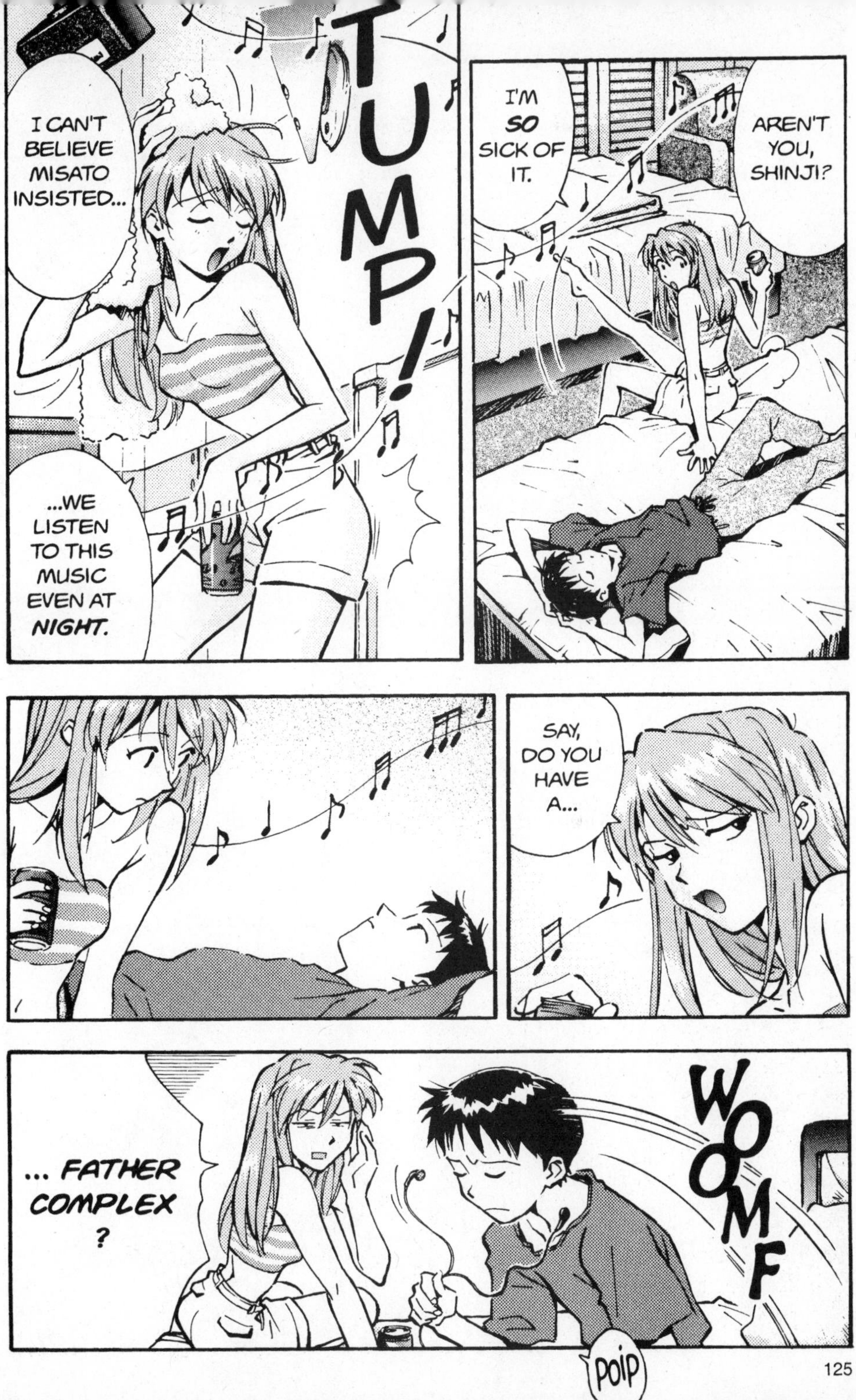
I CAN'T BELIEVE MISATO INSISTED...
TUMP!
...WE LISTEN TO THIS MUSIC EVEN AT NIGHT.
I'M SO SICK OF IT.
AREN'T YOU, SHINJI?
SAY, DO YOU HAVE A...
... FATHER COMPLEX ?
WOOMF
POIP

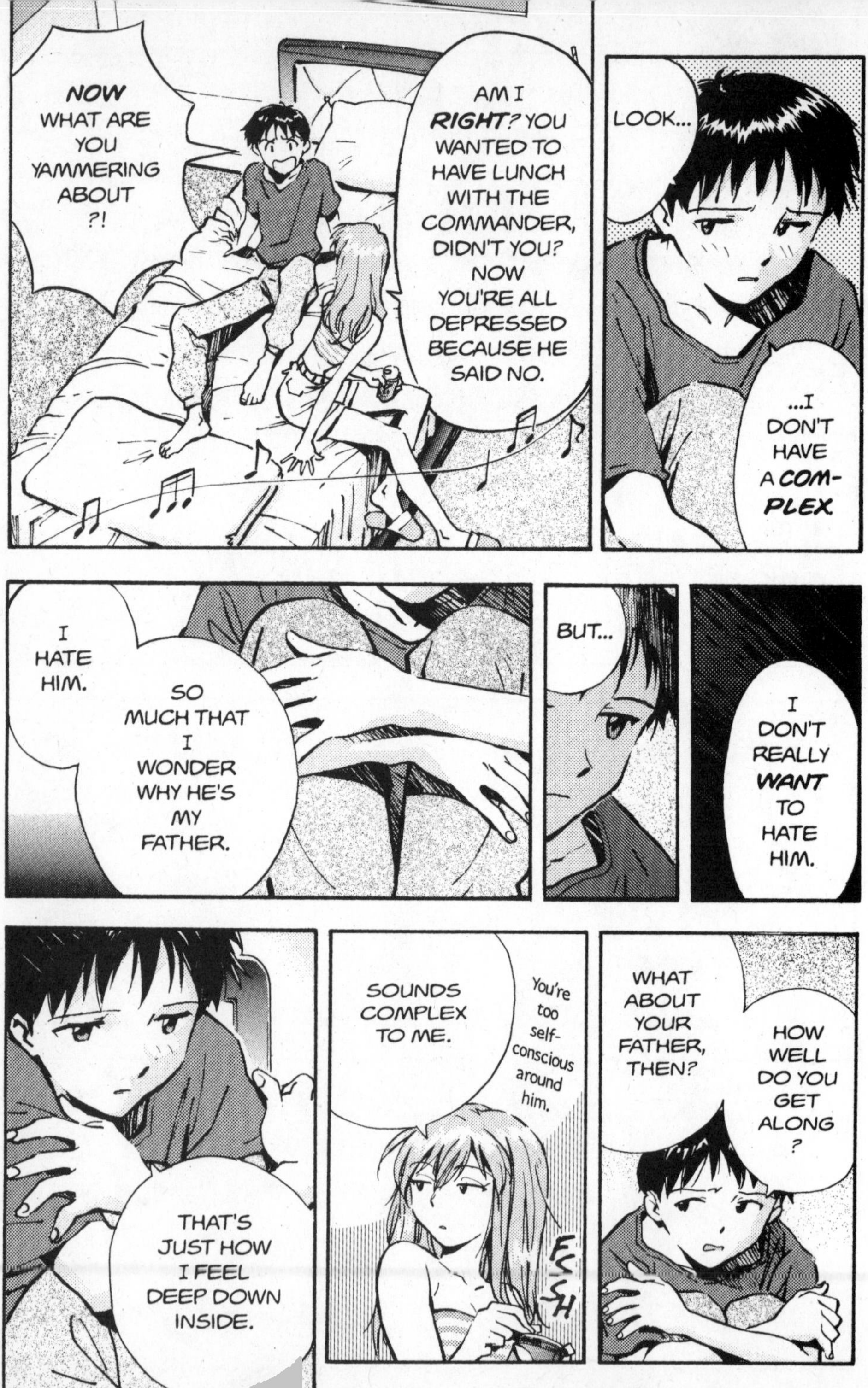
NOW WHAT ARE YOU YAMMERING ABOUT ?!
AM I RIGHT? YOU WANTED TO HAVE LUNCH WITH THE COMMANDER, DIDN'T YOU? NOW YOU'RE ALL DEPRESSED BECAUSE HE SAID NO.
LOOK...
...I DON'T HAVE A COMPLEX.
I HATE HIM.
SO MUCH THAT I WONDER WHY HE'S MY FATHER.
BUT...
I DON'T REALLY WANT TO HATE HIM.
THAT'S JUST HOW I FEEL DEEP DOWN INSIDE.
SOUNDS COMPLEX TO ME.
You're too self-conscious around him.
FSSH
WHAT ABOUT YOUR FATHER, THEN?
HOW WELL DO YOU GET ALONG ?

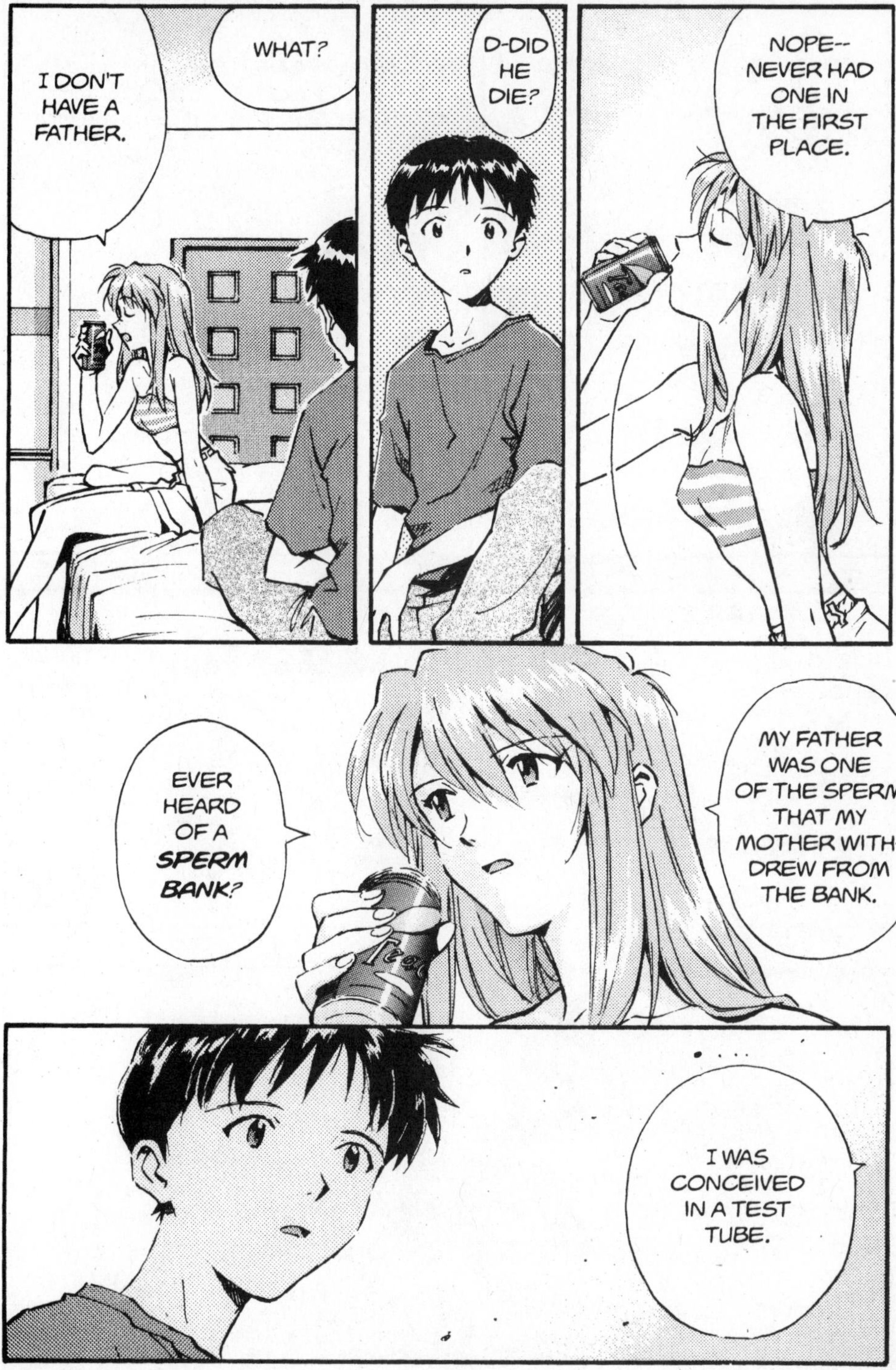
I DON'T HAVE A FATHER.
WHAT?
D-DID HE DIE?
NOPE-- NEVER HAD ONE IN THE FIRST PLACE.
EVER HEARD OF A SPERM BANK?
MY FATHER WAS ONE OF THE SPERM THAT MY MOTHER WITH-DREW FROM THE BANK.
. . . .
I WAS CONCEIVED IN A TEST TUBE.

..... WHAT'S **YOUR** PROBLEM?

WELL... I'D **HEARD** OF IT--

--BUT I'D NEVER SEEN THE ACTUAL RESULTS!

AND LISTEN!

IT WASN'T JUST **ANY** SPERM.

MY MOTHER CHOSE A **VERY** EXCLUSIVE SPERM BANK. THE DONOR PASSED A **STRICT** QUALIFICATION TEST ON ACADEMIC BACKGROUND AND CHARACTER.

OF COURSE, THE WOMEN WHO BUY THE SPERM HAVE TO BE SIMILARLY QUALIFIED AS WELL.

THERE'S SOMETHING **WRONG** WITH A 14-YEAR OLD GIRL TALKING ABOUT ALL THIS **SPERM**..

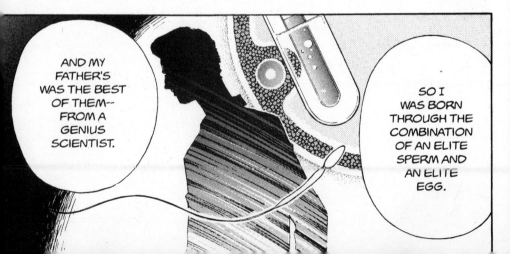

AND MY FATHER'S WAS THE BEST OF THEM-- FROM A GENIUS SCIENTIST.

SO I WAS BORN THROUGH THE COMBINATION OF AN ELITE SPERM AND AN ELITE EGG.

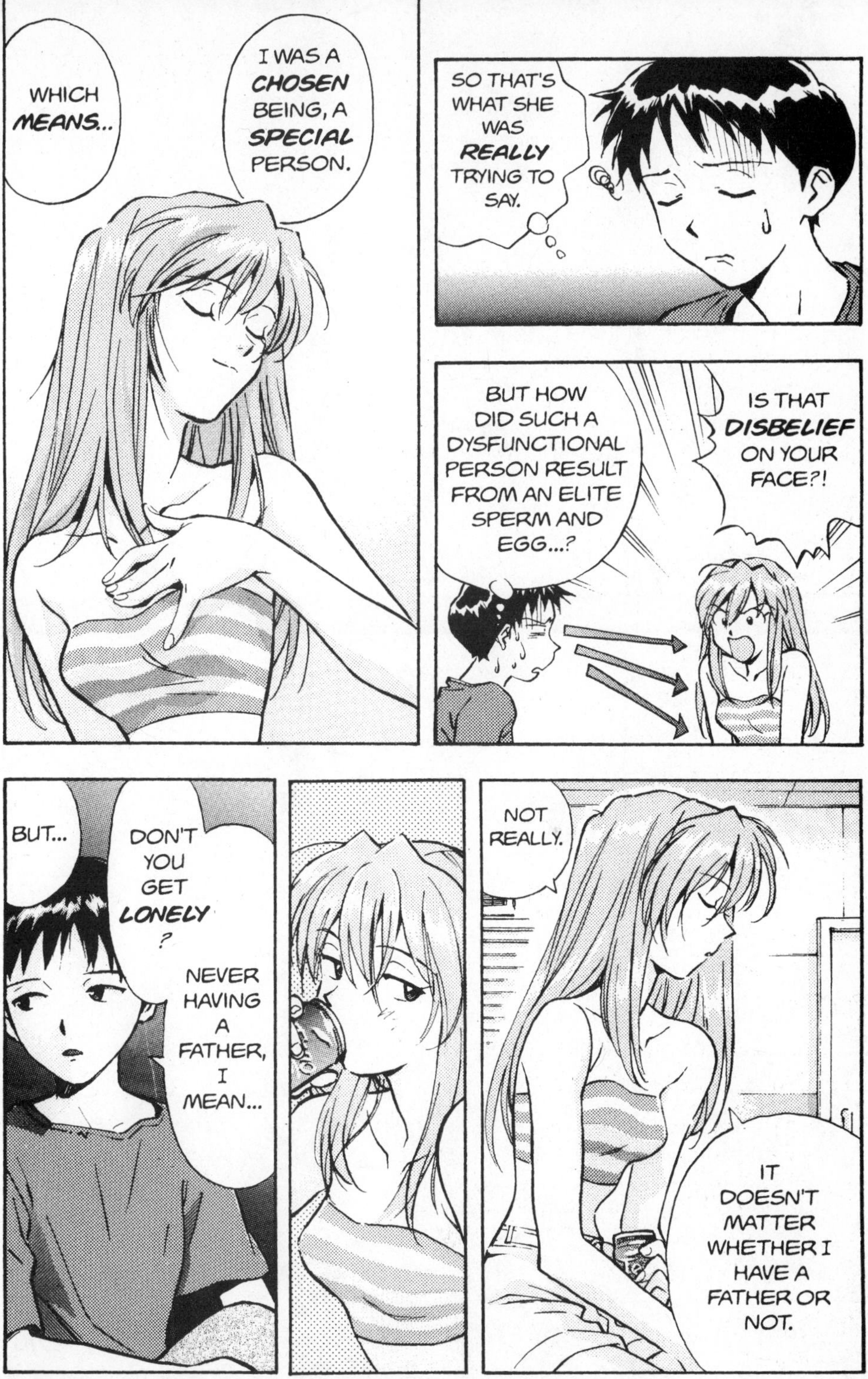

I WAS A CHOSEN BEING, A SPECIAL PERSON.
WHICH MEANS...
SO THAT'S WHAT SHE WAS REALLY TRYING TO SAY.
BUT HOW DID SUCH A DYSFUNCTIONAL PERSON RESULT FROM AN ELITE SPERM AND EGG...?
IS THAT DISBELIEF ON YOUR FACE?!
BUT...
DON'T YOU GET LONELY?
NEVER HAVING A FATHER, I MEAN...
NOT REALLY.
IT DOESN'T MATTER WHETHER I HAVE A FATHER OR NOT.

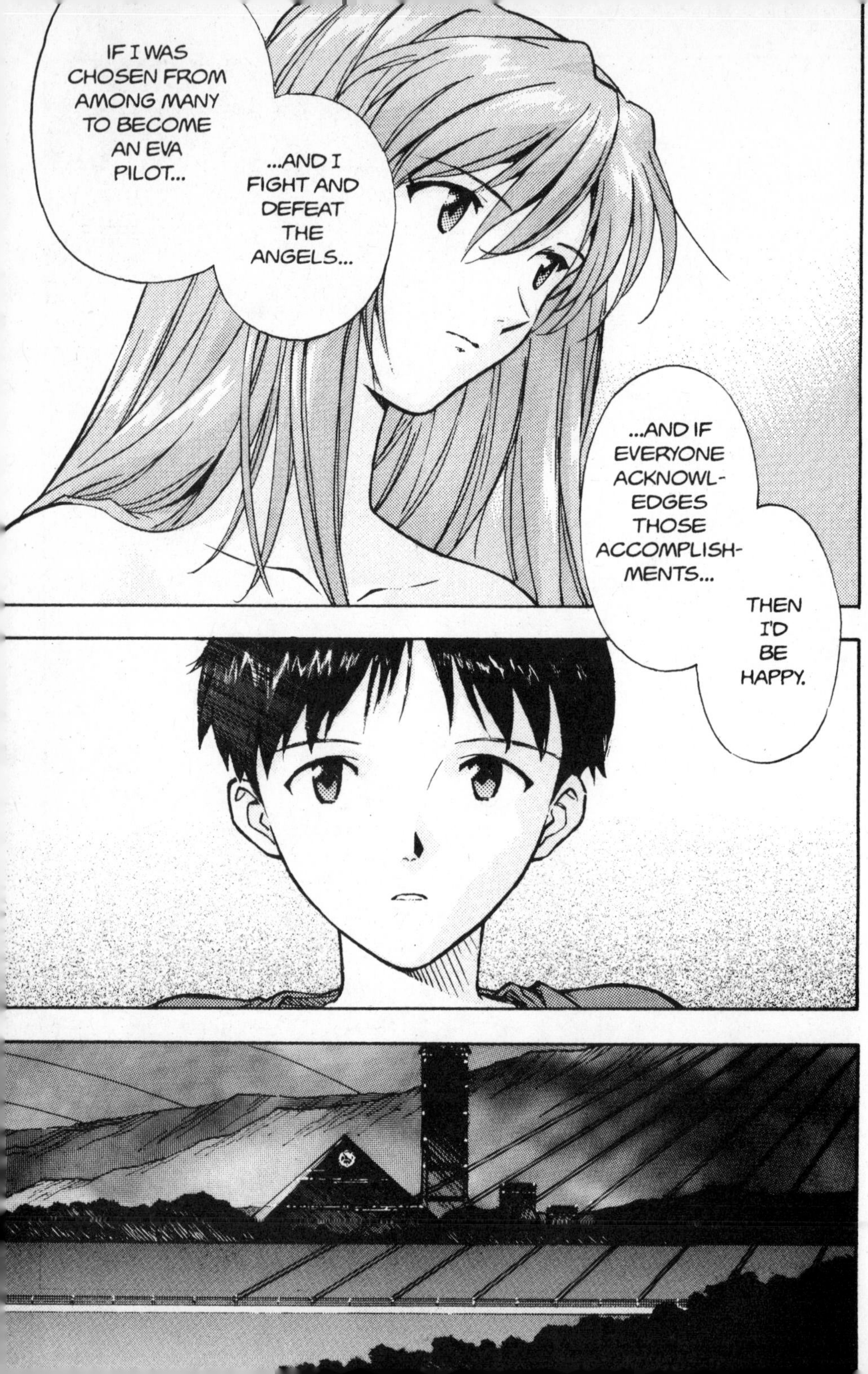
IF I WAS CHOSEN FROM AMONG MANY TO BECOME AN EVA PILOT...
...AND I FIGHT AND DEFEAT THE ANGELS...
...AND IF EVERYONE ACKNOWL-EDGES THOSE ACCOMPLISH-MENTS...
THEN I'D BE HAPPY.

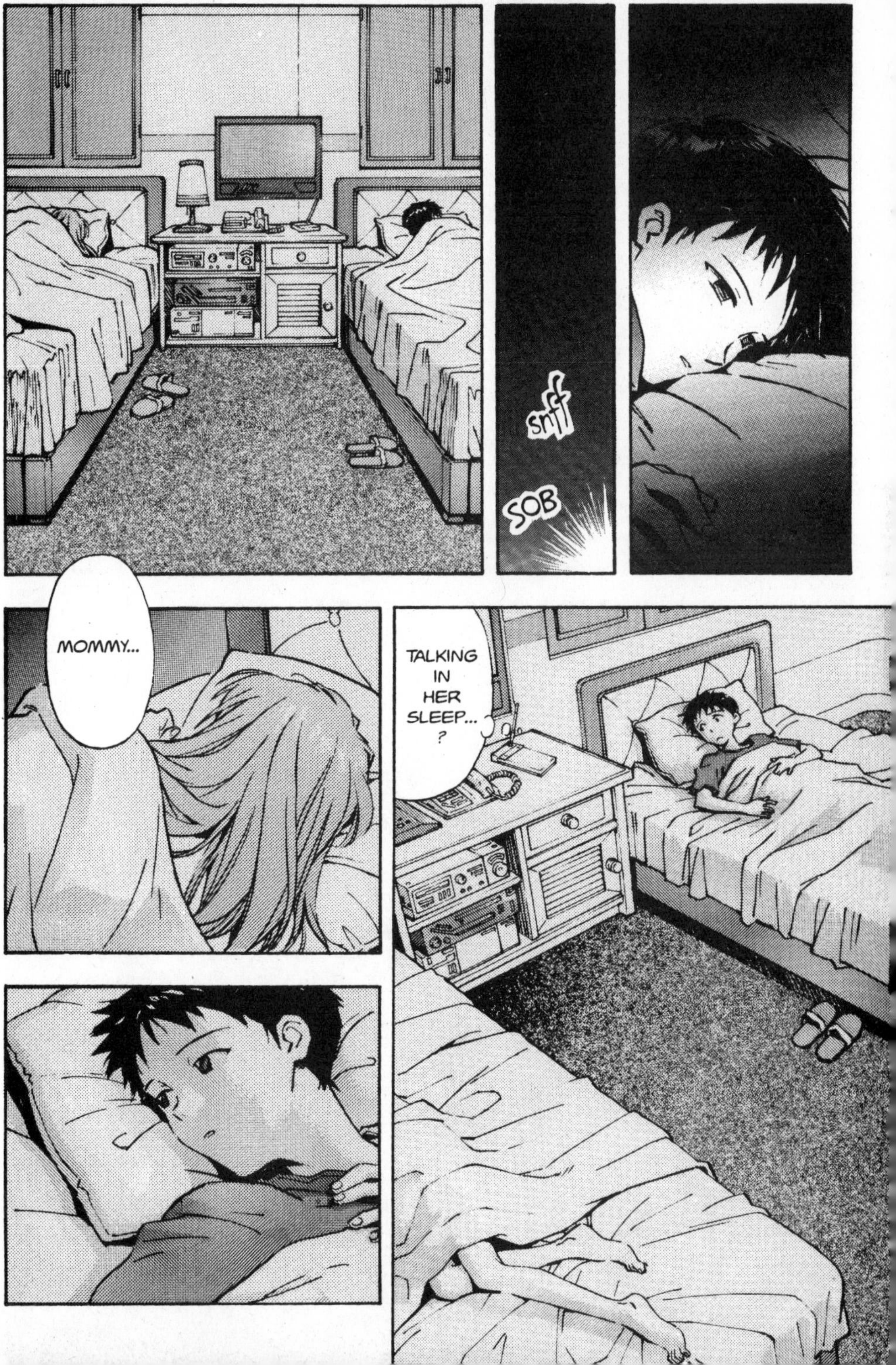
snff
SOB
MOMMY...
TALKING IN HER SLEEP...?

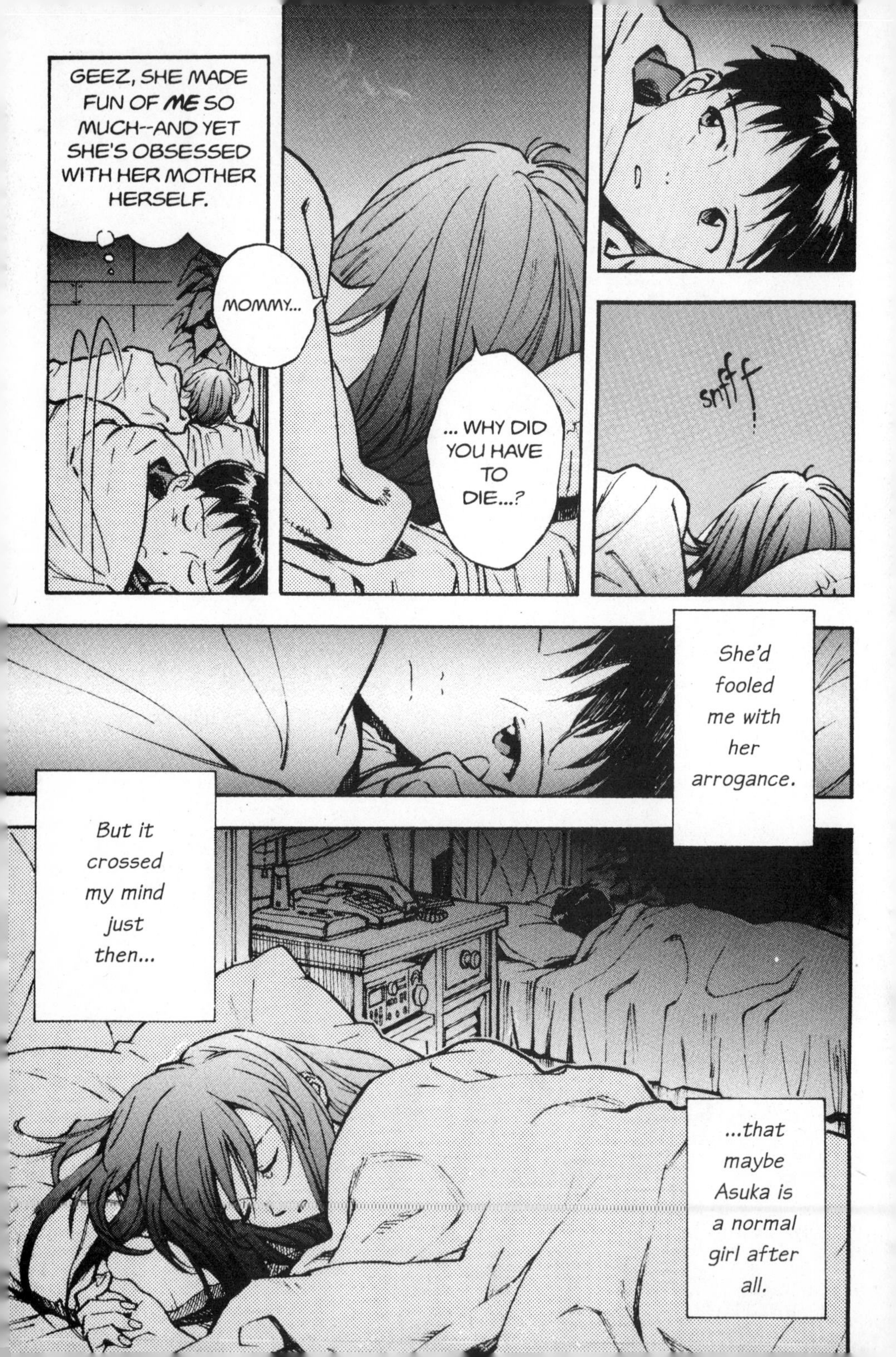
GEEZ, SHE MADE FUN OF ***ME*** SO MUCH--AND YET SHE'S OBSESSED WITH HER MOTHER HERSELF.
MOMMY...
... WHY DID YOU HAVE TO DIE...?
snfff
She'd fooled me with her arrogance.
But it crossed my mind just then...
...that maybe Asuka is a normal girl after all.

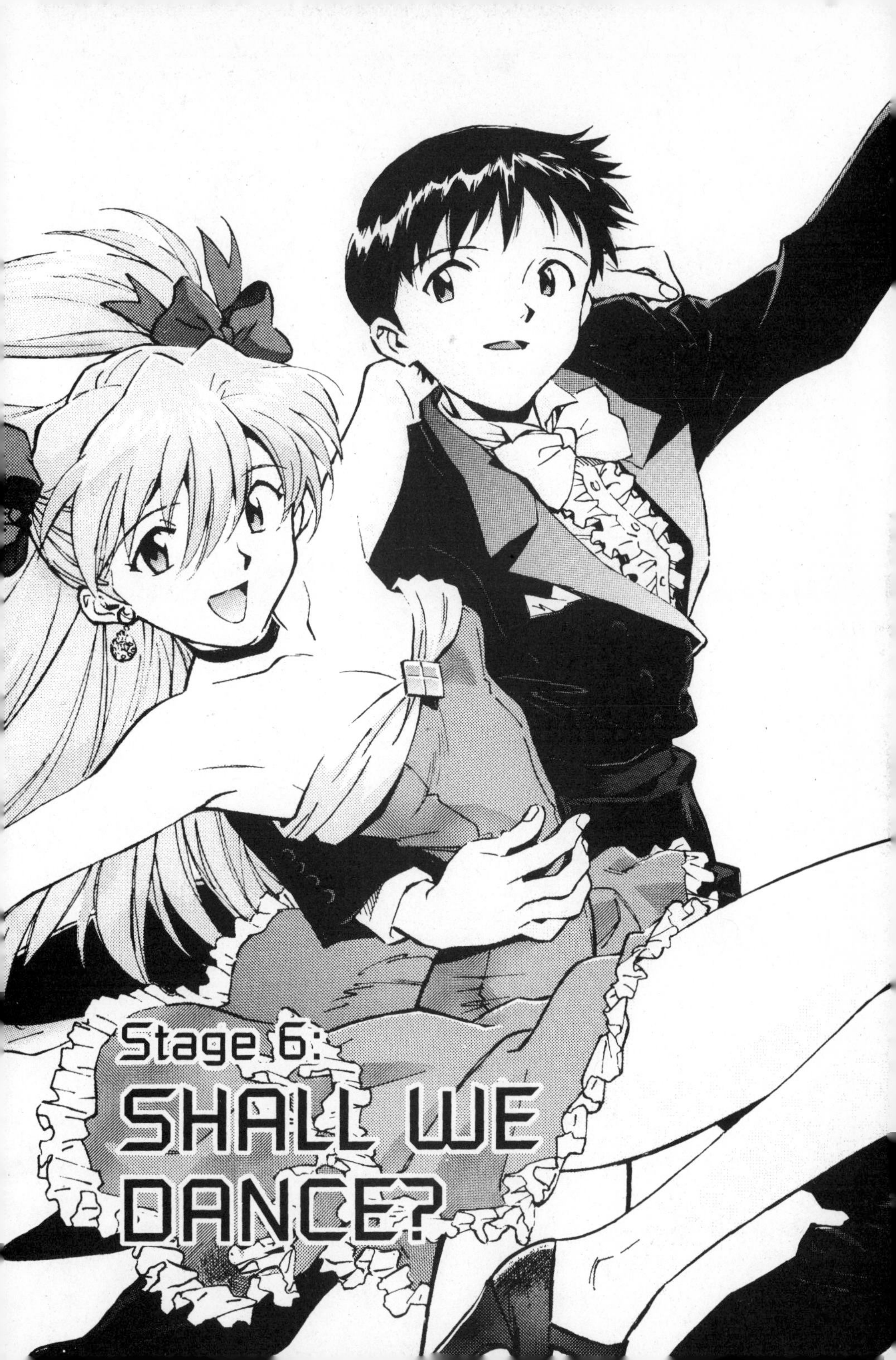
Stage 6:
SHALL WE DANCE?

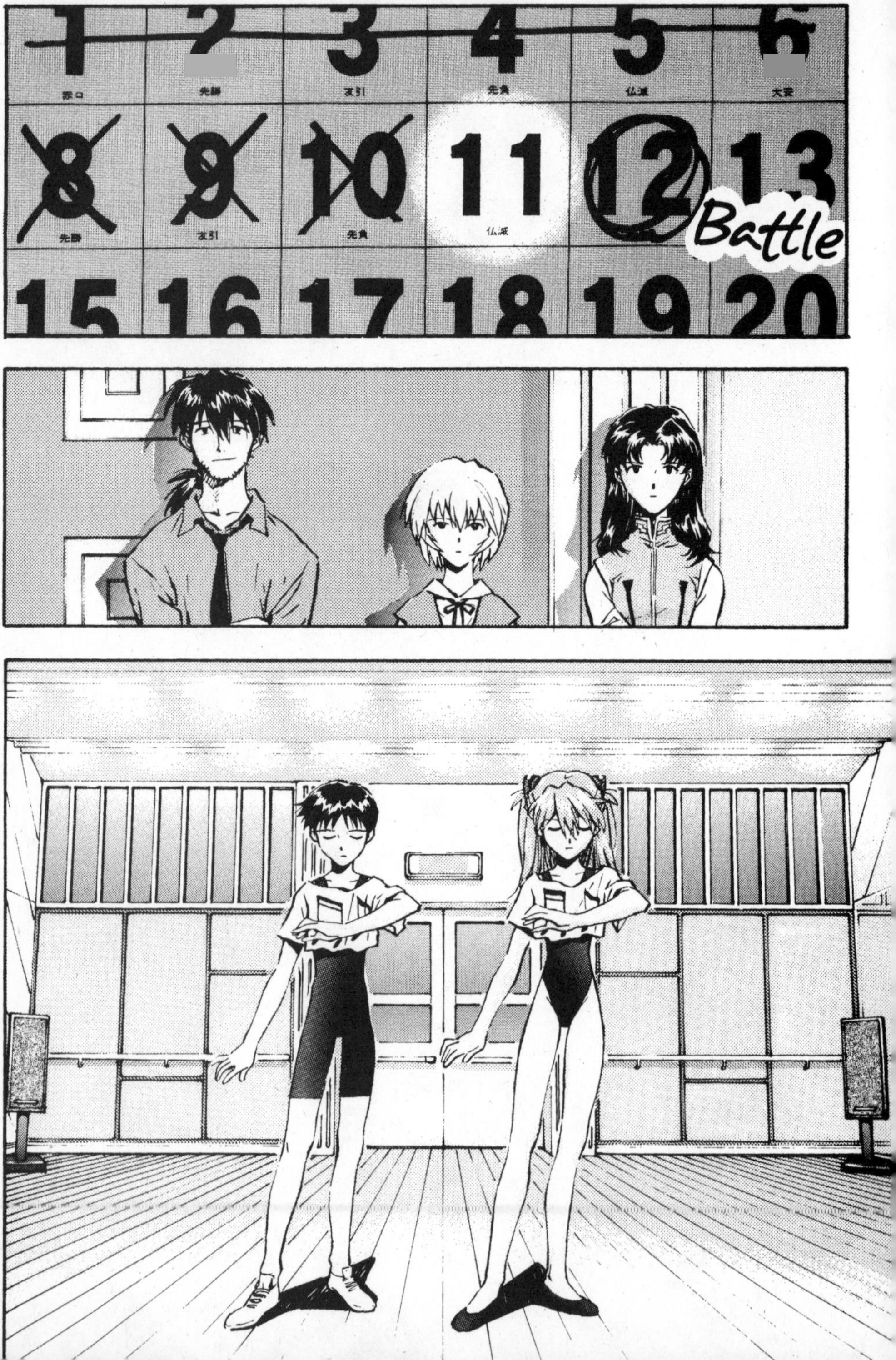
1 2 3 4 5 6
赤口 先勝 友引 先負 仏滅 大安
8 9 10 11 12 13
先勝 友引 先負 仏滅
Battle
15 16 17 18 19 20

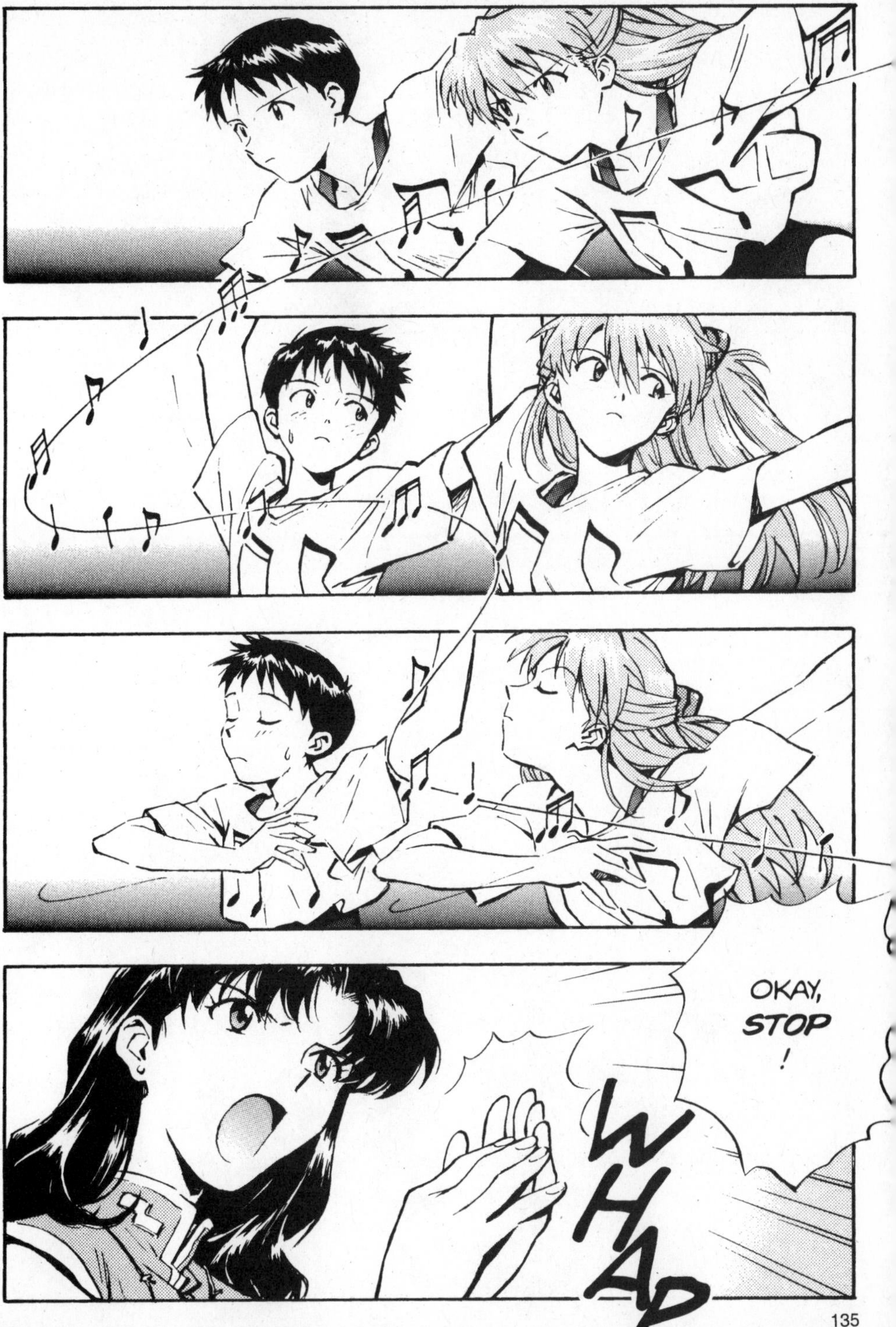
OKAY, STOP!
WHAP

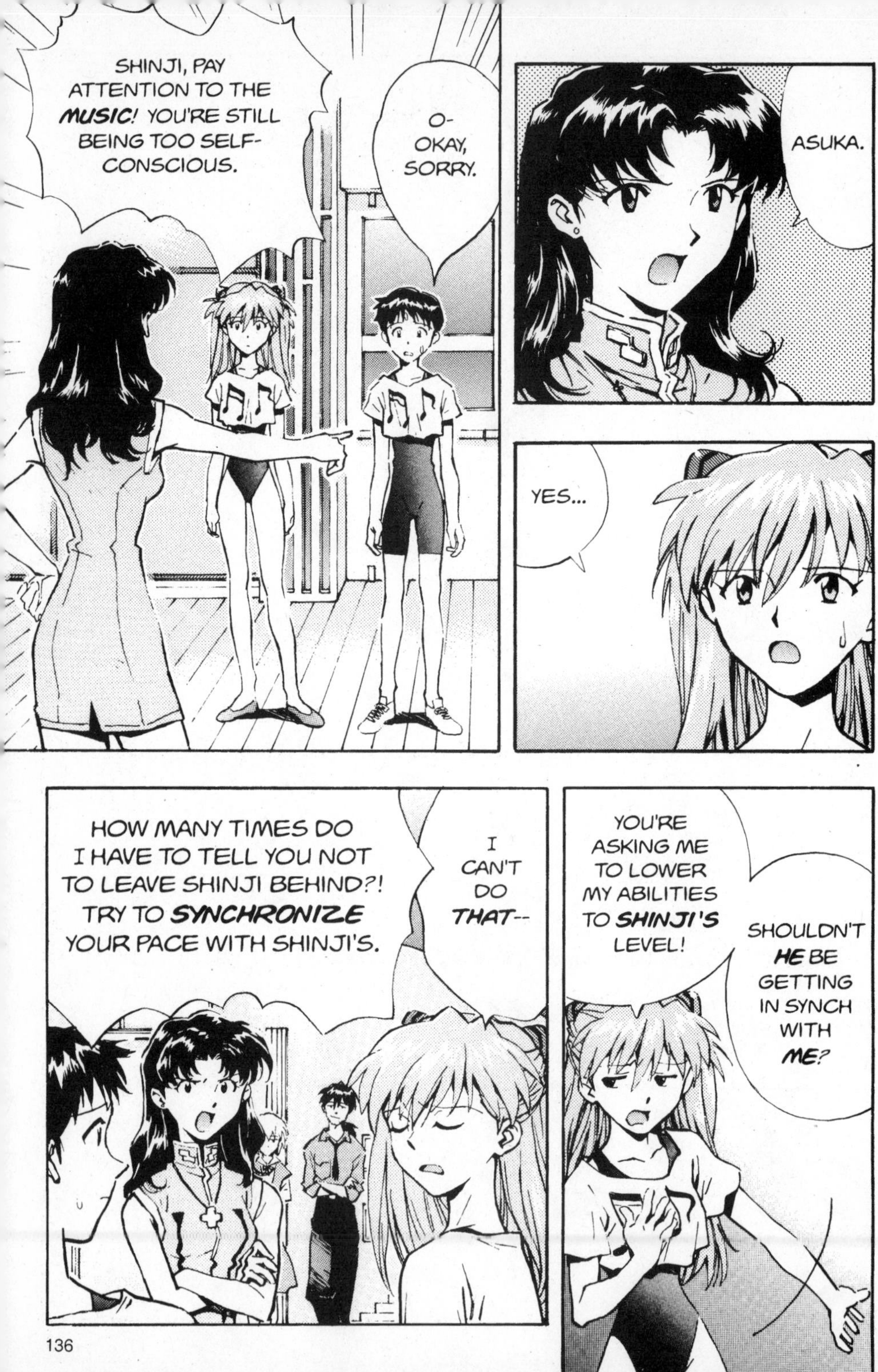
SHINJI, PAY ATTENTION TO THE MUSIC! YOU'RE STILL BEING TOO SELF-CONSCIOUS.
O-OKAY, SORRY.
ASUKA.
YES...
HOW MANY TIMES DO I HAVE TO TELL YOU NOT TO LEAVE SHINJI BEHIND?! TRY TO SYNCHRONIZE YOUR PACE WITH SHINJI'S.
I CAN'T DO THAT--
YOU'RE ASKING ME TO LOWER MY ABILITIES TO SHINJI'S LEVEL!
SHOULDN'T HE BE GETTING IN SYNCH WITH ME?

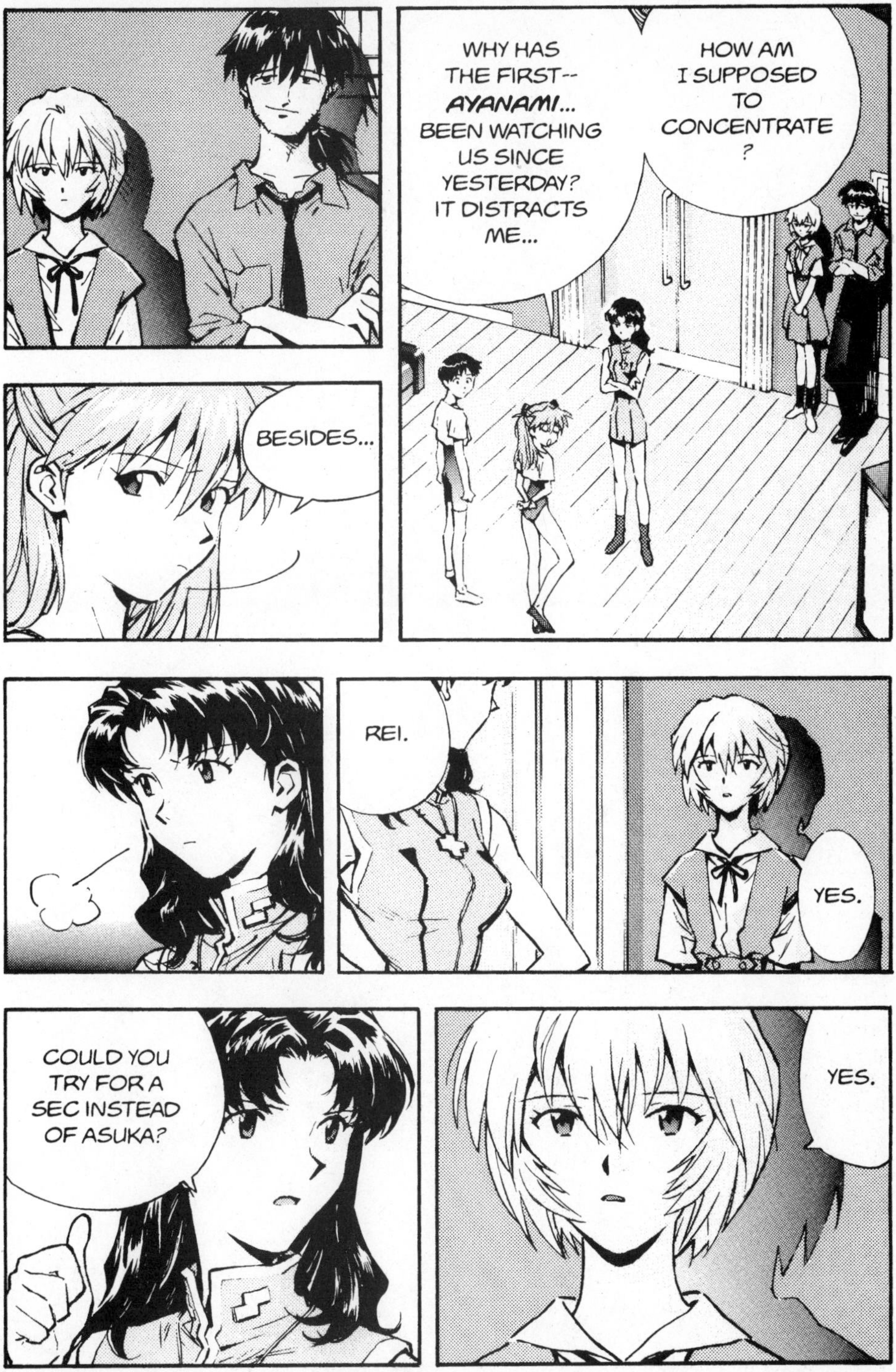

BESIDES...
WHY HAS THE FIRST-- *AYANAMI*... BEEN WATCHING US SINCE YESTERDAY? IT DISTRACTS ME...
HOW AM I SUPPOSED TO CONCENTRATE ?
REI.
YES.
COULD YOU TRY FOR A SEC INSTEAD OF ASUKA?
YES.

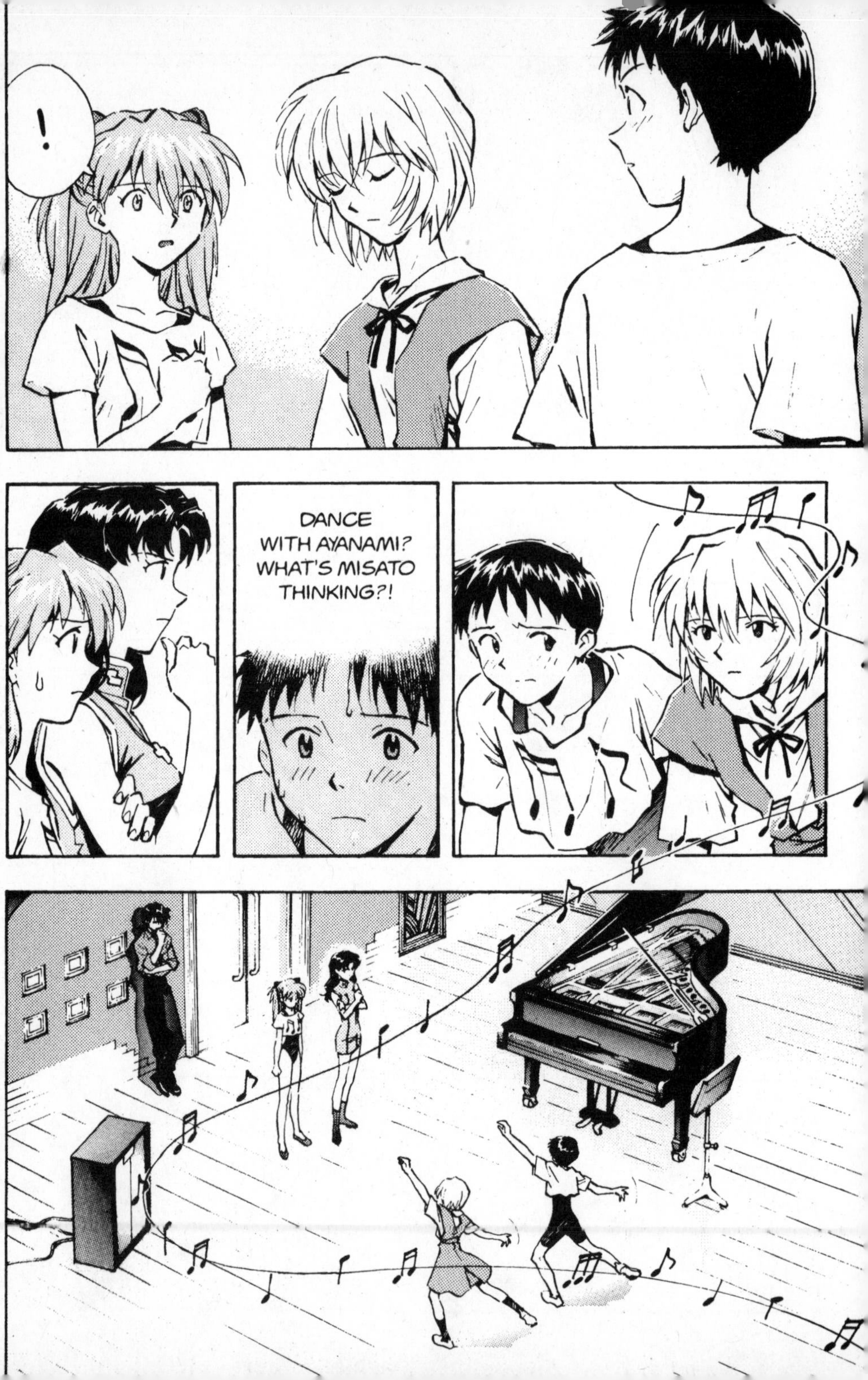
!
DANCE WITH AYANAMI? WHAT'S MISATO THINKING?!

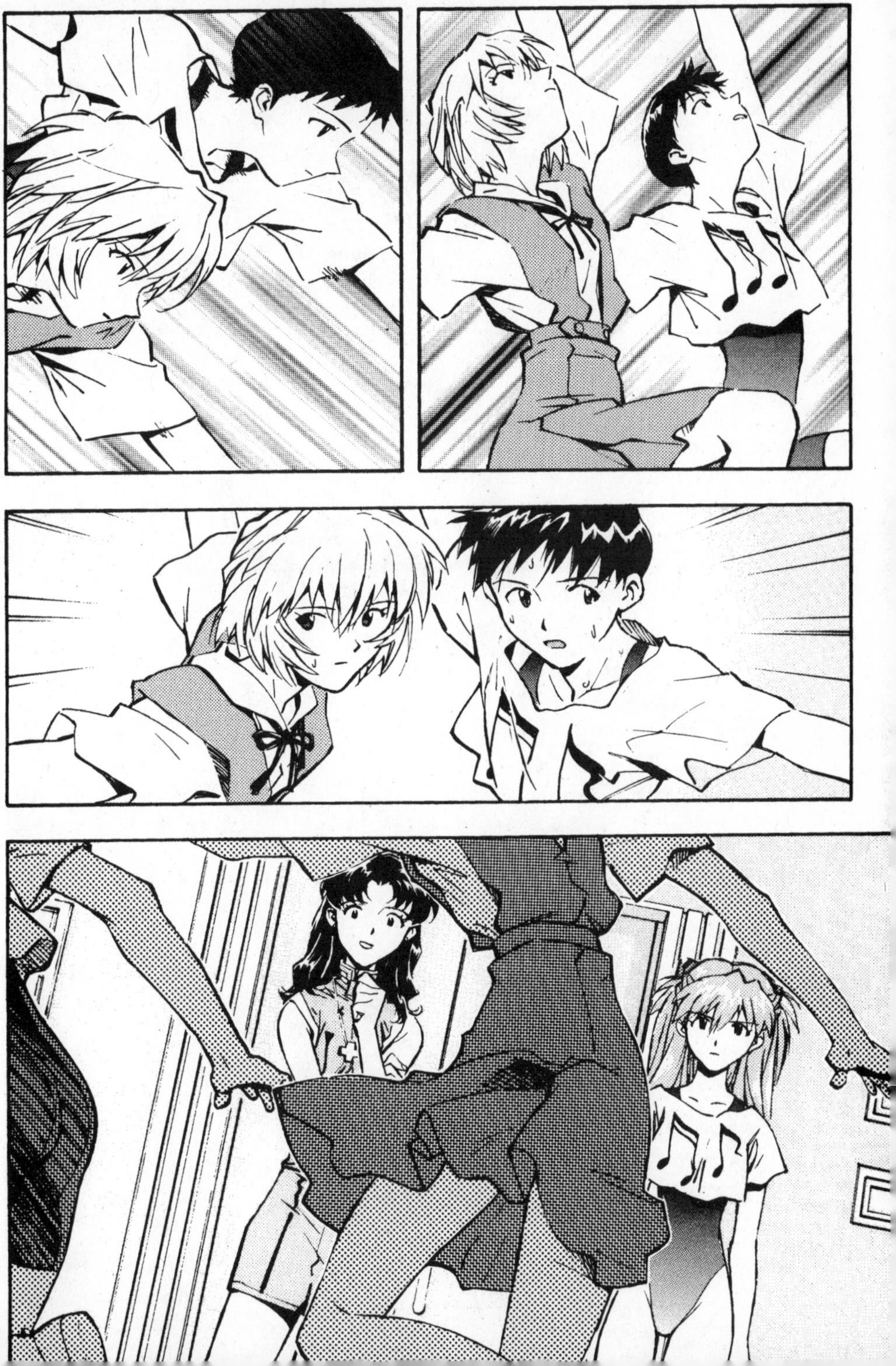

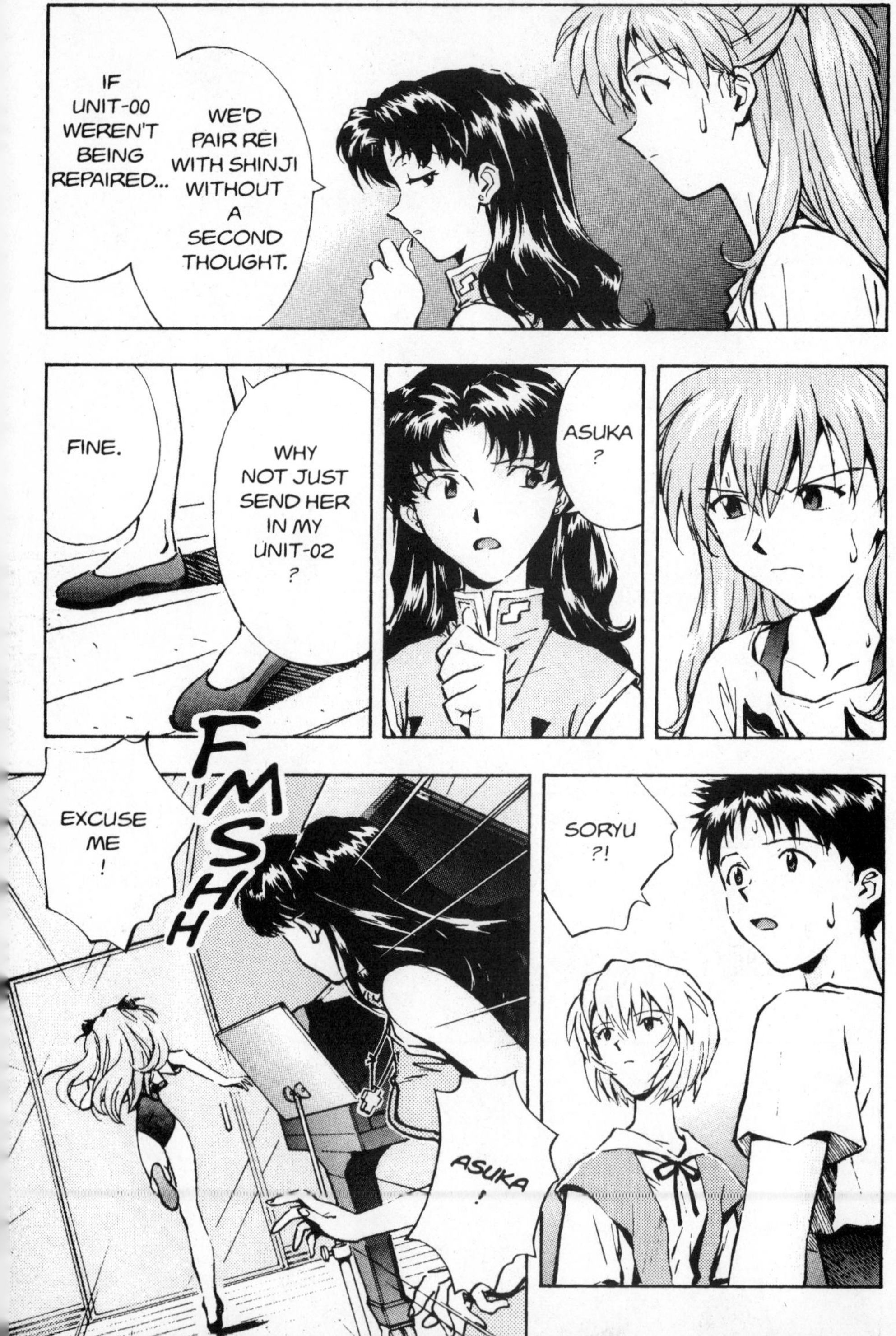
IF UNIT-00 WEREN'T BEING REPAIRED...
WE'D PAIR REI WITH SHINJI WITHOUT A SECOND THOUGHT.
FINE.
WHY NOT JUST SEND HER IN MY UNIT-02 ?
ASUKA ?
EXCUSE ME !
FMSHH
ASUKA !
SORYU ?!

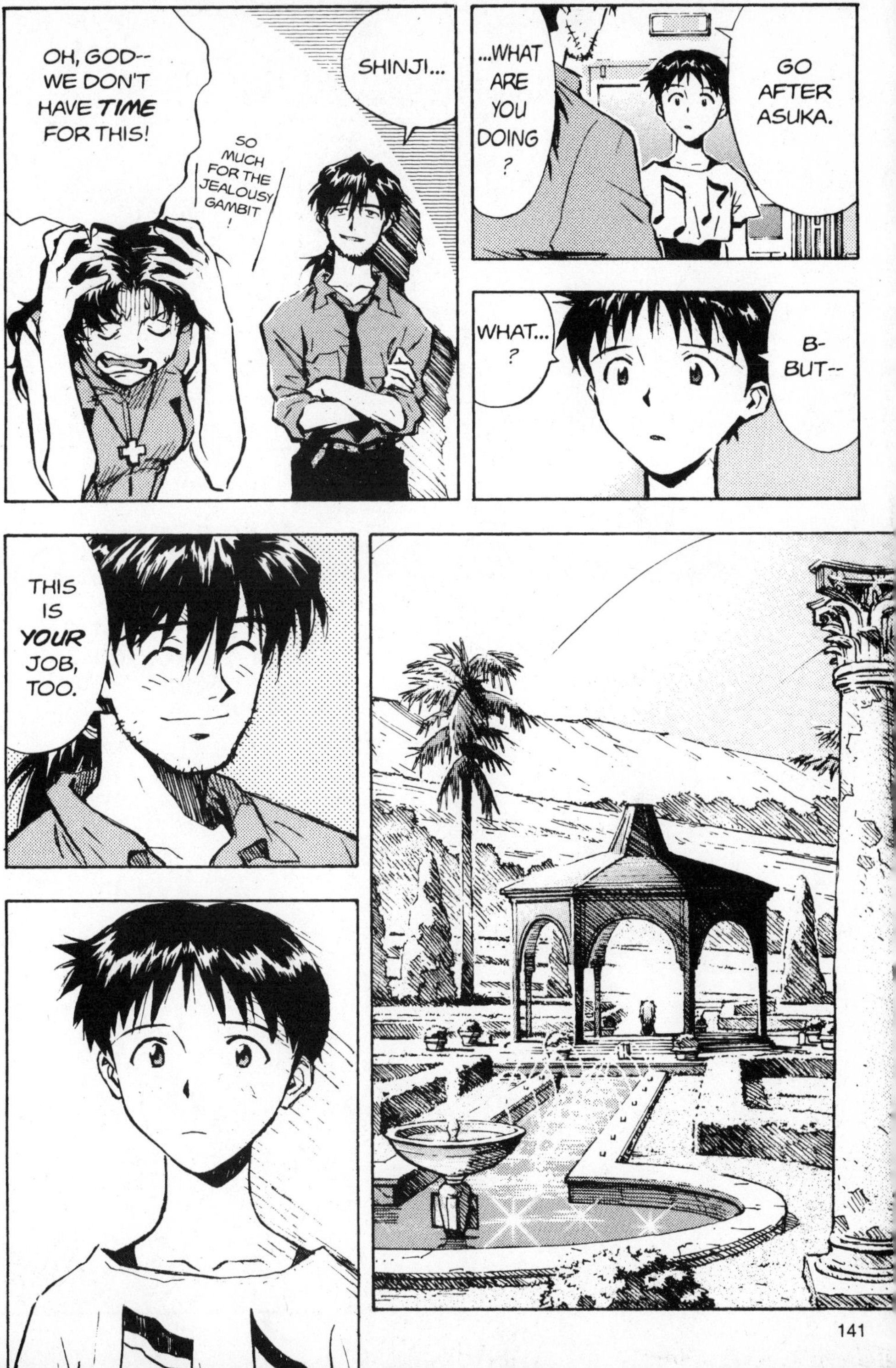
OH, GOD-- WE DON'T HAVE TIME FOR THIS!
SO MUCH FOR THE JEALOUSY GAMBIT!
SHINJI...
...WHAT ARE YOU DOING?
GO AFTER ASUKA.
WHAT...?
B-BUT--
THIS IS YOUR JOB, TOO.

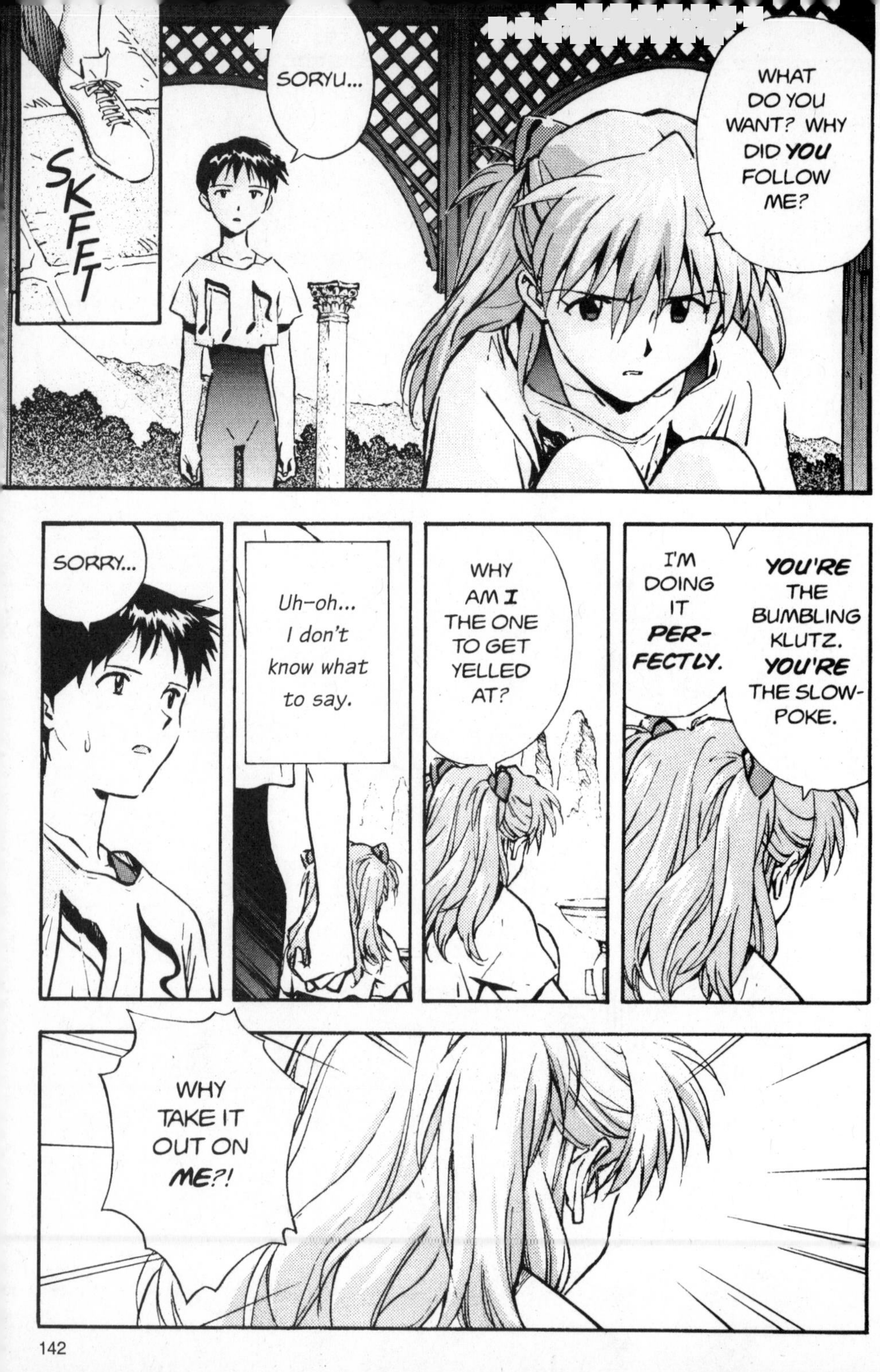
SKFFT
SORYU...
WHAT DO YOU WANT? WHY DID YOU FOLLOW ME?
SORRY...
Uh-oh... I don't know what to say.
WHY AM I THE ONE TO GET YELLED AT?
I'M DOING IT PER-FECTLY.
YOU'RE THE BUMBLING KLUTZ. YOU'RE THE SLOW-POKE.
WHY TAKE IT OUT ON ME?!

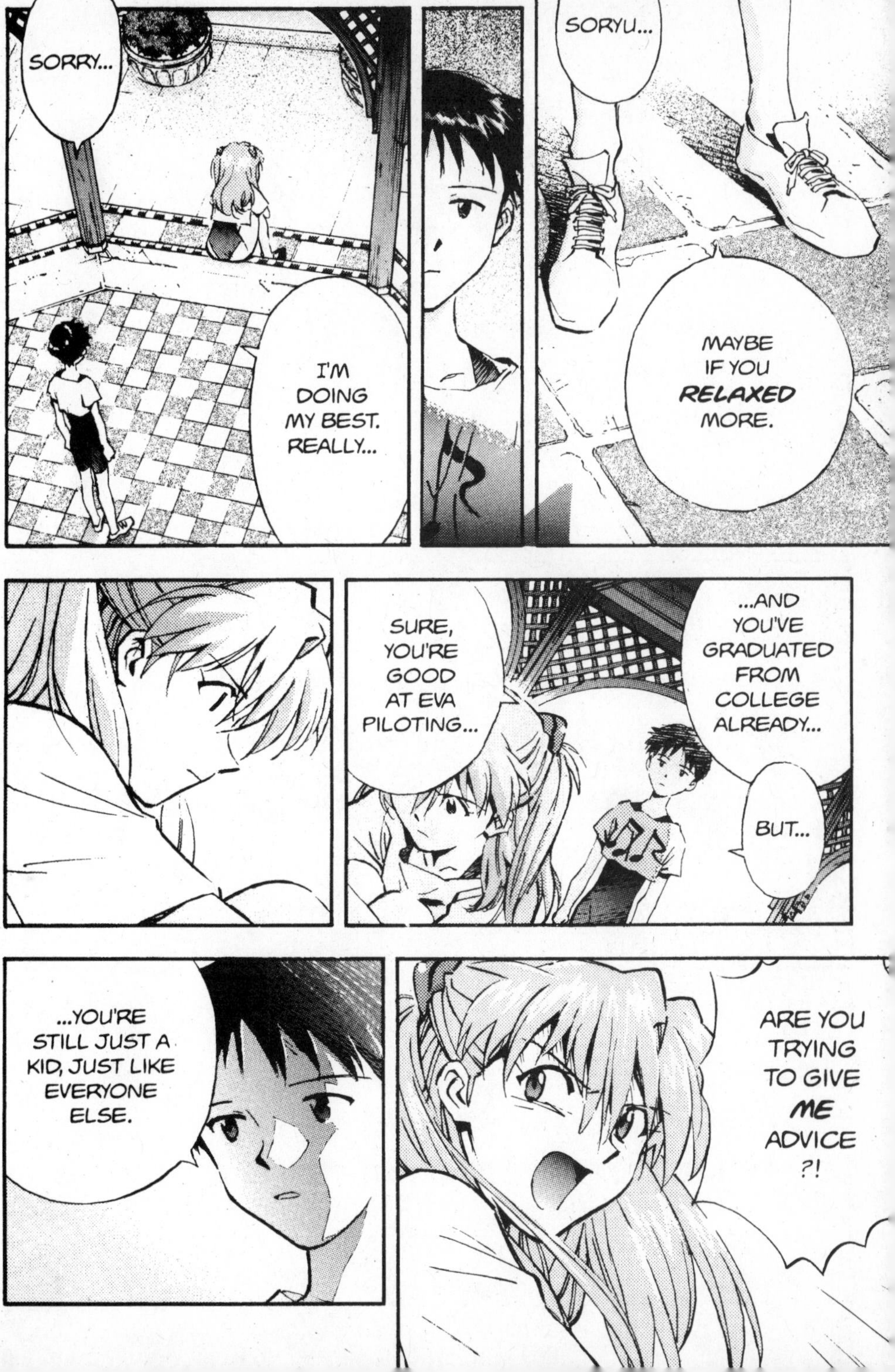
SORRY...
I'M DOING MY BEST. REALLY...
SORYU...
MAYBE IF YOU **RELAXED** MORE.
SURE, YOU'RE GOOD AT EVA PILOTING...
...AND YOU'VE GRADUATED FROM COLLEGE ALREADY...
BUT...
...YOU'RE STILL JUST A KID, JUST LIKE EVERYONE ELSE.
ARE YOU TRYING TO GIVE **ME** ADVICE ?!

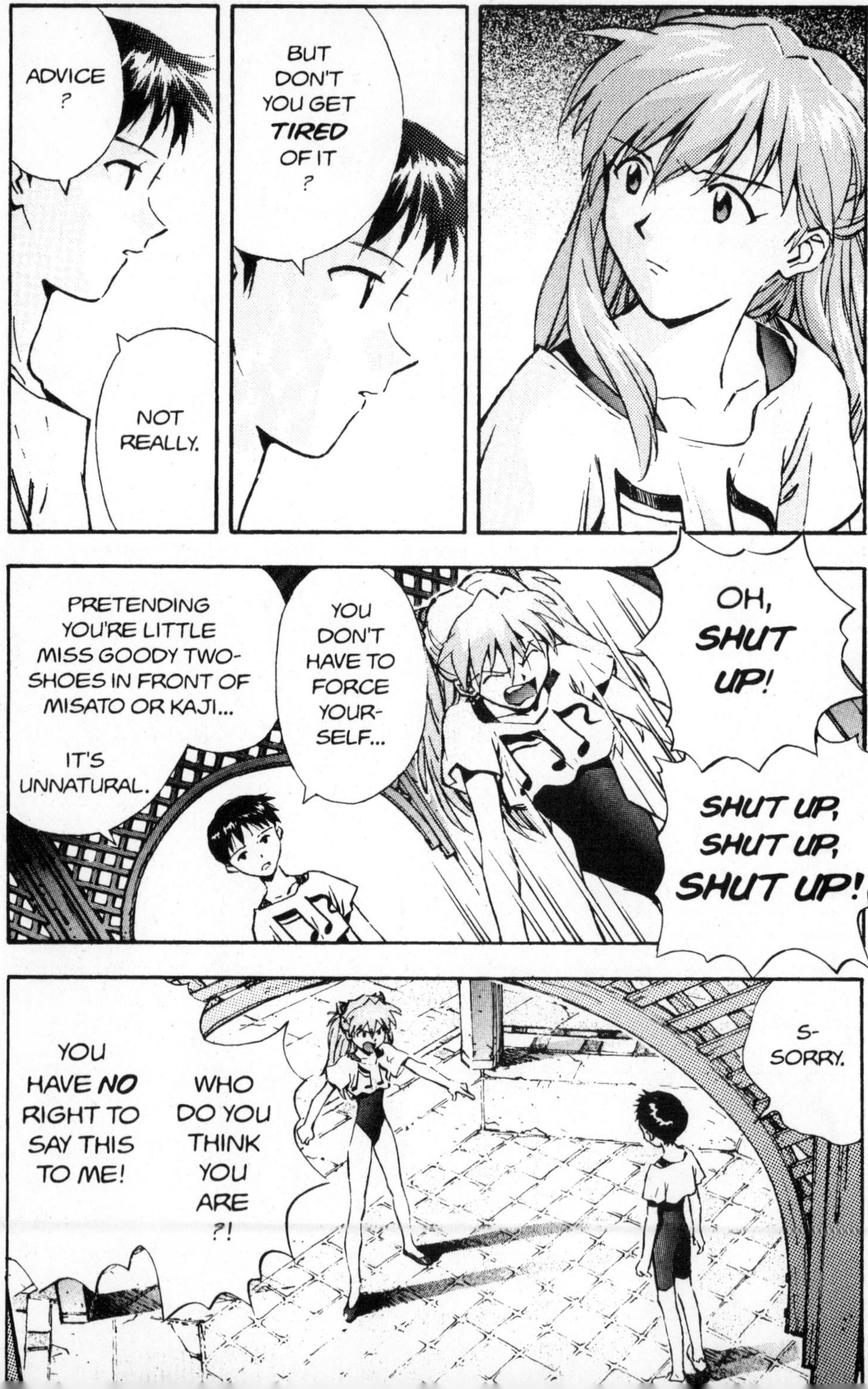
ADVICE?
NOT REALLY.
BUT DON'T YOU GET TIRED OF IT?
PRETENDING YOU'RE LITTLE MISS GOODY TWO-SHOES IN FRONT OF MISATO OR KAJI...
IT'S UNNATURAL.
YOU DON'T HAVE TO FORCE YOURSELF...
OH, SHUT UP!
SHUT UP, SHUT UP, SHUT UP!
YOU HAVE NO RIGHT TO SAY THIS TO ME!
WHO DO YOU THINK YOU ARE?!
S-SORRY.

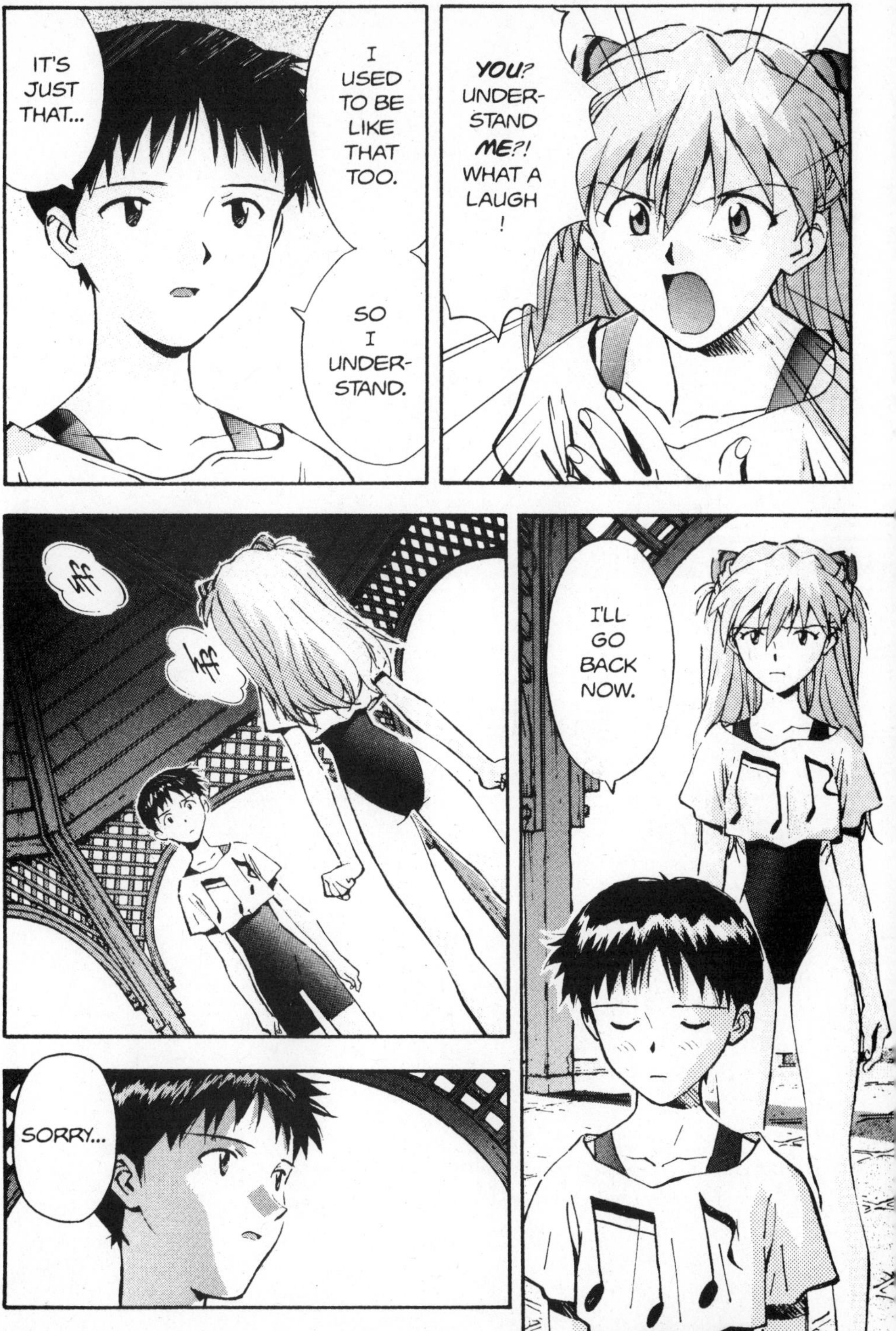
IT'S JUST THAT...
I USED TO BE LIKE THAT TOO.
SO I UNDERSTAND.
YOU? UNDERSTAND ME?! WHAT A LAUGH!
hff
hff
SORRY...
I'LL GO BACK NOW.

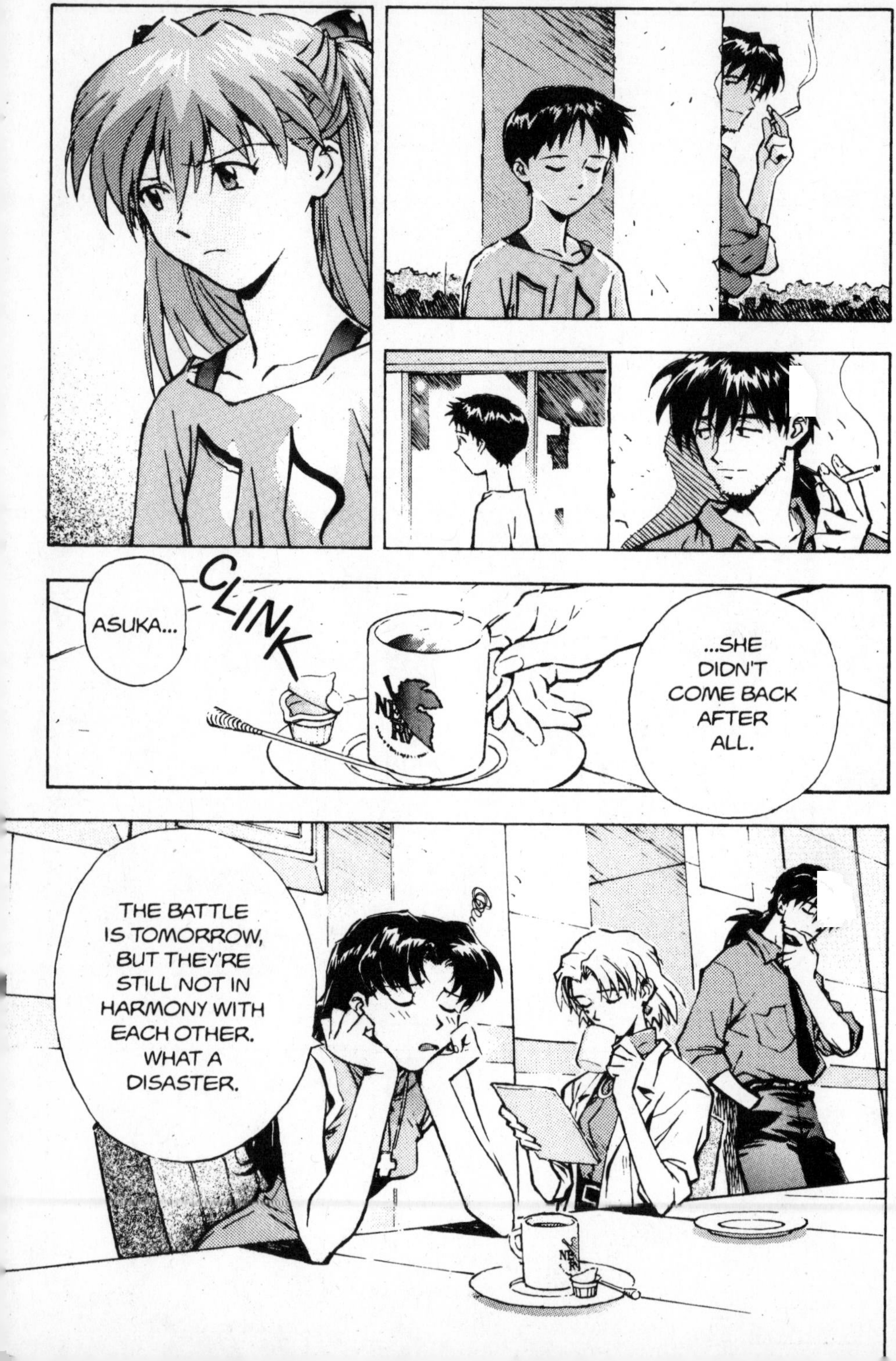
ASUKA...
CLINK
...SHE DIDN'T COME BACK AFTER ALL.
THE BATTLE IS TOMORROW, BUT THEY'RE STILL NOT IN HARMONY WITH EACH OTHER. WHAT A DISASTER.

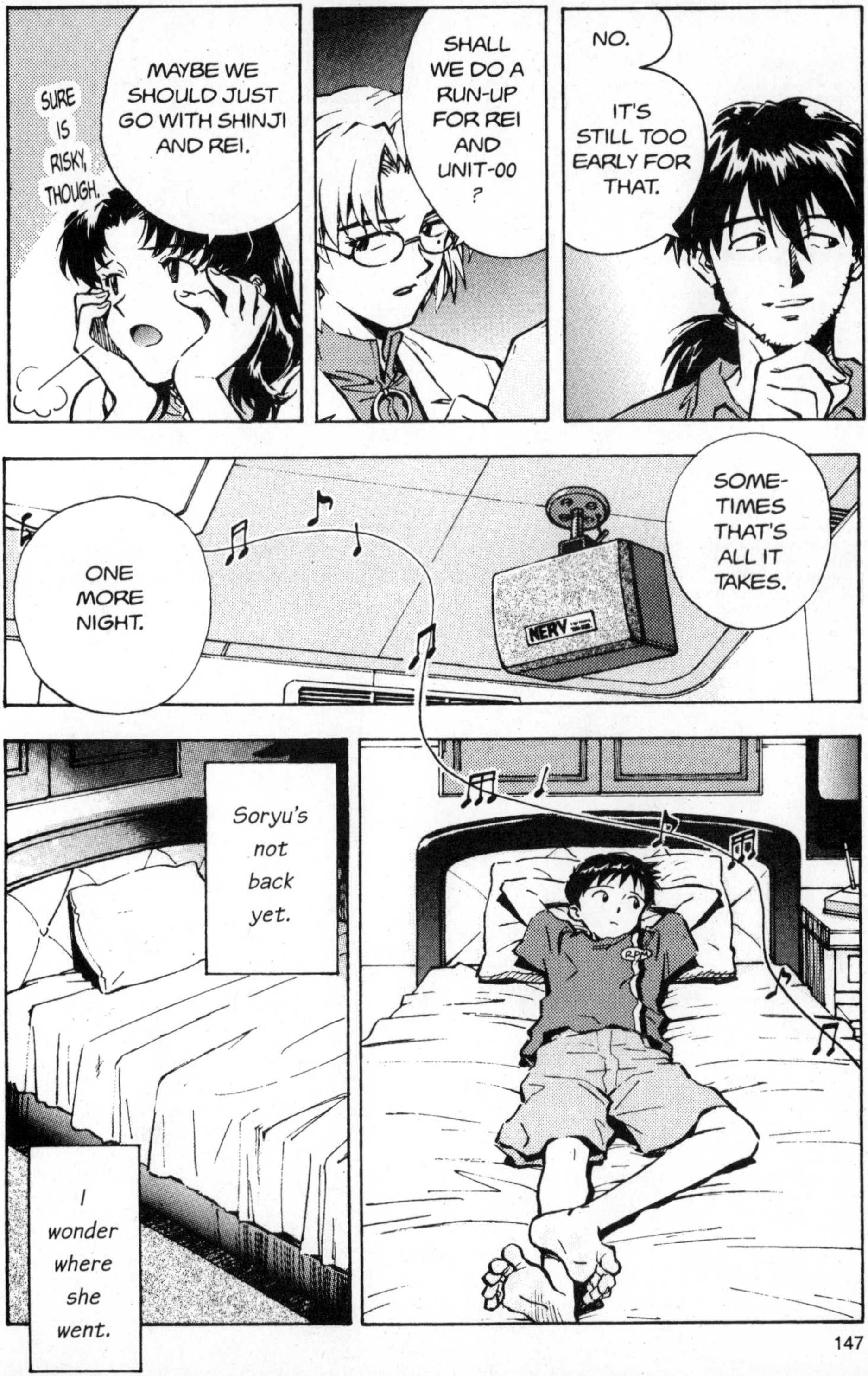
MAYBE WE SHOULD JUST GO WITH SHINJI AND REI.
SURE IS RISKY, THOUGH.
SHALL WE DO A RUN-UP FOR REI AND UNIT-00 ?
NO.
IT'S STILL TOO EARLY FOR THAT.
ONE MORE NIGHT.
NERV
SOME-TIMES THAT'S ALL IT TAKES.
Soryu's not back yet.
I wonder where she went.
RPM

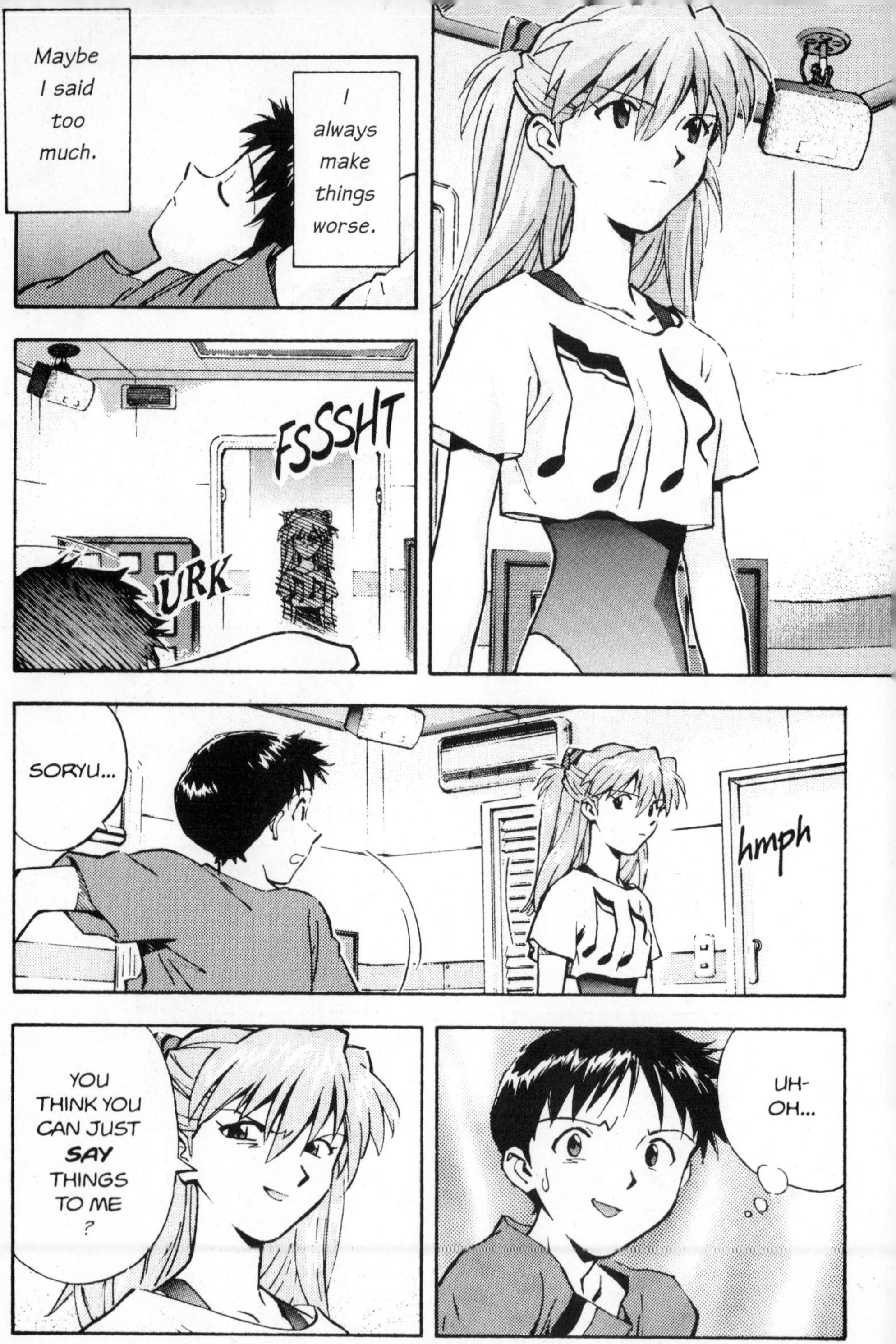
Maybe I said too much.
I always make things worse.
FSSSHT
URK
SORYU...
hmph
YOU THINK YOU CAN JUST **SAY** THINGS TO ME ?
UH-OH...

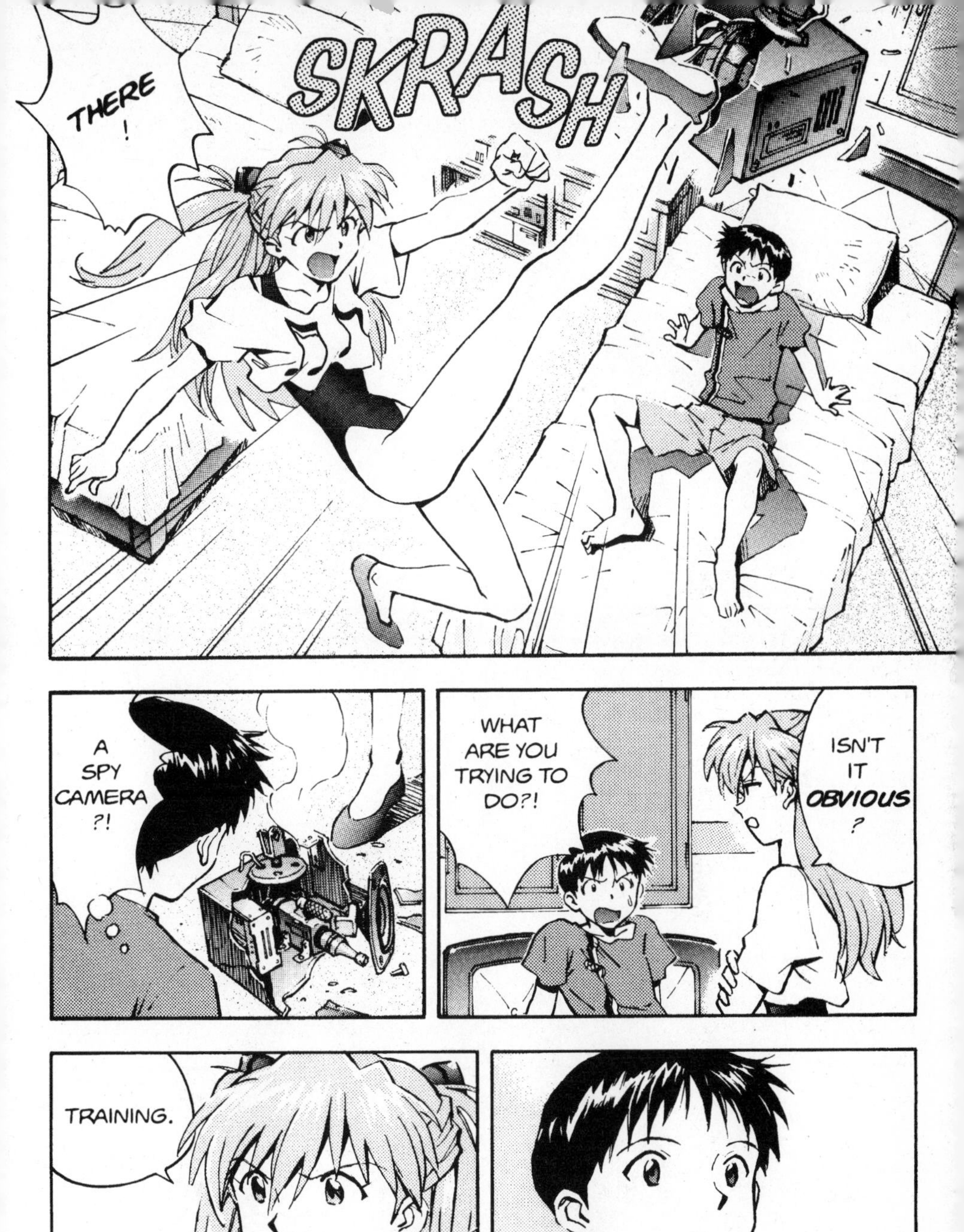
THERE
!
SKRASH
A
SPY
CAMERA
?!
WHAT
ARE YOU
TRYING TO
DO?!
ISN'T
IT
OBVIOUS
?
TRAINING.

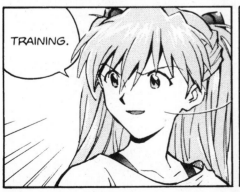

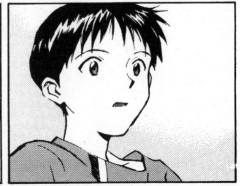

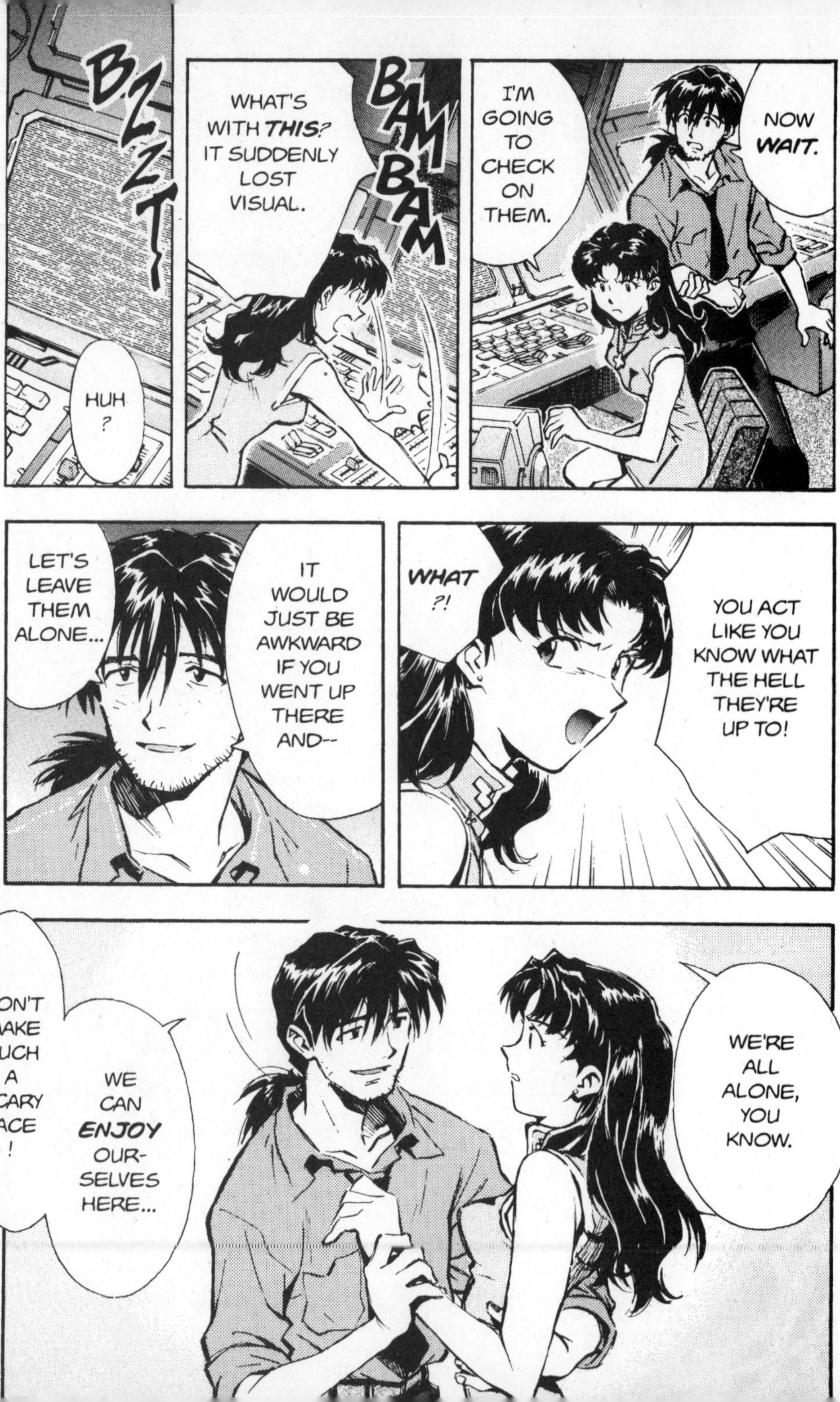
BZZT
HUH?
WHAT'S WITH **THIS**? IT SUDDENLY LOST VISUAL.
BAM BAM
I'M GOING TO CHECK ON THEM.
NOW **WAIT**.
LET'S LEAVE THEM ALONE...
IT WOULD JUST BE AWKWARD IF YOU WENT UP THERE AND--
WHAT ?!
YOU ACT LIKE YOU KNOW WHAT THE HELL THEY'RE UP TO!
DON'T MAKE SUCH A SCARY FACE!
WE CAN **ENJOY** OUR-SELVES HERE...
WE'RE ALL ALONE, YOU KNOW.

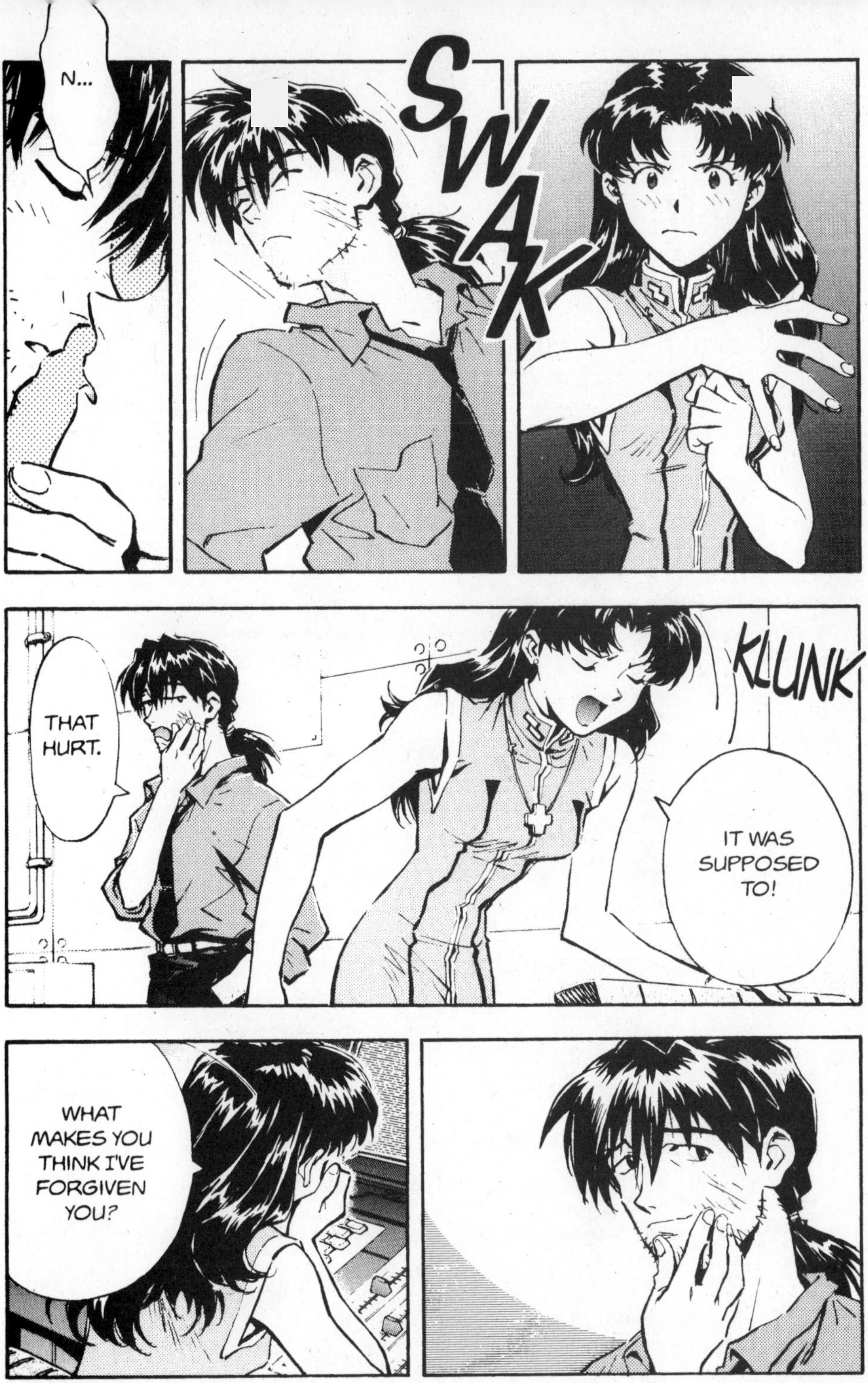
N...
SWAK
THAT HURT.
KLUNK
IT WAS SUPPOSED TO!
WHAT MAKES YOU THINK I'VE FORGIVEN YOU?

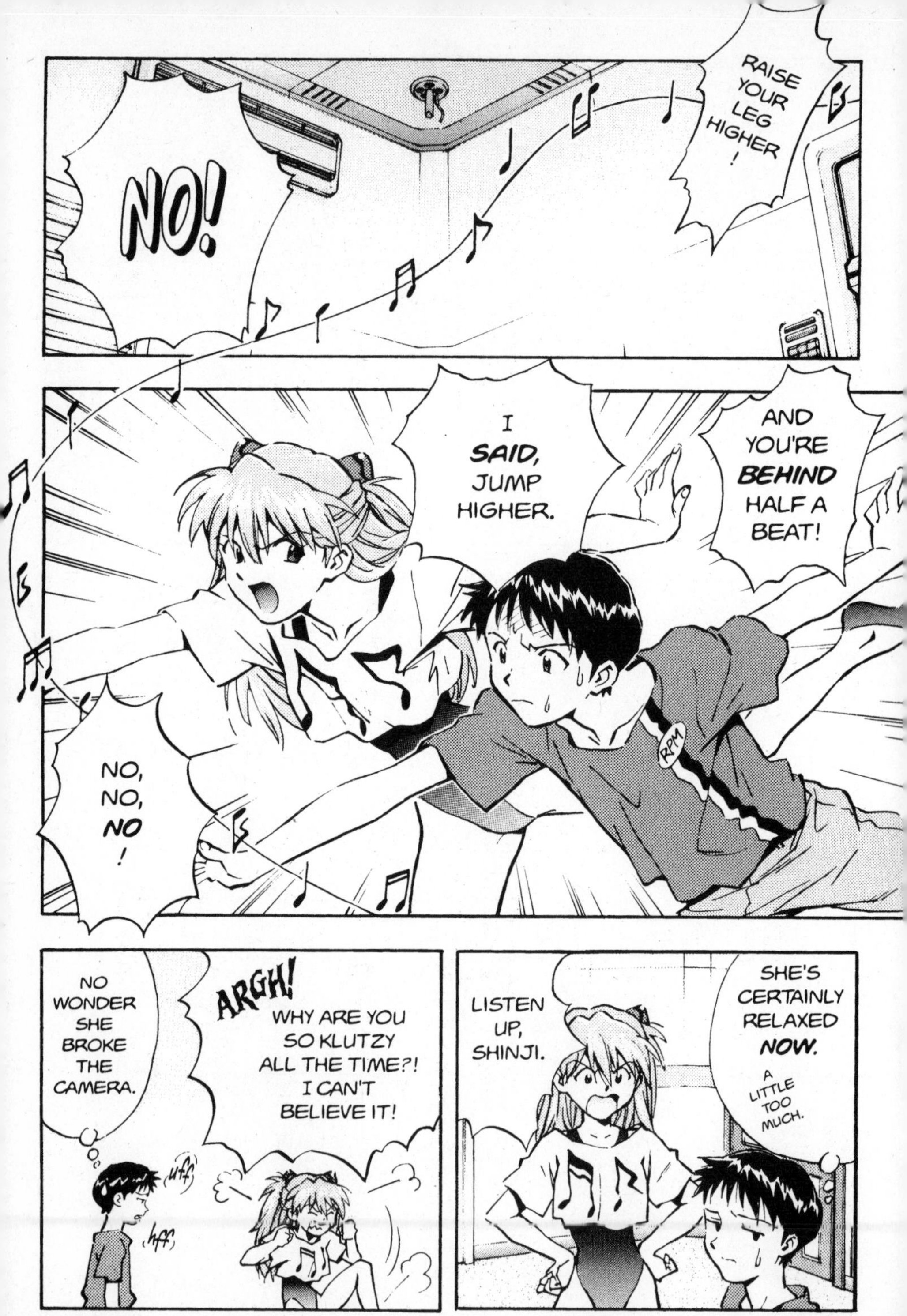

NO!
RAISE YOUR LEG HIGHER!
I SAID, JUMP HIGHER.
AND YOU'RE BEHIND HALF A BEAT!
NO, NO, NO!
NO WONDER SHE BROKE THE CAMERA.
ARGH!
WHY ARE YOU SO KLUTZY ALL THE TIME?! I CAN'T BELIEVE IT!
uff
hff
LISTEN UP, SHINJI.
SHE'S CERTAINLY RELAXED NOW.
A LITTLE TOO MUCH.

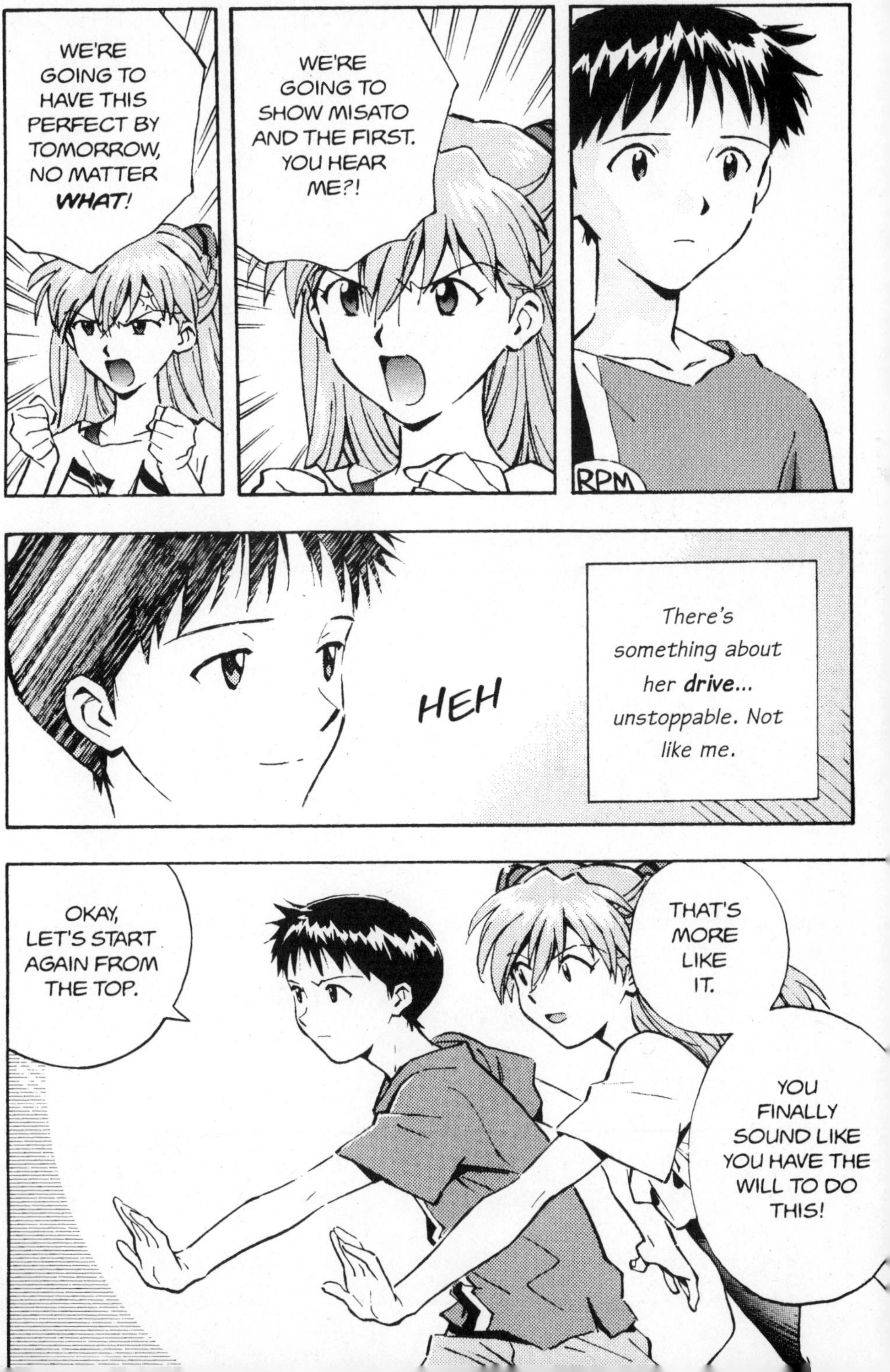
WE'RE GOING TO HAVE THIS PERFECT BY TOMORROW, NO MATTER **WHAT**!
WE'RE GOING TO SHOW MISATO AND THE FIRST. YOU HEAR ME?!
RPM
HEH
*There's something about her **drive**... unstoppable. Not like me.*
OKAY, LET'S START AGAIN FROM THE TOP.
THAT'S MORE LIKE IT.
YOU FINALLY SOUND LIKE YOU HAVE THE WILL TO DO THIS!

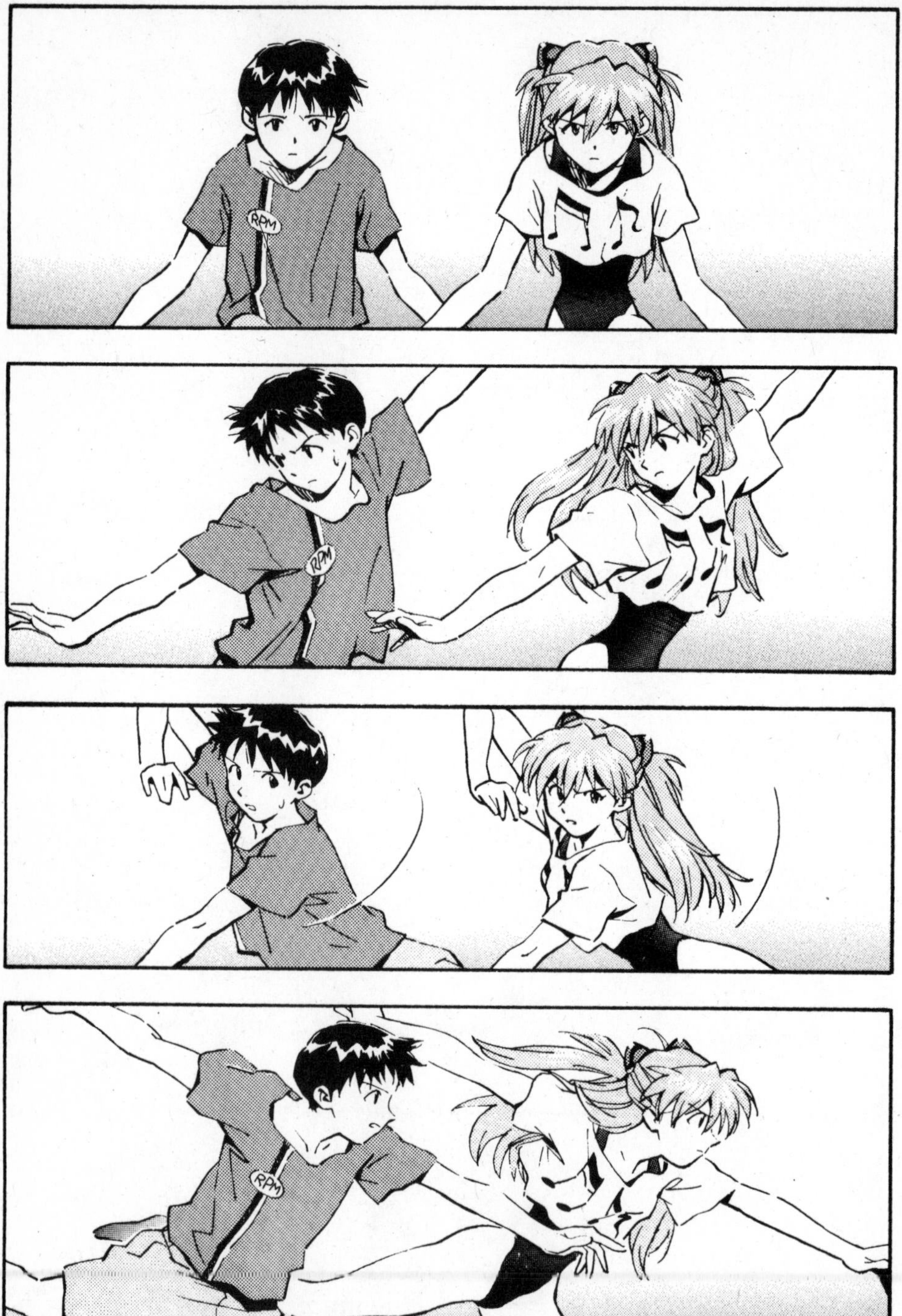
RPM
RPM
RPM

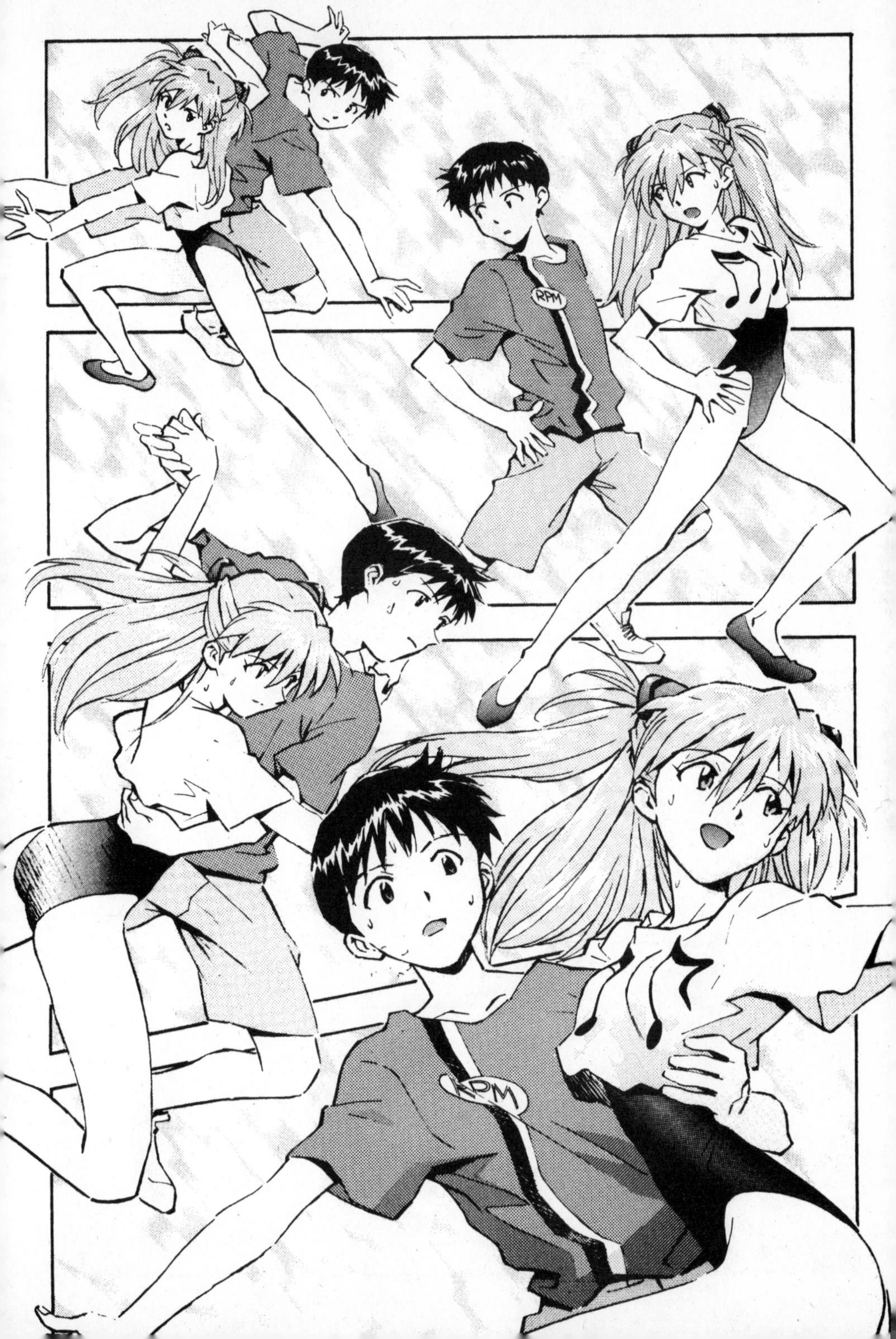
RPM
RPM

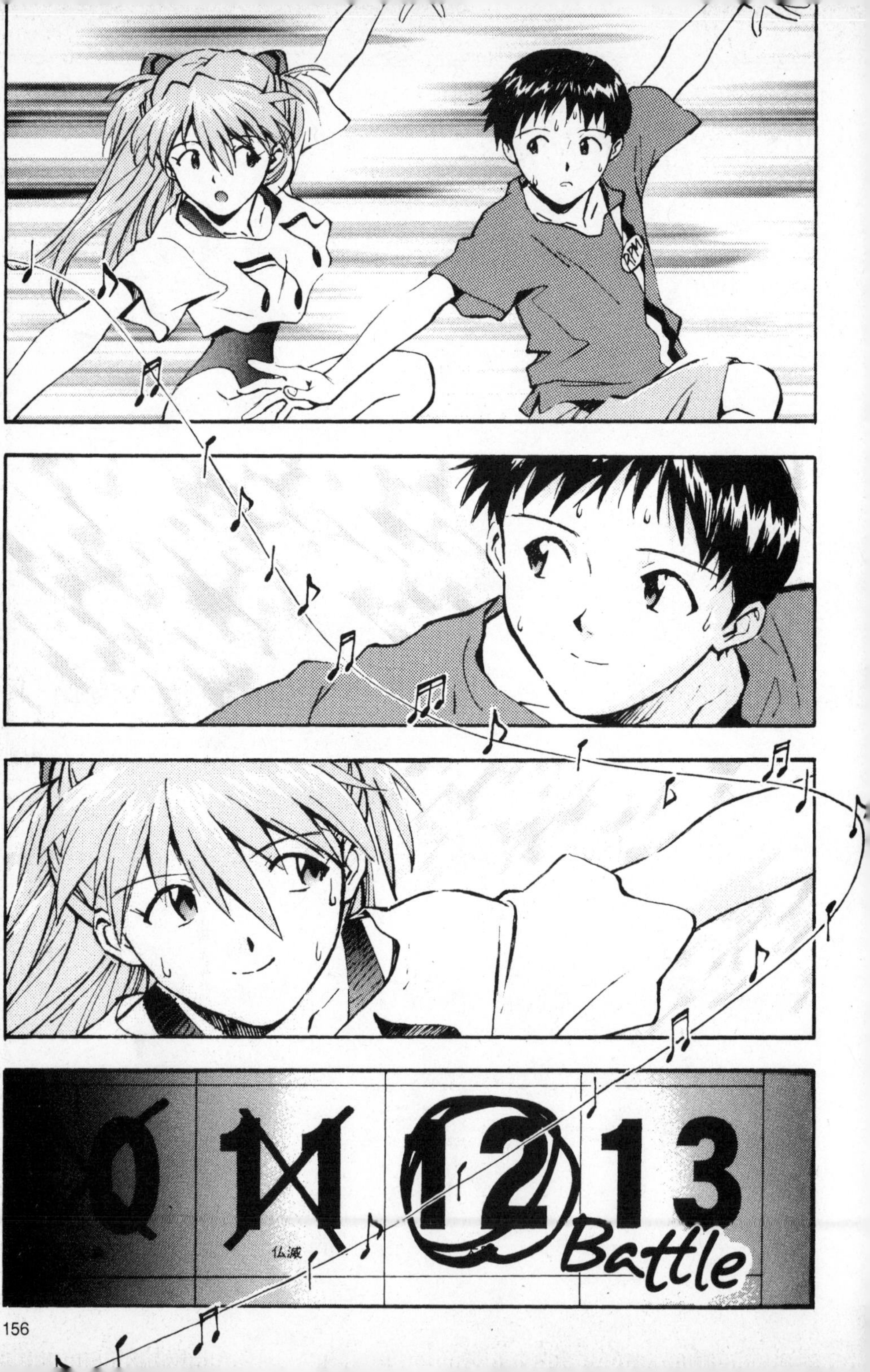

11
12
13
仏滅
Battle

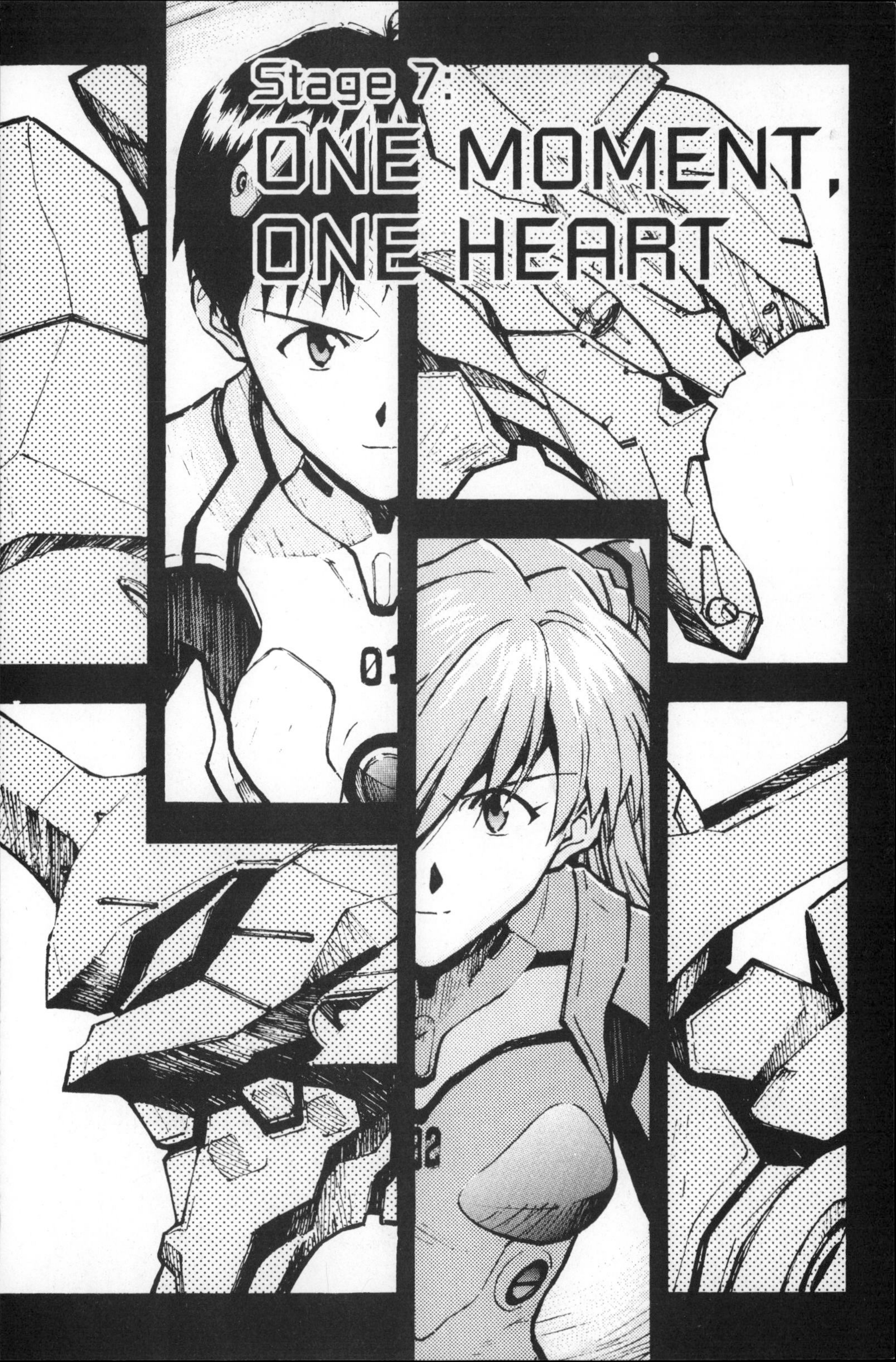
Stage 7:
ONE MOMENT, ONE HEART
01
02

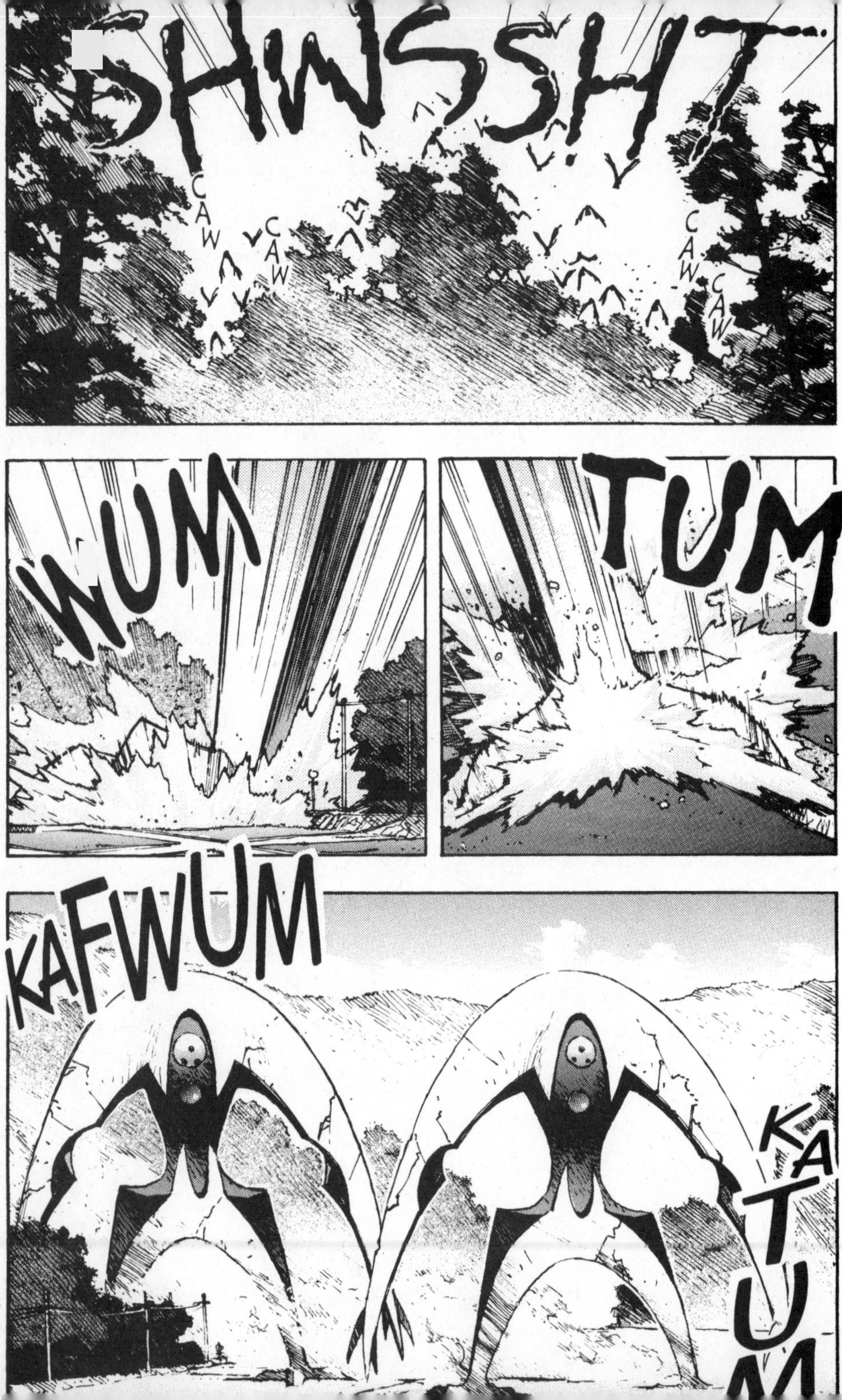
SHWSSHT
CAW
CAW
CAW
CAW
WUM
TUM
KAFWUM
KATUM

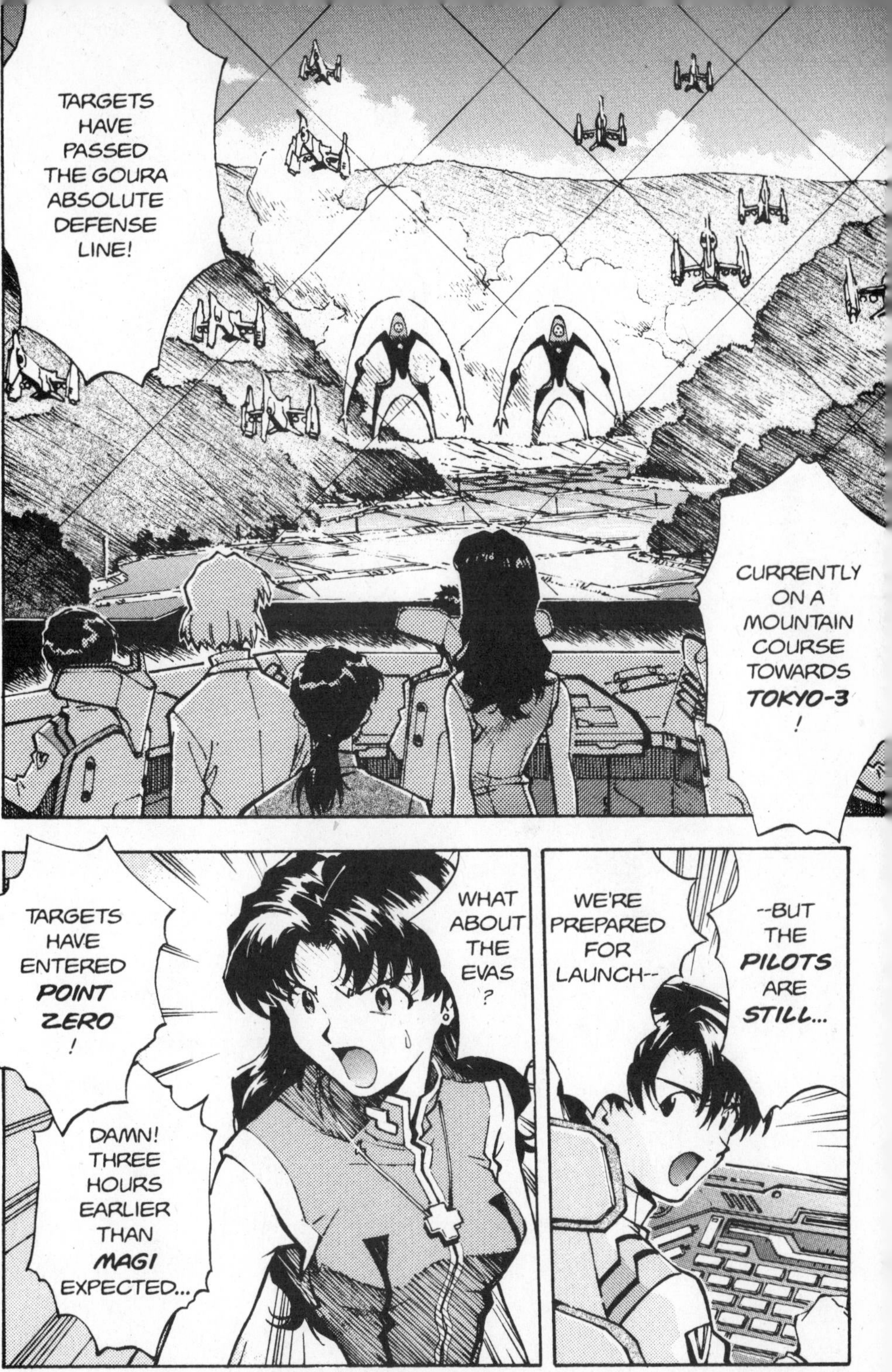
TARGETS HAVE PASSED THE GOURA ABSOLUTE DEFENSE LINE!
CURRENTLY ON A MOUNTAIN COURSE TOWARDS TOKYO-3!
TARGETS HAVE ENTERED POINT ZERO!
DAMN! THREE HOURS EARLIER THAN MAGI EXPECTED...
WHAT ABOUT THE EVAS?
WE'RE PREPARED FOR LAUNCH--
--BUT THE PILOTS ARE STILL...

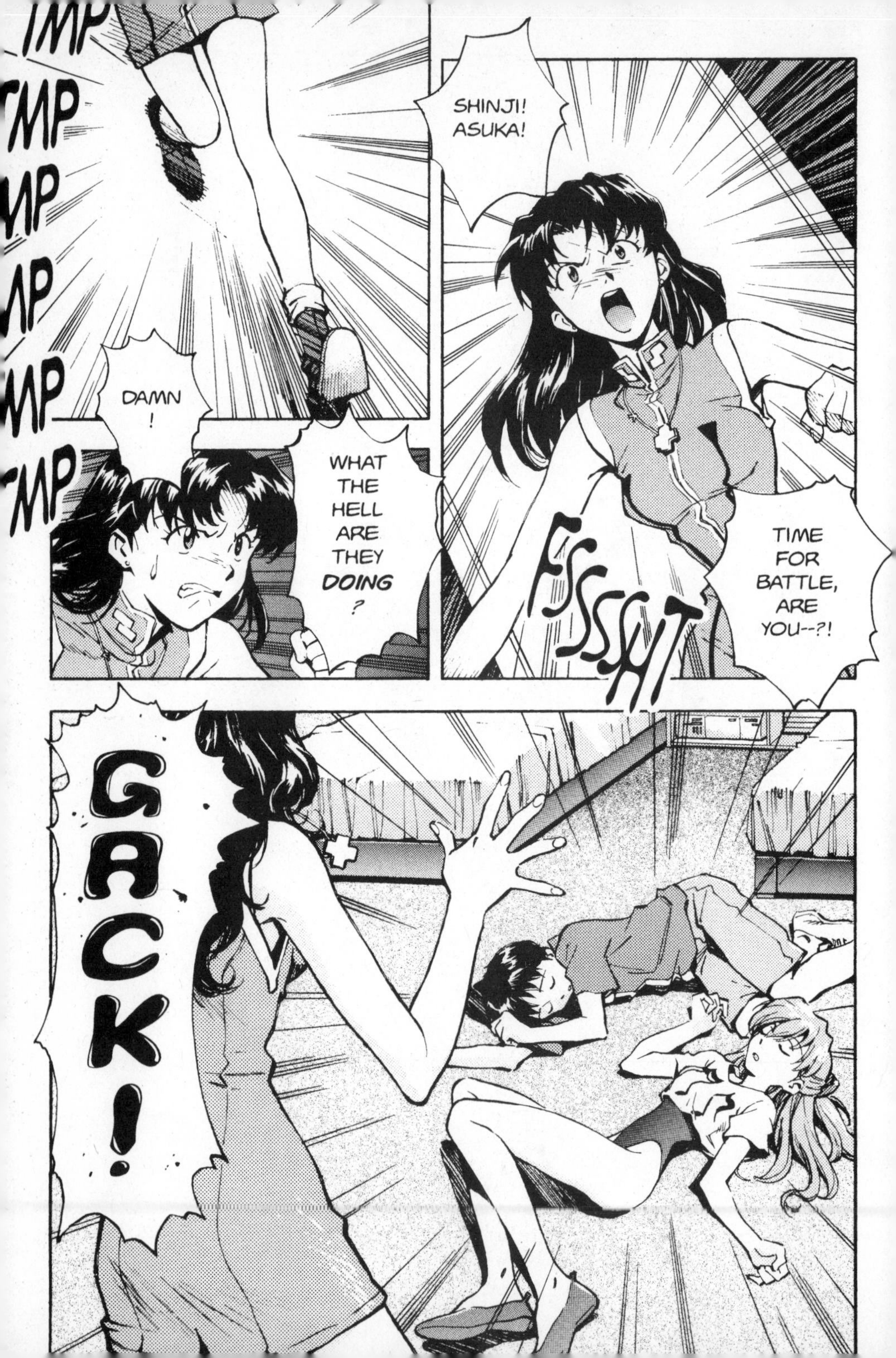

IMP
TMP
MP
MP
MP
TMP
DAMN!
WHAT THE HELL ARE THEY DOING?
SHINJI! ASUKA!
FSSSHT
TIME FOR BATTLE, ARE YOU--?!
GACK!

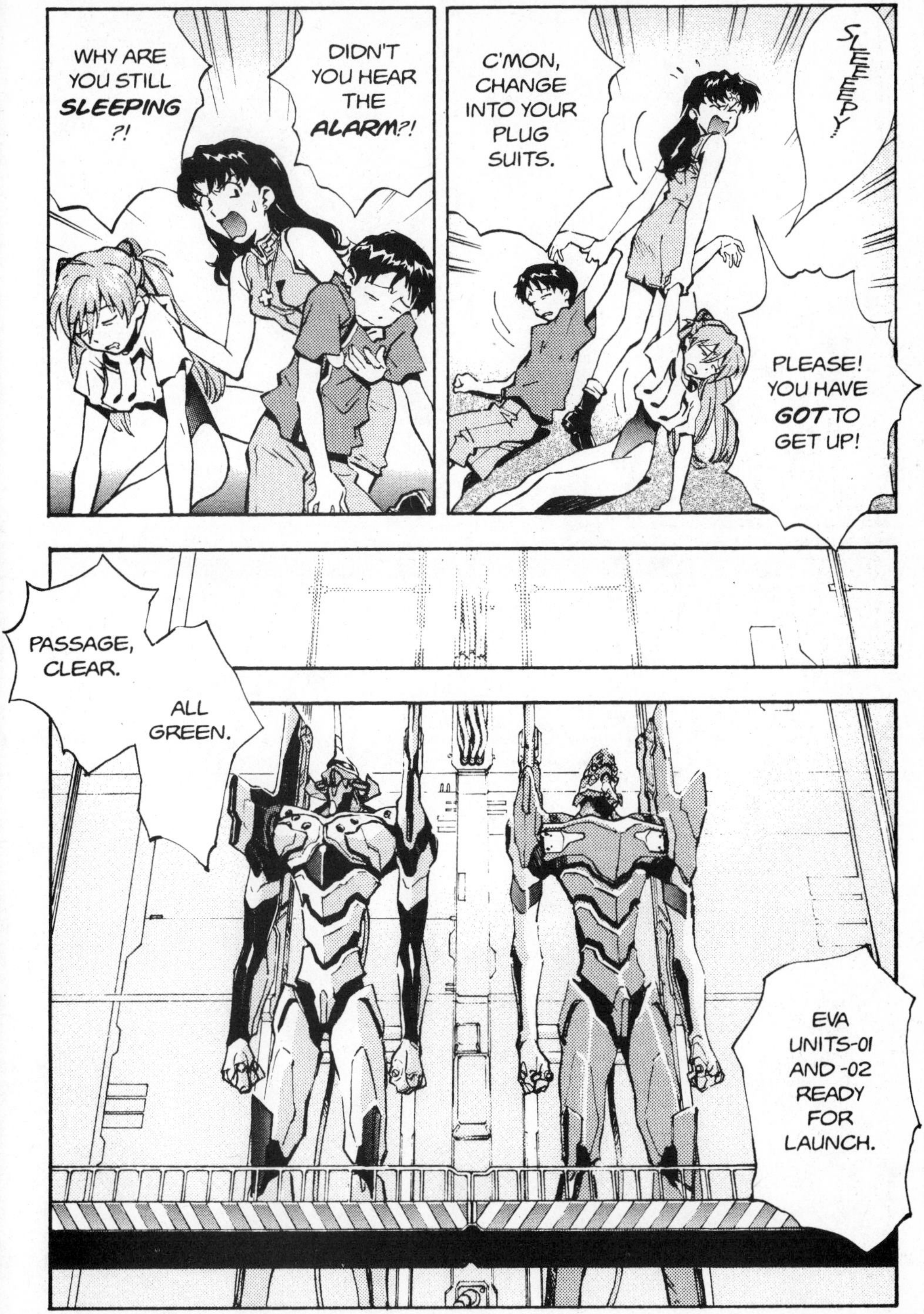
WHY ARE YOU STILL SLEEPING?!
DIDN'T YOU HEAR THE ALARM?!
C'MON, CHANGE INTO YOUR PLUG SUITS.
SLEEEEPY...
PLEASE! YOU HAVE GOT TO GET UP!
PASSAGE, CLEAR.
ALL GREEN.
EVA UNITS-01 AND -02 READY FOR LAUNCH.

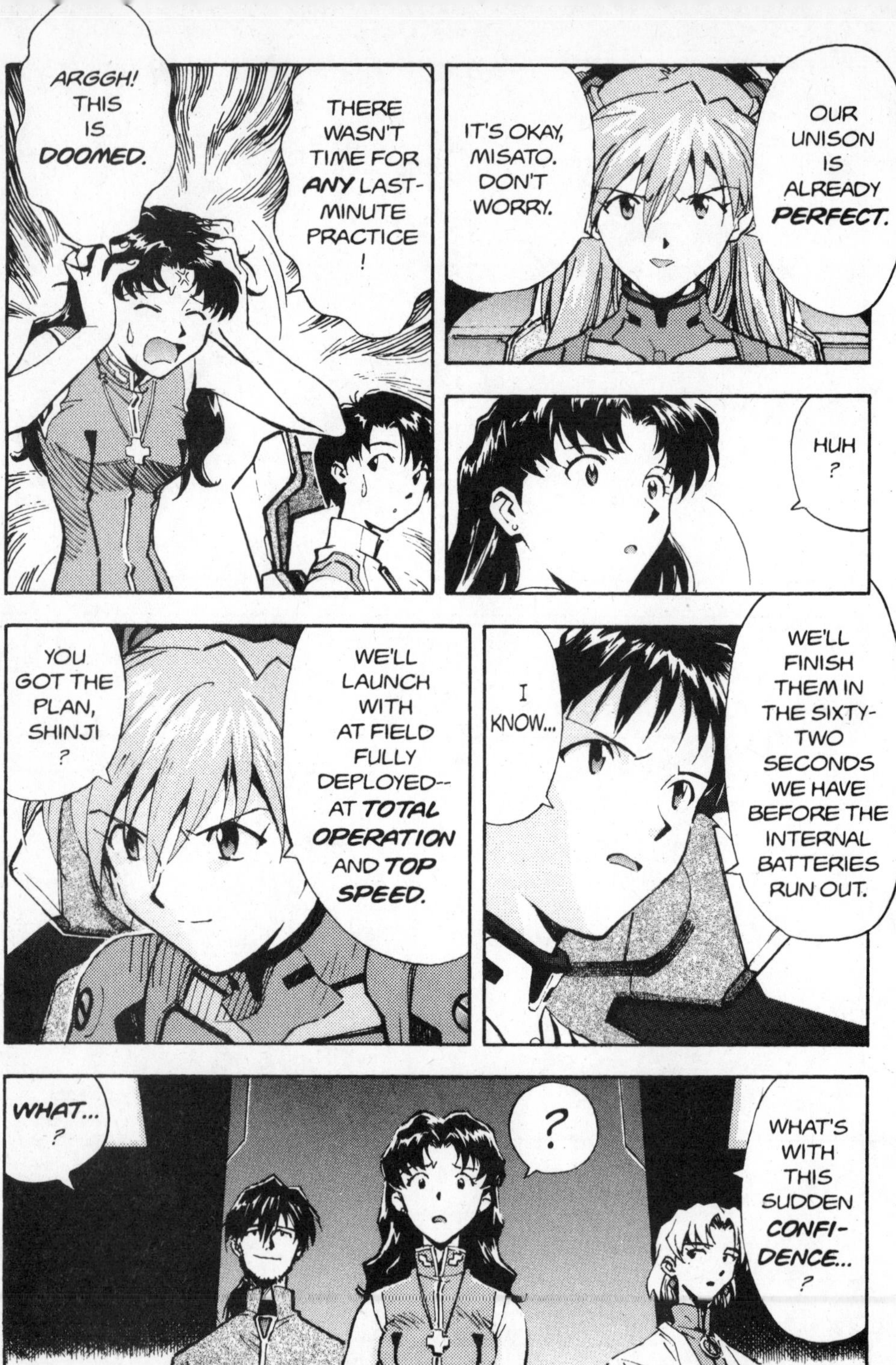
ARGGH! THIS IS **DOOMED.**
THERE WASN'T TIME FOR **ANY** LAST-MINUTE PRACTICE!
IT'S OKAY, MISATO. DON'T WORRY.
OUR UNISON IS ALREADY **PERFECT.**
HUH?
YOU GOT THE PLAN, SHINJI?
WE'LL LAUNCH WITH AT FIELD FULLY DEPLOYED--AT **TOTAL OPERATION** AND **TOP SPEED.**
I KNOW...
WE'LL FINISH THEM IN THE SIXTY-TWO SECONDS WE HAVE BEFORE THE INTERNAL BATTERIES RUN OUT.
WHAT...?
?
WHAT'S WITH THIS SUDDEN **CONFIDENCE...?**

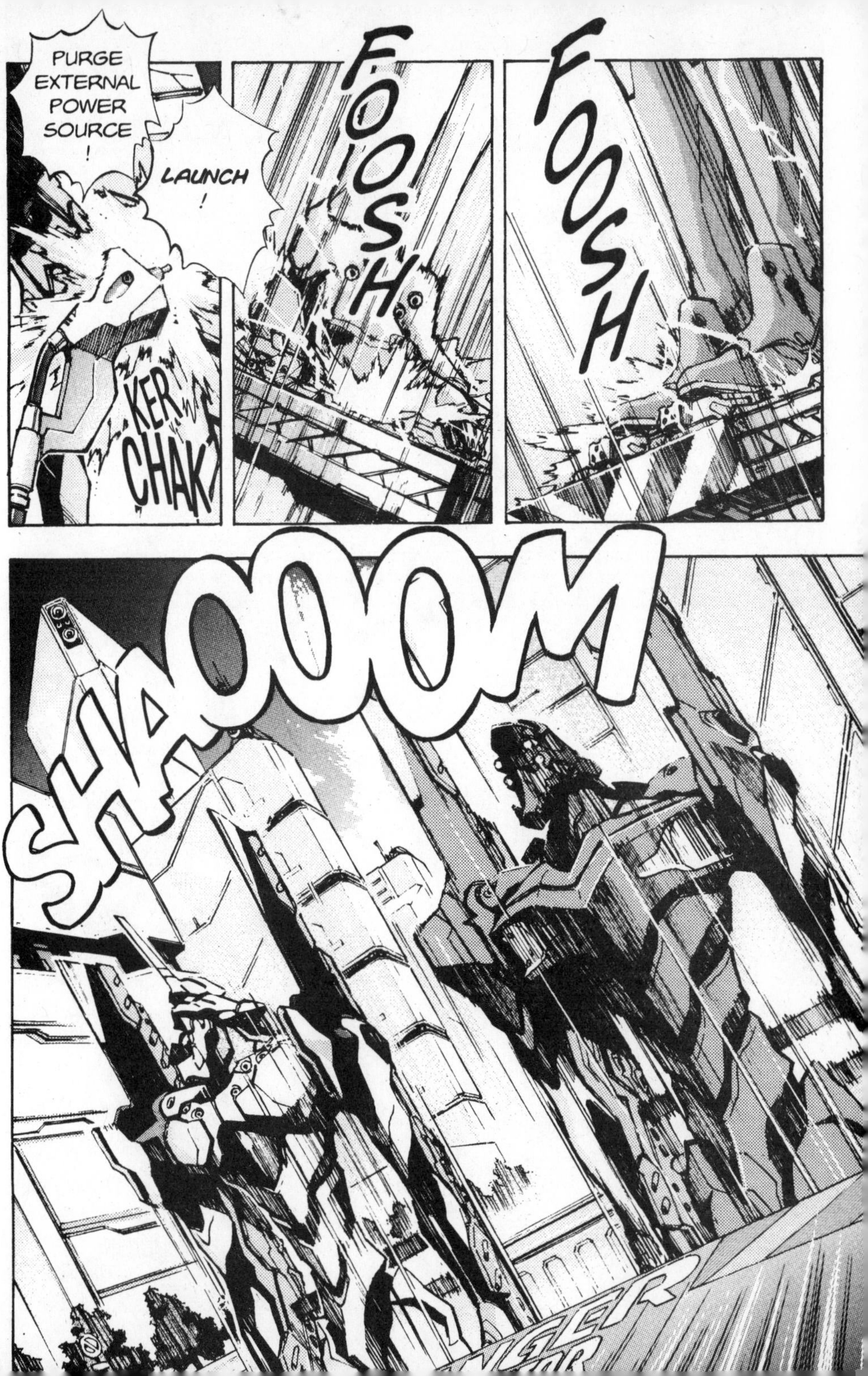
PURGE EXTERNAL POWER SOURCE!
LAUNCH!
KER CHAK
FOOSH
FOOSH
SHAOOOM

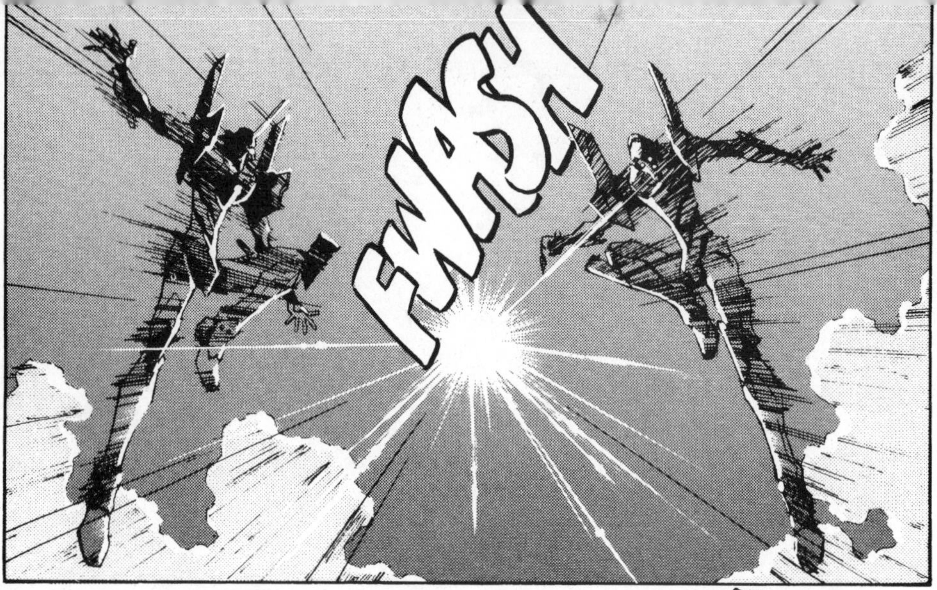
FWAS!

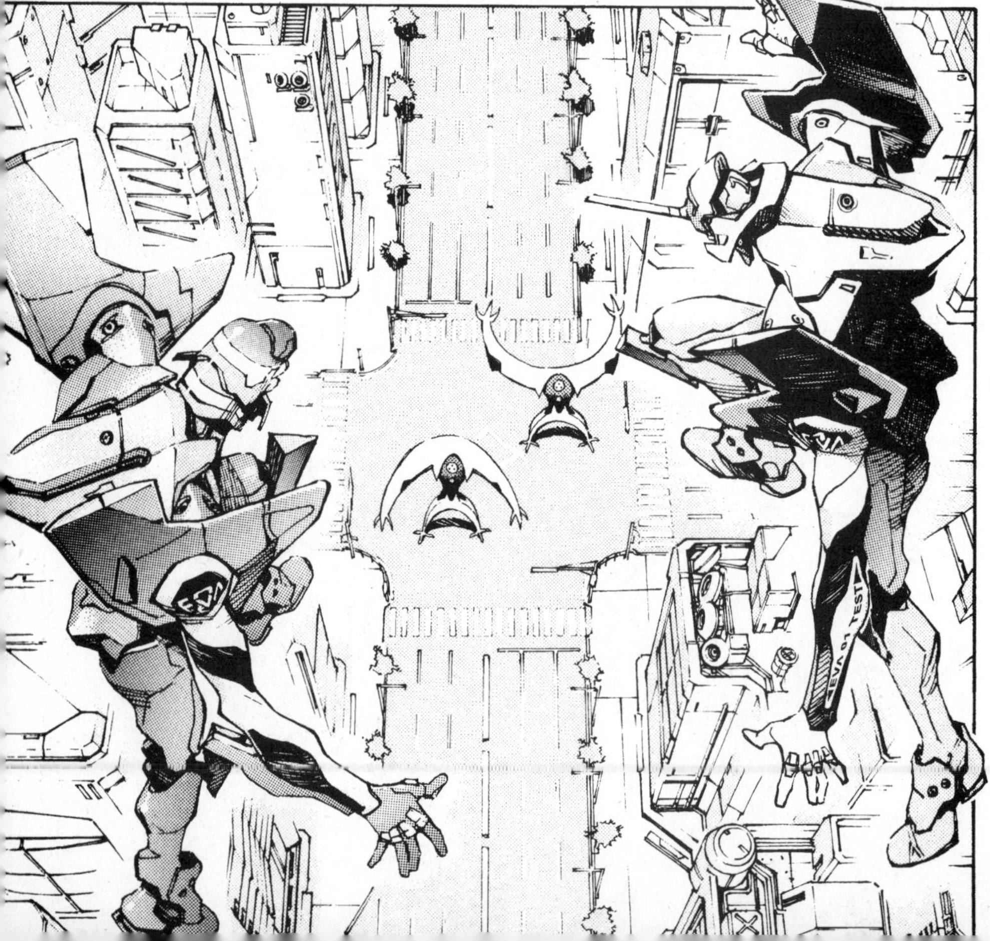
EVA 01 TEST

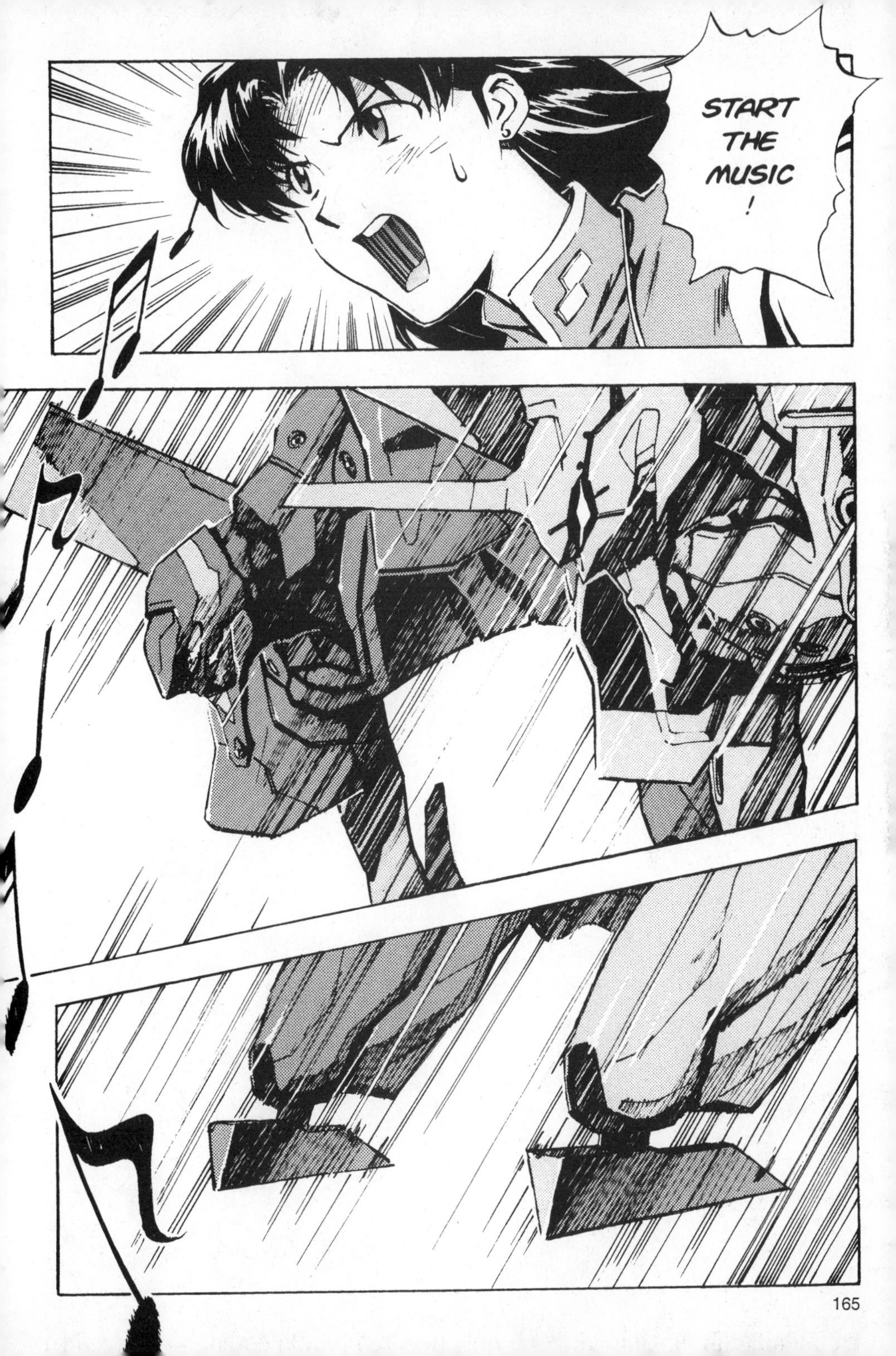
START THE MUSIC !

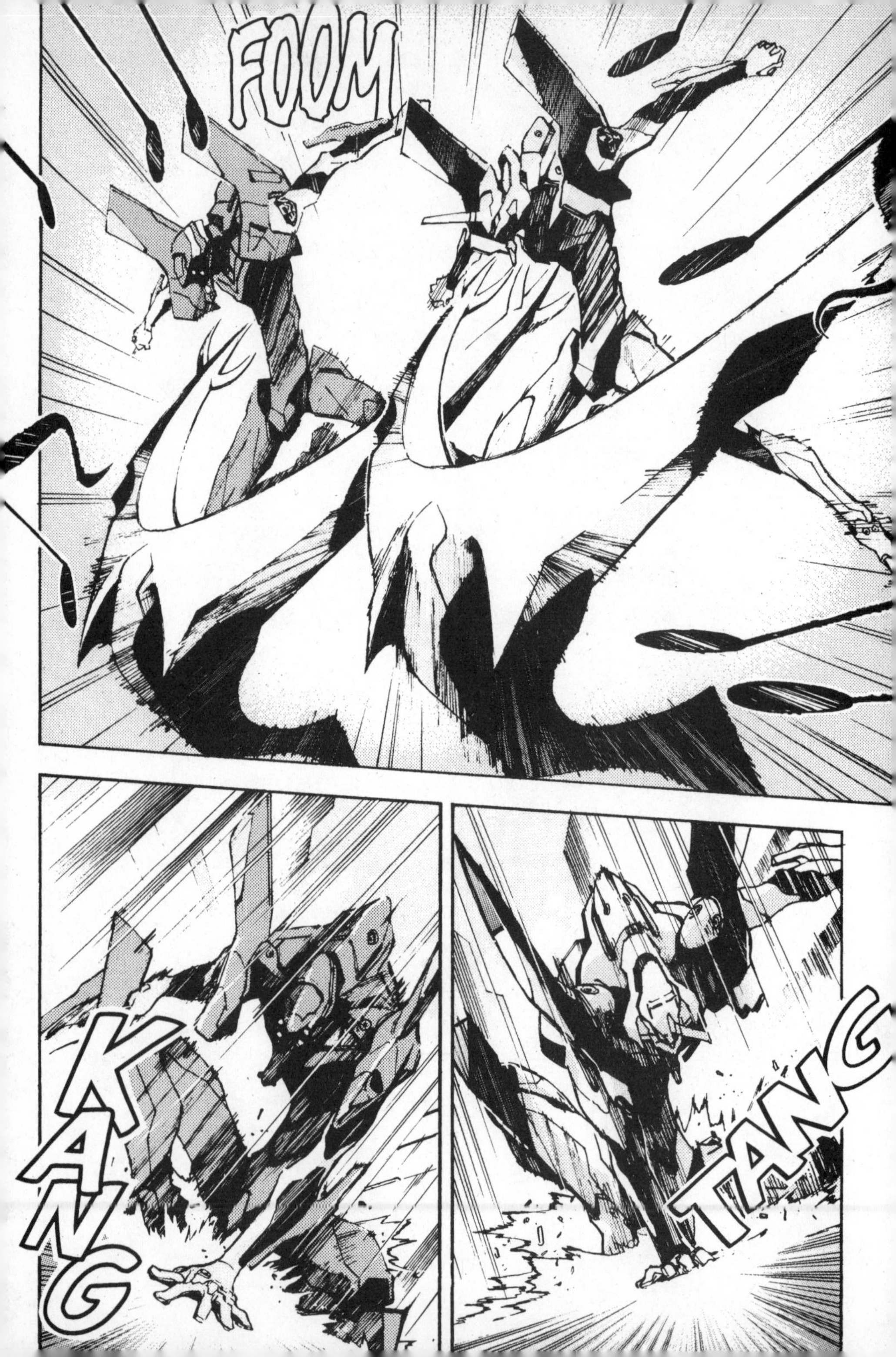
FOOM
KANG
TANG

WOW! PERFECT HARMONY!

THIS LOOKS *GOOD*!

KATONK

CHONK

VWIP

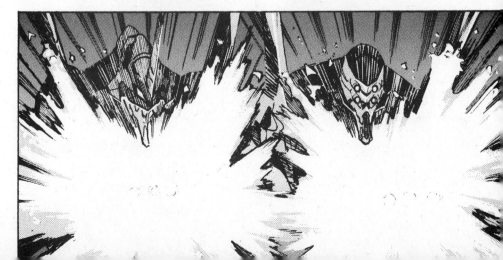

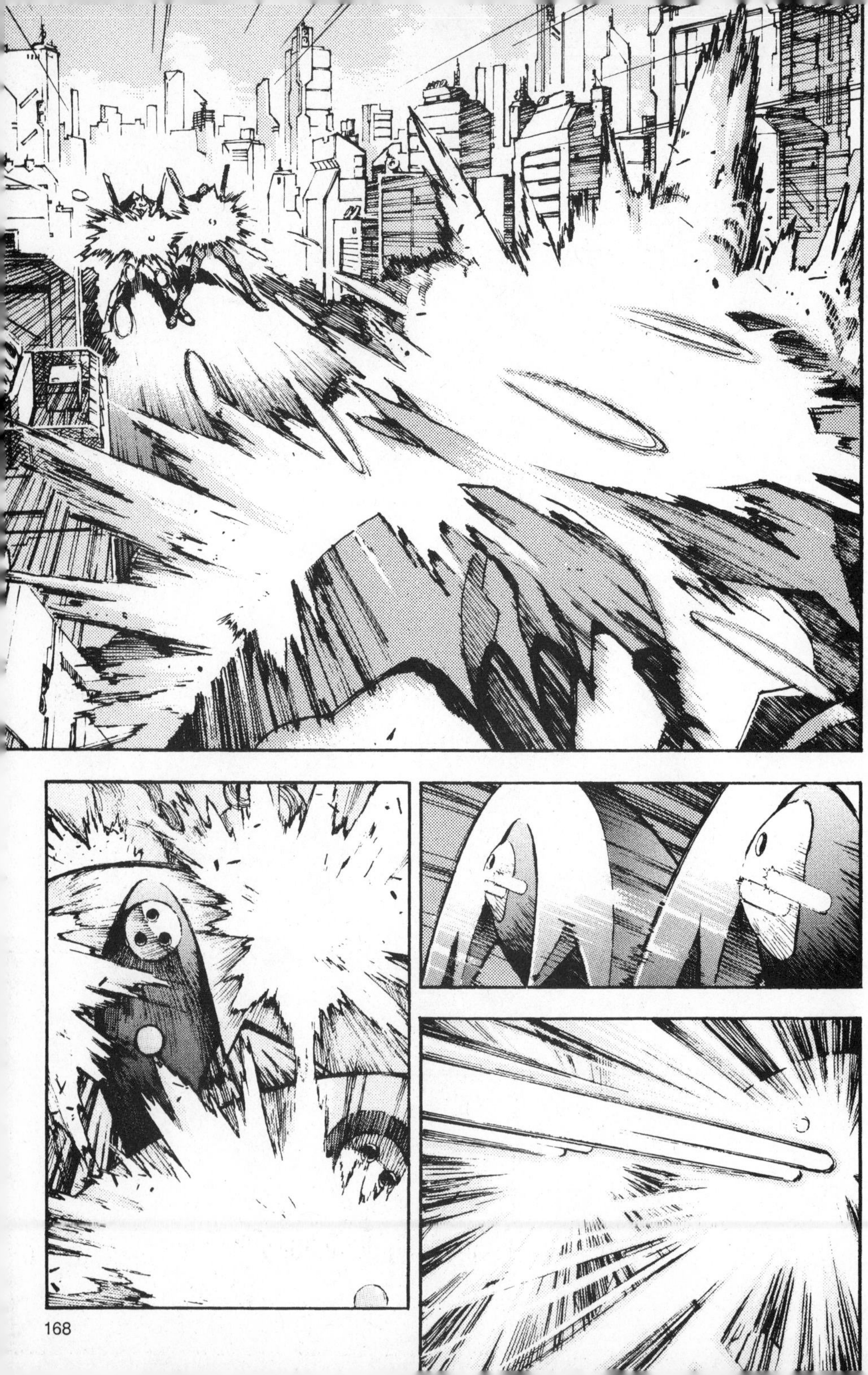

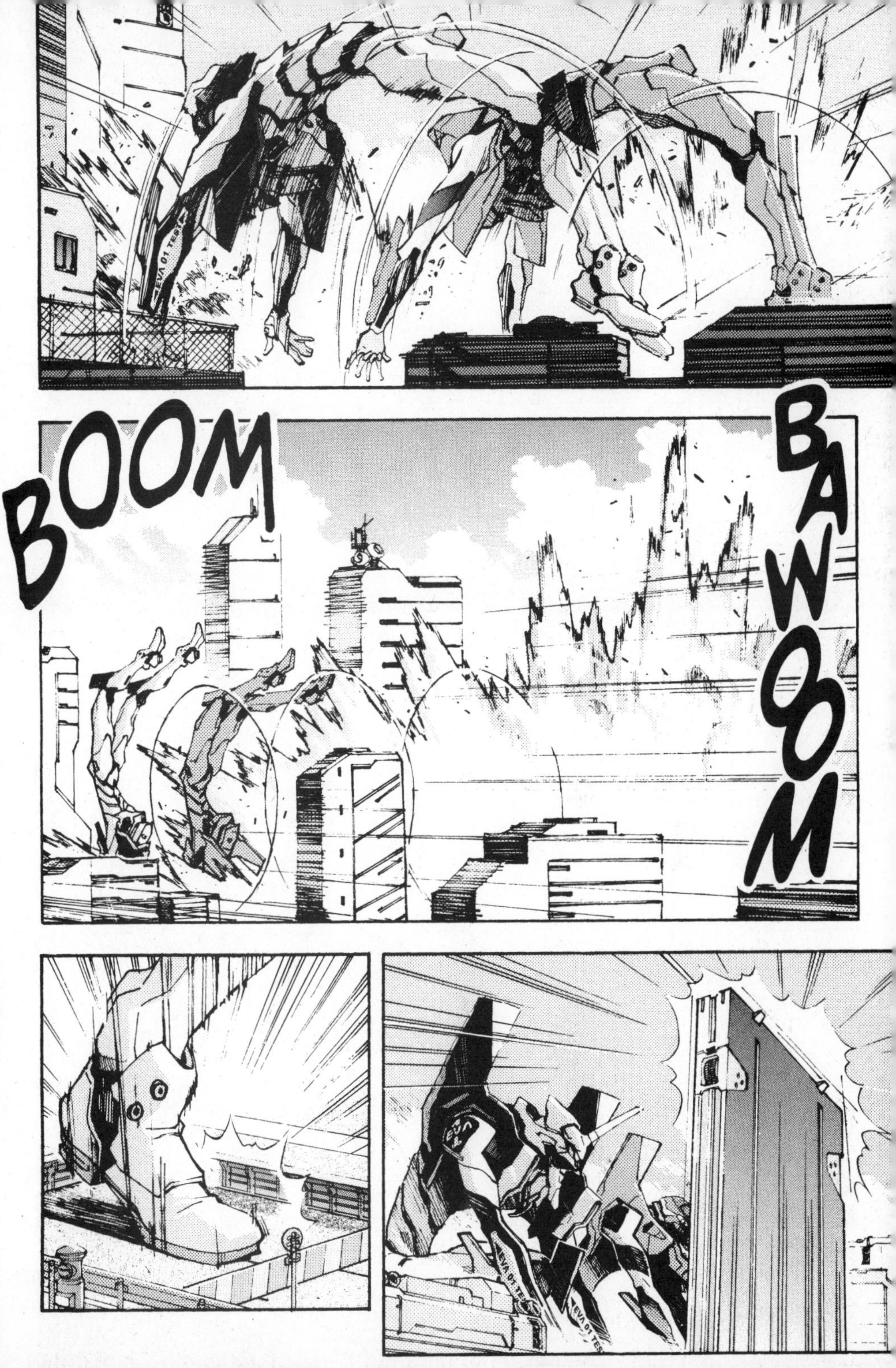
EVA 01 TEST
BOOM
BAWOOM

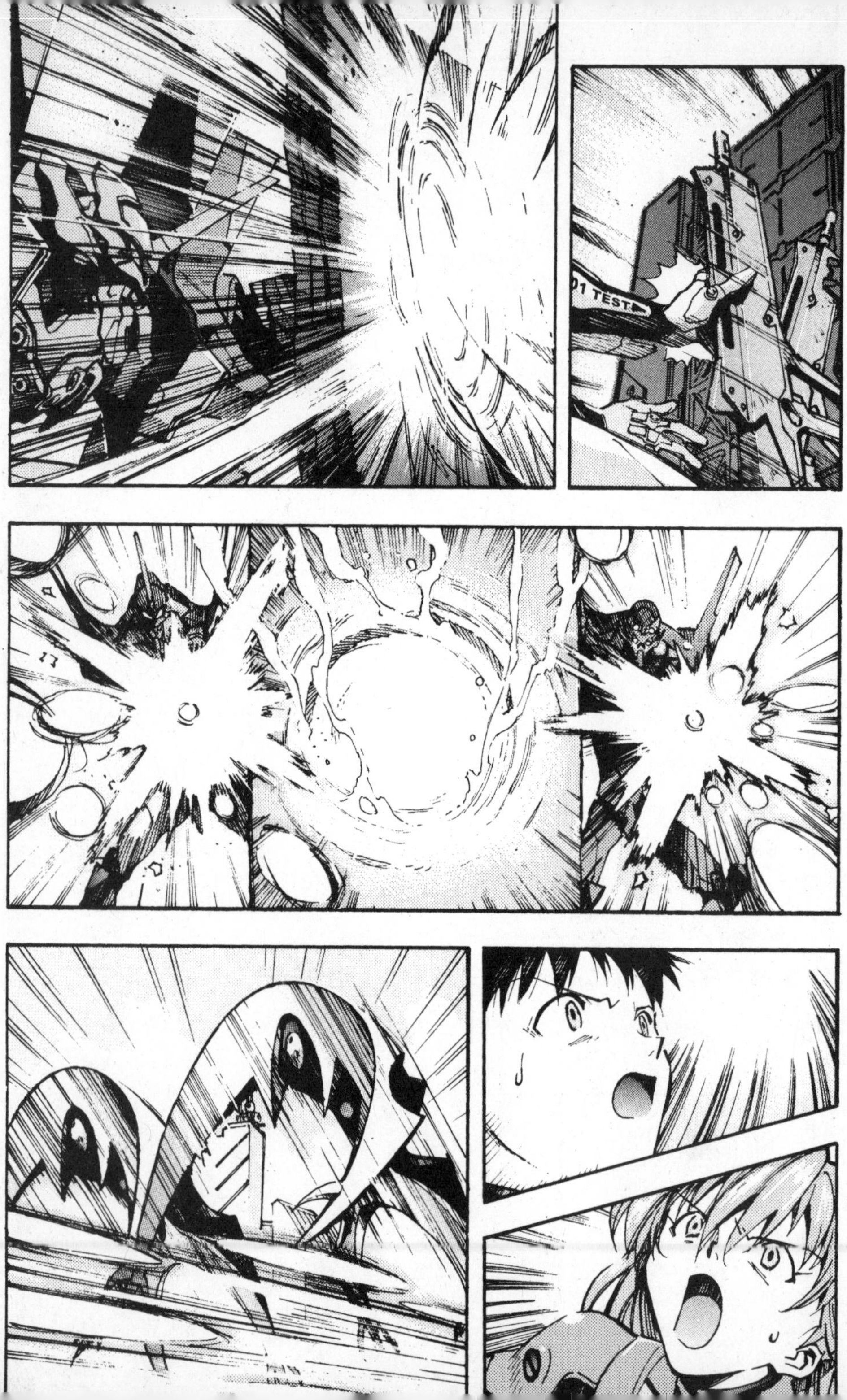
01 TEST

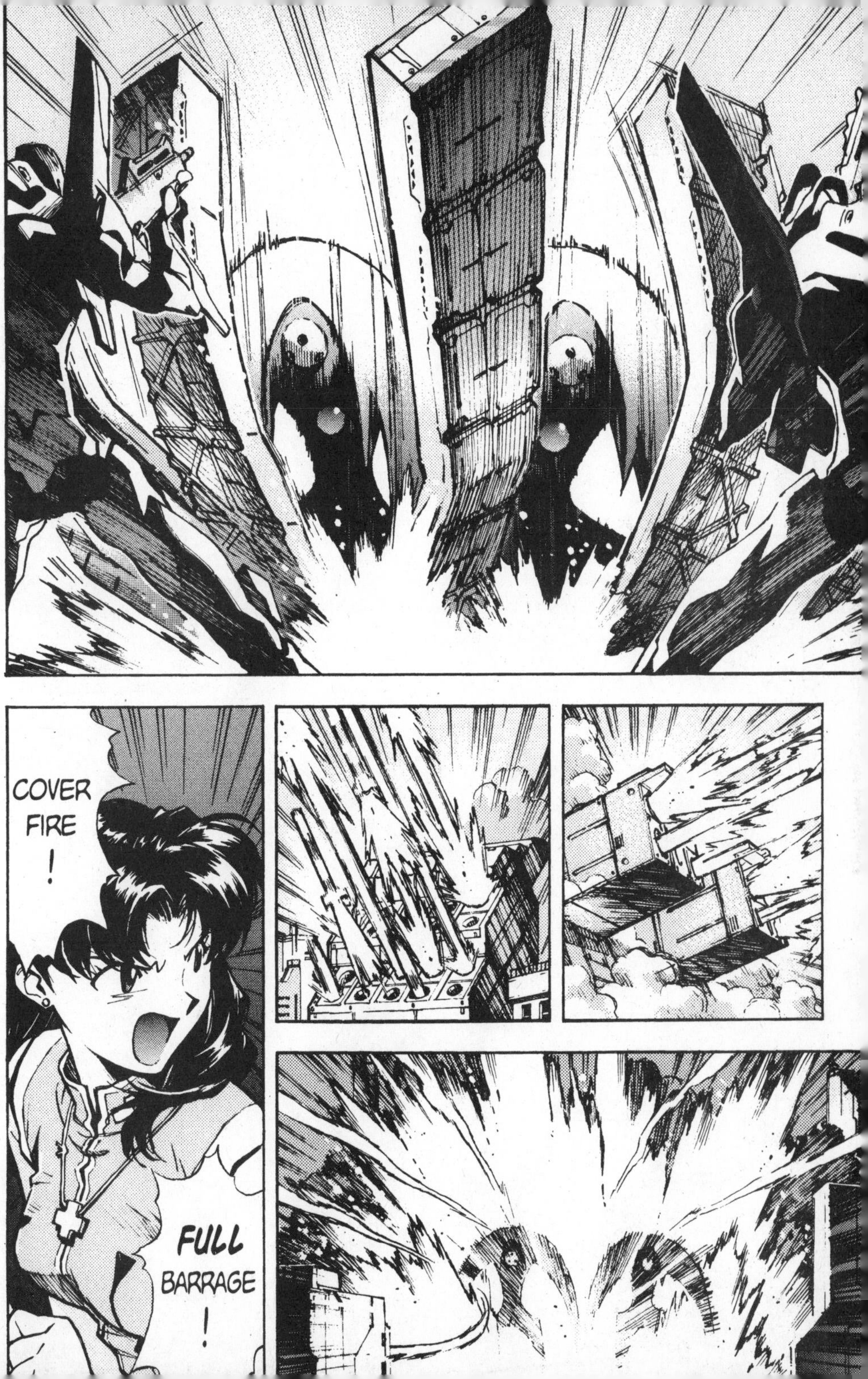
COVER FIRE !
FULL BARRAGE !

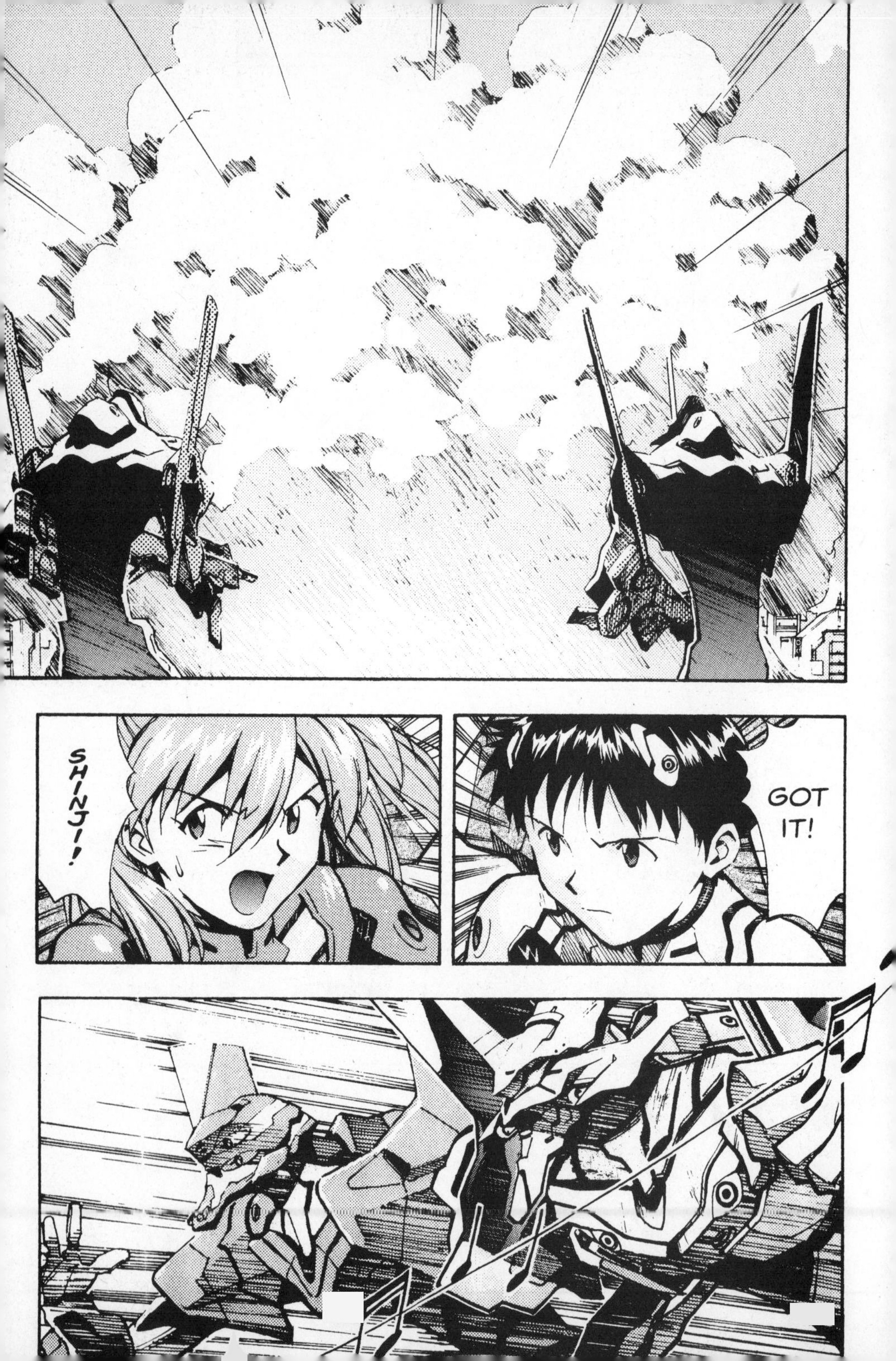
SHINJI!
GOT IT!

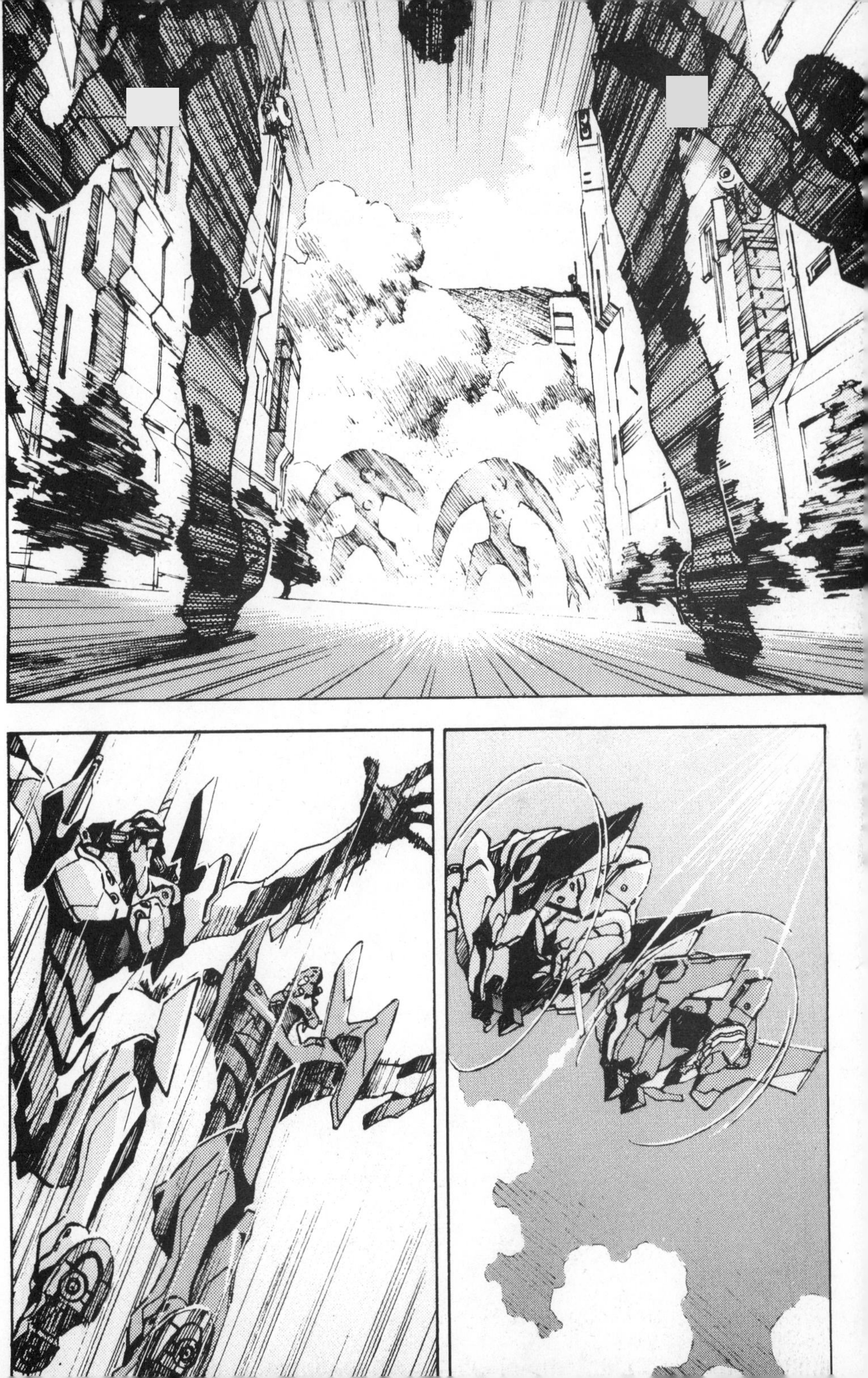

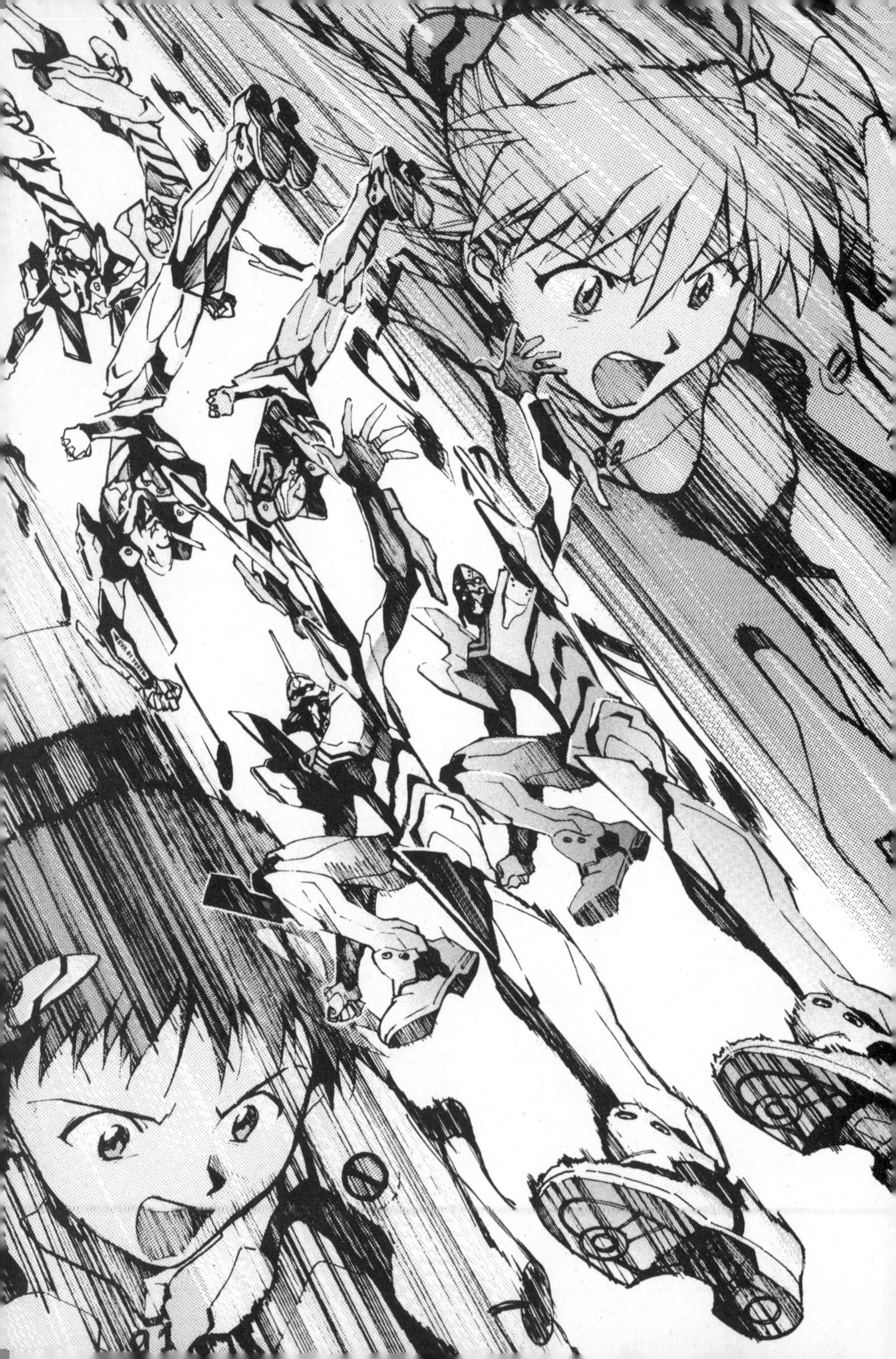

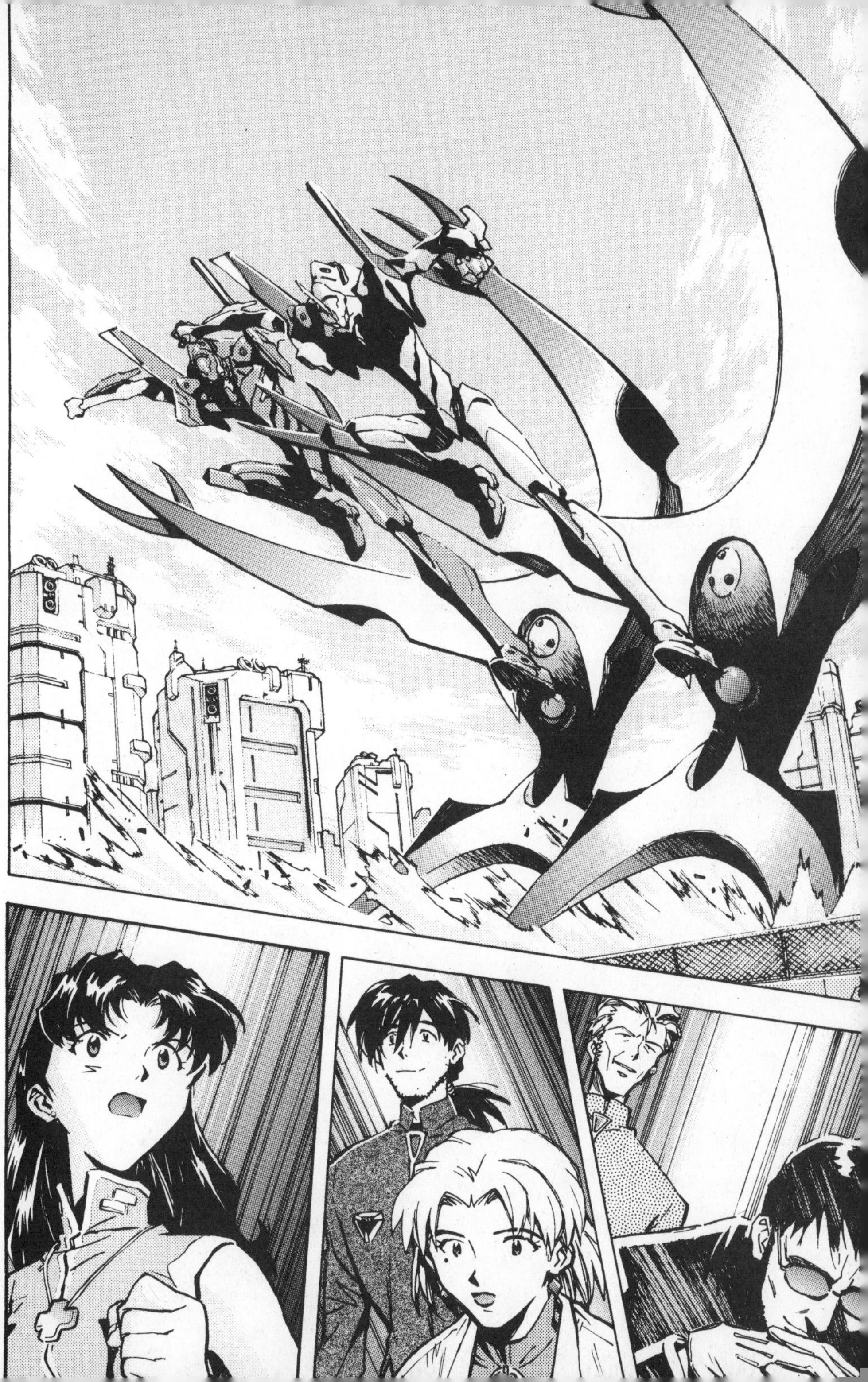

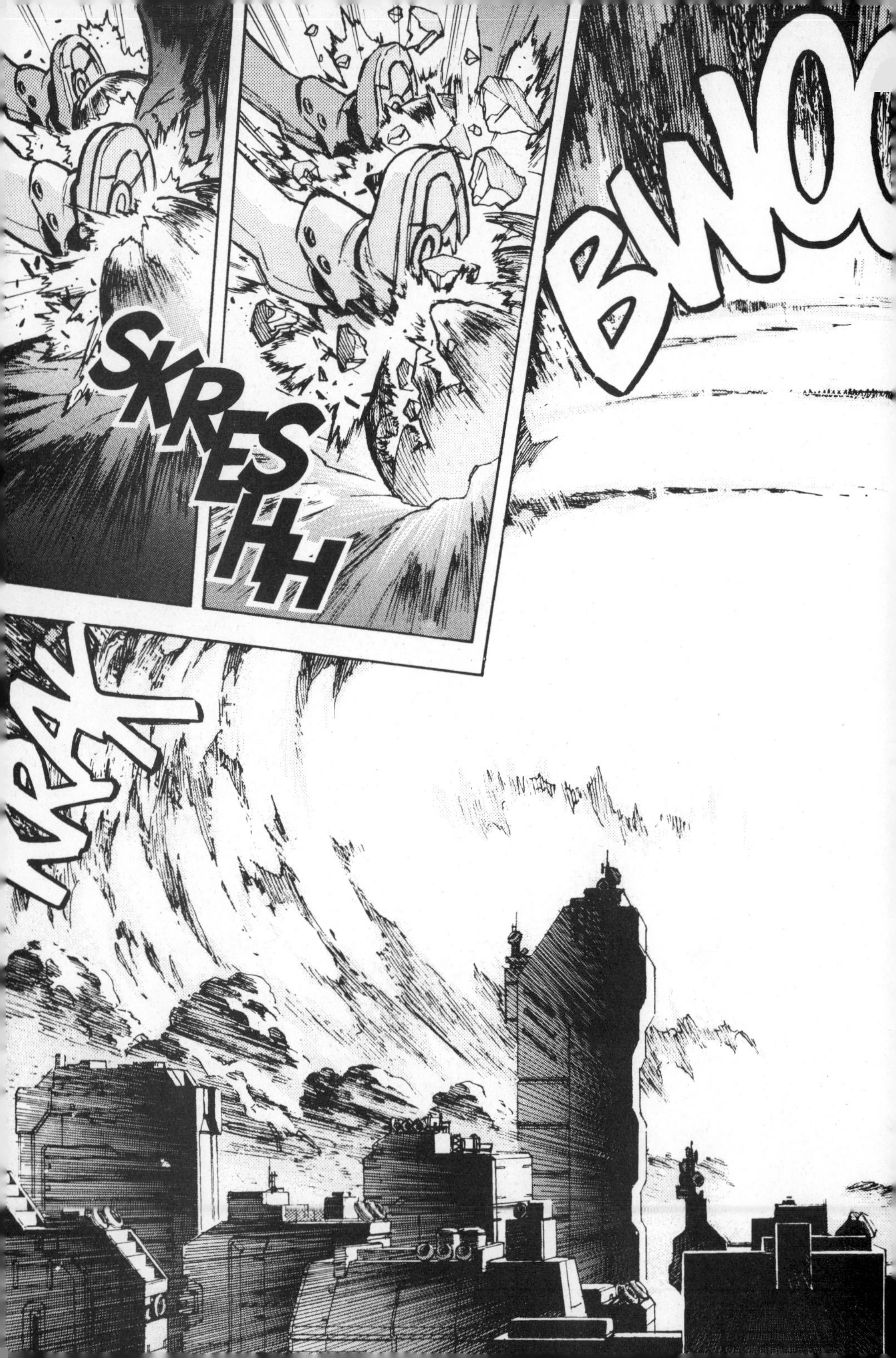
SKRESHHH
BWOO

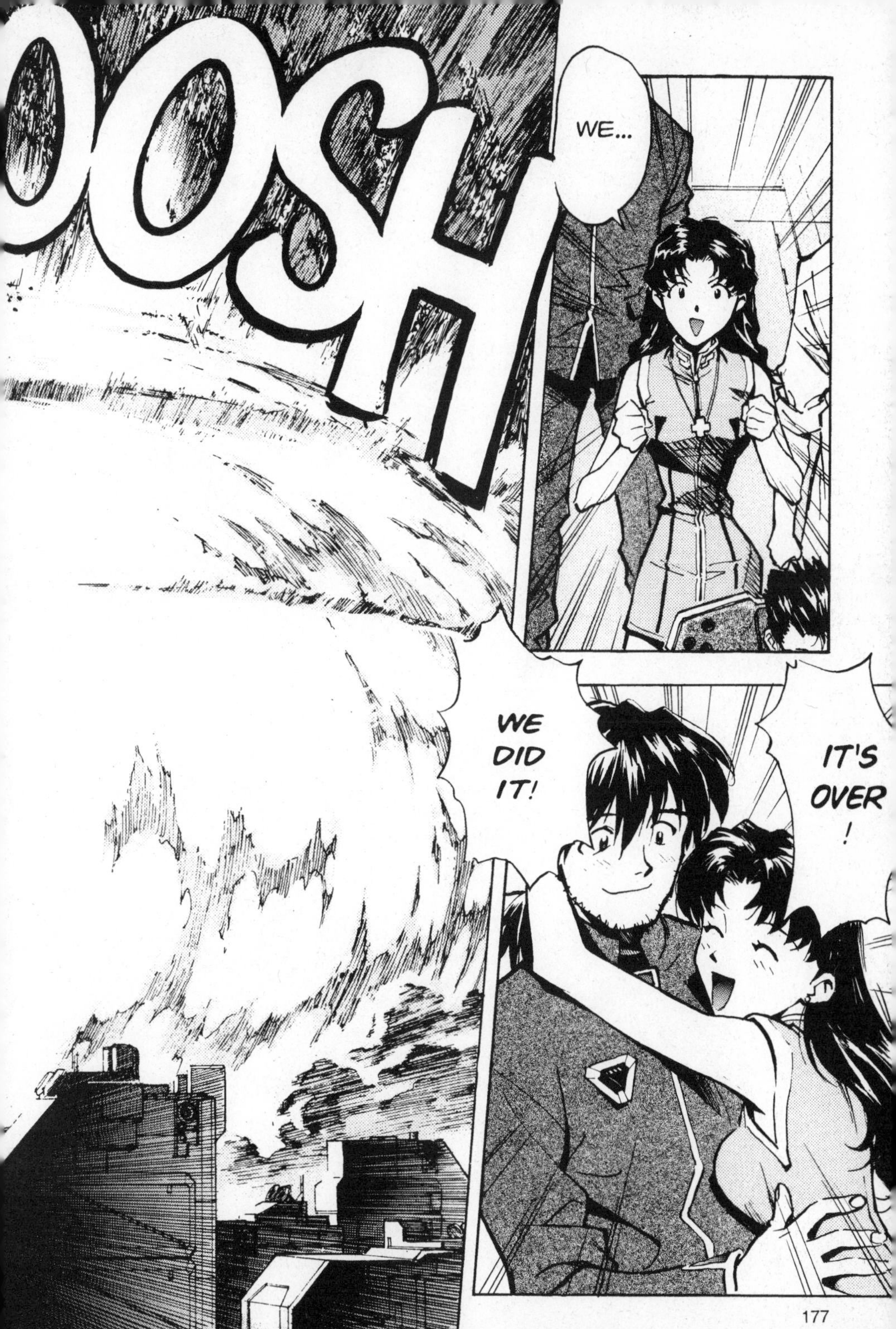
OOSH!
WE...
WE DID IT!
IT'S OVER!

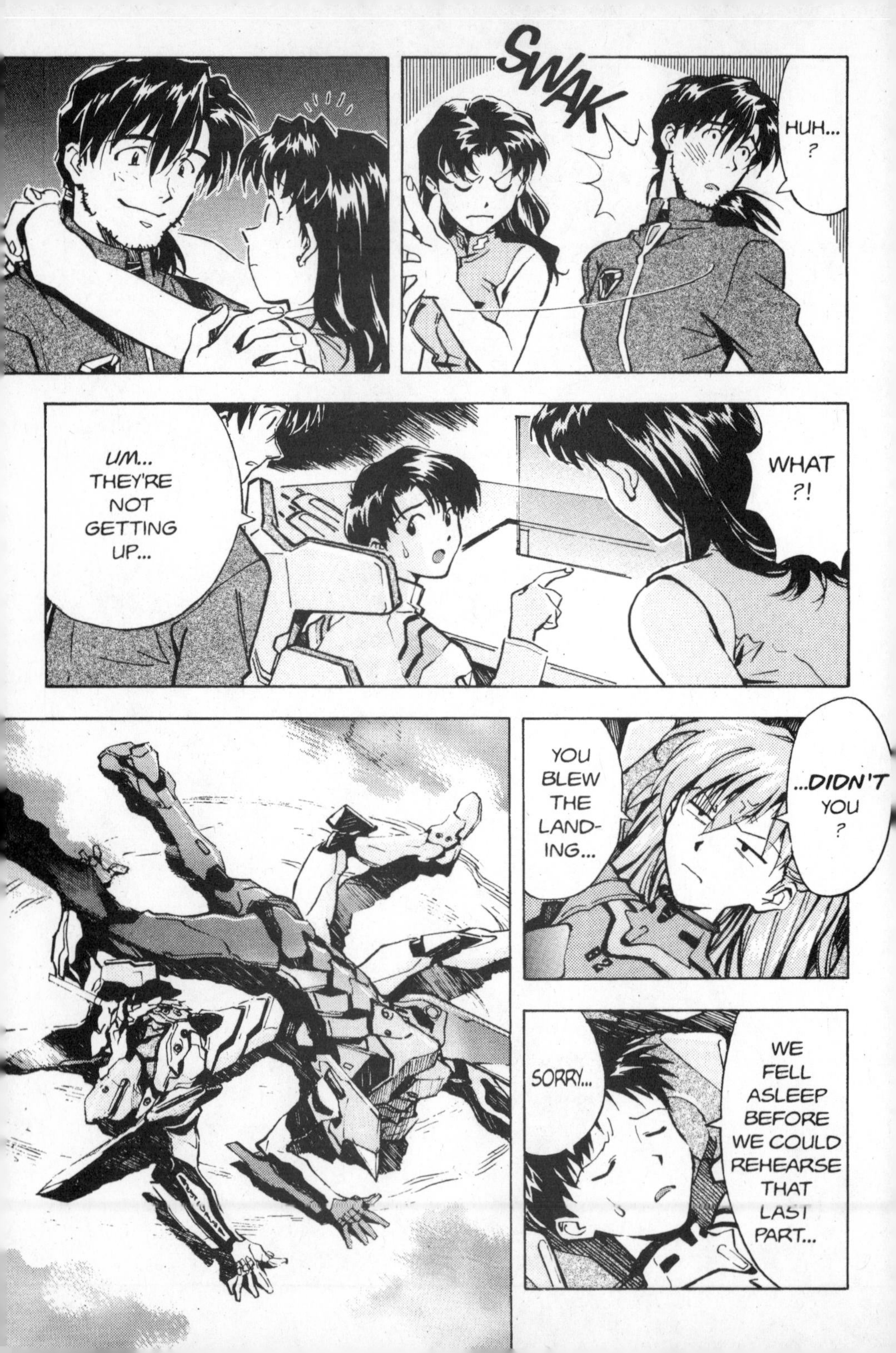
SWAK
HUH... ?
UM... THEY'RE NOT GETTING UP...
WHAT ?!
YOU BLEW THE LAND-ING...
...DIDN'T YOU ?
SORRY...
WE FELL ASLEEP BEFORE WE COULD REHEARSE THAT LAST PART...

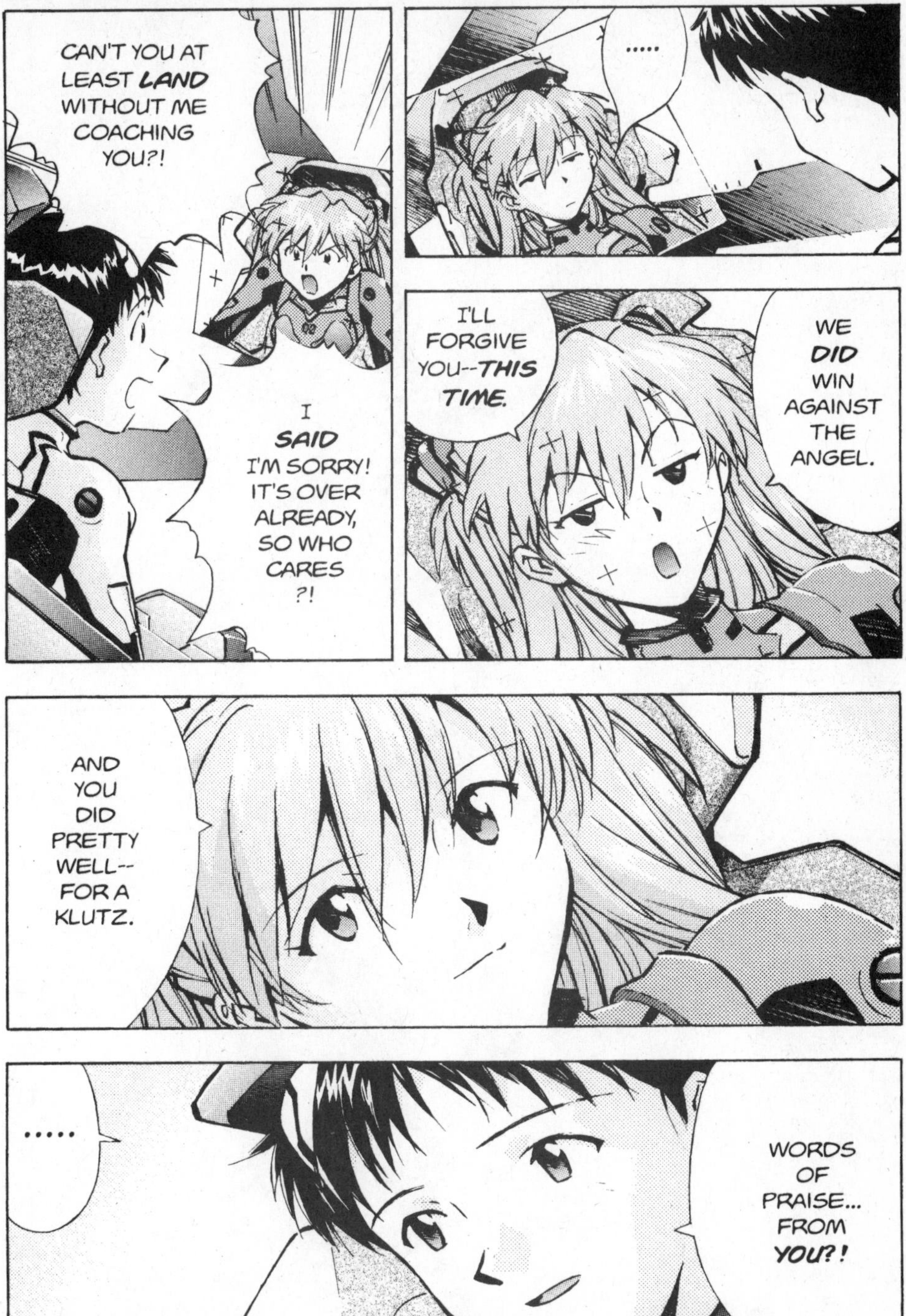
CAN'T YOU AT LEAST LAND WITHOUT ME COACHING YOU?!
I SAID I'M SORRY! IT'S OVER ALREADY, SO WHO CARES ?!
.....
I'LL FORGIVE YOU--THIS TIME.
WE DID WIN AGAINST THE ANGEL.
AND YOU DID PRETTY WELL--FOR A KLUTZ.
.....
WORDS OF PRAISE... FROM YOU?!

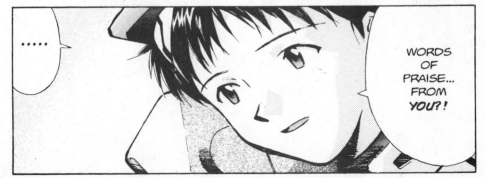

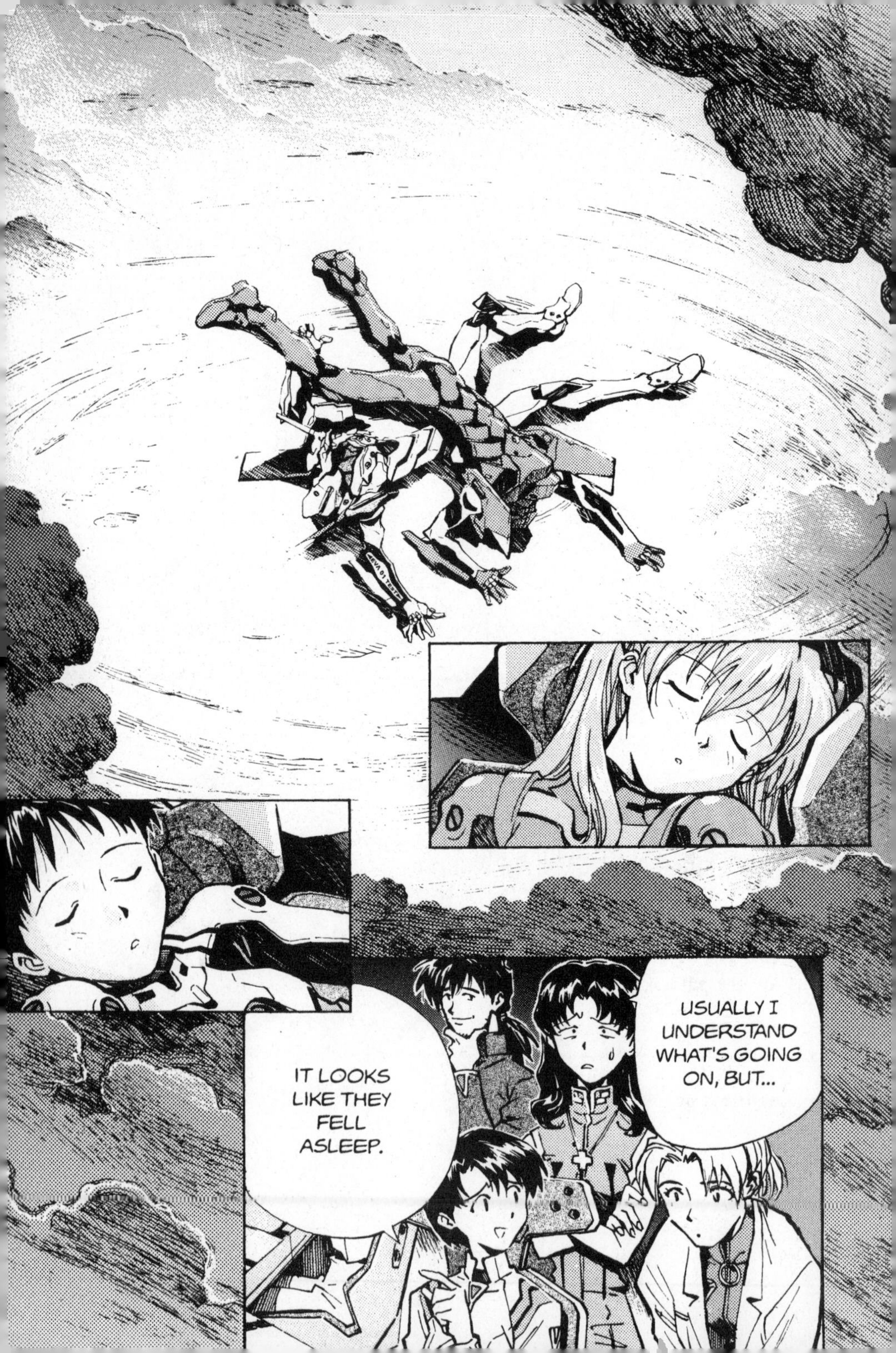
IT LOOKS LIKE THEY FELL ASLEEP.
USUALLY I UNDERSTAND WHAT'S GOING ON, BUT...

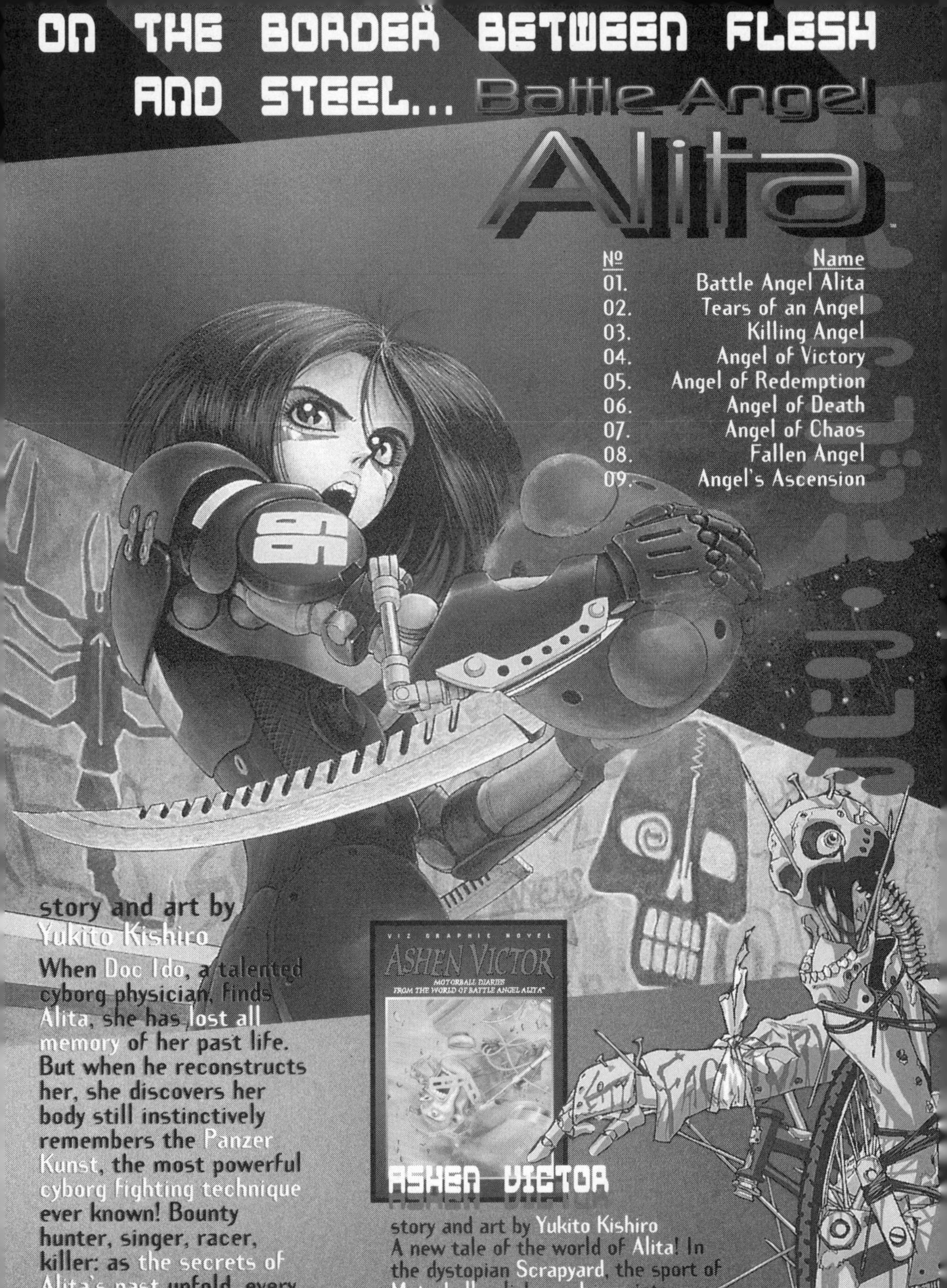

ON THE BORDER BETWEEN FLESH AND STEEL... Battle Angel Alita

story and art by
Yukito Kishiro

When Doc Ido, a talented cyborg physician, finds Alita, she has lost all memory of her past life. But when he reconstructs her, she discovers her body still instinctively remembers the Panzer Kunst, the most powerful cyborg fighting technique ever known! Bounty hunter, singer, racer, killer: as the secrets of Alita's past unfold, every day is a struggle for survival...

ASHEN VICTOR

VIZ GRAPHIC NOVEL
ASHEN VICTOR
MOTORBALL DIARIES FROM THE WORLD OF BATTLE ANGEL ALITA

story and art by Yukito Kishiro
A new tale of the world of Alita! In the dystopian Scrapyard, the sport of Motorball polishes cyborgs into winners ... or grinds them beneath the wheels of competition and death.

step over the edge

japan edge

The Insider's Guide to Japanese Pop Subculture

"The time is ripe. Already many of Japan's pop signifiers have firmly twisted their way into the Western world..."
—Patrick Macias

"The ultimate, most sincere subculture will always be the individual."
—Carl Gustav Horn

LIVE

ANIME
ACTION
MUSIC
MANGA
NOISE

The hottest guide to anime, manga, Japanese music, and more, written by fans whose lives were changed by it! Four young writers share their passion for Japan in a mix of guidebook and autobiography with insights for both new and experienced otaku. Includes tons of artwork; reading, viewing, and listening guides; historical information and current news. Confessional, daring ... step across the Pacific and over the edge!

by Carl Gustav Horn, Mason Jones, Patrick Macias and Yuji Oniki

black & white, 200 pages
$19.95

CADENCE BOOKS VIZ

ARMAGEDDON FILLS THE CRUMBLING SKY

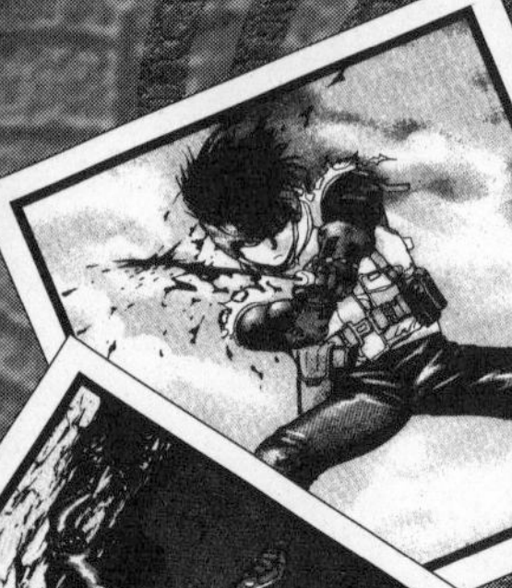

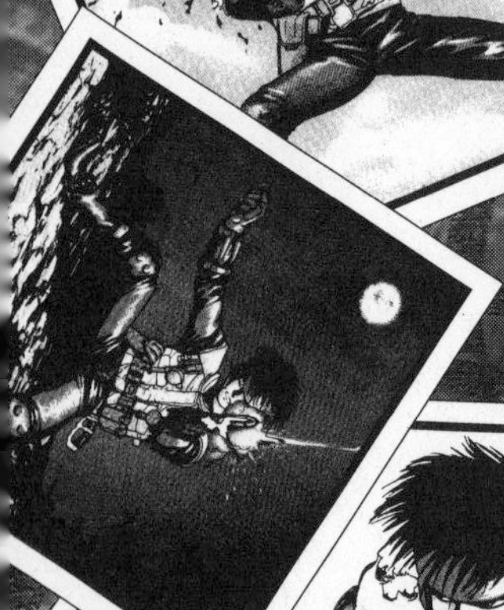

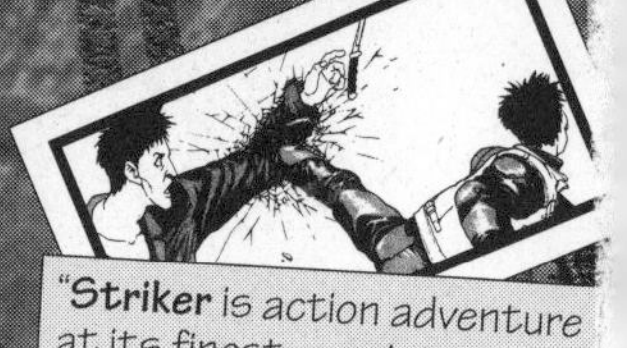

On the threshold of the new millennium, private armies scour the Earth for super-advanced ancient technologies and artifacts. The powers of these artifacts could usher humanity into a new golden age. . .or destroy it utterly.

"**Striker** is action adventure at its finest. . .an interesting, way-out slugfest full of cool tricks, wild characters, and intense action."
—***Comic Buyer's Guide***

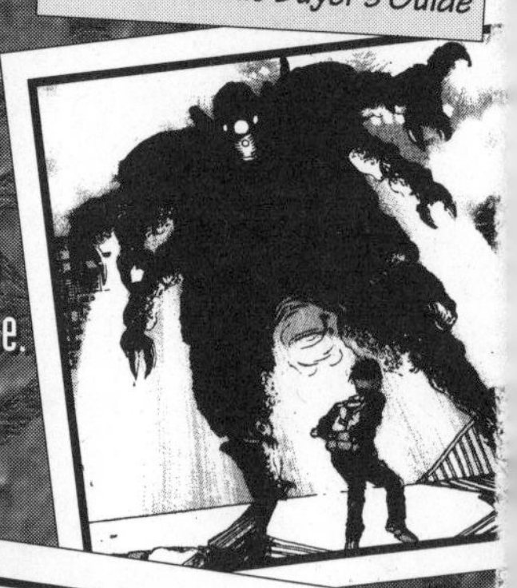

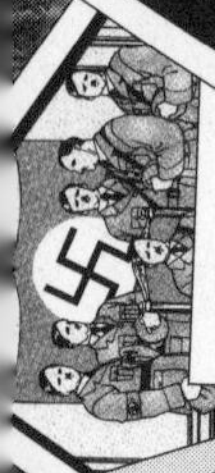

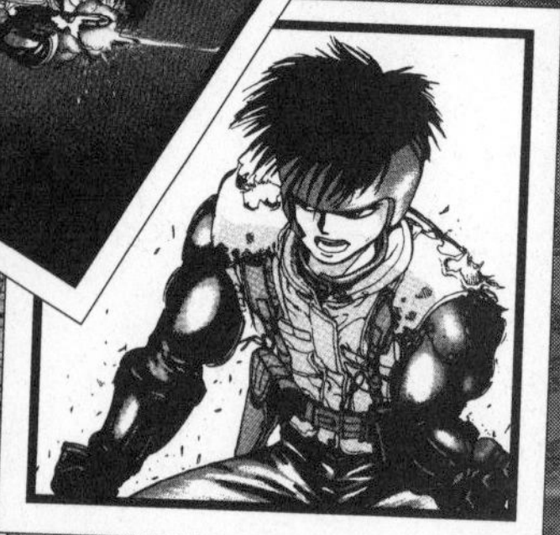

One teenager is all that stands between us and the apocalypse. How does he feel about it?

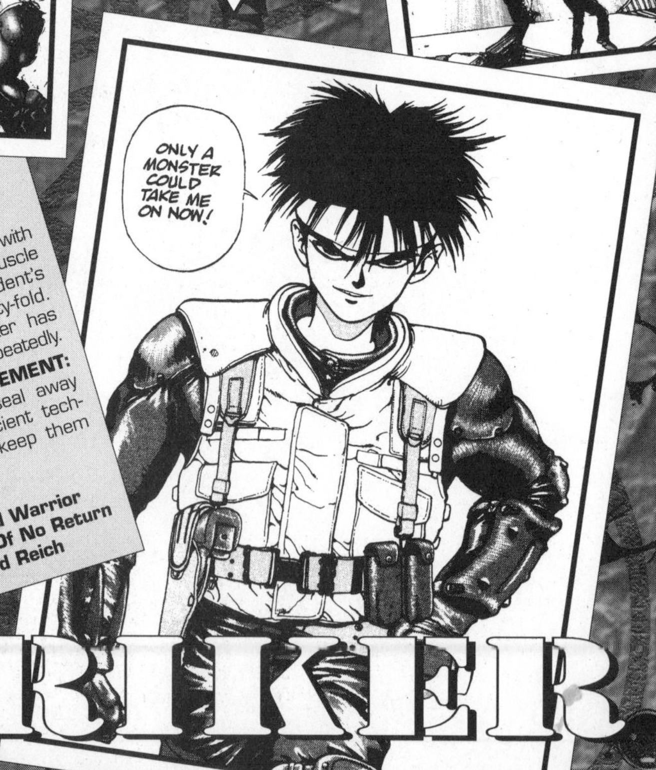
ONLY A MONSTER COULD TAKE ME ON NOW!

PERSONNEL FILE

NAME: Yu Ominae

CODE NAME: Striker

EMPLOYER: Arcam Foundation

SPECIAL ABILITIES: Outfitted with Arcam's Omihalcon armored muscle suit, this high school student's strength is multiplied thirty-fold. Arcam's top operative, Striker has proved his mettle in battle repeatedly.

ARCAM'S MISSION STATEMENT: To find and destroy or seal away extremely dangerous ancient technology and artifacts to keep them out of the wrong hands.

MISSION REPORTS:
Striker: The Armored Warrior
Striker: The Forest Of No Return
Striker vs. The Third Reich

STRIKER.

VIZ GRAPHIC NOVELS.